GOVERNING SUBJECTS

This introduction to the study of politics highlights the ideas of key thinkers to illustrate how our whole lives are politically conditioned and subject to governance. Looking across every major component of the discipline—at law and institutions, markets and power, and culture and identity—this book encourages students to engage in critical thinking by evaluating arguments for their internal coherence and explanatory power. In addition, it helps them learn to think holistically as it demonstrates that none of these domains can be adequately understood without analyzing the other two. Indeed, the better we understand the connections between these three major areas of politics and governance, the better we understand politics as a whole.

Isaac D. Balbus is Professor of Political Science at the University of Illinois at Chicago. He is the author of four previous books and has won several awards for excellence in teaching.

GOVERNING SUBJECTS

An Introduction to the Study of Politics

Isaac D. Balbus

University of Illinois at Chicago

Routledge
Taylor & Francis Group

NEW YORK AND LONDON

First published 2010
by Routledge
711 Third Ave, New York, NY 10017

Simultaneously published in the UK
by Routledge
2 Park Square, Milton Park, Abingdon, Oxon OX14 4RN

Routledge is an imprint of the Taylor & Francis Group, an informa business

© 2010 Taylor & Francis

Chapter 28 is a revised version of Chapter 10 in *Mourning and Modernity: Essays in the Psychoanalysis of Contemporary Society* (New York:
Other Press, 2005), pp. 131-146 and is reproduced by kind permission
of the publisher.

Typeset in MinionPro by
Prepress Projects Ltd, Perth, UK

Library of Congress Cataloging in Publication Data
Balbus, Isaac D.
Governing subjects : introduction to the study of politics /
Isaac D. Balbus.
p. cm.
Includes bibliographical references.
ISBN-13: 978-0-415-99889-5 (hardback : alk. paper)
ISBN-10: 0-415-99889-1 (hardback)
ISBN-13: 978-0-415-99890-1 (pbk. : alk. paper)
ISBN-10: 0-415-99890-5 (pbk.)
[etc.]
1. Political science. I. Title.
JA66.B27 2009
320--dc22

ISBN10: 0-415-99889-1 (hbk)
ISBN 10: 0-415-99890-5 (pbk)
ISBN10: 0-203-88144-3 (ebk)

ISBN13: 978-0-415-99889-5 (hbk)
ISBN 13: 978-0-415-99890-1 (pbk)
ISBN13: 978-0-203-88144-6 (ebk)

FOR MY SON, SIMON

CONTENTS

PREFACE AND
ACKNOWLEDGMENTS

The seeds of this study were planted many years ago. In 1995 a series of faculty meetings devoted to the mission of the Department of Political Science at the University of Illinois at Chicago culminated in the conclusion that our undergraduate program should emphasize "three substantive dimensions of politics—law and institutions, markets and power, and culture and identity"—and that this emphasis would enable us to build "bridges to other social sciences and humanities disciplines . . . as a central part of an interdisciplinary liberal arts education."[1] Shortly thereafter I was (in my capacity as Undergraduate Director) able to persuade my colleagues that we should develop a new, required introduction to the study of politics that was organized around the categories of our mission statement and that was consistent with its interdisciplinary commitment. This was to be a (relatively) small-section course that was team-taught twice a semester by four tenured or tenure-track faculty, each of whom would have primary responsibility for one part of the course, including a one-week introduction and a two-week conclusion that I taught for several years. The course was first taught in the fall of 1996, and over the course of nine years it managed to engage the participation of almost one-half of the faculty of the Department.

In 2005 the team-taught course met the budgetary axe and was transformed into a singly taught, large-section lecture class that was taught once a semester. Since that time I have taught it once a year. My version of the course is still organized around the categories of the original course: over the course of the semester I devote eight lectures each to Law and Institutions, Markets and Power, and Culture and Identity. I cover a great deal of ground in each of these sections of the course—some of my students complain that I cover too much ground—but with only four weeks to devote to each of them there is, of course, a great deal of important material that I cannot include. Inevitably, the decision to include or exclude material is based at least as much on my own familiarity with that material as it is on its intrinsic significance. For example, in the section on Law and Institutions, I include the rule of law, the separation of powers, political parties, elections, and civil society, but I exclude Congress, the presidency, and bureaucracy. Similarly, and as the language of the previous sentence anticipates, most of my concrete, empirical references in that section and many in the remaining two sections are to the United States. Like any teacher, I teach what I know best, and there is much that I do not know. Thus the limits of time and my competence combine to yield a course of considerable but selective scope.

The same is true of the book that is based on this course. Twenty-four of its twenty-eight chapters are revised versions of the lectures I give in my introductory course. Four entirely new chapters rethink the material in the previous twenty-four but add relatively little new empirical content. Thus the content coverage of this book is as selective as the coverage of my course. More complete coverage would have required a much longer book, and this one is plenty long enough already. The reader will have to judge for herself whether the depth of the discussion compensates for the gaps in its breadth.

Since *Governing Subjects* is based on the course to which I have referred, my first thanks must go to the graduate students who have helped me teach it. Anika Bishka, Daniel Bliss, Clifford Deaton, John French, Dimitra Katsikidis, and Shannon Nelson have all served admirably as teaching assistants, helping Friday students make sense of my fast-paced Tuesday and Thursday lectures. Two of my research assistants, Clifford Deaton and Tony DiMaggio, read and commented usefully on earlier versions of the manuscript, and another assistant, Zach Gebhardt, contributed in innumerable and indispensable ways to its latest incarnation.

A number of friends and colleagues also deserve thanks for having read earlier drafts, including Ron Bayer, Dick Simpson, David Ingram, and Steven Engelmann. Their positive reactions helped persuade me that the revisions recommended by the readers for Routledge were worth the time and effort they would require. Steven was particularly helpful in encouraging me to revise in the direction on which I finally decided. And my editor at Routledge, Michael Kerns, was thoughtfully supportive from the beginning to the end of this project.

So was my family. My daughter Shayla read and responded enthusiastically to the first five or six chapters. My wife Mary listened to many of the lectures that, in modified form, found their way into this book, and never begrudged the time that writing it took away from her and our five-year-old son Simon. And Simon—although he asked more than once when I would be done with those "boring endnotes"—seemed delighted that his daddy was writing a book. Especially when he learned that it would be dedicated to him.

Chicago, Illinois
March, 2009

GENERAL INTRODUCTION

I have written this book as an *alternative* introduction to the study of politics. That adjective is intended to underscore the difference in both its content and its form from other such introductions. Consider first its content. Under the heading of "politics" I consider a range of material that is considerably broader than more conventional, less capacious treatments of that subject. The title, *Governing Subjects*, was chosen, in part, to signal its unusual political breadth. If, as Michel Foucault famously argued, governance[1] entails the "conduct of conduct,"[2] then not only government, or the state, but also factories, schools, churches, families, and even, Foucault insists, "souls" should be treated as sites of governance, as the subject matter of political study. This is the tack I take in this book. Although the first part, "Law and Institutions," is generally confined to the description and analysis of governance within the state, the second part, "Markets and Power," is devoted to the study of governance within what are usually considered to be "economic" and other (supposedly) non-political arenas. In the second part, then, we will learn that what is more typically studied under the rubrics of "economics" or "sociology" can—and to my mind should—be studied by the student of politics as well.

In the third and fourth parts of this book the scope of politics becomes broader still. In Part III, "Culture and Identity," we will encounter material that is more conventionally considered to be the subject matter of anthropology or cultural studies but that, to my mind, raises fundamentally important issues of governance that the student of politics cannot afford to ignore. And in Part IV, "Conclusion," I treat relationships within the individual psyche (the Greek word for "soul") as well as the relationship between humans and (non-human) nature as relationships of governance, drawing on Kleinian psychoanalysis and ecologically inspired social theory to clarify those relationships.

The reader will gather from what has been said so far that this book might be considered as much an introduction to the social sciences in general as an introduction to political science in particular. This is why I have sub-titled it as an introduction to the study of politics rather than an introduction to political science. Insofar as it understands itself as a *discipline*, political science is committed to isolating the study of politics from the study of other dimensions of social and individual life, which it happily leaves to the other disciplines, including the ones to which I have already referred. Like all academic disciplines, it disciplines the mind to think partially or segmentally rather than organically or holistically. But I start, with the great nineteenth-century German philosopher Georg Hegel, from the assumption that the "truth is the whole," that is, from the assumption that it is impossible to understand any given part of society without understanding its connections to all the other parts. It follows that this book is more properly a *critique* of political science than an introduction to that discipline, so the reader who is looking for a treatment of the current state of that discipline will have to look elsewhere. At the same time, however, the reader who looks elsewhere will discover that there is considerable overlap between the current configuration of the discipline of political science and the questions and issues raised in this book.[3] Thus even the reader whose interests are less interdisciplinary than mine will find a good deal of material to fit within his disciplinary focus.

It also follows from what I have said that the organizing categories of this book should not be understood to represent entirely separate parts of political reality. The fact that I have divided the text into "Law and Institutions," "Markets and Power," and "Culture and Identity" should not imply, in other words, that any one of these subjects can be adequately understood in the absence of an understanding of the other two. Rather the better we understand the connections among "Law and Institutions," "Markets and Power," and "Culture and Identity," the better we understand any one of them. Thus in the introduction to Part II I show that the search for answers to questions that remain open in "Law and Institutions" requires that we explore issues to be considered in "Markets and Power," and in the introduction to Part III I suggest that the quest for a fuller understanding of some of the issues considered in "Markets and Power" necessarily leads us to the subject of "Culture and Identity." And in the introduction to Part IV I demonstrate how the issues that remain unresolved in all three previous parts point us in the direction of the psychoanalytically informed treatment of psyche and (non-human) nature as sites of governance that I develop in the conclusion. But a more complete treatment of all the important interconnections among the different domains would require another book, and I have more than enough to do in this one.

The title, *Governing Subjects*, was also chosen to signal the multiple meanings of governance. The first definition of the noun "subject" in my *Webster's New World Dictionary of the American Language* is "a person under the authority or control of, or owing allegiance to, another." Thus on this meaning of "subjects" *Governing Subjects* refers to people who are *subjected* to authority or control, to those who are governed *by* others or (as we shall see) other forces. In either case the emphasis here is on the person as *acted on* rather than acting. As Foucault puts it, governance refers to "modes of action, more or less considered and calculated, which . . . *act upon* the possibilities of action of other people."[4] The ambiguity introduced by the phrase "more or less considered and calculated" is worthy of pause. Does this phrase mean that the "conduct of conduct" requires a "conductor" who consciously directs the conduct, or can there be the direction of conduct without a director, governance without a governing intention? In this book I resolve the ambiguity in favor of the latter interpretation, and for the following reason. Governance, Foucault argues, "structure[s] the possible field of action of others,"[5] and it is surely the case that the field of possibilities open to actors is structured as much by *structures*—more-or-less stable patterns of relations—as it is by any intentional efforts to affect that field. This is perhaps most obvious in the case of the governing role of culture, which we routinely recognize whenever we speak of a person's identity or sense of self being shaped by the culture or sub-culture she inhabits. But it is also true in the domain of the state, where the rules of institutions significantly affect the outcomes that emerge from them, and in the domain of the economy, where the life-chances of individuals are regularly and dramatically affected by the unintended consequences of market interactions. We might want to argue that it would be better for as many outcomes as possible to be the result of the conscious intentions of individuals, but to make this a defining criterion of "governance" would be to neglect the myriad ways that individual conduct is in fact guided by impersonal forces. Thus, to repeat, by "governance" I mean to include anything that people have (at least at one point in time) created that affects the conduct of their conduct.[6]

My reference above to the "conscious intentions of individuals" evokes yet another meaning of the term "subject." In philosophy a "subject" is a being with consciousness, someone who has subjective experiences. Because subjects in this sense have consciousness, they are able to act *on* the world rather than merely be acted on *by* the world: they are subjects rather than objects. Thus the idea of subjectivity is closely linked to the idea of active *agency*. And as active agents people are capable of govern*ing* as well as being governed. Thus the title *Governing Subjects* evokes the possibility that the governed and the governing might be one and the same, that is, the possibility of *democracy*. This is a possibility that will be explored throughout this book, when I consider not only the problem of the democratization of the state but also the democratization of the economy and (what might be called) the democratization of culture.

The meaning of democracy is thus a central focus of *Governing Subjects*. But there is an even more intimate connection between democracy and this book. There is an important sense in which it owes its very existence to the efforts of people to democratize the state, the economy, and the culture. If not for post–seventeenth-century (and continuing) struggles to first liberalize and then democratize the state, the issues considered in the part on "Law and Institutions"—the meaning of the rule of law, the relationship between the rule of law and the separation of powers, the relationship between judicial review and democracy, the meaning of representation, the role of political parties, elections, and civil society—would simply not exist. Similarly, without the post–eighteenth-century (and ongoing) movements to democratize the economy, the chapters in the part on "Markets and Power" that examine the relationships between the market and human nature, the market and human freedom, the market and justice, and (most obviously) the market and democracy could not have been written. Finally, the counter-cultural struggles of the 1960s and the new social movements that followed in their wake were surely the necessary condition for the critical comprehension of modern culture and identity to which the third part of this book, "Culture and Identity," is devoted. Thus do three centuries of struggles by governing subjects find their way into the structure of a book with the same name.

To generalize the point: conceptual categories are historical products; theory owes its existence to the practice on which it reflects and (possibly) affects. And there is another, perhaps less obvious, point that follows from the conjunction between this one and one that I have already made. You will recall that I claimed that the better we understand the connections among "Law and Institutions," "Markets and Power," and "Culture and Identity," the better we understand any one of these supposedly separate domains. Our understanding of "Law and Institutions," for example, is necessarily improved by our understanding of its connections with "Markets and Power" and "Culture and Identity"; our knowledge of the former develops in proportion to our knowledge of the latter. Now, if this is true, and it is also true that our knowledge of "Markets and Power" and "Culture and Identity" is (as I argued above) dependent on the post–eighteenth-century and post-1960s struggles to democratize those two domains, then it follows that those political struggles have been responsible for (what I claim is) the progressive improvement in our understanding of "Law and Institutions." Thus there is an intimate connection between political development, understood as democratization, and the development of knowledge. Truth, in short, emerges as the outcome of an historical process.

This reference to "truth" is likely to be greeted with more than a little skepticism by those who read with post-modernist eyes. As we shall see, post-modernism teaches us to "deconstruct" claims to truth by disclosing (what it takes to be) their invariably dangerous political effects. Claims about human nature—about what it means to be a "subject"—are suspect because they inevitably establish a "norm" that incites individuals to measure themselves and to which many in fact will never measure up. The claim to speak the truth about the subject, in other words, necessarily subjects them to a "regime of truth" by which they are either "normalized" or excluded. Thus even to speak of *the* subject is to participate in his subjection.[7]

It follows that a post-modernist will be as wary about claims of cultural development as she is about claims of individual development. Cultures, it would seem, can only be evaluated as more or less developed according to the degree to which they facilitate a genuinely good life, but the notion of a genuinely good human life is merely another way of describing a theory of human nature.[8] And a theory of human nature—an account of what it means to be a human subject—is exactly what the post-modernist resists. There is some justification for this resistance, as the history of Western thought is replete with accounts of human nature that (whether deliberately or inadvertently) transform norms that *are* culturally and historically specific into supposedly universal ones, converting contingency into inevitability in the process. But I do not think it is helpful to respond to this risk of ethnocentrism or "essentialism" with a relativism that precludes the possibility of cross-cultural critique. Rather the "trick," it seems to me, is to develop an account of human nature that transcends the either/or of ethnocentrism versus relativism. I allude to this account at various points throughout the first three parts of this book, but do not flesh it out until the concluding part.

Thus *Governing Subjects* closes with a theory of individual and cultural development, one that (to repeat) leans heavily on both Kleinian psychoanalysis and ecology in its effort to establish what it means to be a human subject. As we shall see, the extension of the Kleinian claim that *reparative* inclinations and capacities are the measure of individual development to the problem of cultural development enables us to identify the (all-too-often ignored) emotional preconditions for the realization of ecological ideals. This eco-psychoanalytic answer to the question of what it means to be a human subject is, of course, only one among many different and competing answers, and I do not expect that mine will go uncontested. My hope instead is that it will be taken as a contribution to a dialogue in which we all need to be engaged.

This commitment to dialogue also distinguishes the *form* of this book from that of other introductory texts. With two exceptions, each chapter in the first three parts of this book introduces you to at least two opposing positions on the issue that is central to that chapter. Thus you will become familiar with many of the most important debates in the history of thinking about politics and will learn that the study of politics is itself contested political terrain.

I am by no means a neutral participant in this contest, but I do make every effort to present positions with which I disagree fairly and accurately. I take seriously Hegel's injunction to "enter into the strength" of the arguments of one's adversaries, that is, patiently to summarize, and carefully to consider the merits of, their positions, before subjecting them to internal or external critique. By "internal critique" I mean an evaluation that does not question the fundamental assumptions underlying a theory but rather merely considers whether, or the extent to which, the theory is both internally consistent and empirically useful. By "external critique" I mean an evaluation that contests the fundamental assumptions underpinning a theory in the name of different, competing assumptions. Proper respect for the position of one's theoretical opponent requires, I believe, that external critique be preceded by internal critique. It is all too easy to reject a theory from the "outside," that is, by simply—and arbitrarily—dismissing the assumptions on which it is based. This would simply be a case of not taking the theory seriously enough—not sufficiently entering into its strength—to evaluate it on its own terms. And no intellectual *development* is possible if opposing assumptions merely confront each other like ships passing in the night. But if the critic can demonstrate that the theory (that is the object of her critique) cannot in fact do what it sets out to do, because it lacks either internal consistency or explanatory power, then there is a good *reason* for rejecting the assumptions on which it is based in favor of alternative assumptions. Thus only a compelling internal critique can, in my judgment, justify the move toward external critique. That is why I wait until the last part of this work to speak in my own voice.

There is, finally, a connection between this respectful relationship to other texts and what I would consider a respectful relationship to other *people*. Just as the responsible reader neither suspends his judgment in favor of the judgment of an (idealized) author nor subjects that author to an (ultimately arbitrary) external critique, so the responsible individual refuses either to subordinate himself to, or dominate over, the other individuals with whom he interacts. In both cases respectful treatment requires that the self simultaneously affirm its connection to, yet difference from, the other. Dependence on the other and assertion of the self can and should go hand in hand. That is, I trust, the ultimate message of both the form and content of this book.

Part I

LAW AND INSTITUTIONS

1

LAW AND THE RULE OF LAW

The subject of this chapter is the nature of law and thus the meaning of the rule of law. The question, in other words, is what is law? But why should we care about this question? One answer—a relatively shallow one—is that political scientists have always included the study of law making, law application, and law adjudication—the activities of legislators, administrators, and judges—within the scope of their discipline. This answer is shallow because it begs the question of whether the discipline of political science as traditionally constituted *should* exist in the first place. But there is a more important answer, which is that, as individuals who are expected to obey the law and as citizens who are expected to make the law (if only indirectly through representatives whom we elect), all of us—even people with no particular interest in the discipline of political science—ought to know what it is that we are supposed to both obey and create. What is it, exactly, that obliges us to obey the law? What, if anything, distinguishes legal obligation from other forms of obligation to which we routinely submit—for example the obligation to keep a promise, the obligation to care for a sick relative, or the obligation not to lie? How do we determine whether those who are charged with the responsibility of making laws in our name are properly discharging their responsibility, and therefore deserve our support, or are acting *unlawfully* and therefore should be called to account? It would seem, then, that we need to answer the question "What is law?" if we want to be responsible individuals and responsible citizens.

One answer with a distinguished if dubious pedigree is that the *law is nothing but the command of the sovereign*. This is the answer given in the middle of the seventeenth century by the great English political theorist Thomas Hobbes, who argues in his master work *Leviathan* that individuals by nature seek ever greater power over others and that an all-powerful ruler—either a single man or a body of men—is therefore necessary to prevent individuals from living in constant fear of death at the hands of other individuals. The ruler must, in other words, be sufficiently powerful to be able to persuade individuals that the costs of aggressively, violently imposing their will on others outweigh the benefits because doing so would lead to swift and severe punishment at the hands of the ruler. Hobbes assumes, then, that given what he takes to be the aggressive

3

nature of human beings[1] the only thing that will oblige them to obey the law is fear of punishment, and that this fear of punishment will be sufficiently intense only if the sovereign is not constrained by the law but is rather its exclusive source.

This essentially Hobbesian concept of law is taken over almost two hundred years later in the work of John Austin, who defines a legal system as "a situation in which the majority of a social group habitually obey the orders backed by threats of the sovereign person or persons, who themselves habitually obey no one."[2] For Austin, then—as he puts it—"command and duty are correlative terms"[3]: my duty to obey the command of the ruler extends no further than, is exhausted by, my desire to avoid the "evil"—the punishment—that would follow if I disobeyed it. As many have pointed out, this means that Austin is unable to distinguish the situation of legal obligation from the situation of being obliged to hand over my money to a gunman who commands that I hand it over.[4] But this reduction of legal obligation to *coercion* ignores the fact that people may obey the law for a variety of different motives, and often do so even when the chances of being punished for violating it are slight, or even nonexistent. Some people obey the law because they believe it is right to do so even if they judge that the chances of being caught if they break it are extremely remote.[5] Some governments—not all, as we have all-too-recently discovered—obey international law even if, as effectively remains the case, there is no sovereign body capable of enforcing it. The command theory of law cannot explain why this is the case.

This can be put another way. Americans learn from a very early age that this is supposed to be a "government of laws, not men." This implies that the law cannot merely be *anything* that men decide, that the men who make the law are not "above" the law but must rather be constrained or limited by it. Thus law cannot be reduced to, equated with, the mere command of the sovereign. Consider the phrase the "rule of law," which American political leaders celebrate and, recently, have attempted to export. If law were nothing but the command of the ruler, then this phrase would be redundant, since law would be *defined* in terms of rule. If the phrase has any meaning, in other words, it can only be because the law—once again—limits or is supposed to limit the commands or will of the ruler: as Joseph Raz has argued, not just any sovereign commands, but only those that are general, prospective rather than retroactive, relatively stable, etc., are consistent with the rule of law.[6] More on this shortly. For now I want to raise the question: Why *should* the will of the ruler be constrained, especially if—as in the case of a democracy—the law issues or is supposed to issue from the will of the people? Why should the rule of law trump the will of the people? How can popular sovereignty—the power of the people—be reconciled with the limits on the power of the people that the law imposes?

One answer is that at one time—the time of the founding of the constitution—*the people decided that there should be limits on the subsequent power of the people,* that certain spheres of individual action—typically referred to as "rights"—should be exempt from popular, that is, governmental, interference or control. Thus, according to this line of reasoning, democracy or popular sovereignty and the limits of the rule of law are ultimately consistent because the people originally decided to impose those limits on themselves. But this argument only raises two closely related additional questions. First, why should subsequent generations be bound by the decisions of an earlier generation? Why should we be limited by the limits imposed by people we never knew and in whose decision we never participated? And, second, even if we could satisfactorily answer that question—even if we were to argue, for example, that the constitution gives us the right to amend the constitution and that if we choose not to we can be presumed to give our current consent to the limits it imposes on us—what authorized the founders of the constitution to create the constitution in the first place? The constitution authorizes the subsequent exercise of power, but an exercise of power was necessary in order to create the constitution. What then ultimately justifies the constitution that subsequently justifies the limits on the sovereign (power of the people)?

The answer of the legal positivist is *nothing*. Thus H. L. A. Hart argues that the law rests on an ultimately arbitrary basic norm or "rule of recognition,"[7] a rule or norm that creates and legitimates the law but that cannot itself be rationally justified. Thus for the positivist there is nothing inherently *moral* about the rule of law: the "rights" it creates are purely conventional in the sense that they are granted by a convention—a rule of recognition—that itself has no natural or essential basis. Rights, in the language of our day, are merely "social constructions." But this argument seems unsatisfactory, since it leads to the conclusion that the obligation to obey the law, whose immediate or proximate source is the constitution or rule of recognition, is *ultimately* as arbitrary as Hobbes's or Austin's command of the sovereign. Why should I obey the law if the convention or norm that establishes the law cannot itself be justified or legitimated?

The (modern) natural law approach to law answers this question by denying that the constitution or rule of recognition is an arbitrary social construction and arguing instead that the "rights" that it recognizes and guarantees are rights that are inherent in what, in a pre-feminist age, was called the Nature of Man. Thus the natural law theorist claims that the constitution or rule of recognition that limits the power of the people by subordinating it to the rule of law is legitimate to the extent that the rights it grants are *natural rights*, or what today are sometimes called universal human rights. According to the natural law tradition, then, the ultimate justification for the rule of law is natural law: human law is legitimate, is only *truly* law, if and when it expresses and reinforces human nature, or what are understood to be the essential purposes of human life, the enduring content of what it means to be human. Only natural law in this sense, it is argued, justifies both the binding force of the constitution on subsequent generations and the creation of that constitution in the first place.

But this argument only raises the question—the very thorny question—of what precisely is human nature? If true law must be consistent with and contribute to human nature, then we would need to agree on the answer to this question—what is human nature?—in order to agree about what constitutes true law. But even passing familiarity with the history of Western political thought alone reveals there is anything but consensus with respect to the question of human nature. Are people essentially rational beings, or are they essentially appetitive creatures, driven by their passions or appetites? Are they social or a-social, or even anti-social? Cooperative or competitive? Or some combination of all these attributes? Do we side with Plato, Hobbes, Rousseau, or Marx on human nature? The persistence of profound disagreements among those who follow each of these thinkers, as well as many others, suggests that agreement on what constitutes human nature is—to say the very least—very hard to come by, even within the context of a Western tradition that traces its roots back to Ancient Greece. When we recognize—as we should—that this tradition is only one among many others, the likelihood of universal agreement on human nature becomes even more remote. In short, if we need to agree on human nature in order to agree on what constitutes a genuine law, then we are unlikely to agree on what the law really *is*.[8] To restate this problem in a way that ties it to the problem of the legitimation of the constitution or ultimate rule of recognition: if the constitution that justifies the rule-of-law limits on popular sovereignty can itself be justified only through a successful appeal to natural law, and what constitutes natural law is intrinsically controversial, so that the appeal to natural law is bound to fail, then it would appear that the effort to justify the rule of law must fail as well.

Are there any alternatives to the unsatisfactory either/or of positivist versus natural law approaches to the law? Positivism effectively denies any connection between the law and morality by arguing that legal obligation is, at bottom, based on norms or rules that have no intrinsic moral content. Natural law effectively collapses the distinction between law and morality by arguing that law is *only truly law* if it expresses and reinforces moral purposes that express and reinforce human nature. There *are* in fact intermediate positions, positions that argue the case for a certain connection between law and morality without—they believe—taking recourse to inherently controversial claims about human nature. The author of one of these positions is Joseph Raz, a contemporary legal theorist who argues that the rule of law possesses a "moral virtue" even if it falls far short of embodying a full-scale and complete morality, even, in fact, if it is consistent with and doesn't discourage the existence of a number of moral evils in the society that it governed by it. To understand this claim, consider a partial list of the principles that, according to Raz, "can be derived from the basic idea of the rule of law":

1   "All laws should be prospective, open and clear." Prospective: a retroactive law, proscribing and penalizing some past action even though it was legal at the time it was undertaken is not a genuine law. Open: "The law must be open and adequately publicized": individuals should be able to determine

what the law is if their actions are to be guided by it. Clear: individuals cannot be guided by the law if they are uncertain of its meaning.

2   "Laws should be relatively stable." People need to know the law for "long-term planning." And if the laws are frequently changed people will live in "constant fear that the law has been changed since they last learnt what it was."

3   "The making of particular laws should be guided by open, stable, clear and general rules." General: laws must apply to general classes or categories of individuals and not single out particular individuals or make invidious distinctions among them. The generality of the law is closely related to its commitment to formal equality, that is, in David Ingram's word, it "treat[s] everyone as equally subject to the law and equally capable of rationally abiding by it."[9]

4   "The independence of the judiciary must be guaranteed." Courts must apply the law rather than act for other reasons, and for them to apply the law they must be "free from extraneous pressures and independent of all authority save that of the law."[10]

Raz argues that these and other principles required by and embodied in the rule of law have moral value in part because they serve to check some (but not all) forms of the arbitrary exercise of governmental power. But the most important reason "for valuing the rule of law," he tells us, is that the rule of law "respect[s] human dignity." It does so by providing a "stable, secure framework for one's life and actions" that enables one to "choose styles and forms of life, to fix long-term goals and effectively direct one's life towards them." It thereby treats humans as "persons capable of planning and plotting their future," and respects their dignity by "respecting their autonomy, their right to control their future."[11] Raz emphasizes, however, that this minimal "moral virtue" of the law does *not* guarantee that the law will be used for good and just purposes. One can imagine all kinds of bad laws that are prospective, open, clear, stable, and applied to individuals by an independent judiciary. In fact Raz claims that:

> a non-democratic legal system, based on the denial of human rights, on extensive poverty, on racial segregation, sexual inequalities, and religious persecution may, in principle, conform to the requirements of the rule of law better than any of the legal systems of the more enlightened Western democracies. This does not mean that it will be better than those Western democracies [but merely that] it will excel in one respect: in its conformity to the rule of law.[12]

It seems to me that there are two problems with this argument. First, Raz argues that a principled commitment to human dignity is embodied in the rule of law but claims at the same time that the rule of law is compatible with the racial, sexual, and religious indignities to which he refers. How can the law respect human dignity if it authorizes racism, sexism, religious persecution, etc.? Do not these forms of inequality or domination preclude the very "autonomy" and the right to "control their future" that Raz insists are endorsed by the rule of law? If Raz is right to insist that the principle of human dignity is fundamental to the rule of law, then it would seem that the rule of law should *rule out* these forms of injustice. This suggests that the connections between the rule of law on the one hand and justice or morality on the other may be more extensive than Raz believes. Maybe the rule of law is not such a minimalist moral virtue after all.

But to say this is not to say that its moral virtues are universal. Raz seems to assume that "human dignity," understood as respect for people's "autonomy and their right to control their future," is an uncontroversial moral good. But a commitment to individual autonomy and the right of individuals to control their future is not a commitment that is likely to be shared by those who inhabit traditional cultures—or even sub-cultures within our own culture—for whom dependence on rather than autonomy from others—for example dependence on elders—is a value and for whom the commitment to control the future is a form of blasphemy that arrogates to human beings powers that only God can exercise. The principle of individual dignity embodied in the rule of law, in other words, is arguably a culturally and historically specific principle rather than a universally recognized moral good. To put this another way, to certain people the rule of law is an affront to, rather than an affirmation of, their sense of what it means to be human.

The point is, then, that Raz simultaneously *underestimates* the moral implications of the rule of law and *overestimates* the universality of these moral implications. This brings us, finally, to the position of Ronald Dworkin, who, influenced by the eminent early nineteenth-century philosopher Georg Hegel, insists *both* on the pervasive presence of concrete moral principles animating the formal rule of law *and* on the historically specific nature of these principles. On the one hand, Dworkin argues that "legal systems consist of laws in the narrow sense (prescriptive rules) and unstated moral principles that lay out a philosophy of government that can be seen as justifying the system as a whole."[13] Here Dworkin echoes Hegel, for whom law or the state is "objective mind," that is, shared ideas about individuals, their purposes, and their social relations that are, as it were, materialized or embodied in legal institutions and decisions. Thus for Dworkin the obligation of a judge is to interpret a law that cannot unambiguously or easily be applied to a new or "hard" case in the light of his understanding of the shared ideas—the underlying moral philosophy—that "explains the legal system as a whole."[14] In so doing the judge both expresses his commitment to the law (rather than acting extra-legally, as positivists such as Hart claim) and contributes to its further development. The judge, we may say, simultaneously transmits and transforms the legal tradition he inhabits.

To say this is to say—against natural law theorists—that the principles that underwrite the legal system or the rule of law are not timeless and universal rules of reason but rather evolving rules of that particular form of reason that is embedded in that legal system. There are many questions that can be and have been raised about this concept of historical reason, one of which—the problem of ethnocentrism—we will come to much later in this book in the part on Culture and Identity. At this point however I want to close this chapter with a different although related one. Dworkin, like Hegel, assumes that the law expresses and reinforces *shared* ideas or principles, overarching ideals—such as the principle of "equal concern and respect for all"—to which all at least implicitly subscribe. But what if even this ideal, rather than expressing what Rousseau in *On the Social Contract* calls the General Will, is merely a particular will in a general disguise; what if, in other words, the ideas embodied in the law express not the interests of all but rather the interests of a dominant group or class? What if, as Marx argued in *The German Ideology*, the "ruling ideas in every epoch . . . are the ideas of the ruling class; [what if] the class which is the ruling *material* force of society, is at the same time its ruling *intellectual* force"?[15] Even if we reject Marx's claim as overstated, merely to take it seriously is to suggest that Dworkin may assume too much consensus and too little conflict in the evolution of the law. In other words—and to conclude—Dworkin's historical reason may have a history—a history of struggle among contending groups and classes—that is very different from the one he depicts.

2

THE SEPARATION OF POWERS

In this chapter I address the question: Does the rule of law—whose outlines we examined in the previous chapter—require the separation of powers? The American political answer to this question would appear to be a definite "yes." Everyone knows—or *thinks* they know—that the American political system is based on a separation between the legislative, executive, and judicial branches of government, each of which is staffed by different individuals who are chosen in different ways.

James Madison gives the classical American defense of this arrangement in *Federalist Papers 47, 48, 49,* and *51,* which along with all the other numbers were designed to persuade the American people—or at least the white, male, literate part of the American people—that what eventually became the Constitution of the United States should in fact be adopted. Since Madison in *Federalist 47* refers approvingly to "the celebrated Montesquieu" as "the oracle who is always consulted and cited on this subject,"[1] it is fitting that my analysis of the separation of powers begins with a summary of the argument on its behalf made by that mid–eighteenth-century French political thinker.

The subject of Book 11 of *The Spirit of the Laws* is the political arrangements most conducive to the protection of liberty. In paragraph 1 of chapter 3 Montesquieu defines liberty as "the power of doing what we ought to will, and in not being constrained to do what we ought not to will." Although clearly designed to distinguish liberty from license or what Montesquieu calls "unrestrained freedom" or "do[ing] what they please,"[2] this definition is not terribly helpful and may even be dangerous. It is not helpful because it begs the question of exactly *what* people ought to will, and it is dangerous because it is open to the interpretation that, since it is the law which tells people what they ought to do, liberty is nothing other than obeying the laws, which laws can of course be oppressive. But this interpretation is clearly not intended by Montesquieu, who makes it clear in paragraph 1 of chapter 4 that liberty and "the abuse of power" are incompatible.[3] Thus abusive or arbitrary laws are inconsistent with liberty, and a charitable interpretation of his definition—repeated in paragraph 2 of chapter 3 as the "right of doing whatever the laws permit"[4]—would be that liberty, for Montesquieu, consists in conforming to those laws that are consistent with the features—examined in chapter 1 above—that the rule of law requires. For all practical purposes, then, Montesquieu identifies liberty with the rule of law.

So for Montesquieu the problem of protecting liberty becomes the problem of ensuring the rule of law, of preventing abuses of governmental power. His solution to this problem starts from the assumption—based, he says, on "constant experience"—that "every man invested with power is apt to abuse it," and that, therefore, "to prevent the abuse of power, 'tis necessary that by the very disposition of things power should be a check to power." By his very nature the individual seeks to maximize his power—"he pushes on till he comes to the utmost limit"[5]—and therefore we cannot rely on his reason, conscience, or anything else *within* him to restrain its unlimited exercise. Rather the only effective restraint on the power of the individual must come from the *outside*, in the form of the resistance he encounters from the exercise of the power on the part of other individuals. Power can be checked only by power. These, of course, are contestable assumptions, and much later in this book we will have occasion to contest them. But for now I want simply to point out that these are the assumptions on which Montesquieu's subsequent argument on behalf of the separation of powers rests. For Montesquieu, in other words, the separation of powers is supposed to ensure that "power should be a check to power," which is—supposedly—the only way to prevent "the abuse of power" and thus to protect the rule of law and the political liberty it entails.

By the "separation of powers" Montesquieu means a governmental arrangement in which "the law is made by a legislative body, administered by a separate executive, and applied against citizens only by an independent judiciary."[6] It is easy to understand why the rule of law requires an independent judiciary, and in fact we saw in first chapter that Raz makes an independent judiciary one of the criteria for the existence of the rule of law. Raz's position is anticipated by Montesquieu, who tells us:

> there is no liberty, if the power of judging be not separated from the legislative and executive powers. Were it joined with the legislative, the life and liberty of the subject would be exposed to arbitrary control; for the judge would then be the legislator. Were it joined to the executive power, the judge might behave with all the violence of an oppressor.[7]

Clearly there is no way that judges can determine whether or not the laws are sufficiently prospective, open, clear, general, etc., and whether these laws are being fairly executed or administered, if judges are subordinate or beholden to the power of law-makers and administrators. Thus it is difficult to dispute the claim that judicial power must check legislative and administrative power, and that the judicial power must therefore be separate from the legislative and executive power, if the rule of law is to prevail.

But it is less clear, it seems to me, why the rule of law requires that legislative and executive powers be similarly separate from each other. Montesquieu claims that "when the legislative and executive powers are united in the same person, or in the same body of magistracy, there can be then no liberty, lest the same monarch or senate enact tyrannical laws, to execute them in a tyrannical manner."[8] Here the argument seems to be that legislators would have a greater incentive to enact abusive laws if they also executed them, but Montesquieu does not explain why this should be the case. Perhaps he assumes that if legislators were more certain that the oppressive laws they were contemplating would be effectively executed—because *they* would be executing them—they would be more likely to pass those laws. Perhaps, in other words, they would be more likely to pass laws targeting their political enemies if they were in a position to make sure that those laws would actually hit their target. But the task of administrators is to "faithfully execute the law," so it's not clear why they would have to be effectively identical to the law-makers for the oppressive designs of the latter to be implemented. And, as long as there were an independent judiciary, presumably there would already be a check on both legislative and administrative abuses. So—once again—it's not clear why the rule of law requires that legislative and executive functions be structurally separated.

This lack of clarity is reflected in the fact that Montesquieu—just three paragraphs after the one in which he insists on the abuses necessarily attendant to the union of legislative and executive powers in the same hands—argues that "most kingdoms of Europe enjoy a moderate government, because the prince who is invested with the two first, i.e., legislative and executive powers, leaves the third [judicial power] to his subjects." It is only when all "three powers are united in the [prince's] person" that the "subjects groan under the weight of tyranny and oppression."[9] Here Montesquieu suggests, against his own argument, that the real problem is the absence of an independent judiciary—when all three functions, judicial, legislative, and executive, are united in the same hands—rather than the mere absence of separation between legislative and executive functions.

Montesquieu's well-known praise for the British constitutional system inadvertently leads to the same conclusion. At one point, he offers an example of the supposedly dangerous integration of executive and legislative functions: "if ... the executive power was committed to a certain number of persons selected from the legislative body, there would be an end to liberty; by reason the two powers would be united, as the same persons would actually sometimes have, and moreover would always be able to have, a share in both."[10] But what Montesquieu failed to realize is that this description *exactly applies* to the very English system that he takes to be a model case of liberty and the rule of law: already by the middle of the eighteenth century, and continuing to this day, the leader of the political party that wins a legislative majority normally becomes the prime minister, who then selects the members of his cabinet, that is, executive department heads, from the members of his party who serve in the legislature. Thus in the British system of government the leader of the legislative branch is also the leader of the executive branch: there simply is no structural separation of legislative and executive powers. If, as Montesquieu argues, liberty and the rule of law flourish in Britain, then the separation of legislative and executive powers cannot be necessary for liberty and the rule of law. Montesquieu cannot have it both ways.

If Montesquieu's mistake about the British system demonstrates that the separation of powers is not in fact a *necessary* condition for the rule of law, his own arguments suggest that a strict separation of powers is not even a *sufficient* condition for the rule of law. Remember that Montesquieu assumes that the separation of powers enables a checking of power by power that militates against abuses of power. But when he gives examples of the mutual checking of legislative and executive powers he makes it clear that this checking in fact presupposes a certain degree of *shared* power between these two branches. Thus he argues that, on the one hand, the "executive power . . . ought to have a share in the legislature by the power of refusing," that is, should have the power to veto legislation, and that, on the other hand, the legislature should have the right to "examine and punish," that is, impeach and convict, "a subject entrusted with the administration of public affairs [who] may infringe the rights of the people, and be guilty of crimes which the ordinary magistrates either could or would not punish."[11] So it turns out that checking of power by power, necessary according to Montesquieu for liberty and the rule of law, actually requires that the executive exercise a legislative function—the veto—and the legislature exercise a judicial function—impeachment. In fact, reflection reveals that a certain sharing or mixing of powers is logically entailed by the notion of one power checking another. How could one power *limit* the power of a second power without exercising at least some of the power that is normally reserved for that second power? A complete structural separation of powers would thus appear to be logically inconsistent with the checking of power by power. This suggests that Montesquieu is really making a case for a certain *combination* of separation and sharing among the three branches of government. What is implicit with Montesquieu, we shall see, is made much more explicit by Madison.

Before we come to Madison, a final point about Montesquieu. It is possible to infer from some of his observations about the different *interests* represented by the three different branches of the British government that he understands that even an ideal combination of separation and sharing among those branches would not be sufficient to produce the mutual checking of their power to which he is committed. According to Montesquieu, the British monarch

> represented social interests different from those of the legislature; the legislature, in turn, composed of two houses, was to represent the aristocracy and the bourgeoisie respectively, while the judiciary . . . was to represent everybody . . . since the judges ought to be the accused [sic] peers.[12]

Montesquieu's emphasis on the importance of a certain degree of social diversity or pluralism appears to signal his awareness of the following problem: if all three branches of government represented, or were controlled by, the *same social group*, the mere legal or organizational separation among those branches would in no way secure the mutual checking of effective power among them. To avoid this problem Montesquieu complements his constitutional principle of the (incomplete) separation of powers with what Franz Neumann calls the "sociological principle of balancing social forces."[13]

This however raises the following problem. Montesquieu argues that the "three powers should naturally form a state of repose or inaction. But as there is a necessity for movement in the course of human affairs, they are forced to move, but still to move in concert."[14] But how can they "move in concert" if each branch checks the other because each branch represents different, conflicting social interests? The mutual agreement among all three branches supposedly required for political action or movement would appear to be precluded, or at least significantly impeded, by the very disagreement among social groups that is supposed to be a prerequisite for the mutual checking of power on which liberty and the rule of law supposedly depend. Thus Montesquieu's argument for a combination of constitutional and social pluralism appears, at bottom, to be an argument for what we today call political *gridlock*, for limiting the power of the people, acting through their government, to change their society. Doesn't Montesquieu say as much when he claims that "the three powers should *naturally* form a state of repose or inaction"? Doesn't this amount to the assertion that the best government is the *least* government?

This brings us to Madison, who, writing in 1788, relies on arguments from Montesquieu as well as arguments of his own to make the case for the particular combination of separation and sharing of powers in the proposed new constitution for the United States of America, which was subsequently adopted in 1789. In *Federalist 47* Madison dismisses objections to the proposed constitution that proceed from the assumption that the separation of powers must be absolute. He points out that Montesquieu argued, as we have seen, for only a *relative* separation of powers consistent with *some* sharing of powers, and that this "blending" was in fact consistent with American political traditions already affirmed in the existing constitutions of the separate, now American, states. Starting from the Montesquieuan assumption that "power is of an encroaching nature, and that it ought to be effectually restrained from passing the limits assigned to it," *Federalist 48* goes on to assert that in a "representative republic, where the executive magistracy is carefully limited" (in contrast to what he calls "a democracy, where the people . . . are continually exposed by their incapacity for regular deliberation . . . to the ambitious intrigues of their executive magistrates") the greatest danger of "encroachments" comes from the "enterprising ambition" of the "legislative department."[15] It is, above all, this department that must be "effectually restrained" from invading the prerogatives of the other two, which is exactly what happened, Madison argues, when the legislatures of Virginia and Pennsylvania usurped the powers of either the judiciary or the executive of those states.[16] This Madisonian insistence on the primacy of legislative abuses rests on the assumption that a legislative assembly "is sufficiently numerous to feel all the passions which actuate a multitude, yet not so numerous as to be incapable of pursuing the object of its passions, by means which reason prescribes,"[17] that is, on the assumption that an elected legislature is dangerous precisely insofar as it *effectively represents the passions of the people*.

This distrust of (the passions of) the people is also on display in *Federalist 49*, in which Madison considers, and dismisses, the very different proposal for addressing abuses of governmental power offered by Thomas Jefferson. Jefferson proposed periodic constitutional conventions called into being by any two of the three branches of government for the purpose of "altering the constitution or *correcting breaches of it*." Rather than relying on what we have come to call the "checks and balances" that Madison defends, Jefferson argues that:

> whenever any one of the departments may commit encroachments on the charted authority of the others . . . it seems strictly consonant to the republican theory to recur to the same original authority [of the people], as the people are the only legitimate fountain of power.[18]

Madison rejects this appeal to the power of the people on a number of grounds, including his belief that frequent appeals to the people would "deprive the government of that veneration which time bestows on every thing, and without which perhaps the wisest and freest governments would not possess the requisite stability," and his even greater fear that such periodic appeals to the people would entail "the danger of disturbing the public tranquility by interesting too strongly the public passions."[19] In short, Jefferson's proposal is *too democratic*; it places more power in the hands of the people than is warranted by a proper understanding of the nature of the passions and their relationship to human reason. In Jefferson's regular constitutional conventions:

> the passions . . . not the reason of the public would sit in judgment. But it is the reason, alone, of the public that ought to control and regulate the government. The passions ought to be controlled and regulated *by* the government.[20]

But the argument that "it is the reason . . . of the public that ought to control and regulate the government" does not sit well with, and in fact would appear to be directly contradicted by, the assumption that underlies Madison's very different proposal for guarding against "encroachments" of governmental power in *Federalist 51*. Here Madison relies not on reason but rather on (conflicting) passions as a check against abuses of governmental, especially legislative, power. He advocates a policy of "supplying, by opposite and rival interests, the defect of better motives" and tells us that "ambition must be made to counter ambition" and that "the private interest of every individual [must] be a centinel over the public rights."[21] Thus the surest guarantee against encroachments of one governmental department over the others "consists in giving to those who administer each department the necessary constitutional means and personal motives to resist the encroachments of the others." To those who would object that this reliance on selfish motives to secure the public interest betrays too little faith in human nature, Madison responds, famously, "what is government itself, but the greatest of all reflections on human nature? If men were angels, no government would be necessary."[22] I will come back to this question—the all-important question—of human nature later in this book. For now it is important only to understand that Madison's defense of checks and balances among otherwise separated powers depends decisively on what might, at the risk of some misunderstanding, be called his "realist" theory of human nature, and that that defense is only as persuasive as this theory of human nature.

You will recall that Madison is particularly worried about encroachments of power on the part of the legislative department. From what he has said so far in *Federalist 51* it would follow that the only way that the other departments can resist legislative encroachments is to be given powers of self-defense commensurate with that danger. Yet Madison argues that "it is not possible to give to each department an equal power of self-defense," since, "in republican government, the legislative authority [since it is through this authority that the people govern] necessarily predominates."[23] The dilemma, then, is that, according to Madison, the greatest danger to liberty comes from that branch of government that ought to be more powerful than the others. How then to restrain (other than by a qualified executive veto, which Madison also favors) the legislative branch without violating the republican principle of legislative supremacy? Madison's answer (following Montesquieu) is that the legislature should be "divide[ed] into different branches; and to render them, by different modes of election and different principles of action, as little connected with each other as the nature of their common functions and their common dependence on the society will admit."[24] Thus the proposed constitution called for direct election of members of the lower house, the House of Representatives, and selection of members of the upper chamber, the Senate, by state legislatures, and based the number of Representatives allocated to each state on the population of that state but allocated two Senate seats to each state irrespective of its population. Madison's supposed solution to the problem of reconciling legislative supremacy with the need to guard against legislative encroachments is to *weaken the legislative body*, to divide it against itself so that it is unable to conquer the other branches. Whether this "solution" leaves anything left of legislative supremacy is of course an open question, a question to which I will return.

Madison does not rely exclusively on "checks and balances" among the branches of the national government as a solution to the problem of how, in his words, "to oblige the government to control itself."[25] He also argues that federalism supplies additional, complementary protections against abuses of governmental authority. By dividing governmental authority between the national government and the state governments, "a double security arises to the rights of the people. The different [viz. national and state] governments will controul each other; at the same time that each will be controuled [thanks to the partial blending of separate powers] by itself." To guard "the society against the oppression of its rulers," it would seem, requires that the rulers be doubly divided against themselves. How would they ever be able to move—as Montesquieu acknowledges they sometimes must move—"in concert"?

Finally, Madison argues that federalism helps not only to "guard the society against the oppression of its rulers, but [also] to guard one part of the society against the injustice of the other part." Here we encounter Madison's famous warning about, and remedy for, the so-called "tyranny of the majority." He worries that, since "different interests necessarily exist in different classes of citizens," a majority "united by a common interest" will render the "rights of the minority . . . insecure."[26] Since the poor are many and the rich are few, it is fair to conclude that Madison's great fear is that a majority of the poor would unite to threaten the property and associated interests of the minority of the rich. This is, many commentators agree,[27] what Madison had in mind when he refers to "an unjust combination of a majority of the whole," which "unjust combination," he believes, a federal republic will discourage by ensuring that "the society . . . will be broken into so many parts, interests and classes of citizens, that the rights of individuals or of the minority will be in little danger from interested combinations of the majority."[28] And the "extended republic of the United States" will guarantee that this necessary "multiplicity of interests and sects" will flourish. Thus "the larger the society, provided it lie within a practicable sphere, the more duly capable it will be of self-government."[29]

However this is, it must be said, a peculiar notion of *self*-government. Although the explicit target of Madison's attack is majority *tyranny*—unjust combinations of a majority—the solution he proposes effectively precludes the possibility of majority *rule* itself. The governmental and social divisions that, according to Madison, will work to prevent the formation of an unjust majority coalition would equally work to prevent the formation of *any* majority coalition. Is Madison's anti-majoritarianism consistent with his commitment to "republican government"? Can a form of government designed to thwart the will of the majority be said to be a form of self-government?

The answer of Jean-Jacques Rousseau in *On the Social Contract* is "no," as long as what is meant by "the will of the majority" corresponds to what Rousseau means by the General Will. The General Will results from all the citizens who participate in its formation asking themselves: Is this (proposed) law consistent with the general or common interest? The only legitimate laws, in other words, are those that issue from the non–self-interested, public-spirited calculations of the assembled body of citizens: "it is uniquely on the basis of this common interest that society ought to be governed."[30] As we have seen, Montesquieu and especially Madison argue, to the contrary, that government should be based on (the conflict among) *private* interests, and they therefore advocate a system of separated powers with checks and balances that is designed to prevent any one private interest from predominating over the other private interests. But the governmental structure they design, I have suggested, also inevitably prevents the articulation and organization of the very common interest whose possibility they contest (thus producing a self-fulfilling prophecy!), the only interest that, according to Rousseau, is the basis of a legitimate government. It should come as no surprise that Rousseau contemptuously dismisses those political theorists who "sometimes . . . mix all [the] parts together, sometimes they separate them. They turn the sovereign into a fantastic body formed of bits and pieces." They fail to recognize that "for the same reason that sovereignty is inalienable, it is indivisible."[31]

3

JUDICIAL REVIEW

The debate over judicial review is as old as the debate over the American constitution itself. Although the power of the Supreme Court to nullify legislative acts by declaring them unconstitutional is nowhere explicitly granted in that constitution, Federalists supporting ratification such as Alexander Hamilton hoped, and anti-Federalist opponents of ratification such as Robert Yates feared, that Article 3, section 2, which declares that "The judicial power shall extend to all cases in law and equity arising under this constitution, the laws of the United States, and treaties made, or which shall be made, under their authority," would be invoked by the Court to justify overturning acts of Congress that were deemed to be inconsistent with other provisions of that constitution. In fact this is exactly what happened, for the first time, in 1803 in *Marbury* v. *Madison* when Chief Justice John Marshall, writing for the Court, declared section 13 of the Judiciary Act of 1789 unconstitutional. Ever since then judicial review has been one of the defining, yet still controversial, features of the American system of government. The controversy boils down to the question of whether, or the extent to which, the nullification of laws passed by elected representatives of the people, by judges who are not elected by the people, is consistent with the republican principle of popular sovereignty, or, more simply, whether or the extent to which judicial review is consistent with democracy.

This was the issue joined by Hamilton in *Federalist 78* and Yates in his "Letters of Brutus." Yates argues that judicial review implies the supremacy of the judicial over the legislative branch of government and that it is therefore inconsistent with republican, or representative democratic, government. Hamilton tries to rebut this argument and to demonstrate that judicial review is an essential "bulwark against the legislative encroachments" that, as we have seen, so worried his colleague James Madison. I will begin with a summary of Yates's position, since his "Letters" were in fact published a few months before Hamilton's *Federalist 78*, which is an explicit rejoinder to some of the arguments in those letters. (I will not focus on Yates's characteristically anti-Federalist preoccupation with the supposed way in which federal judicial review, like other provisions of the proposed constitution, would weaken and ultimately destroy the power of the individual state governments, but rather concentrate exclusively on his claim that judicial review is incompatible with popular sovereignty whether exercised at the state or national level, since that is the issue that is joined by Hamilton in *Federalist 78*.)

Yates's argument, in a nutshell, is that the judicial review (that he believes is) authorized by Article 3, section 2, would entail an unaccountable and therefore illegitimate exercise of tremendous power. On the one hand, and against those who, like Hamilton in *Federalist 78*, would claim that the judiciary, including the Supreme Court, would be confined to the "steady, upright and impartial administration of the laws,"[1] Yates argues in Letter XV that "this court will be authorized to decide on the meaning of the constitution, and that, not only according to the natural and obvious meaning of the words, but also according to the spirit and intention of it."[2] In other words, what we now call "strict constructionism" is effectively impossible, because (as Yates argues in Letter XI) judges "will not confine themselves to fixed or established rules, but will determine, according to what appears to them, the reason and spirit of the constitution":[3] judicial interpretation necessarily requires an interpretation of not merely the letter but also the "spirit" of the laws, and interpretation of the spirit of the laws necessarily leaves room for a great deal of judicial discretion and thus judicial power. Thus there is no way to ensure that judges will not inject their personal or political preferences in the course of determining whether a given law is or is not consistent with the meaning of the constitution.

On the other hand, under the proposed constitution there would be absolutely no check on this inescapable exercise of judicial power. Because (Supreme Court) justices would be appointed for life (contingent on "good behavior"):

> there is no power above them, to controul any of their decisions. There is no authority that can remove them, and they cannot be controuled by the laws of the legislature. In short they are independent of the people, of the legislature, and of every power under heaven.[4]

Thus Yates questions whether there was ever "a court of justice with such immense powers, and yet placed in a situation so little responsible," and concludes that "in the exercise of this power [of deciding upon the meaning of the constitution] they will not be subordinate to, but above the legislature."[5] Hence judicial review is inconsistent with popular sovereignty or republican government.

Although Yates rejects judicial review as a remedy for legislative abuses, he is by no means insensitive to the need to correct those abuses. But he believes that the only way to correct them that is consistent with republican principles is to rely on the people themselves: if the people's elected representatives "determine contrary to the understanding of the people, an appeal will lie to the people at the period when the rulers are to be elected."[6] In short, the people can vote abusive legislators out of office. When, in contrast, the power to remedy the evil "is lodged in the hands of men independent of the people," that is, in the hands of judges "who are not accountable [to the people] for their opinions, no way is left to controul them but *with a high hand and an outstretched arm*,"[7] in other words by forcible measures. Thus judicial review is not only undemocratic, it is also a recipe for political instability.

Hamilton in *Federalist 78* attempts to rebut Yates's case against judicial review in at least two different—and not necessarily compatible—ways. First, he argues, famously, that "the judiciary is beyond comparison the weakest of the three departments of power . . . it may truly be said to have neither Force nor Will, but merely judgment."[8] The claim that the judiciary lacks force clearly refers to the fact that the judiciary is entirely dependent on the executive branch to enforce its decisions. But the claim that the judiciary lacks *will* is less clear and is I think harder to sustain. Presumably Hamilton means that the judiciary is *reactive* rather than proactive: it responds to cases that are brought before it rather than initiates action of its own. But the mere fact that the judiciary decides cases that are brought before it on the initiation of others in no way guarantees that the will of the judges will not be exercised in the course of deciding those cases. In fact Hamilton acknowledges that judges might "substitute their own pleasure [for] the constitutional intentions of the legislature," but argues that this fact in no way counts against judicial review, since the risk that judges might be "disposed to exercise will instead of judgment" is present not only in constitutional interpretation but in ordinary, non-constitutional types of judicial decision making as well: "the observation, if it proved anything, would prove that there ought to be no judges distinct from that [legislative] body."[9] In other words, he attempts to undermine the force of Yates's objection that Supreme Court judges will exercise unaccountable power in interpreting the constitution by arguing that, since this danger is inherent in any type of judicial decision making, Yates's objection logically leads to the (absurd) conclusion that a judiciary independent of the legislature should not exist at all. But surely the consequences of the "substitution of the pleasure [of judges] to that of the legislative body" are far more serious when it comes to the interpretation of the constitution than to ordinary adjudication, so Yates has good reason to be more far more worried about the former than the latter exercise of judicial power. And, to the extent that Hamilton grants that there is a permanent possibility that any judge who "must declare the sense of the law" might be "disposed to exercise will instead of judgment," he undermines his own claim that the judiciary "may truly be said to have neither Force nor Will, but merely judgment." Indeed, it can be argued that judgment—since it presupposes discretion—*always requires* an exercise of will, and that the opposition that Hamilton attempts to establish between "will" and "judgment" necessarily breaks down.

Indeed, Hamilton's other main argument against Yates implies as much. Yates, you will recall, argued that a judicial nullification of a law passed by the representatives of the people would be an exercise of power that was contrary to the will of the people, and thus would be inconsistent with popular sovereignty. Hamilton cleverly parries this objection by arguing, to the contrary, that in upholding the constitution against the legislature the court would be representing the will of the people in opposition to the will of their (supposed) representatives: "where the will of the legislature declared in its statutes, stands in opposition to that of the people declared in the constitution, the judges ought to be governed by the latter, rather than by the former." But this conclusion, according to Hamilton, does not "by any means suppose a superiority of the judicial to the legislative power. It only supposes that the power of the people is superior to both."[10] Thus Hamilton, by equating the court with the constitution and the constitution with the will of the people, is able to argue that an unelected court is actually more responsive to the will of the people—*more democratic*—than the legislatures the people elect.

But this argument is unpersuasive, because Hamilton arbitrarily assumes that any law overturned by the court would be an expression not of the will of the people but rather of their (supposedly unresponsive) representatives. Rather than independently ascertaining the will of the people, he effectively equates the will of the people with the will of the court whenever it acts against the will of the legislature. But one could with as much or even more reason equate the will of people with the will of their elected representatives—which is exactly what Yates does—and thus conclude that when the court overturns a law passed by the representatives of the people the court is contravening the will of the people, and thus undermining democracy. Thus Hamilton's effort to reconcile judicial review with democracy or popular sovereignty is ultimately unsuccessful.

Consequently it has fallen to subsequent legal scholars to wrestle with this problem. In recent years—especially since the 1960s period of so-called "judicial activism"—a number of different approaches to this problem have emerged, only two of which I have space to discuss in this chapter. The first—associated above all with the writings of Judge Robert Bork—is usually referred to as "originalism," which, as the name implies, argues that judges' interpretation of the constitution should be guided exclusively by their understanding of the intent of the original framers of the constitution. Thus, according to this approach, the only legitimate reason for declaring a law unconstitutional would be the incompatibility between that law and "the principles [the framers] enacted, the values they sought to protect."[11] Worried about "activist judges"—for him, Liberal judges—who (supposedly) read their own personal or political preferences into the meaning of the constitution, Bork prescribes deference to the intentions of the framers as the only way to prevent this kind of judicial license and thus to reconcile judicial review with constitutional democracy. Only if judges confine themselves to the meaning of the constitution as it was understood by the framers of the constitution can the power of judicial review be reconciled with the principles of representative democracy, because in this case judges would be guided exclusively by the (popular) intentions that authorized representative democracy in the first place. In the words of Bork, "no other method of constitutional adjudication [than originalism] can confine courts to a defined sphere

of authority and thus prevent them from assuming powers whose exercise alters
. . . the design of the American republic."[12]

But Bork's argument that the intentions—understood as the principles and
values—of the framers should be determinative in judicial review suffers from
a number of serious—I think ultimately fatal—defects.[13] To begin with, there
is no unambiguous way to identify the "principles and values" enshrined by
the framers in the words of the constitution. At the time of the founding, the
American public was in fact deeply divided over the meaning of such values
as freedom and equality. Thus there was no consensus on what the "public at
that time would have understood the words [of the constitution] to mean"[14]
and thus the appeal to a supposedly original understanding cannot suffice to
determine the particular interpretation of the "principle and values" that judges
should apply in deciding contemporary cases. Second, some of the principles
and values that *were* widely accepted are clearly repugnant to modern sensibilities: the constitution legitimated slavery by specifying that, for purposes of
legislative apportionment, slaves should count as three-fifths of a person, and
all women were excluded from citizenship because it was assumed that they
were intellectually inferior to men. Originalist jurisprudence, it would seem,
would require that current commitments to human equality and dignity be
trumped by long since repudiated commitments to racial and sexual inequality.
And it is not clear how an originalist such as Bork could resist this conclusion
without drawing distinctions between acceptable and unacceptable original
"principles and values," a distinction that itself could not be legitimated by an
appeal to origins. Finally, and relatedly, originalists such as Bork never convincingly explain why the interpretations of past generations—in this case the
founding generation—should be binding on present generations, who, after all,
have the benefit of more than two hundred years of political hindsight that was
not available to the founding generation itself.

John Hart Ely attempts to avoid these difficulties of originalism—its problematical assumption of an original consensus as to the meaning of the constitution,
its apparent endorsement of relationships of domination and subordination,
and its arbitrary assumption of the superior wisdom of past generations—by
justifying judicial review as a means of protecting and enhancing democratic
participation. Unelected judges can serve democracy—judicial review is consistent with popular sovereignty—when they strike down laws that "impede the
democratic process,"[15] that limit citizens' political participation. For example,
Ely argues that judges may legitimately overturn laws that discriminate against
so-called "minorities," that place unreasonable limits on popular assembly, or
that make it unnecessarily burdensome for people to vote.[16] In all these cases
judges would be acting to open up closed channels of popular participation and
making it more likely that the will of the people will prevail. Thus insofar as
judicial review is confined to the defense of procedural or "participational" values there is, according to Ely, no inconsistency between judicial review and the
fundamental principle of republican government, namely that people should be

governed only by laws that (through their elected representatives) they impose on themselves.

The problem, however, is that Ely is able to reconcile judicial review and popular sovereignty only at the cost of an overly narrow scope of judicial review. The constitution guarantees any number of rights that are not (directly or obviously) participational—the right not to testify against oneself, the right not to be subject to unreasonable search and seizure, the right freely to exercise one's religion, perhaps the right to privacy, etc.—and Ely's participational defense of judicial review would appear to prevent judges from striking down laws that violate these non-participational rights, thus leaving them unprotected from the tyranny of an unprincipled majority. It is of course possible to respond to this danger with the argument that the rights to which I have just referred, as well as others, are ultimately essential for political participation—that they are, in effect, "participational" in an extended sense of that term—and should therefore be protected through judicial review. But the difficulty here is that, since virtually any right could be considered participational, we would be left with no effective way to delimit or justify the scope of judicial review. Moreover, in the name of "participation" more rights could be read into the constitution than are actually set forth in that document. For example, because gross economic inequality obviously impedes equal political participation, a court that was committed to enhancing participation could well conclude that laws permitting the unequal acquisition of wealth, e.g., laws that protect private property in the means of production, were unconstitutional. Equalizing the distribution of wealth might indeed be a desirable political outcome, but if we believe in democracy presumably we believe that this outcome should be produced by elected representatives of the people rather than by unelected judges.

The general point I am making is this: if we construe the meaning of "participation" strictly, then the scope of judicial review in the name of participation would be much too narrow, but if we construe it broadly then in the name of participation a court could claim an entirely unlimited scope for judicial review and effectively assume the role of policy-makers, that is, usurp the legislative function that ought properly be left to the people and or their elected representatives. Thus it seems to me Ely's "participationalism" is no more successful in reconciling judicial review with popular sovereignty than is Bork's originalism.

What Bork's and Ely's positions have in common—despite the obvious differences between them—is what Ingram calls a "backward-looking"[17] concept of democratic legitimation. That is, they both assume that the decision of the court is final and that a prior justification for its finality must be found. Bork finds this source to be the (publicly articulated) intentions of the framers: judicial review is legitimate only if it is consistent with those intentions. Ely defines this source as democratic procedure: judicial review is legitimate only if it protects popular participation. It may be that if we think of democratic legitimation in this way there is no effective way to legitimate judicial review. If we assume that the decisions of the Court are final—a case of the will of unelected judges trumping the will of elected representatives—then we will inevitably conclude that these decisions are in tension with democracy, and will look for ways to reduce that tension by limiting the scope of judicial review. But limiting the scope of judicial review means limiting the ability of judges to protect *and* expand our rights in a way that reflects our developing moral sensibilities.

In contrast, what Ingram calls a "forward-looking"[18] concept of democratic legitimation might offer a more promising approach. If we think of the outcome of a judicial review as not a final, definitive result but rather a contribution to an ongoing democratic dialogue among judges, legislators, judicial scholars, the press, and the general public, then the legitimacy of the judicial outcome cannot be evaluated independently of the evaluation of this multifaceted democratic dialogue to which the judicial opinion is only one important contribution. This assumption of a dialogue between judges and other political actors implies, of course, that there is space for legislative and other democratic responses to the decisions of those judges, including amending the constitution, changing the composition of the court by the election of a President who is committed to that goal, publishing critiques of majority judicial opinions that give voice to the opinion of dissenting justices, demonstrating in front of the Supreme Court, etc. To the extent that this space exists and is occupied by people who listen to and perhaps even learn from each other, to the extent that judicial review helps to engender a robust and respectful conversation about how a society should be organized, judicial review can be considered to be consistent with, indeed to be an important contribution to, the democratic process. But this conclusion presupposes that we think of democracy as a process of society-wide *delibera-tion* rather than as a mere method of making decisions based on majority rule or the counting of votes. These conflicting conceptions of democracy are the subject of the next chapter.

4

CONCEPTIONS OF DEMOCRACY

"Thick" versus "Thin"

As we have seen, the controversy surrounding judicial review centers on the question of whether judicial review is or is not consistent with democracy. But we have yet to explore the meaning of the term "democracy." In fact democracy has long been a contested term within the discipline of political science. The Greek root of the term is the word *demos*, which means "people," so everyone agrees that democracy means rule by or of the people. But ever since the middle of the eighteenth century, and beginning with Rousseau's arguments in *On the Social Contract*, political theorists have debated whether democracy requires that the people should rule directly or merely indirectly, by means of their own participation or through the participation of those they choose to represent them. This theoretical debate, of course, has contemporary political implications: our evaluation of actually existing democracies such as the American government and the government of other mainly Western societies will depend decisively on what side we take on this debate. If we accept the case for representative democracy, then we will be more-or-less satisfied with the democratic character of these types of governments. But if we agree with the partisans of participatory democracy, then we will inevitably come to the conclusion that such governments, despite their conventional designation, are not in fact authentically democratic, and that many dramatic, far-reaching changes would have to be made before their people would actually be able to rule.

The definition of democracy in Robert Dahl's *Polyarchy: Participation and Opposition* reflects his conviction—justified elsewhere in his voluminous writings—that the government of a large-scale, modern society must be largely *representative* in nature. "I should like to reserve the term 'democracy'," he tells us, "for a political system one of the characteristics of which is the quality of being completely or almost completely *responsive* to all its citizens."[1] The criterion of responsiveness implies, of course, that the political system or government is *different* from the citizens and that in an ideal democracy the government will, in Dahl's words, "continue over a period of time to be responsive to the preferences of its citizens," that is, to *represent* those preferences. In order for this to happen, "all full citizens must have unimpaired opportunities . . . to formulate their preferences," to "signify their preferences to their fellow citizens and the government," and "to have their preferences weighed equally in the conduct of the government,"[2] which, in turn, requires the freedoms and institutional arrangements that we typically associate with the principles if not the practice of representative democracies. This distinction between principles and practices is important to Dahl, for he recognizes that "no large system in the real world is fully democratized" in the sense of his definition, and he therefore reserves the term "polyarchy" for those "real world systems" that are rather closer to than farther away from his democratic ideal.[3]

It is important to underscore, however, and once again, that Dahl's ideal is a representative and not a participatory democracy. Even though he considers "participation" along with "opposition" to be one of the "two theoretical dimensions of democratization," he confines "participation" to the role of "controlling and contesting the conduct of the government."[4] In other words, for Dahl "participation" either ensures that the government is responsive or challenges it when it is not. He does *not* include the "conduct of the government" itself in what he means by "participation." This is one reason why this concept of participation or citizenship is often referred to as "thin": citizens are expected to formulate and express their political preferences—to tell government what they want—but they are not expected to participate in the more demanding task of actually governing, of deliberating over those preferences and transforming them into laws they are obliged to obey.

As Benjamin Barber points out in *Strong Democracy*,[5] this limited or thin conception of democratic citizenship presupposes a number of contestable assumptions about the nature of individuals and the relationships they form. Like many political theorists, Barber refers to these assumptions as "Liberal," which in this context means something different from the contemporary meaning of "Liberal," understood as an ideology that is opposed to "Conservative." (In fact much of the contemporary debate between "Liberals" and "Conservatives" takes place within the framework of these assumptions.) Liberal political theory—from Thomas Hobbes to John Rawls—assumes that individuals are not naturally communal beings but are rather by nature self-interested—in Rawls's words, "mutually disinterested"[6]—in the sense that they experience others merely as the means to their private purposes or as the obstacles to the fulfillment of those purposes. Individuals need other people to get what they want but they also fear that other people will prevent them from getting what they want. Given this supposedly inevitable experience of the other as instrument or obstacle, social interactions are assumed to be naturally both instrumental and competitive. Whether because individuals are naturally aggressive or because they fear, and therefore attempt to preempt, the aggression of others, there is a permanent possibility that individuals will harm other individuals in the course of their self-seeking pursuits. Liberal political theory assumes, in other words, that there is an inevitable conflict between the claims of individual self-interest and the claims of society for self-protection, or between "freedom" and "law and order." Given this assumption, finally, it follows that the function of politics—understood as the government or the state—is to facilitate the pursuit of individual self-interest and to resolve conflicts among different self-interests, and thus to protect society from the consequences of their immoderate or violent pursuit. Hence Barber's characterization of the Liberal conception of politics as "zookeeping."[7]

This can be put in a different, less colorful, way. For Liberal political theory, politics is always a *means* or an instrument for implementing already existing preferences and for resolving conflicts among them. It is *not* something that creates or shapes these preferences in the first place. Politics is not essential to the development of the individual; it merely serves to implement or regulate what she is assumed *already*—prior to and independent of politics—to want. Starting from this assumption, specifically democratic Liberal political theory treats democracy as a preferred form of interest representation and conflict resolution. In other words, since politics in Liberal theory is a realm of need *implementation* rather than need *creation*, democratic politics can be representative in character. The task of democratic legislators, in short, is to represent—to re-present or present again—the already existing wants of their individual constituents, the wants that their constituents have already presented to them. Thus democracy is defended as the best method for ensuring that individuals get what they already want: because democratically elected representatives are, in principle, accountable to the people, they have an incentive (which autocratic legislators lack) to support policies and programs—to make laws—that reflect the (supposedly) pre-existing interests of the people. Political scientists committed to this Liberal democratic model often disagree over whether or the extent to which elected representatives are in fact accountable to the people, but this debate presupposes a common identification of democracy with representative democracy, which presupposes, in turn, and once again, a conception of politics as a realm of need implementation rather than need creation. To put this another way, it presupposes that individuals develop their needs and form their preferences entirely independently of their activity as citizens. Or, as Barber pithily puts it, "politics . . . become[s] what politicians do; what citizens do (when they do anything) is vote for the politicians."[8]

What for Barber is a harshly critical observation is for Joseph Schumpeter—writing forty years before Barber in the 1940s—blithely accepted as an inevitable fact of political life, and, in fact, actually incorporated into his definition of democracy. In *Capitalism, Socialism and Democracy* Schumpeter argues that we should abandon what he calls the "classical theory" that makes "the selection of representatives . . . secondary to the primary purpose . . . to vest the power of deciding political issues in the electorate" because that theory "attribute[s] to the electorate an altogether unrealistic degree of initiative" and ignores the (supposed) fact that "collectives act almost exclusively by accepting leadership."[9] If, in contrast, we are properly skeptical of the capacity of the people for "initiative" and appreciative of the need for "leadership" we should "make the deciding of issues by the electorate secondary to the election of the men who are to do the deciding." Thus "the role of the people is [merely] to produce a government." Hence his famous—or infamous—definition of democracy: "that institutional arrangement for arriving at political decisions in which individuals acquire the power to decide by means of a competitive struggle for the people's vote."[10]

If Dahl's conception of democracy is already "thin," Schumpeter's, we might say, is positively anorexic. With Dahl, at least, and as we have seen, the *responsiveness* of the government to its citizens is the defining measure of its democratic character. But Schumpeter's definition makes no reference whatsoever to responsiveness, and we are not entitled to infer from his emphasis on a "competitive struggle for the people's vote" that he means implicitly to include "responsiveness" as a democratic criterion. In fact Schumpeter makes it clear that he does *not* believe that democratic political competition guarantees, or even is likely to produce, "responsiveness." After drawing an analogy between economic and political competition—an analogy that transforms representatives into political entrepreneurs who "bid" for the support of the "political consumers" and that is the starting point for contemporary "rational choice" theories of political behavior—he tells us that political competition

> does not exclude the cases that are strikingly analogous to the economic phenomena we label "unfair" or "fraudulent" competition or restraint of competition. And we cannot exclude them because if we did we would be left with a completely unrealistic ideal.[11]

In other words, just as unfair or fraudulent economic competition allows producers to ignore or de-emphasize the preferences of consumers, so collusive arrangements among apparent political competitors—such as, for example, an agreement, perhaps all too frequent, to exclude certain issues from the electoral competition—precludes the possibility of political accountability or responsiveness, but without in any way casting doubt on what Schumpeter takes to be the existence of democracy. He even argues that the existence of democracy is perfectly compatible with what he calls a "faked" or "manufactured will" of the people:

> The ways in which issues and the popular will on any issue are being manufactured is exactly analogous to the ways of commercial advertising. We find the same attempts to contact the subconscious [and to create] favorable and unfavorable associations which are the more effective the less rational they are ... Thus information and arguments that are really driven home are likely to be servants of [the] political intent [of the leaders].[12]

Because "the people can in the short run be fooled step by step into something they do not really want," we should realize that "in reality they neither raise nor decide issues but that the issues that shape their fate are normally raised and decided for them."[13] Of course much of this may be an accurate description of what actually happens in the contemporary societies that we habitually refer to as "democracies." The problem is not that Schumpeter recognizes these facts, but that he treats them as inevitable and even builds them into his conception of democracy. In the process a substantive distinction between democracy and autocracy, political freedom and political slavery, becomes difficult if not impossible to draw. Why should we care about preserving or defending democracy if even indirect rule by or of the people is impossible?

Schumpeter's inability to draw anything but a purely formal distinction between political freedom and political slavery unwittingly testifies to the prescience of Rousseau's caustic critique of the slavish nature of political representation and the Liberal theory of human nature that supports it. In *On the Social Contract* he contests, to begin with, the assumption that a society is nothing more than a collection or aggregation of self-interested individuals whose individuality and preferences somehow antedate the formation of that society. He insists, to the contrary, that the individual is a *social* being: it is only because of his participation in a society—what we today call his or her socialization— that "his faculties are exercised and developed, his ideas broadened, his feelings ennobled and his whole soul elevated."[14] In addition to the "private interests" that distinguish individuals from one another, they are (or should be) united by a social bond that is formed by the common interests that they share. And, we have already seen in chapter 2, Rousseau argues that "it is uniquely on the basis of this common interest that society ought to be governed."[15]

Thus for Rousseau, in contrast to Liberal political theory, the function of politics is not to facilitate and regulate the expression of private interests but rather to ensure that the public interest will prevail. As we have also seen, the public interest will prevail only if what Rousseau calls the General Will prevails, that is, if the laws by which the citizens are governed are the result of a process of decision making in which all citizens participate and in which they all ask themselves: Is the (proposed) law in the general interest or not? Thus the General Will is general in a twofold sense. It is general as to its *object*: only insofar as individuals transcend self-interest and act on behalf of (what they take to be) the general or common interest do they truly function as *citizens* rather than merely private persons. And it is general as to its *formation*: "any formal exclusion destroys the generality."[16] To experience genuine freedom *all* the citizens who are obliged to obey the laws must participate in the formation of those laws, because, according to Rousseau, freedom is nothing other than "obedience to the law one has prescribed for oneself."[17]

This means that, for Rousseau, representative democracy is a contradiction in terms and is in fact a recipe for political slavery. If a good political society can only be a society governed by the General Will, then a good political society cannot avail itself of representatives who would substitute their will for the will of the people:

> Sovereignty cannot be represented for the same reason it cannot be alienated. It consists essentially in the general will, and the will cannot be represented . . . The deputies of the people, therefore, are not nor can they be its representatives; they are merely its agents. They cannot conclude anything definitively. Any law that the people in person has not ratified is null; it is not a law. The English people thinks it is free. It greatly deceives itself; it is free only during the election of members of Parliament. As soon as they are elected, it is a slave, it is nothing.[18]

This claim that any legitimate law must be ratified by the people in person stands as an enduring challenge to representative democratic theory and practice. Thus Rousseau can be considered, in certain respects and with certain qualifications I do not have space to detail,[19] a theoretical progenitor of the contemporary partisans of direct or participatory democracy, whether the Students for a Democratic Society who in their Port Huron Statement of 1962 demanded a "democracy of individual participation [in which] the individual share[s] in those social decisions determining the quality and direction of his life,"[20] or Benjamin Barber, who, two decades later, argued the case for a "strong democracy" in which "all of the people govern themselves in at least some public matters at least some of the time."[21] To "govern themselves," Barber insists, people "must develop a form of political consciousness that will enlarge [their] understanding and sympathies . . . and *transform* them into citizens capable of reassessing themselves and their interests in terms of . . . newly invented communal norms and newly imagined public goods."[22] Thus for Barber, in contrast to the Liberal tradition, the public "reformulation and reconceptualization" (and not merely the representation and/or regulation) of individual needs lies at the heart of politics, and an authentically democratic politics would demand that all citizens have frequent opportunities to participate in this deliberative, transformative process.[23]

Like Rousseau, then, Barber has a much "thicker," more demanding conception of citizenship than Schumpeter or even Dahl. Rousseau, for one, drew catastrophic conclusions from the failure of the citizens to meet such demands:

> As soon as public service ceases to be the main business of the citizens, and they prefer to serve with their pocketbooks rather than with their persons, the State is already close to ruin . . . as soon as someone says *what do I care?* about the affairs of the State, the State should be considered lost.[24]

There is no room for any doubt, then, about what Rousseau would have to say about the American and other states in which civic privatism and political apathy are increasingly the order of the day.

Rousseau tells us that in a well-constituted state, in contrast:

public affairs dominate private ones in the minds of the citizens. There is even less private business, because since the sum of common happiness furnishes a larger portion of each individual's happiness, the individual has less to seek through private efforts.[25]

This claim raises the question, of course, of whether capitalism and a "well-constituted state" are compatible, since capitalism encourages, perhaps even requires, individuals to seek their happiness through "private efforts." I will return to this question in the "Market and Power" part of this book. At this point I will leave you with two others. First, Rousseau himself lists the "immenseness of States" as one of the reasons for the introduction of representative government, and concludes that "I do not see that it is henceforth possible for the sovereign [i.e., the people] to preserve the exercise of its rights . . . unless the City [Rousseau's term for an association of citizens] is very small."[26] As many have argued after him, Rousseau here suggests that direct or participatory democracy may be unworkable in large-scale societies and that, since most people on the face of the earth now live in large-scale societies, the time for direct or participatory democracy may have passed.

It would be difficult to dispute the conclusion that millions of people separated by thousands of miles cannot possibly "in person ratify" the laws by which they are governed. "In person," no, but why not the "direct" and "simultaneous" participation of the multitude that computer-mediated communication makes possible?[27] Or, alternatively, and more radically, why not a reversal of the trend toward ever-bigger societies in the name of what Kirkpatrick Sale calls "human scale"?[28]

Rousseau acknowledges that not only scale but also *time* is a crucial participatory resource. He reminds the reader that the remarkably participatory nature of ancient Athenian and Roman democracies was purchased at the price of slavery: it was only because slaves did so much of the work that citizens had the time and energy for direct participation in the popular assemblies and the other affairs of state.[29] Now Rousseau was no defender of slavery—in fact, earlier in *On the Social Contract* he strenuously argues against it[30]—but he does not clarify how direct democracy might be possible without it. What we can say, I think, is this: people would have to work a lot *less* to participate in politics a lot *more*. This also raises the question of the compatibility between capitalism and participatory democracy, since it is an open question whether dramatic, or even significant, reductions in the working day, week, or year are possible in the context of a system that is predicated on the principle: grow or die. This, too, is a question to which I will return when I discuss the relationship between the state and the economy later in this book.

5

THE CONCEPT (AND REALITY?) OF REPRESENTATION

In the last chapter we saw that partisans of direct democracy such as Rousseau and Barber call representative democracy into question in the name of a vision of a society in which, to once again quote Barber, "all the people [directly] govern themselves in at least some public matters at least some of the time." But the fact is that we live today in a largely if not exclusively *representative* system, and even Barber's ideal—direct democracy with respect to *some* matters *some* of the time—implies a continuing need for political representation, even if it is supplemented by a number of more directly democratic features. So representation will inevitably remain a central feature of those political systems we call democratic for a long time to come, perhaps even forever. Thus it would seem to be important to understand precisely what we mean by political "representation." What does it mean to say that an elected official, and a legislator in particular, represents her constituents? To put this question another way, what conditions would have to be satisfied before we could confidently describe the American or any other contemporary political system as genuinely representative?

As Hanna Pitkin points out in *The Concept of Representation*, political scientists have been divided on this question for almost as long as there have been representative—or supposedly representative—democratic systems. She identifies two polar opposite positions which have framed the debate over the meaning of political representation. One school of thought is committed to the idea that an elected representative is merely a delegate or agent of the people who elect him, in the sense that his duty is merely to reflect faithfully whatever happen to be their wishes. On this concept of political representation, then, the representative should be bound by the *mandate* or instructions of his constituents, and thus violates his obligation if he acts in any way independently of their wishes. Thus the representation-as-mandate position effectively reduces representation to responsiveness: elected law-makers represent their constituents to the extent that they respond to their wishes.

The so-called "independence theorists," in contrast, argue that the role of representatives is to serve the *welfare* rather than wishes of their constituents. Since, according to Pitkin, "a constituency is not a single unit with a ready-made will or opinion on every topic ... a representative cannot simply reflect what is not there to be reflected."[1] In other words, it is often difficult if not impossible to determine exactly what the will of the people *is* that the representative is supposed to represent. And even if that will *could* be determined, their will is not necessarily identical to their welfare; what they wish is not necessarily the same as what is in their interest (a point to which I will return) and thus the representative whose duty it is to serve their interests cannot be bound by their wishes. Finally, if she *were* bound by their wishes, it would prevent her from properly fulfilling the responsibilities of a legislator, which include the "formulation of issues, the deliberation and compromise on which decisions should be based."[2] For all these reasons the independence theorists insist that the representative must be free to exercise independent judgment, and that she should be considered a *trustee*—someone with specialized knowledge who acts on behalf—of her constituents rather than someone who is supposed mechanically to register their preferences.

Pitkin argues that even though these positions are "opposite and incompatible" there is nonetheless a sense in which they are both right. The mandate theorist is surely correct to insist that a representative really doesn't deserve that name if he "habitually does the opposite of what his constituents would do." At the same time, the independence theorist is right to argue that the role of legislator regularly requires that the representative be committed to serve the interests of—to do the right thing for—her constituents and that this commitment requires the exercise of her independent judgment. Both positions are *partly* true, Pitkin claims, because "each holds part of the meaning of representation," but both are inadequate or incomplete because "each extrapolates incorrectly from that part."[3] To understand Pitkin's own position, then, we need to understand what she takes to be the "meaning of representation."

She begins with the assertion that "being represented means being made present in some sense, while not really being present literally or fully in fact."[4] The representative, in other words, would be entirely superfluous if the represented were literally or fully present within her, but if there were no presence in some sense of the represented in the activity of the representative then the representative would only be presenting herself and not re-presenting someone else. So Pitkin argues that "the represented must be both present and not present" in the activity of the political representative. The representative, she goes on to say in the very next sentence, "must really act, be independent; yet the represented must be in some sense acting through him."[5] The mandate theorist correctly insists that the represented be present in the activity of the representative, but fails to understand the sense in which complete or full presence of the represented would be inconsistent with the very "concept of representation" itself—would, in other words, eliminate or destroy representation. The independence theorist "gets" the sense in which the represented is not and cannot be fully present in his activity, but doesn't "get" that the represented must nevertheless "in some sense" be "acting through him."

Pitkin's own position purports to be a synthesis of these two polar opposite positions, a synthesis that attempts to incorporate what might be called the "relative truth" of each of them while leaving their errors behind. Thus she concludes that:

> the substance of the activity of representing seems to consist in promoting the interest of the represented . . . but in such a way that he does not object to what is done in his name. *What* the representative does must be in his principal's interest, but *the way* he does it must be responsive to the principal's wishes.[6]

Thus Pitkin, in contrast to both the mandate and independence theorists, incorporates *both* the wishes and the welfare of the represented, and thus both the responsiveness and independence of the representative, into her concept of political representation.

But this implies that it is *possible* for the representative to be both independent from, and responsive to, the wishes of the represented. How can this be? Pitkin's answer to this question turns on the distinction she draws between the interests and wishes of the represented and her understanding of the relationship between them. Although we often equate a person's interests with what he or she wants, Pitkin correctly points out that our everyday linguistic usage also countenances a more objective meaning of the term "interest": when we say, for example, that something is not good for someone even though she wants it, we imply that she doesn't know, or at least doesn't act according to, her own interest. For this reason it is possible to argue that persons have interests whose existence does not depend on their preferences, which preferences may sometimes in fact run counter to those interests.[7] It follows, according to Pitkin, that "representation does not require the principal [the represented] to have formulated 'a will' on issues before the representative, or even to know about them. One can represent others on matters they neither care nor know about." Or again: "The fact is that . . . the represented have no will on most issues, and the duty of the representative is to do what is best for them."[8]

Yet she also tells us that "the constituent's wishes are relevant to [their] interest[s]. Consequently the representative also has an obligation to be responsive to those wishes."[9] Thus, whenever the constituents *do* have an "express will," the duty of the representative is to be responsive to that will. In most cases this will mean, according to Pitkin, that the representative will carry out the wishes of their constituents, but if the representative believes that their wishes are in fact inconsistent with their interests he is not obliged to carry those wishes out, but he *is* obliged to explain to them why he is unwilling or unable to do so. "Responsiveness" in this case requires, in other words, that the representative make himself accountable to his constituents by informing them of the rationale for his unwillingness to be bound by what otherwise might be considered their mandate. Pitkin assumes, without sufficient justification to my mind, that this conflict between the expressed wishes of the constituents and the representative's view of their interest will be the exception rather than the rule. This assumption enables her to conclude that the "representative must act independently in his constituents' interests and yet not *normally* conflict with their wishes."[10]

However, if the conflict between the representative's view of the interest of his constituents and their expressed wishes were *not* exceptional—if they regularly differed—then it would be difficult to see how the representative could both exercise independent judgment and be responsive to the wishes of his constituents. Thus Pitkin's synthesis is ultimately based on the assumption of a *normal* coincidence or harmony between the perceived (by the representative) interests and expressed wishes of the constituents. But, as I have already suggested, she never adequately defends this assumption. Perhaps she tacitly assumes that the policy positions of representatives will generally coincide with the preferences of their constituents because the majority of their constituents have, after all, elected them and might be supposed to share those policy positions. But other political scientists have shown that the electorate is often unaware of the policy positions of the candidates for whom they vote, in part because, in an election between only two major party candidates, the candidates often have an incentive to attract "swing voters" by "moving to the middle" and blurring their policy positions in the process.[11]

It might be possible to argue that the fact that the representative normally wants to be re-elected creates an incentive for him to harmonize his view of his constituents' interests with their wishes, but this argument is not available to Pitkin, who tells us that "the representative's duty, his role as a representative, is generally not to get re-elected, but to do what is best for those he represents."[12] Presumably then she would have to argue that a representative who allowed his view of "what is best" for his constituents to be determined or even significantly influenced by his hopes for re-election would no longer be fulfilling his duty. Thus she could not rely on re-election pressures as the reason for the supposed harmony between the perceived interests and the expressed wishes of the constituents. And it is not clear what other reason might account for that harmony.

The general point is that it may not be as easy as Pitkin thinks for representatives to combine the two commitments that she treats as definitive of representation, namely, once again, independent judgment and responsiveness to the represented. In practice one might have to be sacrificed to the other. Since 1967, when Pitkin's book was published, and especially over the past two decades, the proliferation of regular, even constant polling of constituents carried out by their representatives would seem to suggest that this is indeed the case. The practice of polling allows representatives to determine the wishes of their constituents with respect to a wide range of issues that might be important to them, and thus *appears* to signal a commitment on the part of representatives to defer to those wishes. Indeed, a common contemporary complaint about American legislators is that many of them are increasingly basing their legislative decisions on the results of their polling and sacrificing their independent judgment in the process. The balance between the independent judgment required for the welfare of the represented and the responsiveness to their wishes has, it is argued, shifted significantly in the direction of responsiveness to their wishes.[13] But there is something superficial about this complaint, since it uncritically assumes that polling merely registers or measures a *pre-existing* set of wishes, when it may in fact help to shape or even construct those wishes in the first place. Asking people one set of questions tends to define the questions asked as the important ones, whether or not they really are as important to the constituents as another set of questions that might have been asked. And obliging them to choose among a limited range of answers to those questions encourages them to adopt a position on a policy that they might otherwise never even thought about, one that might be very different from the one they would have held had they thought about it. So the point is that the representative who designs his policy positions to conform to the results of his polling may in fact be conforming those policy positions to a "will" that he has (perhaps unknowingly) helped to create.[14] After many years of regular polling it may no longer be true (four decades after Pitkin wrote) that the represented "have no will on most issues," but whether that will is authentic—whether it is autonomously formed or the artifact of the very methods ostensibly designed to measure it—is an open question. Thus what at first glance looks like increasing responsiveness may in many cases simply provide "cover" for the representative to pursue his independent objectives. And whether these objectives include a commitment to serve the welfare or interests of his constituents is also an open question.

This brings us, all too briefly, to Kenneth Prewitt's and Heinz Eulau's empirical study of the "representativeness" of eighty-two city councils in the San Francisco Bay area. To make a long story very short, they find that what they call a "representative relationship between governors and the governed"[15] is most likely to emerge (a) in larger, more diverse communities in which more interest groups or "attentive publics" are typically found than in smaller, more homogeneous communities; (b) in communities—relatively few in number—characterized by what they call "forced electoral turnover," that is, in which some councilmen are voted out of office and others therefore have to worry that they might be as well; and (c) in communities whose citizens are relatively unsupportive of, relatively dissatisfied with, the performance of the council. To put this the other way around, councils are least representative—councilmen are most likely to "rely on their own sense of what the community needs were"[16]—when the community is small and relatively homogeneous, when the risk of being turned out of office is small, and when "the citizenry is on the whole satisfied with council operations and policies and is apparently giving the council its support."[17]

There are, it should be noted, a number of conceptual and methodological problems with this study. Notice, to begin with, that Prewitt and Eulau define "representativeness" exclusively in terms of "responsiveness." They tell us that they "do not explore here" the issue of whether councils in supportive communities that do not face external pressures are "acting *in the interest* of the represented."[18] Neither do they explore that issue in the case of the "responsive" councils; rather they tacitly assume that if they *are* responsive they must be acting in the interests of their constituents. This means that, although they refer approvingly to Pitkin's book—published just a few years before their article—in fact their reduction of representation to responsiveness captures only one part of what for Pitkin the concept of representation requires. Recall that for Pitkin representation requires a combination of responsiveness *and* the independent judgment necessary to serve the welfare or interests of the represented. For Pitkin, then, the councils that Prewitt and Eulau characterize as representative might or might not be representative depending on whether their representatives exercise independent judgment, and, on the other hand, the councils that they describe as unrepresentative (because relying "on their own sense of what the community needs were") might well be considered representative according to Pitkin's criteria; remember she argues that "representation does not require the principal to have formulated 'a will' on issues before the representative, or even know about them. One can represent others on matters they neither care nor know about." From Pitkin's point of view then, Prewitt's and Eulau's study of "what representatives in fact do" might be a classic case of an "empirical investigation" that "is no less ambiguous in its results than traditional 'normative' controversy," a study that builds in "conceptual ambiguity" into "the questions we ask . . . or the population we interview."[19]

Of course Prewitt and Eulau might respond by arguing that they "do not explore" the question of whether councils are "acting in the interest of the represented" because there is no way empirically or "scientifically" to answer that question: How, they might ask, can we possibly determine or measure the interests of people independently of their expressed preferences? We will come back to this question later in this book when we encounter the concept of "power." For now I think it is fair to say that—whatever the answer to this question— Prewitt and Eulau have sacrificed the concept of representation on the altar of methodological rigor, and quantitative methodology in particular. That is, they have defined the concept in such a way that it can easily be *measured*, losing the richness and complexity of that concept in the process.

This commitment to what can (easily) be measured also explains, I think, some of the methodological limitations of their study. Their study was based on *interviews* with 423 city councilmen. Thus in determining the "representative style" of their eighty-two councils Prewitt and Eulau studied not how councilmen actually *act* but merely how they *say* they act. And there may of course be a difference between words and deeds. Councilmen, in other words, may have an incentive to describe themselves as either more "responsive" or more "independent" than they really are. The only way to tell would be to compare their actual behavior with the expressed preferences of their constituents, but this would obviously require a great deal more time and energy—would be a lot more difficult to determine or measure—than it takes to merely interview councilmen. Similarly, and as Prewitt and Eulau themselves note, to their credit, "although we sometimes speak of community support for the council, we actually are inferring level of support from responses of the councilmen themselves."[20] Here we are entitled to wonder whether this is a legitimate inference. Might not those councilmen who see themselves as acting relatively independently of "interest groups or attentive publics" have a strong incentive to justify or legitimate their "independence" by claiming that it was supported by a satisfied community? The fact that Prewitt and Eulau discover a close correlation between councils that "rely on their own sense of what the community needs were," on the one hand, and high levels of "community support," on the other, could be considered evidence of another example of the way in which representatives "construct" the represented in the very act of purporting to represent them, thus transforming representation into a self-justifying circle.[21] To determine whether or the conditions under which this cycle could be broken would require a very different study from the one that Prewitt and Eulau conducted.

6

POLITICAL PARTIES

It would appear that representative democracy and political parties are two sides of the same political coin: almost everywhere that there are democratically elected representatives there are political parties to which they belong. It is not difficult to understand why this should be the case. The members of a democratically elected assembly (or legislature) who want to pass laws that are opposed by other members of that body will inevitably unite, that is, form a caucus, whose purpose is to maximize the number of votes on which they can rely and thus enhance their chances of passing those laws. The members who are opposed to those laws, in turn, will inevitably form counter-organizations that are designed to maximize *their* voting strength. Since the members of these opposing organizations also generally wish to be re-elected, it is equally certain that they will eventually attempt to employ their embryonic party organizations on behalf of the goal of mobilizing as much support as possible among the voting population. When organized competition within the legislature expands in this way into organized competition for the votes of the electorate, we can speak of the full-blown emergence of political parties. In short, parties attempt to win elections and thus gain for their members and supporters at least a share in governing the society. Thus E. E. Schattschneider, in his 1942 classic, *Party Government*, defines a political party as "an organized attempt to get . . . control of the government."[1]

Although this goal of party control of the government would, in the sense I have outlined, seem to be inherent in the very logic of representative democracy, the founding fathers of the American constitution, and James Madison in particular, were in fact *opposed* to this goal: they did *not* want the government to be controlled by one or more political parties. And Madison was opposed to this goal because he assumed that political parties were, at best, *necessary evils*. Thus in *Federalist 10* Madison *defines* a party or a faction—he, like his colleague Hamilton, uses these terms interchangeably—as:

a number of citizens, whether amounting to a majority or a minority of the whole, who are united and actuated by some common impulse of passion, or of interest, adverse to the rights of other citizens, or to the permanent and aggregate interests of the community.[2]

By Madison's definition, then, a political party is *necessarily* opposed to the public interest: it embodies and promotes *partial* interests—partisan interests—that are inimical to the welfare of the society as a whole.

But if parties are, in this sense, evil, they are also necessary: "the latent causes of faction are . . . sown in the nature of man." And Madison claims that the most important of these causes is economic inequality:

> From the protection of different and unequal faculties of acquiring property [and Madison insists that the "first object" of government is the protection of these faculties], the possession of different degrees and kinds of property immediately results: and from the influence of these on the sentiments and views of the respective proprietors, ensues a division of the society into different interest and parties.[3]

Or, as he puts it more pithily on the next page of *Federalist 10*, "the most common and durable source of factions, has been the various and unequal distribution of property."[4]

Since this as well as other sources of faction or party "are [supposedly] sown in the nature of man," it follows that "the *causes* of faction cannot be removed; and that relief is only to be sought in the means of controlling its *effects*." When the "faction consists of less than a majority," he continues, this is of no great concern, because "the republican principle . . . enables the majority to defeat its sinister views by regular vote." But:

> when a majority is included in a faction [when, in other words, a political party is able to gain the support of a majority of citizens] the form of popular government . . . enables it to sacrifice to its ruling passion or interest, both the public good and the rights of other citizens. To secure the public good, and private rights, against the danger of such a faction, and at the same time to preserve the spirit and the form of popular government, is . . . the great object to which our enquiries are directed.[5]

Here we re-encounter Madison's famous fear of the "tyranny of the majority" that we first encountered in *Federalist 51*. There the danger was "legislative encroachment" on the powers of the other branches of government, and the solution was to weaken the legislature, to divide it against itself. In *Federalist 10* the danger is majority party control, and the solution is to *weaken the power of the majority party*: "the majority . . . must be rendered, by their number and local situation, unable to concert and carry into effect schemes of oppression."[6]

Madison goes on to argue that a "Republic, by which I mean a Government in which the scheme of representation takes place [in contrast to a direct democracy] promises the cure for which we are seeking." It does so, according to Madison, in two different ways. First it works—or so he claims—to

> refine and enlarge the public views, by passing them through the medium of a chosen body of citizens, whose wisdom may best discern the true interests of their country, and whose patriotism and love of justice, will be least likely to sacrifice it to temporary or partial considerations.

In other words he anticipates that (supposedly) wise elected representatives will be generally far less likely to fall victim to the spirit of faction than the ordinary citizens who elect them. But he also realizes that this may not always be the case—that representatives of "factious tempers . . . may betray the interests of the people"—and he therefore argues in favor of a large rather than small republic, in part on the grounds that the large republic is more likely to produce a larger number of "fit" representatives who would serve as "proper guardians of the public weal."[7]

However, as I suggested at the beginning of this chapter, even the most enlightened, public-spirited legislator wants to win—if only to be able to implement the program she believes is needed by the public—and in order to win she will almost always need the support of a party organization. In relying on enlightened representatives to check the spirit of faction Madison fails to grasp the sense in which elected representatives—no matter how enlightened—are therefore actually far *more* likely to embrace that spirit than the citizens who elect them. Thus think it is fair to say that this part of Madison's argument is an exercise in wishful thinking.

But Madison's republican (supposed) solution to the problem of faction does not stop there. He counts not only on public-spirited representatives but also, and above all, on the *multiplicity of interests* that inevitably proliferate in an "extended" republic to prevent the emergence of majority party control of the government. Here I think it is important to cite one of the most frequently cited passages from the *Federalist Papers*—almost in its entirety:

> The other point of difference is, the greater number of citizens and extent of territory which may be brought within the compass of Republican, than of [directly] Democratic Government; and it is this circumstance principally which renders factious combinations less to be dreaded in the former, than in the latter. The smaller the society, the fewer probably will be the distinct parties and interests composing it; the fewer the distinct parties and interests, the more frequently will a majority be found of the same party; and the smaller the number of individuals composing a majority, and the smaller compass within which they are placed, the more easily will they concert and exercise their plans of oppression. Extend the sphere, and you take in a greater variety of parties and interests; you make it less probable that a majority of the whole will have a common motive to invade

the rights of other citizens; or if such a common motive exists, it will be more difficult for all who feel it to discover their own strength, and to act in unison with each other.[8]

There are many things that could be said about this remarkable passage, but in the present context what is essential is this: Madison argues (a) that there will be a "greater variety of . . . interests" in a large republic than in either a smaller republic or an inevitably small direct democracy; (b) that because of this multiplicity of interests—of what we today call pluralism—it will be difficult for a majority to form based on a "common motive"; and (c) even if this common motive and thus this majority exists, it will be difficult for so many people divided by so much distance "to act in unison with each other," that is, for the majority to act effectively and thus gain control of the government. Thus Madison's solution to the problem of (majority) party control of the government is to rely on the multiplicity of interests and thus the (supposedly) "greater variety of parties" in a large republic to prevent "any one party [from] being able to outnumber and oppress the rest."[9]

But—as Schattschneider points out—the social and economic diversity of the American Republic has *not* in fact engendered a "greater variety of parties" and thus has not prevented majority parties from gaining control—or at least a measure of control—over the government. Ever since 1804 almost all presidential elections and most congressional elections have been (for all practical purposes) contests between two major parties, the diversity of whose supporters has not in fact prevented each party from uniting on behalf of a "common motive" or platform that distinguishes itself from the other party and that the winning party generally at least attempts to translate into public policy. So, even if American parties are typically weaker than their European counterparts—even if party control over individual legislatures is far less reliable than in most parliamentary systems—these parties have undeniably played a far more important role in the American Republic than Madison anticipated.

And that, for Schattschneider, is a very good thing. *Party Government*, he tells us, is "devoted to the thesis that the political parties created democracy and that modern democracy is unthinkable save in terms of the parties."[10] Whereas, as we have seen, Madison defines political parties in opposition to the public interest, Schattschneider argues that they are the indispensable servants of that interest. Parties are, in his words, "beneficent instruments of popular government,"[11] and for two main reasons. First, they have been responsible for the progressive *expansion of the electorate* from the time of the founding of the Republic to the middle of the twentieth century: "in the search for new segments of the populace that might [become party supporters], the parties have kept the movement to liberalize the franchise well ahead of the demand"; parties, in other words, "were forced by the competitive situation to make an effort to organize the electorate."[12] Second, parties work to *simplify the alternatives* confronting the voter: "the typical pattern of an election in which there is no party organization," he tells us, "is a multiplicity of candidates and a wide dispersion of votes among the candidates." In contrast, "the characteristic pattern of an election dominated by parties is a drastic limitation of the number of candidates and a high degree of concentration of votes."[13] In other words, it is far easier for the voter to choose between two candidates or even among a limited number of candidates each of whom is associated with a different political party than it is for the voter to choose among a potentially infinite number of candidates with no party affiliation to signal their policy preferences. Moreover, insofar as the party that wins the election attempts to implement those policy preferences, it is far easier to hold elected representatives who identify with those preferences accountable in the next election than if the electorate were obliged to evaluate the performance of the unaffiliated representatives individually and in detail. If you don't like the performance of the political party in power, all you need to know is the party affiliation of the individual representative in order to know whether to re-elect her or not.

The simplification of alternatives promoted by political parties is even more dramatic in what Schattschneider calls the "two-party system" of the United States. He argues that:

> In practice the two-party system means that there are only two major parties, one or the other of which usually has the power to govern . . . and that no minor party is able to become a third major party permanently. The gap between the second major party and the greatest minor party is enormous and insurmountable; no minor party in American history has ever become a major party, and no major party has ever become a minor party.[14]

This two-party system, he tells us, "is the direct consequence of the American election system."[15] This electoral system—which also prevails in Great Britain—allocates only one representative for each legislative district and usually specifies that the candidate who receives a plurality of votes in that district will be the winner of the election. In contrast to an electoral system based on proportional representation (PR), whereby the percentage of seats in the legislature that any given party garners will be roughly equivalent to the percentage of the national vote that party receives, and where voters therefore have an incentive to vote for candidates from a large number and wide variety of parties because they know that the party of their choice will gain representation in the legislature even if their favored candidate receives only a small fraction of the votes cast, in a single-member district, first-past-the post system the party of your choice has to win at least a plurality of votes in any one district before it will gain representation in the legislature. Suppose, for example, that a party competing for representation in the American House of Representatives receives 40 percent of the national vote but that vote were distributed in such a way that it never receives a plurality in any of the 435 congressional districts from which representatives are chosen. In this case 40 percent of the national vote would produce *zero* representatives for that political party. (On the other hand, as Schattschneider points out, theoretically a party could earn only 20 percent of the national vote and, if its support were concentrated in one geographical region rather than dispersed equally over many of them, could wind up with far *more* than 20 percent of the representatives in the House of Representatives.[16]) It is not hard to see—although Madison did not see it—that under this system (in contrast to the system based on PR), voters have no incentive to vote for minor party candidates whom they might otherwise favor, and in fact great incentive to vote against them, because voters realize that (a) only the party of the candidate who wins in a given district will receive representation and (b) minor party candidates have little or no chance of winning in that district. In short, under a single-member district, first-past-the-post system, a vote for a third or fourth party is normally considered a *wasted vote*. And, rather than waste their vote, most voters—if they vote at all—will typically vote for the major party candidate they consider to be the "lesser of the two evils." The American electoral system, then, confronts minor parties with seemingly "insurmountable" obstacles, thereby ensuring the hegemony of two major parties and preventing the translation of American social and economic diversity into the "variety of parties" that Madison wrongly anticipated.

For Schattschneider, once again, this is a good thing, and for two main reasons. First, he argues that "*the two-party system* [in contrast to a multi-party system based on PR] *produces majorities automatically*. Since there are only two major parties actually in the competition for power and these parties monopolize the vote, it is almost certain that one of them will get a majority."[17] Thus in the American (or British) system, governance does not depend on the arduous process of creating a governing coalition—often a most precarious, fragile coalition—*after* the election is over. Second, the two-party system "produces moderate parties." It guarantees that each of the two parties will be large and therefore composed of a variety of often conflicting interests which need to be held together by "compromise and concession." For example, normally the party cannot pursue policies preferred by its extreme left wing or right wing (but does the Republican Party still have a left wing?) without alienating and losing the support of the opposite wing. Thus, Schattschneider concludes, there is an inherent "tendency of the parties to avoid extreme policies."[18]

What for Schattschneider are the virtues of the two-party system are for Lisa Disch its vices. She argues, to begin with, that "to be confronted with an option of voting for one of only two viable candidates is to be forced to cast a vote (if we vote at all) not *for* the candidate we want but *against* the candidate we least prefer," and, pursuing an analogy advanced by Schattschneider between elections and markets, asks "why do voters accept as the ultimate in political freedom a binary option they would surely protest as consumers?"[19] In fact, she tends to interpret the dramatic, long-term decline in American voter turnout as an implicit protest against this "binary option," and thus concludes that "two-party competition has suppressed the electoral participation of dissenting groups and thereby exaggerated the consensual basis of American politics."[20]

Second, and relatedly, she argues that the moderating tendencies of the two-party system celebrated by Schattschneider often militate against the objective of the clear and simple political alternative to which Schattschneider is committed. She points out, for example, that during the 2000 presidential campaign both Gore and Bush "played down the issues that would have set them apart" in an effort to capture so-called "swing voters," confident that their more militant base of voters would continue to support them because they had, so to speak, nowhere else to go. The result was that the two party-system failed "to bring out the difference between them," blurring or even masking rather than simplifying the alternatives with which voters were confronted.[21] Is it not probable, she might ask, that many "swing voters" voted for George Bush because during the campaign he portrayed himself as a "compassionate conservative," even though he went on to pursue what can arguably be described as extreme right-wing policies?

Disch's objective, then, is to call the inevitability or seeming "naturalness" of this "deeply undemocratic" system into question. Against Schattschneider, she argues that the history of electoral fusion—which Schattschneider never mentions—demonstrates that it is possible, even within the framework of the American winner-take-all electoral system, to avoid the "binary option" that she thinks is so oppressive. Fusion allows a third party to nominate a candidate of one of the two major parties as its own candidate as well. It thus enables voters to vote for the party they prefer without having to fear that in so doing they will be wasting their vote. Because separate tallies are kept for the major party and minor party votes for the winning candidate, moreover, the victorious major party is necessarily aware of how much its victory depended on the help it got from the minor party, which increases the leverage of the minor party and encourages the major party to pursue policies that move in its direction, or that at least do not alienate it. One could imagine, for example, a winning candidate endorsed by both the Democratic Party and the Green Party who received a significant portion of her votes on the Green Party line, and who, as a consequence, would be obliged to pursue far more eco-friendly policies than if she ran on the Democratic Party line alone. This would largely have to be an exercise of the imagination, however, because fusion is currently legal in only a few states, and regularly practiced only in New York State. And, as Disch points out, in 1997 the Supreme Court in the *Timmons* case upheld the right of a Minnesota law banning fusion on the grounds that the "traditional two-party system" is sufficiently important to "sound and effective government" that states should be able to protect it "whatever the cost to third political parties."[22] Thus did the court contribute to the reproduction of the hegemony—the supposed inevitability—of the very system that Disch contests.

7

ELECTIONS

In a representative democracy elections are arguably the most important medium through which the will of the people is expressed and thus the principal means by which to hold representatives accountable to the people on behalf of those whom they claim to rule. Genuine electoral accountability presupposes, of course, that the will of the people is formed autonomously from, independently of, the political processes that purport to express that will; if the will of the people were merely a creature of the those who govern, it would scarcely be possible to argue that those who govern are kept in check by or are responsive to that will. Democratic accountability requires an *authentic* popular will. Yet, as we have seen, the authenticity of the popular will is precisely what Joseph Schumpeter, for one, denied: he claimed that what we call the will of the people is often "faked" or "manufactured" in ways that are "exactly analogous to the ways of commercial advertising." Thus, as we also saw, he argues that in a representative democracy elections do *not* in fact guarantee that the representatives will be *responsive* to those they are supposed to represent.

In *The Responsible Electorate* V. O. Key rejects the argument that the will of the voters is "faked" or "manufactured" and argues, instead, that:

> voters are not fools ... in the large the electorate behaves about as rationally and responsibly as we should expect, given the clarity of the alternatives presented to it and the character of the information available to it ... the portrait of the American electorate that develops from the data is not one of an electorate straitjacketed by social determinants or moved by subconscious urges triggered by devilishly skillful propagandists. It is rather one of an electorate moved by concern about central and relevant questions of public policy [and] of governmental performance.[1]

Because, Key argues, elected politicians are aware that the electorate is "moved by concern about ... questions of public policy," they necessarily worry about how their policy performance will affect "their fate at future elections."[2] Thus Key is far more optimistic about the responsiveness of representatives than Schumpeter and other proponents of the "voters are fools," or at least "can be fooled," school of thought.

Key comes to the conclusion that voters are responsible on the basis of a study of the correlations between voting *behavior* in U.S. presidential elections between 1936 and 1960, on the one hand, and the policy positions of voters as measured by surveys of their *attitudes* regularly conducted during that twenty-five–year period. His study is particularly, but by no means exclusively, concerned with the attitude of those voters he calls "switchers," that is, voters who switched either from voting for the Democratic candidate in one election to the Republican candidate in the next or from voting Republican to voting Democratic. In part he focuses on "switchers" because they obviously play "a significant role in a democratic system" by making it possible for one governing party to be replaced by another and thus permitting, if not bringing about, the "major adjustments that occur in the system."[3] But he also concentrates on them because of the conventional assumption that voters who move from one party to another are likely to lack stable policy preferences and are therefore vulnerable to the variety of manipulative, irrational appeals that the "voters can be fooled" school argues are determinative of their voting behavior. Key finds, contrary to that school of thought, that the switchers are, as the title of his unfinished book announces, thoroughly *responsible* voters, in the sense that they express policy preferences which are consistent with the policy positions of the party to which they switch: the great majority who moved from D to R or from R to D in any given two elections indicated (in their responses to the survey questions) that they believed that the party from which they switched no longer held the policy positions which they *continued* to prefer. People say they switched, in other words, because the party to which they switched better represented what they understood to be their interests (and most who didn't switch, Key's so-called "standpatters," also voiced policy preferences that were consistent with the positions of the party to which they remained loyal). Thus Key concludes that American voters are—at least in presidential elections—rational actors rather than irrational fools.

Key recognizes, however, that this conclusion is an *inference* that is not *proven* by his data. Those data demonstrate, as we have seen, a correlation between the political attitudes and the political behavior of voters: voters who switched from one party to another also believed that the party from which they switched no longer reflected their political views. But, as Key himself points out, correlation is not necessarily *causation*. To demonstrate that A and B—in this case policy preferences and voting behavior—usually occur together does not demonstrate that A *causes* B—in this case that the policy preferences caused the voting behavior. Just because darkness and the visibility of the moon are normally found to coexist, this doesn't mean that darkness *causes* the moon to rise. It is in principle possible, in other words, that voters actually switched for entirely different reasons than rational, policy-based ones, and that they merely retrospectively identified their (supposed) policy preferences as the reason for their switch. In principle possible, but, Key argues, most improbable, because if "switchers" are as feckless, as irrational, as the "voters are fools" school describes them, it is highly unlikely they would have sufficiently detailed information to "be able to simulate a pattern of policy preferences"[4] that was consistent with the positions of the party to which they had, for very different reasons, switched. Thus Key argues that it is reasonable to conclude that the voters are reasonable.

Yet Key qualifies this conclusion when he argues, as we have already seen, that "the electorate behaves about as rationally and responsibly as we should expect, *given the clarity of the alternatives presented to it and the character of the information available to it.*" And he amplifies this point—the pun is intended—when he compares an election to an echo chamber:

> The voice of the people is but an echo. The output of an echo chamber bears an inevitable and invariable relationship to the input. As candidates and parties clamor for attention and vie for popular support, the people's verdict can be no more than a selective reflection among alternatives and outlooks presented to them. Even the most discriminating popular judgment can reflect only ambiguity, uncertainty or even foolishness if these are the qualities of the input into the echo chamber.[5]

Here Key acknowledges that the quality or rationality of the voters' "output" depends decisively on the quality of the "input"—the alternatives and outlooks—presented to them. If, for example, the two parties did not present clear alternatives, or if the alternatives they presented were overly narrow in the sense that they excluded important issues that voters might care deeply about, we would have no reason to be confident about the quality of the electoral process and its result. To argue that, given the limited alternatives available to them, the voters were acting as "rationally" and "responsibly" as we should expect is not to say very much, as under those conditions we really shouldn't expect very much "rationality" or "responsibility" at all. So for all practical purposes Key admits that the voters—and the electoral system in which they participate—*may* not be so rational after all. To determine whether it is, it would seem, would require an evaluation of the "input" side of the echo chamber, that is, an appraisal of the quality of the alternatives presented to the voters. But the great weakness of Key's book is that he never even begins to undertake that appraisal. Thus his conclusions about the rationality of the voters remain open to question.

This brings us to a number of works that question, in different ways, the quality of the "input side" of what Key calls the electoral echo chamber. Walter Dean Burnham's by-now classic *The Changing Shape of the American Political Universe*[6]—published in 1965, one year before Key's book—is deeply indebted to, and in effect provides empirical support for, a seminal insight of E. E. Schattschneider in his *Semisovereign People*, which was published in 1960, or eighteen years after his *Party Government*: "the definition of alternatives is the supreme instrument of power; the antagonists can rarely agree on what the issues are because power is involved in that definition."[7] Schattschneider argued that the overwhelming electoral defeat of the Democratic-Populist candidate, William Jennings Bryan, in the election of 1896 produced a dramatic redefinition of the alternatives that would thereafter—at least until 1932—be presented to the American electorate: the smashing defeat of the populist challenge to the power of capital, that is, big business, produced a displacement of (what was prior to 1896) an increasingly salient class conflict and the substitution for that conflict of a sectional or regional conflict that worked to consolidate both the political power of capital outside the South and the conservative and racist planter class within it. What had previously been a lively and remarkably evenly contested two-party competition across almost the entire United States was transformed into a solidly Democratic South and an overwhelmingly Republican North and West, and thus culminated in the effective emergence of one-party government in most states in the Union:

> the extension of one-party areas meant that in 1904 less than one-seventh of the population of the United States lived in states in which the parties contested the election on relatively equal terms, while in 1920 only about 12 million out of 105 million Americans lived in states in which they had a choice between two major parties both of which had a chance to win.[8]

It would not be until the realignment of 1932 and the re-emergence (outside the South) of two-party politics in the midst of the Great Depression that class issues, and especially issues involving the crucial conflict between labor and capital, would re-emerge as alternatives that could be presented to the American electorate. Until that time the largely one-party system functioned to exclude entirely these alternatives from the mainstream of American political life. Schattschneider speculates that the consequence of the electoral realignment of 1896 was the dramatic decline in turnout—the proportion of eligible voters who actually voted—in presidential elections following 1896 compared with the remarkably high rates that typically prevailed prior to that time.

Burnham provides much more empirical evidence to support that speculation. He finds that there has been "a steep decline [in national turnout in both presidential and congressional elections] from 1900 to about 1930, followed by [only] a moderate resurgence since that time." Between 1848 and 1896 the mean or average turnout in presidential election ranged between 75 and 78 percent, and even in "off years," that is, when there were elections for Congress but not for the President, mean turnout ranged between almost 63 and 65 percent. Thus turnout in Northern states prior to 1900 actually approximated turnout in Western European democracies. But between 1900 and 1960 mean national presidential turnout was never higher than 65 percent, and was as low as 52 percent in the years between 1920 and 1928, and off-year turnout ranged between 35 and 48 percent.[9] Since 1962 (the last year fully included in Burnham's data set) moreover, mean national turnout in presidential and Congressional elections has either remained at the same relatively low levels or declined even further (depending on the precise way in which the eligible electorate is defined), confirming Burnham's claim that "the political realignment of the 1930s, while it restored two-party competition to many states outside the South, did not stimulate turnout to return in most areas to 19th century levels."[10]

Burnham's in-depth analysis of turnout in Congressional and state elections in four large Northern American states—Michigan, Ohio, Pennsylvania, and New York—and one so-called border state—Oklahoma—supports his national findings: all five states witnessed "the same pattern of decline in turnout and sharp increases in indices of voter peripherality after 1900."[11] By "indices of peripherality" Burnham means measures that, in addition to mean turnout, indicate what he takes to be a dissociation or a weakening link between citizens and the political system; included among these indices are what he calls "roll-off" and "drop-off." "Drop-off" refers to the difference in the percentage of people voting in presidential as compared with off-year elections. "Roll-off measures the tendency of the electorate to vote for 'prestige offices' but not for lower offices on the same ballot at the same election."[12] Burnham reasons that voters who vote in presidential elections but not in off-year Congressional elections, and voters who vote only for candidates at the top of the ticket, are more "peripherally" involved than so-called core voters, who vote in both kinds of elections and for candidates up and down the entire ballot. And he finds that in all five states both roll-off and drop-off increased dramatically after 1896 along with the equally dramatic declines in turnout. For example, he finds that, whereas during the Civil War era in Michigan more than three-quarters of the eligible electorate were core voters, with only 7 percent voting peripherally (and only 15 percent non-voters), by the 1920s, he tells us, "less than one-third of the potential electorate were still core voters, while nearly one-quarter were peripheral and nearly one-half remained outside the political system altogether," i.e., were non-voters.[13] The Michigan case, like the cases of the other states, is consistent with a national trend that has never been significantly reduced: "at present [1965] about 44 per cent of the national electorate are core voters, another 16 or so are peripheral, and about 40 per cent are still outside the political system altogether."[14]

Thus Burnham concludes that the data point to "the existence and eventual collapse of" a "late 19th century voting universe [that] was marked by a more complete and intensely party-oriented voting participation among the American electorate than ever before or since."[15] This finding, he argues, puts into historical perspective contemporary research that reveals a positive correlation between levels of education and levels of voting. Although it seems to be true now that, within the context of the current American political universe, more highly educated voters are more likely to vote, this positive relationship between education and voting certainly does *not* hold when we compare the current with the pre-1896 "universe." Prior to 1896 most people had far *lower* levels of formal education than after that period, but those lower levels of education did not prevent then from participating in electoral politics with far greater frequency and intensity than people participated after 1896 and right up until today.

This suggests that currently high rates of non-voting among the less educated as well as the poor should not be understood as an inevitable fact of life but rather "that the political system itself is responsible for its [non-voting's] continued existence."[16] Following Schattschneider, Burnham argues that:

> it is difficult to avoid the impression that while all the forms of political democracy were more or less scrupulously preserved, the functional result of the 'system of 1896' was the conversion of a fairly democratic regime into a rather broadly based oligarchy.[17]

"Rather broadly based," because at least half of the eligible electorate typically votes, at least in presidential elections. But an "oligarchy"—which means rule by the few, or the rich—nonetheless, because it becomes difficult if not impossible within this system to offer voters alternatives that might challenge the socio-economic status quo that well serves the rich and ill serves the poor. Burnham never quite says so directly or definitively, but he implies that this absence of meaningful economic alternatives accounts for "the concentration of socially deprived characteristics among the more than forty million adult Americans [the number is much higher forty-five years after Burnham's article was published] who today are altogether outside the voting universe." Non-voting, he leads us to believe, is a sign of a profound alienation "on a scale quite unknown anywhere else in the Western World,"[18] an alienation that is anything but an indication of the rationality of the electoral system. If, following V. O. Key, the rationality of the system is a function of the quality of the alternatives presented to the potential voters, then it would be difficult if not impossible to conclude that the system is rational.

This judgment is shared by Thomas Patterson, who argues in *Out of Order*[19] that the decline of political party control of the *nominating* process and the spread of presidential primaries since the early 1970s have only exacerbated the irrationality of the American electoral system. Although the goal of the McGovern–Fraser Commission was, beginning in 1972, to open up the nominating process to ordinary, rank-and-file party voters and thus to break the control of party leaders over that process, the result of the reforms that the Democratic Party adopted—soon followed by the Republican Party—was anything but the increased democracy that was intended. It did make the nominating process more competitive, in the sense that it allowed for a larger number of presidential hopefuls to compete for their party's nomination. But precisely because there were now so many candidates, who would have to appeal directly to ordinary party voters (and not the party leaders) for support, the candidates were increasingly obliged to rely on the mass media to make their case to the voters. Thus the press increasingly supplanted the party as the organizer of the presidential nominating process. As Patterson argues:

> When the parties established a nominating process that is essentially a free-for-all between self-generated candidates, the task of bringing the candidates and voters together in a common effort was superimposed on a media system that was built for other purposes.[20]

"Other purposes," because journalists, according to Patterson, "are driven by news opportunities, not by political values." Whereas "a party is driven by the steady force of its traditions and constituent interests," the press is preoccupied with the "new, the unusual, and the sensational"[21]—in short, with stories that will sell. Patterson argues that presidential candidates increasingly depend not on the ordinary party voter but rather on media decisions that are driven by considerations other than—indeed opposed to—what the voters need in order to make an genuinely *informed* decision. The outcome of the presidential primaries that will determine the nominee increasingly turns on perhaps irrelevant issues of marital fidelity or whether the candidate ever smoked marijuana, and on more-or-less arbitrary decisions of the press—a politically unaccountable press—to either pump up currently leading candidates or write off currently losing ones. Thus he concludes that "there is no purpose behind an electoral system in which the vote is impulsive and the outcome can hinge on random circumstance or minor issues."[22] If, as Schattschneider claims, "the definition of alternatives is the supreme instrument of power," and the definition of alternatives *begins with* the nominating process, over which the media exercise disproportionate control, then we should be properly skeptical of the claim that the people exercise power within the American electoral system.

8

CIVIL SOCIETY

In the past two decades "civil society" has become an especially hot political topic. Ever since the fall of what passed for Communism in the Soviet Union and its client states, scholars and journalists alike have insisted that the democratization of that and other regions of the world depends decisively on the creation of (a hitherto absent) dense and diverse network of voluntary associations in those societies, even as other commentators, such as Robert Putnam, have bemoaned what they take to be a decline in the number and vitality of these associations in the very nation—the United States—that is typically taken to be the model that the so-called "newly emerging democracies" are supposed to emulate. This near-consensus on the crucial importance of civil society to democracy owes a great deal to the arguments of Alexis de Tocqueville in his two-volume classic, *Democracy in America*, the first volume of which was first translated into English in 1835, shortly following Tocqueville's extended visit to the United States in the early 1830s. So I will begin the analysis of the concept of "civil society" with a summary and critique of the arguments of that aristocratic Frenchman.

On the very first page of *Volume I* Tocqueville informs us that:

> during my stay in the United States, nothing struck me more forcibly than the general equality of social conditions . . . the more I advanced in the study of American society, the more I perceived that the equality of conditions is the fundamental fact from which all others seem to be derived, and the central point at which all my observations constantly terminated.[1]

Tocqueville's observation is likely to strike the contemporary reader who is aware of the systematic racial and gender *in*equality in that era as something of an idealization, but it nevertheless contains an important grain of truth: most white males were small, landowning farmers, and among them the conditions of life and distribution of income *were* in fact remarkably equal, in comparison both with the European societies with which Tocqueville was familiar and with American society from the middle of the nineteenth century down to the present time.

Tocqueville also believes that America is only the most extreme example of a trend toward the equalization of social conditions that he identifies throughout "the whole of Christendom." He is deeply ambivalent about this anti-aristocratic trend. On the one hand, he acknowledges that the old order was in many ways oppressive, and argues that there is, in any event, nothing that can stop the egalitarian struggle against it: "it is universal, it is durable, it constantly eludes all human interference, and all events as well as men contribute to its progress."[2] On the other hand, he thinks that this egalitarian trend has replaced the beneficent "influence of a small body of citizens"[3]—strong individuals who were both independent and committed to the welfare of their communities—with the predominance of weak individuals who are neither independent nor communally oriented.

Thus, to begin with, Tocqueville is wary of the danger that the equalization of social conditions will supplant the traditional aristocratic virtue of obligation to others with naked self-interest. Consider what he says at a number of points in *Volume II*:

> When social conditions are equal, every man is apt to live apart, centered in himself and forgetful of the public.[4]

> Equality . . . tends to isolate them from one another, to concentrate every man's attention upon himself; and it lays open the soul to an inordinate love of material gratification.[5]

> Not only does democracy make every man forget his ancestors, but it hides his descendants and separates his contemporaries from him; it throws him back forever upon himself alone and threatens in the end to confine him entirely within the solitude of his own heart.[6]

At the same time that Tocqueville worries that social equality will dissolve communal bonds and produce individuals who only look out for themselves, he also fears that the dissolution of these bonds will increase the likelihood that these same individuals will succumb to what he calls the "despotic influence of a majority."[7] In *Volume I* Tocqueville claims that:

> Democratic republics extend the practice of currying favour with the many, and they introduce it into a greater number of classes at once: this is one of the most serious reproaches that can be addressed to them . . . In that immense crowd which throngs the avenues to power in the United States, I found very few men who displayed any of that manly candor, and that masculine independence of opinion . . . of former times, and which constitute the leading feature in distinguished characters wheresoever they may

be found. It seems . . . as if all the minds of the Americans were formed in one model, so accurately do they correspond in their manner of judging.[8]

In short, social equality leads to an overdependence on *what others think* even as it transforms them into strangers with whose welfare the self-interested individual is entirely unconcerned. Tocqueville is perceptive enough to recognize that egotism and conformism can—and he argues, in the United States, do—go hand-in-hand. And the tendency of social equality to produce weak, conformist individuals both encourages and is reinforced by the growth in the power of the state: weak individuals are obliged to depend more and more on the state to "produce . . . the commonest necessaries of life,"[9] and the more they come to depend on the state, the weaker, and thus more vulnerable to the despotic power of the majority—exercised through either public opinion or the state—they will become.

Since Tocqueville argues, as we have seen, that the trend toward social equality is irreversible, it follows that it is not possible to ameliorate the twin problems of egotism and conformism to which social equality gives birth by attempting to reverse that trend. The solution to those problems lies rather in the formation of an active, vibrant civil society—voluntary associations that mediate between the individual and the state—abundant evidence for which Tocqueville happily discovers in the United States:

> Americans of all ages, all conditions, and all dispositions constantly form associations. They have not only commercial and manufacturing companies, in which all take part, but associations of a thousand other kinds, religious, moral, serious, futile, general or restrictive, enormous or diminutive. The Americans make associations to give entertainments, to found seminaries, to build inns, to construct churches, to diffuse books, to send missionaries to the antipodes; in this manner they found hospitals, prisons, and schools. If it is proposed to inculcate some truth or foster some feeling by the encouragement of a great example, they form a society. Wherever at the head of some new undertaking you see the government in France, or a man of rank in England, in the United States you will be sure to find an association.[10]

According to Tocqueville, these flourishing voluntary associations temper or moderate the self-interest of the individual *and* help protect him against the tyranny of the majority to which he would otherwise succumb. They moderate self-interest by fusing personal interest with the interest of the association to which he belongs. Tocqueville claims that:

> In their political associations the Americans . . . daily acquire a general taste for association and grow accustomed to the use of it. There they meet

together in large numbers, they converse, they listen to one another, and they are mutually stimulated to all sorts of undertakings. They afterwards transfer to civil life the notions they have thus acquired and make them subservient to a thousand purposes. Thus it is by the enjoyment of a dangerous freedom [unrestrained liberty of association] that the Americans learn the art of rendering the dangers of freedom less formidable;[11]

and that:

Feelings and opinions are recruited, the heart is enlarged, and the human mind is developed by no other means than by the reciprocal influence of men upon one another. I have shown that these influences are almost null in democratic countries; they must therefore be artificially created, and this can only be accomplished by associations.[12]

Participation in voluntary associations "enlarges the heart" and "develops the minds" of individuals who would otherwise remain wholly preoccupied with themselves; they are schools of citizenship that teach individuals to identify their welfare with first the welfare of their group and then, Tocqueville believes, the welfare of the community as a whole. Thus by "connecting the notion of right with that of private interest,"[13] the institutions of civil society mitigate the egotistical tendencies of an egalitarian society.

These institutions also serve, according to Tocqueville, as protection against the tyranny of the majority, especially as exercised through the overweening power of the state. He avers that:

At the present time, the liberty of association is become a necessary guarantee against the tyranny of the majority . . . There are no countries in which associations are more needed, to prevent the despotism of faction or the arbitrary power of a prince, than those which are democratically constituted. In aristocratic nations, the body of the nobles and the more opulent part of the community are in themselves natural associations, which act as checks upon the abuses of power. In countries in which these associations do not exist, if private individuals are unable to create an artificial and a temporary substitute for them, I can imagine no permanent protection against the most galling tyranny.[14]

And he claims that:

No sooner does a government go beyond its [proper] political sphere and to enter upon this new track than it exercises, even unintentionally, an insupportable tyranny; for a government can only dictate strict rules, the opinions which it favors are rigidly enforced, and it is never easy to discriminate between its advice and its commands . . . Governments, therefore, should not be the only active powers; associations ought, in democratic nations, to stand in lieu of those powerful private individuals whom the equality of conditions has swept away.[15]

Thus the voluntary associations of civil society provide alternative centers of power to the state and thus reproduce under very different conditions the protection from centralized governmental control previously provided by the members of the aristocracy.

Although, as we have seen, Tocqueville assigns to voluntary associations both the goal of transforming the egotistical individual into the public-spirited citizen, on the one hand, and the goal of protecting that individual from the tyranny of the majority as exercised through the state, on the other, it is not difficult to understand that these two goals may in fact sometimes conflict, and that under certain circumstances it may not be possible to reconcile them. The idea that voluntary associations serve as "schools of citizenship," so to speak, presupposes a congruence or compatibility between what is learned in these "schools" and the requirements of citizenship in a liberal democratic society. But if—as is often the case—the values of the voluntary association are incon-sistent with the values of a liberal political order in which all are considered equal in the eyes of the law, then the goal of preparation for citizenship cannot be accomplished without state interference with that voluntary association. Consider the issue of exclusionary membership clauses—membership rules that exclude people on the basis of race, gender, or religion—in such volun-tary associations as private schools, law firms, labor organizations, or fraternal groups such as the Jaycees. The Supreme Court of the United States has upheld state laws banning racial and gender discrimination in such organizations as *not* violating the First Amendment right of freedom of association as long as the state law does not "significantly affect the members' ability to carry out the purposes of the organization."[16] Under these conditions, in other words, the power of the state to enforce anti-discrimination laws that reflect and express the egalitarian values of a liberal democratic society trumps the right of the voluntary association to determine who will be its members. But a voluntary association that is prevented by the state from determining its own member-ship could scarcely be said to provide protection against the power of the state but would instead be obliged to defer to that power. To put this the other way around: the function of protecting the individual from what Tocqueville calls "majority tyranny," as exercised through the state, presupposes the autonomy of the association from the state, but that autonomy opens up the possibility that the association will fuse *not* self-interest and right, but rather self-interest and wrong or injustice.

Thus it seems to me that John Ehrenberg is correct to conclude in his *Civil Society: The Critical History of an Idea* that "civil society can just as eas-ily impede democracy as advance it, and the history of American segregation should give antistatist advocates of localism and community [that is, of civil society] considerable pause," and that "taken by itself, 'civil society' can serve freedom or reinforce inequality. There is nothing inherent that drives it toward plurality, equality, or participation."[17] If, for example, the internal structure of the association is authoritarian rather than democratic, then that association could hardly be considered a school for democracy. If the composition of the association is ethnically or racially homogeneous, there is, similarly, no reason to assume that participation in it will "enlarge the hearts" and "develop the minds" of its members. And, citing Grant McConnell's research in *Private Power and American Democracy*, Ehrenberg argues that hierarchical organization and homogeneous membership all too often characterize the voluntary associations that are wrongly celebrated in what he calls the "neo-Tocquevillean orthodoxy."[18]

Ehrenberg also points out that these associations tend to reflect, and reinforce, the extreme economic inequality—generally unanticipated by Tocqueville[19]—of contemporary American society. He cites the recent study of American political participation, *Voice and Equality*, which concludes that, for the most part, "civil society is a sphere of economic inequality and privilege."[20] Because the poor lack the time, money, and education to participate in them, most voluntary associations are joined by the rich, or at least the relatively well-off: thus the power of these associations is more likely to heighten economic inequity than it is to contest it. Or, as Schattschneider famously noted in his *Semisovereign People*, "the flaw in the pluralist [neo-Tocquevillean] heaven is that the heavenly chorus sings with a strong upper class accent."[21]

So it should not be surprising that Ehrenberg is far less concerned than Robert Putnam about the apparent decline in recent decades in American participation in voluntary associations. In his influential 1995 article "Bowling Alone: America's Declining Social Capital"[22]—which he subsequently expanded into a book with the same title—Putnam cites a large body of research that demonstrates that civic engagement—membership in political parties, labor unions, the PTA, women's and fraternal organizations, etc.—has dropped dramatically since the 1960s or 1970s. For Putnam this means that what he calls "social capital"—defined as "features of social organization such as networks, norms and social trust that facilitate coordination and cooperation for mutual benefit"[23]—has likewise declined. He worries, in other words, that America (and possibly other Western countries as well) is losing the "vibrant civic life"[24] that, he argues, following Tocqueville, has played such an important role in the health and stability of its democratic system.

Putnam's article has generated a lively debate over whether "social capital" has in fact "significantly eroded over the last generation."[25] Some of his critics claim that he ignores or underestimates the importance of new types of voluntary associations whose rise has accompanied the decline of the more traditional types.[26] In fairness to Putnam, he does in fact briefly consider what he calls these "countertrends"—such as the remarkably broad participation in support groups, twelve-step or otherwise, and the "electronic networks" in which millions of Americans participate online, but he concludes, perhaps prematurely and unpersuasively, that these groups do not engender nearly as much social capital—social trust and civic engagement—as the groups they seem to be replacing. Other critics, such as Ehrenberg, call into question Putnam's admittedly tentative explanation for the decline of those groups he details. Included among the factors Putnam considers to be an important part of the explanation are the movement of women into the labor force, the increasing fragility of the American family, and the privatizing of leisure resulting from television, the VCR, and the personal computer.[27] Noticeably absent from this list, Ehrenberg complains, is the de-industrialization of inner cities—"when jobs disappear ... so does civic life"—as well as the fact that employed Americans have been working longer and harder only to find that "half [of them] have lower real incomes today [1999] than in 1973 ... Surely overworked families are at least as credible an explanation for civic decline as watching a lot of television."[28] So, just as he argued that civic participation is determined by class position, so he argues that its decline is also class determined. Whether these two arguments are consistent is unclear. But what is clear is that, for Ehrenberg, the politics of civil society is largely determined by the capitalist market economy. Thus his work is a convenient bridge to the next part of this book, which is devoted to "Markets and Power."

Part II

MARKETS AND POWER

INTRODUCTION

The preceding chapter is by no means the only chapter in Part I that has left us with questions that will be explored further in the next part of this book. In fact most of the chapters in "Law and Institutions" raise issues whose resolution requires that we consider the material to be covered in "Markets and Power." A brief review of those issues should make this clear.

You will recall that our discussion of the meaning of law in Chapter 1 led us to consider the distinction between merely conventional or positive law and natural law, and that the concept of natural law obliged us to allude to a longstanding debate about human nature that is anything but over. More specifically, I referred briefly to the question of whether human beings are by nature social or a-social, cooperative or competitive. This question is taken up in Chapter 9, "Human Nature and the Market," in the form of an argument between Adam Smith, perhaps the most celebrated defender of the "natural-ness" of a competitive, market economy, and Karl Polanyi, well known for his claim that a competitive market mentality is a relatively rare exception to the general rule of the subordination of individual self-interest to social obligation.

You may also remember that chapter 1 closed with a brief reference to Marx's assertion that law serves the interest of the ruling class rather than "respects human dignity" (Raz) or embodies "concern and respect for all" (Dworkin). In the context of a specifically capitalist society this comes down to the claim that law serves the interest of the capitalist class. Even to understand, much less evaluate, Marx's claim about what the law really *is*, we need to know what is meant by the term "capitalist class," and to understand that term we obviously need to understand what is meant by "capitalism." A number of chapters in the next section of this book are designed to contribute to these understandings. Chapter 10, "Freedom and the Market," examines the debate between the Fried-mans, for whom capitalism is a system based on purely voluntary exchange, and Marx, for whom capitalism is a system based on alienated, and therefore fundamentally unfree, labor. Chapter 12 on corporate governance includes Doug Henwood's account of both the competing and the common interests of the various sectors of the contemporary American capitalist class. And in chapter 11 on corporations and the state, Charles Lindblom advances what is, in effect, a modern-day version of Marx's thesis that that class is inevitably the ruling class in a capitalist society. These chapters are not designed to offer a definitive answer to the question "What is law?" but they should make it clear that an answer to this question requires an understanding of the economy—the capitalist market economy—with which the law is closely connected.

As we shall see, the chapters in Part II that I have just cited also shed light on questions that arose in chapter 2 with respect to the separation of powers. You will remember that Montesquieu (a) effectively equated liberty and the rule of law and (b) argued that the separation of powers was necessary for both. Now, if we accept Lindblom's (implicitly Marxist) claim in chapter 12 that the laws that issue from the modern state generally support what he calls the "privileged position" of business (that is, of capital), then Montesquieu's equation of the rule of law and liberty is vulnerable to Marx's argument in chapter 10 that genuine freedom and capitalism are mutually exclusive. To put this another way, the only way that we could agree with Lindblom yet disagree with Marx is to defend the Friedmans' argument in chapter 10 about the inseparable connection between capitalism and freedom. In either case the evaluation of Montesquieu's equation demands that we enter into the debate that is summarized in that tenth chapter.

Similarly, we saw that Montesquieu argued that the separation of powers— the (incomplete) separation between the legislative, executive, and judicial branches of the government—was necessary but not sufficient for liberty and the "checking of power by power" that liberty supposedly required. His confidence that the separation of powers would "prevent the abuse of power" was based on the assumption that the three different branches of the (British) government represented different and competing socio-economic groups or classes. To put this the other way around: Montesquieu implicitly recognized that, if all three branches of government were controlled by the *same* group or class, there would be no political pluralism and thus no liberty to be had. And this class monopoly is exactly what Marx in the nineteenth century and Lindblom in the twentieth assert. *If* they are right, then we have reason to be far less sanguine than Montesquieu about the connection between liberty—even as understood by Montesquieu—and the separation of powers.

Madison's defense of the separation of powers in chapter 2 reinforces this point. He endorsed that separation (along with federalism) as an antidote for a "tyranny of the majority" that amounted in practice to the rule of the many without property over the few with property. That this was Madison's chief worry is reinforced by his insistence in *Federalist 10* (examined in chapter 6) that "the protection of different and unequal faculties of acquiring property . . . is the first object of Government" and that "the most common and durable source of factions, has been the various and unequal distribution of property." If the "first object of Government" is to protect the (supposedly inevitably) unequal distribution of property, and the unequal distribution of property inevitably gives rise to "factions" that contest that inequality, then there would be every reason for the propertied to worry about the "tyranny" of the majority and to propose and put in place institutional guarantees against it. What Madison never says explicitly is nonetheless implicit in his argument: the separation of powers serves the interest of the propertied. Here he is very close to, and in fact anticipates, Marx, for whom "the unequal distribution of property" (in what Marx will call the "means of production") is also "the most common and durable source of factions," or what Marx calls classes. The great difference, of course, is that Marx will call into question the unequal distribution of property and associated "factions" that Madison simply took for granted. Marx's critique of capitalism in chapter 10 is thus at once an extension of, and a challenge to, the political sociology of James Madison.

Perhaps most obviously, much of the material to be covered in Part II speaks directly to the debate over the meaning of democracy detailed in chapter 4. Recall that Rousseau insisted that in a well-constituted state "public affairs dominate private ones in the minds of the citizens" and that "as soon as someone says *what do I care?* about the affairs of the State, the State should be considered lost." Like Benjamin Barber more than two hundred years later, Rousseau decried an individualism or civic privatism that precludes a citizen's a full-throated commitment to the common interest. Whatever the differences between Adam Smith and Marx, we shall see that both of their accounts of a market economy emphasize the very privatism against which Rousseau railed. Both will paint a picture of individual consumers who interact with others principally for the purpose of maximizing their individual consumption. The fact that Smith assumes that self-interest in this sense is natural and inevitable whereas Marx argues that it is the unfortunate result of a system of alienated labor that can and will be overcome should not obscure the fact that they both contest the compatibility of a capitalist market economy with the "thick" democracy to which civic republicans such as Rousseau and Barber are committed.

Lindblom's neo-Marxist argument in chapter 12, moreover, will lead us to question whether even the "thinner" ideal of democracy developed by Dahl in his *Polyarchy* can be realized in the context of a capitalist market economy. Recall that for Dahl a polity is democratic to the extent to which it is "completely or almost completely responsive to all its citizens." Now, if Lindblom's argument about the "privileged place" of business is correct—if, in other words, the government in a capitalist society is necessarily far more responsive to the interests of corporations than it is to the interests of "all its citizens"—then we would have to conclude that polyarchies are not in fact very democratic. This is, in fact, exactly what Lindblom concludes. This conclusion brings us back to Schumpeter, whose definition of democracy, you will recall, excludes any reference to "responsiveness" and reduces it to a political system "in which individuals acquire the power to decide by means of a competitive struggle for the people's vote." Lindblom, then, would appear to share the anti-democratic skepticism of Joseph Schumpeter.[1]

But not, interestingly enough, Robert Dahl. We shall see in chapter 13 that Dahl argues, in *After the Revolution?*, published around the same time as his

Polyarchy, that a market economy can in fact accommodate a considerable expansion in the scope of democracy. That market economy, however, would no longer be a *capitalist* market economy: Dahl envisions a transformation in the internal governance of competitive enterprises from rule by managers who are (at least in principle) accountable to banks and shareholders to rule by managers who are elected by the workers of those enterprise. We will encounter, in other words, a case on behalf of the extension of the norms of democracy into the place where most adults spend the better part of their waking hours, namely the workplace. But it will still be a case for representative rather than direct or participatory democracy.

Dahl's case for what might be (and sometimes is) called market socialism is based on the principle that all those who are affected by the decisions have a right to participate (at least indirectly) in making those decisions. Once we recognize, as Dahl does, that in a globalized economy the decisions of any one large enterprise may well affect the lives of millions, if not billions, of people separated by hundreds, if not thousands, of miles, the difficulties of implementing the principle of affected interests become immediately apparent. Some system of global governance whose reach is commensurate with the global effects of economic decisions is clearly in order, but whether or the extent to which that system would be compatible with the continuing sovereignty of individual nation-states is less than entirely clear. This is a question on which I touch, albeit briefly, in chapter 14 on globalization and governance.

What is clear is that the vast scale of globalized democracy only further strengthens the case for the inevitability of representative democracy (even if it is complemented by more directly democratic participation). This brings us back to Pitkin's analysis of the concept of representation in chapter 5. You will remember that she argued that the representative should combine independent judgment about the interests of her constituents with responsiveness to their wishes, and she assumed that—but does not adequately explain why—any conflict between the former and the latter will be an exception to the general rule of harmony between them. From what I have already said about Lindblom's account in chapter 12 it should already be clear that the "independent judgment" of the elected representative may be much harder to come by than Pitkin imagines. Lindblom will claim that on matters of major importance the representative will generally defer to the interests of business, that is, act as their representative, if only because there are good reasons for her to believe that those interests and her interests are one and the same. If this were the case then we might be able to provide a more convincing explanation than Pitkin's of the general rule of harmony between the (supposedly independent) judgment of the representative and the wishes of her constituents. That explanation would run something like this: on major matters there will be harmony between them because the constituents will normally share the view of their representatives that a capitalist market economy is consistent with their interests as consumers. If and when they no longer share this view—or no longer think of themselves principally as consumers—then their wishes will come into conflict with the so-called "independent" judgment of their representatives. Under these circumstances, we should expect that those representatives will attempt to resolve the conflict in a manner that is as unthreatening to business interests as possible. This, in fact, is exactly what Lindblom argues.

This argument will shed new light on the dispute in chapter 6 between Madison and Schattschneider on the role of political parties. We saw that Madison feared that majoritarian parties would "sacrifice the public good and the rights of other citizens," and that he argued that a large republic would prevent the emergence of such parties but still be consistent with "the spirit and form of popular government": he assumed, wrongly, that the social and economic diversity of a large republic would make it difficult for a majority united by a "common motive" either to form or to act effectively. Schattschneider, showed, to the contrary, that the American electoral system virtually guaranteed that social and economic diversity would *not* engender the "greater variety of parties" that Madison anticipated, and that the system would, instead, produce the very majoritarian parties that Madison dreaded. But, Schattschneider argued, that system would produce *moderate* majority parties that tend to "avoid extreme positions." Thus, for Schattschneider, we have nothing to fear from, and every reason to be thankful for, the majority parties of the "two-party system."

Thus the opposition between Madison and Schattschneider is, at bottom, a fight within the family: they simply disagree on the means necessary to achieve an end on which they entirely agree, namely the elimination of "extreme" threats to the "public good" and "private rights." As we have seen, there are good Madisonian reasons to translate these threats to "the public good" and "private rights" as "attacks on the propertied," or, in Lindblom's terms, on business. If so, then Schattschneider's account of moderate majoritarian political parties can be read as one possible solution to the problem of ensuring the "privileged place" of business while preserving "the spirit and form of popular government." From this perspective, the political parties that are, for Schattschneider, "beneficent instruments of popular government" also appear to be important instruments of capitalist *legitimation*. (What goes for political parties, of course, also goes for the elections they both organize and contest.) This, I think, is at least one of the things that Lisa Disch had in mind when she argued that "two-party competition has suppressed the electoral participation of dissenting groups and thereby exaggerated the consensual basis of American politics."

This brings us, finally, to questions about the role of civil society. We saw in chapter 8 that John Ehrenberg, following Schattschneider and McConnell, argued that "civil society is a sphere of economic inequality and privilege," and thereby cast doubt on the beneficent functions that Tocqueville assigned to that sphere. Tocqueville, you will recall, claimed that the associations of civil society "enlarge the heart" and "develop the minds" of their otherwise self-preoccupied members, and thereby "connect the notion of right with that of private interest." Yet Tocqueville himself gives us a good reason to be as skeptical of this claim as

Ehrenrberg. In an infrequently cited chapter of *Democracy in America, Volume II* entitled "That Aristocracy May be Engendered by Manufactures," Tocqueville inveighs against a manufacturing division of labor that forces the "workman" to focus "every day upon the same detail," makes him "more weak, more narrow-minded and more dependent," and ultimately transforms him into a "brute." "What can be expected," he asks, "of a man who has spent twenty years of his life making heads for pins?"[2] Surely not that he or she becomes the individual whose heart is "enlarged" and whose mind is "developed" through his or her participation in voluntary associations!

This suggests either that Tocqueville expected that the voluntary associations in which he placed so much faith would be composed of people who were not "workmen," or that the "schools of citizenship" function he assigned to voluntary associations cannot possibly be fulfilled. He tries, in effect, to avoid the second alternative by arguing that the "manufacturing aristocracy which is growing up under our eyes ... is one of the most confined and least dangerous"; he appears to assume that the majority of American citizens will not be ruled by that aristocracy, and will not, therefore, suffer the debilitating consequences of that rule. His assumption, in others words, is that most Americans will be able to participate in, and benefit from, the voluntary associations he applauds. Yet at the same time he acknowledges that "the demand for manufactured commodities becomes more general and more extensive" and warns that "if ever a permanent inequality of conditions and aristocracy again penetrate into the world, it may be predicted that [manufacturing] is the channel by which they will enter."[3] Thus he worries that the potentially positive contributions of the voluntary associations of civil society might eventually be overwhelmed by the alienating consequences of the capitalist market economy. This, as we shall see in Part II, is exactly what Marx argues.

9

HUMAN NATURE AND THE MARKET

It is difficult to overestimate the enduring influence of Adam Smith's *The Wealth of Nations*, which was first published in England in 1776. In it Smith articulates assumptions about the relationship between human nature and the market that underlie not only the contemporary discipline of (mainstream) economics but all those approaches to the study of human beings—including so-called rational-choice theory in political science—that are based on essentially economic assumptions. By "economic assumptions" I mean the assumptions (a) that humans are motivated above all by individual gain, and (b) that they are sufficiently rational to know how to maximize it. It follows from this "expectation that human beings behave in such a way as to achieve maximum [monetary] gains" that a market economy in which "all production is for sale on the market and . . . all incomes derive from such sales"[1] will be considered both natural and inevitable. Living as we do in a capitalist market society, we tend to take this for granted: since individuals are, by nature, rationally-self interested—in more colloquial language, since they necessarily "look out for number one"—it follows that the only rational economic system is one in which the chief incentive for the production and distribution of goods and services is personal monetary gain. In short, many of us simply take it on faith that a market economy is, if not the only possible economy, the only one that will really ever work. This tacit assumption merely echoes what Adam Smith and his many followers—including, as we shall see, Milton Friedman and Friedrich Hayek, whose work we will encounter in the next two chapters—have explicitly argued, and celebrated, ever since 1776. Unfortunately for them it turns out that the celebration was, and is, premature: as Karl Polanyi, relying on the research of many twentieth-century historians and anthropologists, persuasively points out, the assumption of the naturalness and therefore the inevitability of a market economy is simply and entirely *wrong*: "previous to our time no economy ever existed that . . . was controlled by markets."[2] But before I come to Polanyi, first let me summarize the essentials of Adam Smith's famous second chapter of his *Wealth of Nations*.

In this chapter Smith looks for an explanation of the division of labor—different people doing different kinds of work, and different kinds of work sub-divided in turn into different tasks performed by different people—from which, he tells us in the very first sentence of chapter 2, "so many advantages are derived." He finds this explanation in "a certain propensity in human nature," namely "the propensity to "truck, barter and exchange one thing for another."[3] Since, he elaborates, "in civilized society [each individual] stands at all times in need of the cooperation and assistance of great multitudes," and since "it is vain for him to expect [this help] from their benevolence only"[4]—because, in other words, other individuals are likely to be as self-interested as he—it follows that he will gain their much-needed "cooperation and assistance" only if

> he can interest their self-love in his favor, and shew them that it is for their own advantage to do for him what he requires of them. Whoever offers to another a bargain of any kind [and "truck" means to "negotiate or bargain"], proposes to do this. Give me that which I want, and you shall have this which you want, is the meaning of every such offer; and it is in this manner that we obtain from one another the far greatest part of those good offices we stand in need of. It is not from the benevolence of the butcher, the brewer, or the baker, that we expect our dinner, but from their regard to their own interest. We address ourselves, not to their humanity but to their self-love, and never talk of them of our own necessities, but of their advantages.[5]

According to Smith, this "trucking disposition"—this disposition to get what we want from others by giving them what they want—works to produce the division of labor in the following way. He imagines a particular hunter in a tribe of hunters and shepherds who "makes bows and arrows . . . with more readiness and dexterity than any other," and who soon discovers that it is in his interest to concentrate exclusively on making bows and arrows and to exchange his surplus of bows and arrows with his companions for cattle and venison rather than to take the time to hunt for them himself:

> he finds . . . that he can in this manner get more cattle and venison, than if he himself went to the field to catch them. From a regard to his own interest, therefore, the making of bows and arrows grows to be his chief business.[6]

And, of course, the shepherd who is better at herding than making bows and arrows comes to the conclusion that it would be also be in his interest to focus exclusively on herding, since he realizes he can get more bows and arrows by exchanging his surplus cattle or venison for the bows and arrows made by his more expert fellow tribesman rather than by making them himself. So Smith concludes that:

> the certainty of being able to exchange all that surplus part of the produce of his own labour . . . for such part of the produce of other men's labour

as he may have occasion for, encourages every man to apply himself to a particular occupation, and to cultivate and bring to perfection whatever talent and genius he may possess for that particular species of business.[7]

Thus does the division of labor grow inevitably out of an equally inevitable propensity to "truck, barter, and exchange."

Notice that Smith's argument rests on the assumption that people will always want to produce a *surplus* over and above what they need for themselves and that this assumption, in turn, is based on the even more fundamental assumption of the motive of human profit or *gain*: it is only because the hunter wants *more* meat than he could otherwise procure for himself that he has an to incentive to produce more bows and arrows than he needs (so that the surplus bows and arrows can be exchanged for beef and venison), and it is only because the shepherd wants *more* bows and arrows than he could otherwise make that he has an incentive to rear more cattle and deer (so that the surplus cattle and deer can be exchanged for bows and arrows). To put this the other way around, if the hunter and shepherd didn't both *want more than they currently have* there would be no incentive for either of them to produce a surplus, thus no possibility of exchange, and no creation of a division of labor based on exchange. This is the sense in which Smith's entire argument—and all subsequent economic arguments on behalf of the proposition of a natural, inevitable link between market exchange and the division of labor—rests on the assumption—the entirely undefended assumption—that by nature Man is a maximizer, that is, that people naturally seek gain, or always want more than they have.

It is precisely this assumption of natural gain that Karl Polanyi debunks. He insists that:

> in spite of the chorus of academic incantations so persistent [following the reception of Smith's late–eighteenth-century work] in the nineteenth century [and, we can add, today as well], gain and profit made on exchange never before played an important part in human economy. Though the institution of the market was fairly common since the later Stone Age, its role was no more than incidental to economic life.[8]

Polanyi's argument turns on the distinction he draws between *markets* and a *market economy*. By a market he simply means "a meeting place for the purpose of buying and selling."[9] Markets in this sense have always existed, but a market economy—which he defines as "an economic system controlled, regulated, and directed by markets alone"—is a very recent phenomenon, dating, he argues, to the beginning of the nineteenth century in Western Europe. Until that time, markets were never "more than accessories of economic life,"[10] the great bulk of which was organized according to very different principles from the market and very different motives from individual profit or gain. More specifically, Polanyi shows that the production and distribution of goods and services in all societies—Western and non-Western alike—prior to the nineteenth century was governed by the principles of what he calls reciprocity, redistribution, and householding.

I will discuss them briefly in reverse order, beginning with householding, by which Polanyi means "production for one's own use."[11] Although Polanyi argues, against more orthodox assumptions, that householding in this sense is probably not as old as either reciprocity or redistribution—he doubts whether householding existed during the time of hunting and gathering societies and dates its emergence to the development of more advanced agriculture—it has nevertheless been a centrally important mechanism for the production and distribution of goods in many kinds of otherwise fundamentally different societies. For example, both the small independent farmer in pre-industrial Colonial America and the peasant under the thumb of his lord in pre-capitalist, feudal Europe produced most of what they consumed and consumed most of what they produced in and for their families. In other words, they did *not* procure most of what they consumed by exchanging a surplus of what they produced (even though some small portion of what they produced may have been taken to the market to be exchanged for other goods that made up a relatively small fraction of what they consumed). Production for use is thus production for oneself and one's family, and it therefore presupposes the existence of the family, understood as a "closed group." Autarchy, or the closed, more-or-less self-sufficient group, is, in other words, the pattern of social organization that is associated with the householding principle. And *subsistence*, not gain, was the primary motivation of householding.

Redistribution is a distributive principle even older than householding, as it is, Polanyi tells "present to some extent in all human groups."[12] Redistribution, as the name implies, exists wherever producers—be they hunter and gatherers or peasants living either under ancient kingdoms or in feudal conditions outside of Western Europe—are obliged to deliver a certain portion of what they produce to whomever is the leader of their community, which leader then stores that portion and determines how and to whom it will be distributed. Notice that redistribution implies a division of labor—between the producers who produce what will be redistributed, those who collect that product and turn it over to the leader, the leader, and, finally, those who help him redistribute the product among his subjects—even though the motive of gain is entirely absent, thus refuting Smith's claim that the motive of gain explains the origins of the division of labor. There is no "trucking, bartering or exchanging" that occurs within the circuit of redistribution, because redistribution implies the existence of a central authority with sufficient *political* power to dictate what and how much will be produced for redistribution and exactly how that redistribution will be carried out. Thus the principle of redistribution requires the organizational pattern of what Polanyi calls "centricity," or the existence of a central, determining political authority.

Householding and redistribution are easy to understand, in part because even within the context of a contemporary market economy such as ours we have examples of each: for example the do-it-yourself movement as a modern form of householding, and the redistributive effects of government fiscal policy (perhaps, in recent years, more from the poor to the rich than from the rich to the poor). But it is more difficult to get our minds around the third distributive principle, which Polanyi calls "reciprocity," because the logic of reciprocity is not only different from but *directly* opposed to the motive of gain—the desire always to acquire *more*—that dominates a modern market economy. Many if not most preliterate, tribal societies produce and distribute their goods through a system of *gift exchange* in which each member of the tribe is expected to give away (rather than consume or accumulate) what he or she produces to other members of the tribe, secure in the knowledge that those other members will at some point reciprocate in kind. In such a community, Polanyi points out, "the idea of profit is barred; higgling and haggling is decried; giving freely is acclaimed as a virtue; [and] the supposed propensity to barter, truck, and exchange does not appear."[13] Nor is the accumulation of a surplus possible, as any goods that cannot either be given away or individually consumed are normally consumed or destroyed communally in lavish public festivals that anthropologists call the Potlatch. And yet, once again, the absence of the motive of gain goes hand-in-hand with what is often a very complex and extended division of labor, in which, as Polanyi puts it:

> the striking "duality" which we find in tribal subdivisions lends itself to the pairing out of individual relations and thereby assists the give-and-take of goods and services in the absence of permanent records . . . Little is known of the origins of "duality"; but each coastal village on the Trobriand Islands [for example] appears to have a counterpart in an inland village, so that the important exchange of breadfruit and fish, though disguised as the reciprocal distribution of gifts, and actually disjoint in time, can be organized smoothly.[14]

Thus what Polanyi calls "symmetry" is the organizational pattern connected to the principle of reciprocity.

It is important, once again, to emphasize just how much "gift exchange" is at odds with the motive of gain or profit. In a market economy based on the motive of gain, generally speaking the more (money) people gain, the more powerful and prestigious they become. In a society based on gift exchange, in contrast, the person who is able to *give the most away* is typically the most powerful and prestigious person. The so-called "Big Man," in other words, is the not the one who *takes* but the one who *gives*. This does not imply that the motives of the Big Man are entirely altruistic. To the contrary, the source of his power is (among other things) precisely that he is able to "place the recipients [of his gifts] under an obligation,"[15] that is, to make them feel indebted to him. But to say that in such societies individuals increase their social power, prestige, and reputation through giving things away is to say something very different from saying that they maximize their power, prestige, and reputation by *accumulating* those things. In the latter case the individual accumulation of material things tends to become an end in itself; in the former case—in societies governed by gift exchange—the individual, in Polanyi's words, "acts so as to safeguard his social standing, his social claims, his social assets [and] values material goods only in so far as they serve this end."[16]

All three of the distributive principles—reciprocity, redistribution, and householding—that regulated the production and distribution of most goods and services in all human societies until the nineteenth century subordinate that production and distribution to social or political obligations: reciprocity subordinates it to the obligation to give goods and services away to socially determined partners, redistribution subordinates it to the obligation to deliver goods and services to a central political authority, and householding subordinates it to the obligation to provide for the members of one's family. This is the sense in which Polanyi is able justly to conclude that "man's economy, as a rule, is submerged in his social relationships."[17]

This conclusion should make us aware of just how profound an exception to this general rule a market economy is. "The control of the economic system by the market," Polanyi argues, "means no less than the running of society as an adjunct to the market. Instead of economy being embedded in social relations, social relations are embedded in the economic system."[18] By "social relations . . . embedded in the economic system," Polanyi means a society in which "all transactions are turned into money transactions,"[19] that is, in which all factors of production—including land and human labor—become or are treated as commodities whose prices are supposed to be determined exclusively by the relationship between the demand for and the supply of those commodities. It is, in short, only under these conditions that, as Marx put it poetically in *The Communist Manifesto*, the social and cultural values that prevailed in pre-capitalist societies are "drowned . . . in the icy waters of egotistical calculation."[20] Or, as Polanyi puts it less poetically, the great transformation to a market society "implies a change in the motive of action on the part of members of society: for the motive of subsistence [as well as other pre-market motives] that of gain must be substituted."[21]

This substitution and the transformation that was both its cause and its consequence did not happen easily or automatically. Against those scholars— mainly economists—who *do* recognize that a market economy is a relatively recent phenomenon but who argue that it developed more-or-less naturally from its pre-market predecessors, Polanyi shows that the emergence of the market economy was the result of a complex process in which the *state* played an absolutely indispensable role: "internal trade in Western Europe" (where the market economy first emerged), he tells us, "was actually created by the intervention of the state."[22] It took specifically political intervention, the exercise of state power, in order to overcome the traditional, feudal or semi-feudal obstacles to the formation of the necessary market in land and labor power. Thus the irony of intense hostility to the state on the part of free-marketeers or libertarians is that the economic system they idealize owes its existence to the actions of the state they demonize.

There is, finally, another reason why, according to Polanyi, the proponents of laissez-faire—governmental non-interference with the economy—are misguided. A market economy, we have seen, requires that both land and labor power be treated as commodities that are bought and sold like any other. But if they really were treated exclusively as commodities, human beings would be "robbed of the protective covering of cultural institutions" and left to "perish from the effects of social exposure," ultimately dying "as the victims of acute social dislocation." And if the land were likewise treated "nature would be reduced to its elements, neighborhoods and landscapes defiled, rivers polluted," etc. Thus, he insists, "to allow the market mechanism to be the sole director of the fate of human beings and their natural environment . . . would result in the demolition of society."[23] Society thus *inevitably* attempts to protect itself from these disastrous consequences of an unregulated market economy by acting through the state to regulate the economy. Hence Polanyi's conclusion is that the idea of an entirely self-regulating market economy is a fiction, and a dangerous one at that. Wherever there is a market economy, in other words, there will be a regulatory relationship between the state and the economy, between market and (political) power. The nature of this relationship will be the subject of the remaining chapters of this part.

10

FREEDOM AND THE MARKET

The next several chapters, as I mentioned at the very end of chapter 9, will be devoted to the relationship between the market economy and the state. I begin with the argument of Milton and Rose Friedman in *Free to Choose* on behalf of laissez-faire, that is, in favor of an extremely limited role of the government vis-à-vis the economy. To anticipate: they argue that a market economy is the only way of organizing the production of good and services that is consistent with both freedom and efficiency, and that governmental regulation of that economy is therefore both oppressive and inefficient. A market economy respects freedom of choice because production and distribution are based exclusively on purely voluntary exchanges between producers and consumers. And a market economy is efficient because its price system ensures that supply and demand will equilibrate, that is, balance out, so that the result of those supposedly voluntary exchanges is that the people who enter into them will normally get what they want.

My focus in this chapter will be on their argument on behalf of the freedom of the market. The Friedmans' assumption that market exchanges are a form, indeed the only form, of voluntary exchange goes hand-in-hand with their assumption that political mechanisms for the distribution of goods and services are necessarily *involuntary*. Although they acknowledge that "to some extent government is a form of voluntary cooperation,"[1] they repeatedly identify governmental influence over the production of goods and services with the properly criticized "command method" that predominated in centrally planned economies such as the former Soviet Union. This identification in effect produces the following equation: the market is to the state as freedom is to coercion. It is this equation that underlies their laissez-faire position, namely their argument, following Adam Smith, that the role of government should be limited to (a) the defense against internal and external coercion, carried out by the police and military respectively; (b) a legal order or administration of justice whose function is to mediate disputes among the parties to voluntary market exchanges; and (c) the provision of large-scale public goods, for example, highways, bridges, and other infrastructure necessary for the functioning of the market economy but which the market itself is generally unable to provide.[2] Note that this list excludes a wide range of modern governmental regulations that we have come to take for granted; in the Friedmans' ideal political-economic world, there would be no minimum wage, no social security, no environmental protection, and no workplace safety laws. According to them, all of these governmental regulations, and many others as well, substitute a centralized political decision for the millions of voluntary individual decisions (based on the price mechanism) and thus replace the free workings of the market with the coercion of the state.

Since this (what is now called conservative) conclusion ultimately rests on the equation "the market is to the state as freedom is to coercion," there are two different ways that it can be contested. One would be to question the Friedmans' identification of the state with coercion or unfreedom, to suggest that this identification fails to distinguish between republican or democratic governments on the one hand and autocratic or even totalitarian governments on the other, and to argue that there is surely a difference between governmental regulations that result from a democratic process and those that do not. If we assume, following Rousseau, that we are free when we obey laws that we impose on ourselves—and this, in principle, is what we do in a democratic form of government—why should we conclude, with the Friedmans, that governmental regulation of the economy is necessarily a form of unfreedom? Why not conclude, to the contrary, that, if the governmental regulations are the result of genuinely democratic deliberations, those regulations reflect the wishes of a free political people?

The other way to dispute their laissez-faire position would be to question their identification of the market with freedom, their assumption that market exchanges are not only a form, but also the *only* possible form, of voluntary economic exchanges. Having encountered Karl Polanyi, we should already be skeptical of the second, stronger of these claims. We know from Polanyi that gift exchange is an equally voluntary form of exchange that has prevailed in many different early, pre-capitalist societies. If the Friedmans acknowledged this point, perhaps they might respond by qualifying their claim to read as follows: market exchanges are the only form of voluntary economic exchanges that is possible in a *modern* society. But perhaps this dismissal of the possibility of a modern form of gift exchange would be premature. It might be argued, for example, that the exchange of (much of) the information on the Internet is a modern form of gift exchange. People voluntarily upload information into cyberspace that will be shared without cost by a potentially almost infinite number of consumers who also inhabit that space, secure in the knowledge that they will eventually be able to download without cost useful information voluntarily supplied by many of those same people. The production and consumption of "informational goods" over the Internet—at least to the extent that the Internet has not yet been entirely commercialized or commodified—would thus appear to be a form of exchange that is voluntary yet non-market, thus calling the Friedmans' equation of voluntary and market into question.

So much for the Friedmans' claim that market exchanges are the only possible form of voluntary exchange. But what about their weaker claim, namely that they are at least *a* form of voluntary exchange? Are all market exchanges necessarily voluntary? Consider what is perhaps the most fundamental market exchange in a capitalist or market economy, namely between the worker who sells his labor power and the employer who buys it. The Friedmans assume that this exchange is voluntary in the sense that worker is not obliged to sell his labor power to any particular employer; if he or she does not like the price, that is, the wage, that one employer is offering, he can always offer that labor-power to another employer somewhere else who is offering a better price for it. Similarly, if workers don't like the conditions under which they would have to work for one employer they can always find different, better conditions working for another employer. Thus the possibility of *exit* from one job to another guarantees the voluntary nature of any one particular job.

But what if the conditions of work are essentially the same in all the jobs for which the worker has the necessary skills? In this case, it would seem, there is no meaningful possibility of exit, since conditions would be the same no matter where the worker would "choose" to work. And, of course, he *must* work if he wants to survive. To anticipate Marx: can we really speak of a purely "voluntary exchange" if the worker's only choice is either to work under conditions that he detests or to die? And, even if the worker *is* able to find better working conditions or higher wages somewhere else, what if that "somewhere else" is hundreds or even thousands of miles away from his home, family, and friends? Is the worker really "free" to take any job if the cost of that decision is breaking the bonds that have tied him to the fellow members of a human community? To anticipate Marx once again, should alienation from others be the price of individual freedom?

This, you may recall, was one of the consequences, deplored by Polanyi, of pretending that labor-power is a commodity that is bought and sold like any other. The Friedmans, in contrast, never even begin to consider that cost. Instead they simply take the commodification of labor-power for granted. They assume, in other words, that the worker "sees his work as a way to get the goods and services he want[s],"[3] that is, as a means to the end of consumption rather than an end in itself. This instrumental assumption, in turn, underlies their critique of governmental efforts to determine or even influence the distribution of income. Thus they ask, "if what a person gets does not depend on the price he receives for the services of his resources, what incentive does he have to seek out information on prices or act on the basis of that information," and "If your income will be the same whether you work hard or not, why should you work hard?"[4] These questions presuppose that the work is *not* intrinsically satisfying, because if it were—if the worker *enjoyed* his work—presumably he *would* have an incentive to work hard and well even if his wage did not depend in part, or even at all, on the intensity or quality of his or her work. To put this another way, only if we assume a natural aversion to work does it follow that the worker will work hard only if she knows that her income will depend on how hard she works.

At one point the Friedmans admit that workers may not in fact always view their work in this instrumental way. They say that:

> information about prices . . . may not even be the most important informa-
> tion, particularly about how to use one's own labor. That decision depends
> in addition on one's own interests and capacities [and] on the advantages
> and disadvantages of an occupation, monetary and nonmonetary. Satisfac-
> tion in a job may compensate for low wages.[5]

This admission constitutes their implicit awareness that labor-power is *not* a commodity like any other, because, if it were, information about its price *would* be the most important determinant of the worker's disposition of his labor-power: workers would *never* work for a lower price than their labor-power might be able to fetch on the market if they viewed their labor in exclusively instrumental terms. That they sometimes do sacrifice the wage to what the Friedmans call "job satisfaction" suggests that they do not in fact always need the carrot of higher wages or the stick of lower wages to get them to work hard and well. But this observation necessarily calls into question the Friedmans' argument against governmental efforts to influence the distribution of income, since that argument was based on the assumption that work is *not* intrinsically satisfying. Perhaps more importantly, the observation implies that, even in a society based on what Marx calls alienated labor, the need for unalienated labor persists.

This brings us directly to Marx's essay on "Estranged Labour," written in 1844 when Marx was 26. In this essay Marx claims, as I have already inti-mated, that the exchange between the worker who sells his labor-power and the capitalist who buys it is anything but a "free" exchange. He argues, instead, that this exchange entails a profound, fourfold alienation of the worker from what Marx takes to be his human nature: (1) the alienation of the worker from the objects he produces, and thus from nature; (2) the alienation of the worker from his own laboring activity, and thus from himself; (3) the alienation of the worker from what Marx calls his "species-being"; and (4) the alienation of the worker from every other worker. For Marx, each of these dimensions of alienation necessarily implies all the others—they are different aspects of the same reality—and thus it is only analytic convenience that justifies Marx's—and my—separate treatment of them. And each dimension of alienation implies a corresponding dimension of (what Marx takes to be) human nature in the light of which the indictment of "alienation" is issued.

1: The Alienation of Workers from Their Products

In the ordinary course of events, the worker who sell his labor-power to the capitalist is obliged to give up any and all control over the critical decisions concerning the objects he will produce: the quality, quantity, and destination of those objects are determined not by the worker but rather by the capitalist (or his agent) to whom the worker sells his labor-power. Growing up in a capitalist society we are likely to treat this separation or alienation of the worker from his products as an inevitable fact of economic life, but for Marx this seemingly mundane, inescapable fact actually entails both a profound "loss of reality" for the worker and his "object-bondage."[6] Under ideal conditions, Marx assumes, humans are able to see themselves in the world they have produced; they can affirm their creative powers by experiencing the (built) environment as an extension of their own purposes: "through and because of this production, nature appears as *his* work and his reality . . . he contemplates himself in a world that he has created."[7] But under capitalism (or, for that matter, any hierarchically organized system of production) workers are unable to experience the produced world as an extension of *their* purposes, because what they produce is a reflection not of those purposes but rather of the purposes (above all, profit) of the capitalist. Thus the break in the link between the purposes and products of the workers makes it impossible for workers to recognize themselves in the world they have produced, and the world becomes alien to them.

Moreover, Marx claims, the very world from which workers are alienated comes back to haunt and dominate them:

> This *alienation* of the worker in his product means not only that his labour becomes an object, an *external* existence, but that it exists *outside him*, independently, as something alien to him, and that it becomes a power of its own confronting him; it means that the life which he has conferred on the object confronts him as something hostile and alien.[8]

The perverse consequence of the fact that workers do not control the objects they produce, in other words, is that these objects (appear to) take on a life of their own and come to dominate the lives of those who have produced them. Produced objects assume inordinate power precisely because—or so Marx argues—workers have exercised no power over the process of producing them: it is as if we attempt to compensate for our loss of control and creativity in the process of *producing* objects by *consuming* as many of them as possible. Thus under capitalism life becomes devoted to the maximum accumulation of "stuff": as Marx puts it in the essay "Private Property and Communism," also written in 1844, "in place of *all* [the] physical and mental senses there has . . . come the sheer estrangement of *all* these senses—the sense of *having*."[9] This means that, for Marx, the capitalist worker is humanly *impoverished* irrespective of the level of his wage or income. The "consumer society" is not a good society no matter how much—or for that matter, how equally—people can consume.

2: The Alienation of Workers from Their Laboring Activity

We have seen that the Friedmans assume that work is (principally) a means to the end of income, in other words, that it is generally *not* intrinsically satisfying. Marx argues that this instrumental conception of work faithfully reflects the way that most work is structured and experienced under capitalism, but emphatically denies that work must always be this way. According to Marx, labor—at least in principle—is far more and other than a mere means to fulfill fixed material needs; rather it is *the* medium within which humans transform their world and transform themselves. Labor for Marx, in short, is both world and self constituting. As such it is—or should be—an intrinsically valuable, satisfying, life-affirming activity. But capitalist labor is anything but:

> [L]abour is *external* to the worker, i.e., it does not belong to his essential being; . . . in his work, therefore, he does not affirm himself but denies himself, does not feel content but unhappy, does not develop freely his mental energy but mortifies his body and ruins his mind. The worker therefore only feels himself outside his work, and in his work feels outside himself. He is at home when he is not working, and when he is working he is not at home. His labour is therefore not voluntary, but coerced; it is *forced labour*. Its alien character emerges clearly in the fact that as soon as no physical or other compulsion exists, labour is shunned like the plague. External labour, labour in which man alienates himself, is a labour of self-sacrifice, of mortification.[10]

Capitalist labor, then, is "mortifying"—life-denying—rather than life-affirming. It is something the worker *has to* do rather than something he *wants* to do, and therefore cannot reasonably be considered to be voluntary or free. The measure of its "forced" or coercive character is that workers are able to feel "at home"—at one with themselves—only when they are not working, even though when they are not working they are usually doing something, for example, "eating, drinking, [or] procreating,"[11] that is, at least according to Marx, less distinctively human than labor. And, since they are not "at home" at work, when they don't have to work they typically avoid it "like the plague." To say this is to say that capitalism creates a fundamental split—or alienation—between work and life: workers feel that when they are working they are not really living and that life really begins only when work ends. Thus the "consumer society" is also the "Thank-God-It's-Friday" society.

3: The Alienation of Workers from Their "Species-Being"

Humans are "species-beings," according to Marx, because they alone are capable of creative, and therefore, genuinely free, activity. Whereas all (other) animals, Marx claims, produce instinctively—"under the dominion of immediate physical need"[12]—and therefore produce the same thing, over and over again, a human being (Marx argues in *Capital*) produces *imaginatively*—he "raises his structure in imagination before he erects in reality"[13]—and is therefore capable of producing entirely new and different things. Thus human labor is distinctive insofar as it unites conception and execution. But under capitalism conception and execution go their separate ways: the capitalist (or his representative) conceives (plans), and the worker executes. Workers are generally unable to erect in *their* imagination a vision of the product before producing it, and thus their work becomes repetitive and quasi-instinctual. In the process they lose what Marx takes to be their distinctive "advantage" over (other) animals: "conscious life-activity."[14] And, since for Marx, conscious life-activity is synonymous with "free activity," workers under capitalism could scarcely said to be genuinely free.

4: The Alienation of Workers from Other Workers

"An immediate consequence of the fact that man is estranged from the product of his labour, from his life-activity, [and] from his species-being," Marx asserts, "is the *estrangement of man* from *man*."[15] The structure of the capital–wage labor relationship cannot but engender instrumental, competitive relationships among those who are caught up in that structure.

Consider, to begin with, what Marx takes to be the most fundamental relationship in a capitalist society, the relationship between capitalist and worker. Clearly neither party to the relationship experiences it as an intrinsically rewarding social interaction: for the capitalist the worker is merely a means to the end of maximum profit, and for the worker the capitalist is only a means to the end of his wage or income. Relationships among members of the capitalist class are similarly instrumental, since each one knows that the success of the other's business can mean the failure of one's own. Finally, in a system in which people must work in order to survive and work is not guaranteed, every worker is a potential threat to the survival of every other worker. Thus the system encourages people to experience others as pure means to the realization of their selfish ends, or as obstacles to the fulfillment of those ends, and thus discourages people from experiencing themselves as what they really are, namely, according to Marx, *social beings* the quality of whose individuality depends decisively on the quality of their interactions with others.

Each of the dimensions of alienation I have reviewed, it should be clear, implies a criterion that an unalienated—and therefore genuinely free society— would have to satisfy. If workers are alienated by virtue of their lack of control over the critical decisions concerning what they produce, in an unalienated society workers would have to participate in the making of those decisions. To say this is to say that the division of labor between rulers and ruled in the process of production would have to be overcome. How—and whether—industrial democracy or worker self-management might be possible is an issue over which much ink has been spilled, and I will consider it briefly in chapter 13.

Similarly, if work that is merely a means to an external end is inherently alienating, then it would follow that in an entirely unalienated society all work would be intrinsically rewarding, an end in itself. Is it really possible that all the work that was necessary to satisfy the needs of the future society could be structured to make it possible for individuals to enjoy it, and to experience themselves as free, because creative, "species-beings"? Marx himself was deeply ambivalent on this question, answering both "yes" and 'no" at different points in his writings.[16] And is Marx correct to assume that individuals are social beings who flourish under cooperation and suffer under competition? It is of course true that capitalism greatly rewards egotism, but, if we assume, as Marx tends to, that egotism is merely a product of capitalism, then it would seem to be difficult if not impossible to explain why a system that so encourages egotism was created in the first place. To explain that, might we not need to supplement Marx's focus on the social side of human nature with a recognition of its a-social or even anti-social side? This is a question to which I will return in the concluding part of this book.

The foregoing questions have to do with whether Marx's ideal could ever be realized. But it is also possible, of course, to raise questions about the integrity of the ideal itself. I have space to ask only one. We have seen that Marx assumes that, under ideal conditions, "nature appears as [Man's] work [and] he contemplates himself in a world that he has created." Here Marx celebrates the modern Western commitment to *mastery over nature* that he shared with so many of his political and theoretical opponents. Is it possible that Marx's critique of capitalism is insufficiently radical, that he takes on board a Western industrial world-view that we now might have good reason to call into question? Is such a thoroughly anthropocentric—human-centered—world-view consistent with the creation of an ecologically sound society? I will have more to say about this world-view first in the part of this book devoted to "Culture and Identity" and then in its conclusion.

11

JUSTICE AND THE MARKET

In this chapter I summarize and contrast two very different positions on the relationship between justice and the market. John Rawls argues in his enormously influential *A Theory of Justice*, published in 1971, that justice demands public policies that could well significantly alter the distribution of income and wealth that would otherwise be produced by the normal, everyday operations of a "free-market" economy. Friedrich Hayek, writing a decade earlier than Rawls in *The Constitution of Liberty*, claims to the contrary that any such redistributive efforts on the part of the state would be fundamentally *unjust*. The fact that they come to such diametrically opposed positions suggests that their concepts of justice are, in fact, very different. This is indeed the case.

I begin with Hayek's so-called "Libertarian" argument against distributive justice.

His argument, in a nutshell, is that distributive justice is an oxymoron, or a contradiction in terms. This argument actually entails two different although related claims: (a) it makes no sense to describe any existing distribution of income or wealth as either just or unjust and (b) the effort to use the state to rectify or mitigate what is (wrongly) perceived to be an unjust distribution of income or wealth would actually be unjust. To understand the first of these claims, consider the following:

> Justice . . . is a concept which . . . ought to be confined to the deliberate treatment of men by other men. It is an aspect of the intentional determination of those people's lives that are subject to such control. Insofar as we want the efforts of individuals to be guided by their own views about prospects and chances, the results of the individual's efforts are necessarily unpredictable, and the question as to whether the resulting distribution of incomes is just *has no meaning*.[1]

Thus Hayek's conclusion that "the question as to whether the . . . distribution of incomes is just has no meaning" is based (a) on the assumption that it makes sense to refer to outcomes as either just or unjust only in the case of those outcomes that are the result of the "deliberate treatment of men by other men" or

84

their "intentional . . . control" and (b) on the assumption that the outcomes of a market economy are *not* in fact the result of the deliberate treatment by or intentional control of others, but rather of the individuals' "own views about [their] prospects and chances" and their "individual efforts."

Notice the circularity in this argument. It is of course true that, in the context of a market economy in which governmental regulation is largely if not entirely absent, most economic outcomes are not the result of the "deliberate treatment" or "intentional control" of others, but this begs the question of whether a market economy is justified in the first place. If, to put this the other way around, economic outcomes *were* significantly influenced by governmental decisions, then Hayek would have to concede that the question of justice *did* apply to the distribution of income. In other words, if we assume the existence of a laissez-faire, market economy, then of course it follows that the "question . . . whether the resulting distribution of income is just has no meaning," because in a pure market economy the distributive principle is, as Hayek emphasizes repeatedly, "to each according to his or her value" to others as measured by the price they are willing to pay; that is, the individual's labor contribution is treated exclusively as a commodity, but this simply sidesteps the question of whether the distributive principle of "to each according to his value as measured by his price" *should* prevail. Thus, up to this point at least, Hayek's defense of a laissez-faire market economy would appear to presuppose the existence of the very economy he is attempting to defend.

But elsewhere in his book Hayek does make one positive argument in favor of this distributive principle (other than those he makes in order to justify his second claim, namely that any other distributive principle, and any redistributive principle in particular, would be unjust). He argues that:

> If the remuneration [the wage or salary] did not correspond to the value that the product of a man's efforts has for his fellows, he would have no basis for deciding whether the pursuit of a given object is worth the effort and risk. He would necessarily have to be told what to do, and some other person's estimate of what was the best use of his capacities would have to determine both his duties and his remuneration.[2]

We have seen this argument before: it is the same argument that the Friedmans made on behalf of laissez-faire. That argument, I suggested in the previous chapter, is based on the assumption that work will be done, or done well, only if the worker is offered a sufficiently attractive external or extrinsic reward, in other words, on the assumption that work is never its own, intrinsic reward. To put this another way, the distributive principle for a pure market determination of the wage or salary—the distributive principle that treats labor-power as a commodity whose value is determined like the value of any other commodity, namely by the demand for it as measured by its price—presupposes that labor is always nothing but what Marx calls alienated labor, a mere and sometimes mortifying means to the end of consumption rather than an inherently satisfying creative activity. Thus if we agree with Marx's critique of alienated labor we will necessarily take issue with Hayek's argument up to this point.

This brings us to his second argument, namely that the political promotion of socio-economic equality—the effort of the government to redistribute income—would be unjust. It would be unjust, according to Hayek, because it would necessarily be inconsistent with the individual liberty and the equality before the law that for him are the central—indeed exclusive—features of a genuinely just society. Listen to Hayek:

> From the fact that people are very different [whether by nature or nurture] it follows that, if we treat them equally, the result must be inequality in their actual position, and that the only way to place them in an equal position would be to treat them differently. Equality before the law and material equality are therefore not only different but are in conflict with each other; and we can achieve either the one or the other, but not both at the same time. The equality before the law which freedom requires leads [necessarily] to material inequality . . . the desire of making people more alike in their condition cannot be accepted in a free society as a justification for . . . discriminatory coercion.[3]

So according to Hayek the government would have to violate the principle of equality before the law—would have to treat individuals differently, and some individuals preferentially—in order to assure them more "equal positions in life." And to do so would be an assault on the very individual liberty that the rule of law protects. For example, if we eliminated inheritance—the right of parents to transfer their property and other assets to their children (which is surely an important mechanism for the inter-generational reproduction of economic inequality) on the grounds that it would be unfair for a child of a rich family to have a better start in life than a child of a poor family, we would be denying parents the freedom to "equip the new generation as well as they can"[4] and undermining the family as a stable, inter-generational unit in the process. If we attempt to enforce equality in early education, so that all could "be assured an equal start and the same prospects," this would mean nothing less than the

> government . . . should aim at controlling all conditions relevant to a particular individual's prospects and so adjust them to his capacities as to ensure him of the same prospects as everybody else. Such deliberate adaptation of opportunities to individual aims and capacities would, of course, be the very opposite of freedom.[5]

Notice that Hayek sets up a stark either–or: either the freedom of an unregulated market economy or the unfreedom of governmental regulation of the market economy. But at least at one point he acknowledges that certain redistributive measures undertaken by the state that reduce inequality may be consistent with liberty, and may even be "preferable," even though never *demanded* by justice:

> Wherever there is a legitimate need for government action and we have to choose between different methods of satisfying that need, those that incidentally also reduce inequality may well be preferable. If, for example, in the law of intestate succession [the law governing the distribution of property in the absence of a will] one kind of provision will be more conducive to equality than another, this may be a strong argument in its favour.[6]

Although, as we have already seen, Hayek generally argues that governmental efforts to promote economic equality necessarily violate individual liberty, here he suggests that the state may in fact pursue certain redistributive policies that do not compromise the "basic postulate of a free society, namely the limitation of all coercion by equal law." It would appear then, that he oscillates between an extreme laissez-faire position that assumes that *any* governmental effort to promote social and economic equality is, by definition, inconsistent with liberty and the rule of law—a position, for example, that would rule out a progressive income tax—and a more flexible, vaguer position that argues that redistributive measures are either desirable or not—but once again, never *demanded by justice*—depending on whether they preserve liberty and equality before the law or not.

This brings us to the arguments of John Rawls, who, like Hayek, accepts what he calls the "priority of liberty" or equality before the law, but, unlike Hayek, argues that justice requires that liberty be harmonized with the principle that any inequalities (resulting from governmental policies) must be to the advantage of all, and to the least advantaged members of society, in particular.

Rawls' two principles of justice read as follows:

> First: each person is to have an equal right to the most extensive basic liberty compatible with similar liberty for others.
> Second: social and economic inequalities are to be arranged so that they are both (a) reasonably expected to be to everyone's advantage, and (b) attached to positions and offices open to all.[7]

Since Rawls argues that these two principles—the liberty principle and what he calls the "difference" principle—"would be chosen in [what he calls] the original position,"[8] it is important to begin with a summary of his account of that position.

The "original condition" is a hypothetical situation, a thought experiment not unlike the "state of nature" of seventeenth- and eighteenth-century Social Contract theorists, in which individuals are assumed (a) to have different, competing interests that they wish to advance (and to be "mutually disinterested");

(b) to be equally rational, equally capable of making and evaluating arguments about their interests; and (c) to decide under what Rawls calls a "veil of ignorance" that prevents them from knowing, among other things, their social or economic status, their particular position relative to the particular positions of everyone else. The veil of ignorance thus prevents them from making a decision based on what Rawls believes are morally irrelevant considerations such as accidents of birth or social circumstances. In other words, since, under the veil of ignorance, the individual is unaware of whether he or she is rich or poor, he or she will not be tempted to choose principles of justice that would either favor the rich or favor the poor. To put this in Rawls's language, "since all are similarly situated and no one is able to design principles to favor his particular condition"—since no one knows his particular position—we can be sure that the principles of justice would be the result of a "fair agreement or bargain."[9] So, when Rawls asserts that the two principles of justice he introduces would be chosen in the original position, he means that equally rational individuals who seek to advance their own interests but are ignorant about their particular place in society relative to others would agree to both the liberty principle and the "difference" principle.

Although I will focus on Rawls's treatment of the difference principle, it is important to note that he agrees with Hayek on the importance, indeed the priority, of the liberty principle. That is, he argues that it would always be unjust to trade off liberty for more social and economic equality. But unlike Hayek—or at least the more extreme version of Hayek's position—Rawls argues that certain redistributive measures may be perfectly consistent with the liberty principle. And, against *any* version of Hayek's position, he argues that justice may under certain circumstances *require* those redistributive measures.

The difference principle, to repeat, tells us that only those social and economic inequalities that are to the benefit of all, and the benefit of the least advantaged in particular, are just: "injustice . . . is simply inequalities that are not to the benefit of all."[10] So whereas for Hayek there is no such thing as distributive justice—thus no justifiable limits on the extent of economic inequality—for Rawls inequality is *justifiably* limited by the requirement that the inequality work to the advantage of those who have the least. To put this another way: if, everything else being equal, a lower level of inequality—a more egalitarian distribution of wealth—would benefit the least well-off, then a lower level of inequality is required by the (difference) principle of justice. Thus for Rawls the onus is on those who are well-off to demonstrate that any given increment of their wealth—resulting for example from tax cuts—would also be to the benefit of those who are not well-off—to demonstrate, for example, that those tax cuts would spur investment that would result in better economic opportunities for the poor.

Recall that Rawls claims that the difference principle would be chosen in the original position. His (by now) famous (and much-contested) argument[11] is that if you could turn out to be either rich or poor, but had no way of knowing (under the veil of ignorance) which way you would turn out, it would be most rational of you to select a principle of distribution that allowed for the opportunity to increase your wealth but at the same time ensured that the increase in anyone's wealth did not occur at the expense of, but rather contributed to, the well-being of everyone else, and the poor in particular. But he also argues in favor of what he calls the "tendency to equality"[12] favored by the difference principle on grounds other than the original position. His claim, in other words, is that even individuals who know their position in society would—or should—select the difference principle. It is perhaps easy to see why a poor person—or at least a poor person who didn't suffer from envy—would find this principle to be fair, but why would a wealthy person, for whom the difference principle would probably mean more limits on his wealth than would otherwise exist, agree with this principle?

To answer this question Rawls makes four different although related arguments in favor of the difference principle: (1) an argument for "redress"; (2) an argument for "reciprocity"; (3) an argument for "fraternity"; and (4) an argument for the reduction of "envy." The redress argument goes like this:

> Undeserved inequalities call for redress; and since inequalities of birth and natural endowment are undeserved, those inequalities are to be somehow compensated for. Thus the principle holds that in order to treat all personas equally, and to provide genuine equality of opportunity, society must give more attention to those with fewer native assets and to those born into less favorable social positions. The idea is to redress the bias of contingencies in the direction of equality. In pursuit of this principle greater resources might be spent on the education of the less rather than the more intelligent, at least over a certain time of life, say the earlier years of school.[13]

Notice that Rawls argues that the difference principle "does not require society to try to even out handicaps as if all were expected to compete on a fair basis in the same race," and we can certainly question whether it goes far enough in that direction. But the general point that Rawls makes is that "those who have been favored by nature . . . may gain from their good fortune only on terms that improve the situation of those who have lost out."[14] Thus the difference principle is a *partial compensation* for the accidents of birth and circumstance for which Hayek, in contrast, argues that no redress is desirable. It says, in effect, to the person fortunate enough to have been born into a rich family that it is unjust for you to benefit from this accident of birth unless your benefit is shared with others.

The difference principle also expresses a "conception of reciprocity."[15] It is a principle of mutual benefit: it is based on the assumption that "the well-being of each depends on a scheme of social cooperation without which no one [not even the richest of the rich] could have a satisfactory life." Thus the rich as well as the poor have an obligation to cooperate with the scheme of social cooperation as long as "the terms of the scheme are reasonable."[16] And Rawls argues, as we have seen, that the scheme of cooperation governed by the difference principle is eminently reasonable.

The difference principle is also an interpretation of the principle of "fraternity"—of brotherhood—and, we might add, of "sorority" or sisterhood as well: "the idea of not wanting to have greater advantages unless this is to the benefit of those who are less well off."[17] Thus the difference principle articulates a political version of the concern for others that normally develops and is expressed, for example, in a family.

Finally, a society in which the difference principle prevailed, Rawls suggests, might well *reduce* the envy of the poor of the rich, since there would probably be less inequality than currently prevails. Whereas Hayek claims that egalitarianism is often rooted in envy,[18] Rawls argues that his "moderate egalitarianism" (a) would not increase envy and might in fact decrease it and (b) is *not* motivated by envy, since envy is a condition in which resentment about having less takes the form of a desire that those who have more should also have less, whereas the difference principle says that it is reasonable for those who have less to want those who have more to gain as long as those who have less gain as well.

To conclude. Rawls's distributive principle—to each according to what is in the interest of all—represents an ingenious attempt to reconcile a commitment to others—social obligation—with a commitment to individual freedom. It also attempts to harmonize the commitment to individual freedom with the need to compensate, at least in part, for the natural and social advantages for which individuals themselves are in no sense responsible. In short, it is an effort to solve two related problems that, to my mind, Hayek simply refuses to face. It is also an effort that has generated a wide variety of critical responses,[19] only one of which I have space to mention. I have already intimated that the extent of redistribution required by Rawls's difference principle is, to say the least, not entirely clear. But, even if it could be shown that that principle would indeed require a dramatic or even significant redistribution of income from the rich to the poor, we might question whether such a principled redistribution could ever be put into *practice* by a government in a (capitalist) market economy. This raises the question of the role of the state in a capitalist society, a question to which I turn in the next chapter.

12

DEMOCRACY AND THE MARKET I

Corporations and the State

The question with which we will be preoccupied in this and the next two chapters is the relationship between a market economy and democracy. Charles Lindblom, the author of *Politics and Markets*—the only book under review in this chapter—translates this question into the relationship between private, corporate control of production on the one hand, and actually existing representative democracies, which he, following his colleague Robert Dahl, calls "polyarchies," on the other. His argument, in a nutshell, is (a) that private enterprise market economies are necessary for polyarchies, but (b) that polyarchies, precisely because of their very dependence on those economies, are not in fact very democratic. Both because this argument runs so counter to conventional wisdom and because, to my mind, it is entirely persuasive, I will depart from my usual practice of introducing the reader to at least two different "takes" on the same topic and will concentrate exclusively on what Lindblom has to say.

Let's consider, to begin with, his argument about the necessity of corporate-controlled, private enterprise economies for polyarchies. Lindblom points out that all existing polyarchal systems—that is, once again, all actually existing representative democracies—are associated with "market-oriented" economic systems. In 1977, when Lindblom's book was published, there were *no examples* that combined polyarchal politics with centrally planned economies,[1] and more than thirty years after that date that continues to be the case. On the other hand, Lindblom also notes that in 1977 a majority of market-oriented economies were combined with authoritarian, non-polyarchal governmental systems.[2] Since 1977 many of the examples of this combination that he cites—Spain, Portugal, and most of Latin America—have been transformed from authoritarian governments into polyarchies, but "non-communist Asia" is still market oriented but largely authoritarian, and some formerly (so-called) communist societies such as Russia and perhaps even China have been transformed into market economies but have retained an authoritarian political system. So it remains the case today that there are many combinations of market economies and non-polyarchal political systems, even as it is still true that there are no polyarchal systems that are not market oriented. Wherever there are polyarchies there are market economies associated with them, but wherever there are market economies there may or may not be polyarchies connected with them. A private-enterprise, market economy, in others words, is *necessary but not sufficient* for polyarchy.

This is the two-part puzzle that Lindblom attempts to solve in his book: Why is it that *no* actually existing polyarchy has rejected corporate or market-controlled production in favor of centrally or politically planned production, and why is it that only *some* market-oriented societies have become polyarchies? As to the first of these two questions, Lindblom notes that there is no necessary *logical* connection between polyarchy and market: in principle, "a [polyarchal] society might believe polyarchy to be superior to the market for achieving popular control and hence might displace the market."[3] Similarly, he insists that "logically . . . polyarchy and market are independent."[4] Yet, as we have seen, the first is never actually found without the second. Why then is this the case? Lindblom's answer is that both polyarchal political systems and private-enterprise, market economic systems share a common origin: "the two are *historically* tied together [because] both are manifestations of constitutional liberalism."[5]

By "constitutional liberalism" Lindblom means the commitment in political theory and political practice to the protection and extension of both the economic and the political liberty of the individual, with "liberty" understood as the right of the individual to develop and express her preferences independent of government or state control. "Constitutional liberalism" is devoted, in other words, to what Isaiah Berlin calls "negative freedom," that is, the freedom of the individual from external obstacles, rather than what he calls "positive freedom," namely the socially or political promoted freedom of the individual more fully to develop her human potential.[6] Lindblom claims that the three great revolutionary movements of the seventeenth and eighteenth centuries—the English, American, and French Revolutions—were all dedicated to liberty in the negative rather than the positive sense, all dedicated to the protection of the individual from the overweening power of the state. To the extent that the French and Americans constitutionalists immediately and the English constitutionalists only gradually came to embrace representative democracy, Lindblom points out, they did so because they believed that representative democracy was the best *means* to preserve and enhance individual liberty. (This belief, you will recall, is precisely what Benjamin Barber castigated in his critique of so-called "thin" conceptions of democracy that ignore the centrality of democracy to the development of "positive freedom.") Lindblom argues, perhaps with some degree of exaggeration, that this instrumental conception of democracy is true of "all the great figures in political thought in the [early] modern era": they all saw representative democracy, once again, as an instrument of liberty.[7] It follows that, as Lindblom says, "if in its historical origins polyarchy is an institution for introducing . . . forms of popular control that serve liberty, then it is not at all surprising that men who created polyarchies will also preserve market systems,"[8] which market systems, according to Lindblom, respond to the preferences of consumers and are thus far more consistent with liberty than centralized command economies that either determine or by-pass those preferences. So he concludes "that the liberal notion of freedom was freedom from government's many interventions, and for that kind of freedom markets are indeed indispensable."[9]

This argument also explains why many societies with private enterprise market economies have not in fact adopted polyarchal, that is, representative democratic, political systems. If polyarchy is understood only as a *means* to the end of economic freedom, then it is entirely possible that in some cases powerful elites might conclude that there are better, more efficient, perhaps less dangerous means to achieve that end. That seems to be what has happened in those societies that combine non-democratic, authoritarian forms of political rule with private-enterprise market economies: they have created a legal framework within which contracts can be predictably enforced and market opportunities can be reliably exploited, but they have refused to extend even indirect self-government to their citizens. In short, they are living examples of Joseph Raz's claim that the rule of law can coexist with authoritarian governments that justly deserve the condemnation of small-d democrats.

To put all this another way, the marriage of market economies and polyarchies generally results from powerful popular movements that were committed to each. Insofar as this particular combination depends in this sense on the power of the people, might not that power be exercised in a way that would uncouple polyarchy from a private enterprise market economy and create a different kind of economic system? If, as Lindblom argues, market economy and polyarchy are united only by history and not by logical necessity, in principle couldn't people change that history? And so Lindblom asks: "Can we conceive of a polyarchy arranged to achieve popular control over a government bent on *collective* purposes, one much less committed to the traditional individualistic liberties?," and answers "Yes, it is not difficult."[10] But the fact that this is easily conceivable only raises the question: "Why have no polyarchies, notwithstanding their liberal and constitutional origins, made a significant attempt at a centrally directed authoritative system,"[11] that is, made a significant attempt to transform a corporate-controlled, market economy into politically planned economy? Lindblom's answer is that polyarchies are actually under the control of the "business and property-owning groups" who control the market economy:

> Only if the wealthy (or persons allied with them) exercise at all times in all polyarchies an extraordinarily disproportionate influence on governmental policy can the challenge of central planning to the privileges of property explain the remarkable uniformity of polyarchal hostility to central planning.[12]

Thus we have arrived at Lindblom's second major claim, namely that polyarchies, precisely because of their dependence on market economies, are not in fact very democratic.

This claim is defended at length in chapters that detail the different forms of corporate power or influence over polyarchal governments. In chapter 13 Lindblom argues that big business has a "privileged position" that is "unmatched by any leadership group other than government officials themselves." This argument starts from the assumption that businessmen are "a kind of public official and exercise what, in a broad view of their role, are public functions."[13] By "public functions" Lindblom means

> decisions on the allocation of resources to different lines of production, on the allocation of the labor force to different occupations and workplaces, on plant location, the technologies to be used in production, the quality of goods and services, innovation of new products—in short, on every major aspect of production and distribution,[14]

all of which rest in corporate hands and all of which dramatically affect the lives of the millions of people who are dependent on the system of production and distribution. Thus Lindblom concludes that in a private enterprise market economy "a large category of major decisions is turned over to businessmen . . . and a broad area of public decision making is removed from polyarchal control."[15]

Although this "broad area of . . . decision making" is removed from the control of (polyarchal) government, government officials are nonetheless expected to ensure that the economy operates effectively. They will get credit if the economy does well and take the blame—suffering at the polls—if it does not. Thus it is in the interests of elected governmental leaders to "see to it that businessmen perform their tasks" well. But the constitutional rules of the private enterprise game prevent those political leaders from simply *commanding* corporate performance: "they must induce rather than command."[16] In other words, in order to encourage businessmen to make decisions that will protect or improve the "standard of living [and] economic security"[17] of their constituents, politicians will have to give to businessmen at least a good deal of what they want. What they want includes a vast array of formal and informal public policies, ranging from the infrastructure necessary for the distribution (and sometimes even the production) of their goods and services, to tax breaks that enable them to increase their rates of profit, laws that hamper the organizations of unions, veto power over governmental appointments to regulatory positions, and ready access to the governmental officials they want to see. Because political leaders are aware that the failure to respond sympathetically to business demands for these benefits could well result in corporate decisions that would harm rather than help the economy, they are powerfully constrained to deliver the political goods to the businessmen who make those decisions.

This same fear of losing what is euphemistically referred to as "business confidence" will generally prevent elected politicians from even seriously entertaining proposals that would weaken the power or threaten the interests of business. Although Lindblom doesn't use the term, it would not be far off the mark to describe the relationship between big business and elected political leaders as a form of legalized blackmail: the tacit, never explicitly articulated threat to harm the economy—for example the threat of disinvestment in technology or of relocation to a different community or even country—functions to ensure that business usually gets most of what it wants, and rarely gets what it doesn't want, from the elected and appointed political leaders who are expected to prevent the economic "hostage" from being harmed. This asymmetrical relationship of dependence of politicians on business, Lindblom concludes, is "the fundamental mechanism by which a great deal of business control, unmatched by similar control exercised by any other group of citizens, [inevitably] comes to be exercised over government."[18] This, in short, is how "polyarchies . . . are controlled undemocratically by business and property."[19]

It is important to emphasize that the exercise of business control does *not* fundamentally depend on the lobbying, campaign financing, or any other concrete political *activities* undertaken by individual corporate leaders, which, according to Lindblom, are only a "supplement to its privileged position."[20] In the ordinary course of events these leaders don't have to *do* anything to achieve their "unmatched control": the ever-present threat that they *might* (do something to harm the economy) is sufficient to assure that control. This is what Lindblom has in mind when he argues that:

> Any government official who understands the requirements of his position and the responsibilities that market-oriented systems throw on businessmen will . . . grant them a privileged position. He does not have to be bribed, duped or pressured to do so . . . He simply understands . . . that public affairs in market-oriented systems are in the hands of two groups of leaders, government and business, who must collaborate, and that, to make the system work government leadership must often defer to business leadership.[21]

Lindblom hastens to add that this collaboration often involves conflict as well. Elected politicians, after all, are dependent not only on business but also on the support of the voters, voters who will sometimes pressure them to pursue policies that business would not prefer. When they are caught between the demands of business and the demands of their constituents, politicians will normally try to resolve this conflict in a way that threatens the interests of business as little as possible. Moreover, these conflicts are inevitably about "secondary issues—such as tax rates and particulars of regulation and promotion of business"[22]—rather than over the fundamentals of the private enterprise system itself. Thus the "conflict [between businessmen and politicians] will always lie," Lindblom insists, "within a range of dispute constrained by their understanding that they together constitute the necessary leadership for the system. They do not wish to destroy or seriously undermine the function of each other." It follows that "evidence . . . of conflict between business and government—and [even] of business defeats—is not evidence of lack of [business] privilege."[23]

But the *degree* or extent of business privilege, he suggests, can vary from society to society and over time in any one society. In fact, Lindblom cautiously claims that the relationship between business and government "slowly shifts, decade by decade, in the direction of less privilege for business and more authority for government."[24] That claim did indeed accurately capture the trend of the relationship in the United States, and more generally in the Western capitalist world, from the beginning of the twentieth century to 1977, when Lindblom's book was published. But since that time, and beginning with the so-called Reagan Revolution in 1980, and continuing under George W. Bush, it would seem that, at least in certain respects, the trend has been reversed. The "era of Big Government" is hardly over, but it would be difficult to dispute the claim that business has in the past two decades consistently achieved *more privilege*—greater freedom from regulation, lower tax rates, less interference from unions, and so forth—than it had from the New Deal in the 1930s through the 1970s.[25] And, curiously enough, business has increased its privileged position in large part as the result of concerted efforts on the part of elected governmental leaders to reduce *their own* influence over business.

Although Lindblom did not foresee this reversal, we can imagine how he would try to explain it. If business privilege is the result of the inducements that politicians are obliged to offer to business leaders, and the number and size of inducements is a function of the degree of dependence of politicians on business, then it follows that increased business privilege must be the result of an increased dependence of politicians on business. To put this another way, the threat of business blackmail—the risk of business action that would harm the economy and thus ultimately harm the prospects of politicians—must have become larger and more credible over the past few decades. Lindblom points out that there will always be "some minimum of privilege short of which inducements will fail to motivate business performance," and he illustrates this point by referring to "the demand for privilege that giant multi-national corporations can impose on small nations. Either the demands are met, or the corporation goes elsewhere."[26] What he did not foresee in 1977 is that, under conditions of the globalization that has proceeded apace since that time, it is now the case that "giant multi-national corporations" can now impose this demand on *large* nations, including the United States. In this sense globalization surely increases the dependence of elected politicians on big business, and thus, on the logic of Lindblom's argument, on the scope of "inducements" they are obliged to offer big business. The blackmail price has, in short, gone up. Whether this is a sufficient explanation for conservative efforts to dismantle the regulations and protections of the New Deal and the Great Society is an open question, but it surely is an important part of a satisfactory explanation.[27] Much more on globalization and governance in chapter 14.

13

DEMOCRACY AND THE MARKET II

Corporate Governance

As we saw in the last chapter, and quoting once again from Lindblom, in a private-enterprise market economy "a large category of major decisions"—decisions about the production and distribution of goods and services that dramatically affect the well-being of entire communities and the individuals who reside within them—"is turned over to businessmen . . . and a broad area of public-decision making is removed from polyarchal [that is, democratic] control." Thus the consequences of corporate decisions are public but the individuals who make those decisions—those who govern the corporation—are not accountable to the various publics, including the workers and consumers, who are inevitably affected by their decisions. How then are corporations governed? In *theory* (publicly traded) corporations are controlled by the individuals who own shares in those corporations: the stockholders elect a Board of Directors, whose responsibility, in turn, is to appoint the managers or executive officers of the corporation and to oversee their performance. Thus, although the managers make all the important decisions about the production of goods and services offered by the corporation, the managers are, in principle, accountable to a body—the Board of Directors—that is, in turn, accountable to the legal owners—the shareholders—of the corporation. In principle, but, as Doug Henwood's *Wall Street* amply demonstrates, the *practice* is in fact very different from the principle.

To begin with, the extreme concentration of stock ownership in the United States makes it unlikely that first Boards of Directors and then the executive officers will be influenced by the great majority of the shareholders in their company. The rhetoric of "People's Capitalism" notwithstanding, in 2004, the richest 1 percent of American households owned 37 percent of all the stock in the United States, the next 4 percent owned almost 29 percent, and the next 15 percent owned just over 25 percent. In other words, the top 20 percent of households owned over 90 percent of corporate shares; the remaining 80 percent owned less than 10 percent of those shares. Similarly, although almost half of American households owned some stock in 2004, only 30 percent owned stocks worth more than $10,000, and fewer than 23 percent owned shares worth more than $25,000.[1] Thus the great majority of the shares in any given large corporation are likely to be owned by a relatively small fraction of the total number of shareholders in that corporation. In principle the majority of small shareholders *might* be able to outvote the minority of giant investors, but, as Henwood points out, there are formidable organizational obstacles to a genuine shareholders' democracy: "the difficulty of running an electoral challenge to corporate management gives the 'small organized party' a great advantage over the 'large unorganized one',"[2] and he suggests "that even with visibility, membership, and funding, it's near impossible to get small, dispersed shareholders to act as a unit."[3] Under these conditions it is no surprise that Boards of Directors, and thus the managers they appoint and whose performance they are supposed to monitor, are disproportionately, overwhelmingly, likely to defer exclusively to the largest investors. Thus in practice the government of the corporation is oligarchical, that is, characterized by the rule of the few who happen also to be rich.

This does not mean that the different oligarchies have identical or even consistently compatible interests. To the contrary: as Henwood points out, their interests are in certain respects very different, and this often makes for intense, even vicious conflicts among them.

Shareholders want high stock prices, and the drive of large investors for the highest possible rate of return puts pressure on managers to undertake sometimes risky investments that they might otherwise prefer to avoid, since managers above all want, as Henwood puts it, "a peaceful life with high salaries and minimal external intrusion."[4] So there is in fact a structural conflict of interest between the managers and the large shareholders to whom they are obliged to pay attention. (The recent effort to overcome this conflict of interest, that is, to make managers think more like large shareholders by tying their level of compensation to the stock price of the companies they manage, moreover, as we have seen all too frequently in recent years, only exacerbates the tendency of managers to "cook the books," to inflate the level of profits in order to impress large investors.) And managers are also beholden to the banks and other creditors on whom they depend for the capital necessary to fund their investments, creditors whose interests typically diverge from the interests of shareholders. Creditors, Henwood notes, "want their interest paid regularly and their principal eventually returned," and "high-risk strategies that might pay off in a big gain in a firm's stock price may strike creditors as putting the security of their payment stream at risk."[5] Thus the actual government of most large corporations entails a struggle for power among three main actors: managers, large investors, and banks and other creditors (who are increasingly large investors as well).

Henwood shows that the actual balance of power among these different members of the corporate oligarchy has shifted significantly over time. During the period from the New Deal in the 1930s through the end of the 1960s, managers gained far more control over the governance of corporations than they had earlier exercised. The so-called managerialism of Adolph Berle and

Gardiner Means was the archetypical academic expression of this political-economic transformation. They argued in their enormously influential *The Modern Corporation and Private Property*[6] that the modern corporation was characterized by the *separation of ownership from control*: as Henwood characterizes their position:

> the function of the 19th century owner entrepreneur had been divided in two. Formal ownership was delivered into the hands of thousands, even millions, of dispersed stockholders [while] actual control . . . fell to managers, who, though formally responsible to the stockholders, were in fact largely independent, self-sustaining, and answerable to no one in particular as long as things didn't go badly wrong.[7]

Although Berle and Means, and John Kenneth Galbraith some thirty years later in his *New Industrial State*,[8] clearly exaggerated the significance of this transformation—they argued, wrongly according to Henwood, that increasing managerial autonomy meant that profit maximization was no longer the driving force of the capitalist system—they did accurately describe a relative decline in the power of financial capital relative to the power of the corporate managers. However, as Henwood points out, since the 1970s and under the impact of globalization and deregulation this decline in the power of financial capital—of banks and large investors—has been reversed and it is now (Henwood was writing in 1996) the case that, according to Henwood, large "shareholders are far less passive, boards less rubber-stampish, and managements less autonomous than at any time since Berle and Means. Since the early 1980s, influence from the financial sphere has been greater than at any time since the 1920s."[9] For Henwood, this renewed and intensified financial influence has been most unfortunate. It has produced the intermittent reality and thus the persistent threat of leveraged buy-outs and forced mergers and acquisitions that are driven by Wall Street's obsession with "quick profit growth" and which pressure managers to sacrifice long-term prospects for short-term, and often short-sighted, gains. These buy-outs and mergers, as is common knowledge, are typically accompanied by lay-offs, wage and benefit cuts, and union busting designed to make the firm more "competitive," that is, to increase the value of the company's stock (sometimes so the firm can be resold at an enormous profit). The stocks go up as the workers (and their communities) go down: "what's divine for rentiers [large shareholders]," Henwood asserts, "is bad news for everyone else."[10] And, according to Henwood, "bad news for everyone else" is exactly what we should expect when corporate governance is effectively turned over to—and here he quotes from Charles Wohlstetter, former Chair of Contel:

> a group of people . . . with no proven skills in management, no experience at selecting directors, no believable judgment in how much should be spent

for research or marketing—in fact, no experience except that which they have accumulated controlling other people's money.[11]

Hence Henwood's claim that "outside shareholders serve no useful purposes," which, he concludes, is a very good argument for "turning firms over to their workers."[12]

This conclusion is apt to appear arbitrary in the absence of the kind of independent argument on behalf of self-management or worker-controlled enterprises that Robert Dahl provides in his *After the Revolution*? This argument is based on the assumption that the current form of corporate governance is inconsistent with what he calls the Principle of Affected Interests, namely that "everyone who is affected by the decisions of a government should have the right to participate in that government."[13] Shareholder government, he tells us:

> is an unreasonable denial of the Principle of Affected Interests. Why should people who own shares be given the privilege of citizenship in the government of the firm when citizenship is denied to other people who also make vital contributions to the firm? The people I have in mind are, of course, employees and customers, without whose support for (or acquiescence in) the myriad protections and services of the state the firm would instantly disappear. The Principle of Affected Interests gives these people a strong prima facie case for citizenship.[14]

This case, Dahl argues, is actually far more compelling than the case in favor of shareholder government. Writing in 1970 at the height of managerialism, Dahl argues that "even if the owners of a large firm have the legal right to run it, everyone knows today that they do not and cannot run it . . . To be sure," he continues, "stockholders do retain a nominal right to participate in governing the firm, but they do not and ordinarily cannot exercise that right." (If Dahl were rewriting this paragraph today, he would have to restrict this claim to the "great majority of stockholders" in order to take into consideration the increasingly dominant influence of financial capital, i.e., a relatively few large investors, over the decisions of the firm, of which financial influence he would undoubtedly be as disapproving as Henwood.) Thus Dahl concludes that "the traditional private property view of authority in the corporation denies the right of citizenship in corporate government to all the affected parties except the one group that does not, will not, and probably cannot exercise that right."[15] Because the form of authority within the corporation denies citizenship to "all affected parties"—because, in other words, the internal governance of the corporation is *undemocratic*—there is, for Dahl, no alternative to the conclusion that this form of authority is simply illegitimate.

It was of course precisely this argument that always fueled what Dahl calls the "orthodox socialist" critique of capitalism or private property in the means of production and which culminated in the commitment to public or state ownership of productive enterprises. But Dahl argues that this commitment proved to be no more consistent with the Principle of Affected Interests than capitalism. In practice, state ownership and control of the means of production has meant a system of control within and over individual enterprises from which workers are every bit as excluded as they are under capitalism: workers are obliged to take orders from managers in state-owned enterprises who attempt to fulfill a production quota established by a central plan in which workers themselves have not participated. Thus Dahl concludes that "coordination by governmental control was obviously inconsistent with autonomy and self-government in the firm. What would industrial democracy do to the sacred central plan?"[16] Thus "state socialism" or what was conventionally and misleadingly called "communism" is as inconsistent with "industrial democracy"—as inconsistent with the Principle of Affected Interests as applied to the government of the firm—as is capitalism.

Having concluded that neither capitalism nor state socialism is consistent with the Principle of Affected Interests, Dahl recommends what has come to be called *market socialism* as a system that *would* be consistent with that principle. At first glance market socialism is likely to strike us as an oxymoron—a contradiction in terms—so accustomed are we to associate capitalism with the market and socialism with its elimination. But Dahl's point is that the form of the internal organization or governance of the enterprise, on the one hand, and the form of the coordination among different enterprises and their customers, on the other, are two logically separate issues. Although it is of course true that coordination by the market and the absence of internal democracy converged historically to become market capitalism, in principle nothing would prevent us from uncoupling market coordination from the undemocratic, capitalist form of enterprise governance in such a way as to link the market with democratically organized, worker-controlled enterprises. The basic idea, in other words, is that firms would be controlled—at least, as we shall see, indirectly—by their workers but that these worker-controlled firms would compete with each other, that is, seek profits, by offering goods and services to consumers, the prices of which would be determined by the demand for those goods and services. Thus there is no good reason for socialists to oppose the market, whose operation, according to Dahl, would in fact be the only way to realize the goal of industrial democracy to which socialists have always been committed, in principle if not in practice:

> That the market might be usable under socialism; that if incomes were justly distributed [a big "if" of course], the market might enormously expand opportunities for the exercise of personal choice; that by decentralizing decisions to semiautonomous enterprises the market could provide a powerful force to counter bureaucratic centralization; that far from being the formless, anarchic, antisocial force portrayed by orthodox socialists, the market could be made into a highly sensitive instrument for coordinating

myriads of activities too complex ever to be settled wisely by central planners—all this socialists did not understand.[17]

Dahl goes on to consider a number of objections to the idea of market socialism. To the objection that the Principle of Affected Interests would demand that other interests, for example, of consumers or the general public, be represented in the internal governance of the enterprise, and that a form of what is sometimes calls "interest-group management" would be superior to worker self-management, Dahl responds both by pointing out the great difficulty of determining the precise amount of representation for each affected group and by arguing that the interests of consumers and the general public can be represented in the external governmental controls over enterprises that would—as they are even under market capitalism—still be necessary.[18] To the objection that workers would lack the competence to run their own enterprises, Dahl replies, "I do not see why a board of directors elected by the employees could not select as competent managers as a board of directors served by banks, insurance companies, or the managers themselves."[19] In other words, he envisions worker self-management as a form of representative rather than direct democracy. Dahl concedes that many workers, long used to thinking of their work merely as a means to the end of income for consumption, might themselves lack enthusiasm or even be opposed to such a system, but argues that if they discovered that "participation in the affairs of the enterprise . . . contributed to their own sense of competence and helped them to control an important part of their daily lives, then lassitude and indifference toward participation might change into interest and concern."[20]

There are many other questions that a convincing, full-blown defense of market socialism would have to address.[21] What would prevent worker-elected managers from developing interests of their own that would prevent them from effectively representing their worker constituents, that is, from ruling over rather than on behalf of workers? What would insulate worker-controlled enterprises from the intense pressures for short-term and short-sighted growth that currently issue, as we have seen, from the financial sector? To reduce that pressure, would financial institutions have to be more heavily regulated, perhaps even partly replaced by nationalized banks that would provide capital to worker-controlled enterprises for reasons other than high stock prices? If such banks were necessary, how might it be possible to reconcile their role with the need for genuinely autonomous enterprises?

Would workers themselves—now that their incomes depended directly on the profits made by their enterprise—be tempted to devote a disproportionate distribution of those profits to their wages as compared with investment in new and better technology? Would they be willing to take on new workers even if this might result in a decline in the size of each current worker's individual share of the surplus? More generally, would the pressure to compete with other enterprises for higher profits simply reproduce the inequality and the self-interest—even if now the form of enterprise-group interest—that currently prevails under capitalism, rather than engender the more just distribution of income to which Dahl is committed, and the social solidarity that all socialists have proclaimed as one of their principal goals? These are only some of the questions—the very important questions—that arise if we seriously consider, as I believe we should, the case for market socialism.

14

DEMOCRACY AND THE MARKET III
Globalization and Governance

The issue I address in this chapter is the impact of economic globalization on democracy. On the one hand, the progressive transformation of the entire world into a private-enterprise market economy clearly weakens the capacity of the governments of any one country in that world to control or even regulate the effects of that economy on its citizens. Although students of globalization differ over the *degree* of the decline of state power relative to the power of global capital—some believe that nation-states are still centrally important political actors whereas others see them as increasingly impotent, almost vestigial organs—it would be difficult to deny that globalization has been accompanied by a significant increase in what Lindblom called the "privileged place of business" relative to the government of the nation-state. When the international mobility of capital enables it to move with relative ease from one country to another, the leverage of capital over the state of any particular country—the level of "inducements" that must be offered to it in order to persuade it not to pick up stakes and leave—must inevitably increase. In part this explains why, according to some globalization scholars, "national governments across the globe have been forced to adopt increasingly similar (neoliberal) economic strategies which promote financial discipline, deregulation, and prudent economic management"[1]—in short, to give an increasingly multinational big business more of what it wants. Thus, according to those scholars to whom David Held and Anthony McGrew refer to as the "globalists," "economic globalization increasingly escapes the regulatory reach of national governments,"[2] and thus the democratic control of their citizens.

On the other hand, the "existing multilateral institutions of global governance"—the International Monetary Fund (IMF), the World Bank, and the World Trade Organization (WTO)—have not stepped in to fill this regulatory void. Rather they—especially the IMF and the WTO—"generally advocate and pursue programs which simply extend and deepen the hold of global market forces on national economic life."[3] The IMF has typically made the adoption of free-market economic policies the price of its loans to developing as well as other countries, and the WTO has sought to eliminate barriers to what is called "free trade" and thus to open up additional markets for exports and investments. They have, in other words, attempted to internationalize a system of laissez-faire, one that encourages the free flow of capital and labor across national boundaries but that *dis*courages efforts to regulate that flow in the name of the protection of the rights of workers or the health of the natural environment as obstacles to free trade or what is euphemistically referred to as economic "liberalization." One consequence of such "neoliberal" policies is that consumers in the United States and other advanced capitalist societies benefit from a regular influx of products that are far cheaper than they would be if produced domestically under far better working and environmental conditions. Another consequence, however, is that the wages, working conditions, and environmental conditions under which they are produced in many—not all—of the poorer parts of the world are quite abysmal. Thus, as Joseph Stiglitz, former Chief Economist at the World Bank notes in his important book, *Globalization and its Discontents*, "despite repeated promises of poverty reduction made [by proponents of unregulated globalization] over the last decade of the twentieth century, the actual number of people living in poverty has increased by almost 100 million."[4] And, as I have already suggested, the ever-present possibility that corporations based in Western capitalist societies might decide to produce the same goods and services far more cheaply in those poorer parts of the world necessarily dampens the militancy of Western capitalist workers: faced with the threat of cutbacks and plant closings, those workers are far more likely to accept lower wages and worse working conditions than they otherwise would. This is what people mean when they say that neoliberalism—unregulated globalization—promotes a "race to the bottom."

In many ways, then, we are today in the same political place internationally as we were nationally in the late nineteenth to the early twentieth century. That period was one in which the role of the state of any given capitalist society was mainly limited to creating the conditions that made private capital accumulation possible and thus one in which the state abstained from the regulatory and social welfare policies that would have cushioned the painful effects of what Polanyi calls the Great Transformation to a private-enterprise market economy. In this country it took the economic catastrophe of the Great Depression and the New Deal repudiation of the laissez-faire policies that were, in part, responsible for that catastrophe to put into effect and eventually legitimate the broad range of regulatory and social welfare policies that most of us now tend to take for granted. Thus did American society begin to protect itself against what Polanyi called "the perils inherent in a self-regulating market system."[5]

Global society has yet to protect itself from those perils. To this point the international political system has, as I have already suggested, functioned to make the world safe for private capital, but not for workers or the environment. But people all over the globe are currently struggling in different ways to create an international or multinational political order that would serve to protect people and the earth on which they depend from the untoward effects of globalization.[6] Perhaps the most promising consequence of the globalization of the market economy and the governmental institutions that promote it has been the rise of a "global civil society"—international non-governmental organizations such as Greenpeace, Peoples' Global Action, and Third World Network—and the trans-national social movements that are allied with them—that increasingly contests the neoliberal global regime.

At the risk of some oversimplification, at this point in time this contestation is divided between reformers who seek a fairer, more democratic form of economic globalization and radicals who reject economic globalization in favor of an entirely different kind of global system. The reformers—let's call them the members of the alternative globalization movement—want to rectify the gross economic and political imbalances between what is commonly referred to as the North and the South: they demand (with some recent success) debt relief for poor countries whose huge regular repayments guarantee a permanent condition of underdevelopment, they pressure (also with some success) the World Bank to support sustainable rather than ecologically disastrous development projects, they protest (with less success) IMF policies that tie loans and bail-outs to countries to the dismantling of their social safety net, and they insist (so far with little success) that WTO-sponsored treaties such as the North American and Central American Free Trade Agreements provide protection for workers—for example the right to organize—and the environment—for example a global ban on toxic pesticides—and not just for private capital. They aim, in short, for an international version of the New Deal, one that would—as the New Deal did in the United States—regulate the market economy and thus rescue it from the harm that its unregulated effects necessarily impose on human beings and the other beings with which they share the planet.

They are also committed to a more *democratic* globalization. They point out that major decisions that dramatically affect the lives of millions of people—for example the WTO decision in 2000 to prohibit continued European Union subsidization of banana production in former Caribbean colonies, a decision that threatened to wipe out that industry in a number of those countries—are typically made behind closed doors by officials either disproportionately recruited from, or dependent on, the major Western capitalist powers, and they demand both greater representation of the Global South and greater transparency within the WTO as well as other dominant trans-national political institutions. Some—including Benjamin Barber in his widely read *Jihad vs. McWorld*—have even wrestled with the problem—the very thorny problem—of how to reconcile the need for global institutions whose reach and power would be commensurate with the scope of the global issues with which they will have to deal, on the one hand, with the continuing sovereignty of individual nation-states, on the other. The threat that economic and political globalization poses to national sovereignty has of course been the principal reason for the rejection of globalization by so-called Paleocons such as Pat Buchanan in the United States. Buchanan and his followers worry that American national sovereignty is being eroded by trans-national political institutions that can trump the decisions of American elected officials. Buchanan's concerns are, in my judgment, overstated—after all, most of the institutions against which he rails are deeply dependent on American financial and political support—but he does point to a problem that is all too frequently neglected by the champions of globalization, namely, once again, the tension between internationalism and nationalism, or between universalism and localism. In his *vs. Jihad vs. McWorld* Barber argues that an international *confederation*, modeled on the American Articles of Confederation that preceded the adoption of the Constitution of 1789, would be the best way to reconcile that tension. For example, Article III of that first American constitution, in Barber's words, "provides for the full autonomy of the member states, and honors their independence . . . but also declares that:"

> The said states hereby severally enter into a firm league of friendship with each other, for their common defense, the security of their liberties, and their mutual and general welfare, binding themselves to assist each other against all force offered to, or attacks made upon them, or any of them, on account of religion, sovereignty, trade or any other pretense whatsoever.[7]

Whether Barber's idea of a global confederation is a good one is open to debate. What is not open to debate, it seems to me, is the need to think seriously about the problem for which it is a proposed (if very general) solution. On the one hand, under conditions of globalization Dahl's Principle of Affected Interests requires global democratic political institutions within which the interests of the billions of people who are affected by economic globalization can be represented. On the other hand, as long as nation-states continue to exist—as long as the *nation* is, as we shall see in the next section of this book, an important source of individual identity—these global political institutions would be obliged to coexist and attempt to harmonize with those nation-states. This is obviously both a very important and a very difficult problem to solve.

But for the more radical wing of the movement—those who would not object to being described as members of the *anti*-globalization movement— that problem is not the most fundamental one. The most fundamental problem is rather the transformation of the world into one giant market in the first place. This transformation, it is argued, necessarily entails the destruction of the way of life of indigenous people throughout the world; cultural heterogeneity is lost to an increasingly homogeneous global culture that defines the good life in terms of the maximum accumulation of stuff. Globalization "with a human face," in short, would still be a world-wide consumer society, even if current inequalities in the distribution of consumption were equalized between North and South. A reformed globalization would still merely globalize that condition that Marx calls alienated labor, extending its rigors across the entire planet. And the increasingly frantic pace of life—fast music, fast computers, fast food, etc.—that prevails in the North would likewise be extended to the South, disrupting the traditionally far slower, more relaxed pace of life in those parts of the world. It seems as if speed, as the cultural critic Paul Virilio has argued, is "the hope of the West,"[8] yet ironically our increasing dependence on time-saving devices—on technologies that enable us to do any one thing in less and less time—only seems to leave us with more things to do and thus *more* stressed out with *less* time on our hands to relax or play. "Not enough time to do all the things I have to do" is perhaps the most commonly voiced complaint in those Western societies that have all the material things that a reformed globalization promises to extend to the entire world. Do we want this time-anxiety to become a generalized experiential condition? For that matter, do we really want it for ourselves?

Some radical critics of economic globalization also contest the relationship between human beings and non-human nature that the transformation of the world into a market economy necessarily entails. If global human society becomes a market for the exchange of material goods, can the earth become anything other than a human *resource*, raw material for the production of those goods? Can the experience of non-human nature as an end in itself, an intrinsically valuable entity with which we can commune, withstand the instrumentalizing imperatives of a consumer society? The answer of many anti-globalists in both the North and the South is "no," which is one reason why they have increasingly joined together in order—in their eyes—to save the earth from globalization.

Some of the radical critics also argue that the increasingly virulent fundamentalist backlash against globalization also points to globalization's irremediable defects. Whatever else fundamentalism is, it is also—as we shall see in the concluding chapter of the third part of this book—a reaction against the loss of a sense of the sacred in modern secular societies, a reaction that all too often assumes intolerant, even violent, forms. It follows that fundamentalism's rejection of modernity is likely to persist as long as modernity marches under the banner of a global capitalism that empties the world of any source of meaning other than the meaning of money, under the banner of what Barber calls "McWorld." McWorld and Jihad are, as Barber argues, simply two sides of the same economic–cultural coin: Jihad lives off its hatred of McWorld, and McWorld defines and legitimates itself through its opposition to a Jihad that is assumed to be its only possible—and much inferior—alternative. But Jihad may not be the only alternative to McWorld. In the long run, argue at least some anti-globalists, only a resacralized or "re-enchanted" modernity—a modernity that somehow reconnects us with something beyond ourselves—will be able to gain the support of people whose anti-materialist impulses are currently captured by fundamentalism. Until that time the so-called "clash of civilizations" between modernity and fundamentalism is likely to remain both endless and bloody.

What a "resacralized" modernity might look like is difficult to imagine. As I intimated in chapter 10, even a globalized market socialism might not be up to the task, since there is nothing about a worker-controlled market economy that would necessarily reconnect working people with the world on which they depend. And what workable alternative there might be to the either–or of market versus central planning is anything but clear. At the very least the system of production and distribution would have to embrace a commitment to develop and employ only eco-friendly technologies that enable humans to strike a balance between their claims and the claims of non-human nature, technologies, in other words, that satisfy human needs with the least possible harm to non-human nature. These technologies would "materialize" a fundamentally different relationship to nature than many of the technologies on which globalization currently depends: they would be based on the assumption that humans have a fundamental kinship with, and obligation to, the other beings with which or whom they share the planet. This renewed sense of inter-species solidarity just might be enough to replenish the social world with meaning and thus to defuse the fundamentalist reaction to its loss.

15

THE CONCEPT OF POWER I

The Three Faces of "Negative" Power

The study of power has always been central to the discipline of political science. At a number of points in this book I have referred to the concept of power—for example in chapter 12 when I considered the power relationship between business and government—but I have yet to analyze the meaning of that core, and eminently contested, concept. This is what I aim to do in this and the next chapter. In this one I will examine, with the aid of Steven Lukes, three approaches to the study of power that share what I call a concept of "negative" power. In the next chapter I will consider two otherwise very different approaches to the study of power that nonetheless both rely on a concept of "positive" power. By negative versus positive power, it should be clear, I do *not* mean "bad" versus "good" power. Rather by "negative" power I mean power that *prevents* people from doing what they would otherwise want to do, and by "positive" power I mean power that *enables* or forms those wants in the first place. Whether either prevention or enabling would be considered a good or a bad thing would depend, of course, on one's judgment about the quality of the wants that are being either prevented or enabled.

Steven Lukes tells us in *Power: A Radical View* that "A exercises power over B when A affects B in a manner contrary to B's interests," and that the three views on power that he considers in his short book—what he calls the one-dimensional, two-dimensional, and (his) three-dimensional views—are all "alternative interpretations and applications of [this] same underlying concept of power."[1] This is important to emphasize so that we don't lose sight of the forest for the trees, so to speak: the differences among the three "views" on which he concentrates are very important, but attention to those differences should not obscure the common conception of power—power as the ability of A to prevent B from doing what he or she would otherwise want to do—that they share.

The first view, associated with so-called pluralist approaches to the study of power—which flourished from the 1950s through the first half of the 1960s—argues that power can only be measured by determining who prevails in "the making of decisions on issues over which there is an observable conflict of . . . express policy preferences."[2] Thus pluralist methodology required the researcher to identify a set of supposedly "key issues" in a given society or community, identify the participants in the process of deciding those issues, and determine for each decision, in Dahl's words, "which participants had initiated alternatives that were finally adopted, had vetoed alternatives initiated by others, or had proposed alternatives that were turned down. The participants with the greatest proportion of successes...were then considered to be the most influential,"[3] that is, the most powerful. In other words, the pluralists claimed that power can be measured—therefore can be demonstrated to *exist*—only in situations where there are conflicting preferences, and one individual or group of individuals can be reliably described as more powerful than another individual or group of individuals only if their preferences regularly prevail over the preferences of their opponents. Thus in a widely read, extremely influential article that he wrote in 1958 called "Critique of the Ruling Elite Model," Dahl argued that it would be possible to conclude that a ruling elite or ruling class exists in any given society or community only if "the preferences of the hypothetical ruling elite regularly prevail . . . in cases involving key political decisions in which the preferences of that elite run counter to those" of the members of other groups who participate in those decisions.[4] Perhaps not surprisingly, the political scientists who employed this decision-based methodology never discovered such a ruling elite or ruling class. Rather they typically found that different individuals or groups prevailed on different decisions or issue arenas, and they therefore concluded that political power in American communities was dispersed rather than concentrated, heterogeneous rather than homogeneous—in short, pluralistic rather than dominated by a single elite or class.

Enter Peter Bachrach and Morton Baratz, whose approach to power Lukes labels the "two-dimensional view." In their justly famous article written in 1962, "Two Faces of Power,"[5] they argued, as that title implies, that the methodology of Dahl and the other pluralists enabled them only to capture one face of power to the exclusion of another. They acknowledged that "power is exercised when A participates in the making of decisions that affect B." But they also insisted that:

> power is also exercised when A devotes his energies to creating or reinforcing social and political values and institutional practices that limit the scope of the political process to public consideration of only those issues which are comparatively innocuous to A.[6]

The "other face of power" entirely missed by the pluralists, in other words, was the effort of individuals to prevent certain matters that might be threatening to them from *becoming political issues in the first place*. Because the pluralists insisted that the study of power must begin with overt issues—since for them powerful people were people whose positions prevailed on those issues—their methodology necessarily prevented them from recognizing that the most powerful people are often those who never have to deal with issues they don't want to arise, who are able to prevent certain matters from being seriously considered by public authorities who otherwise might have discretion over those matters. Even if these people don't always prevail in the process of deciding already-existing issues—the only process on which the pluralists focused—they would have to be judged powerful by virtue of their control over what might be called the agenda of serious alternatives. Thus Bachrach and Baratz, unlike the pluralists, took seriously the seminal insight of Schattschneider's that I cited earlier in this book, namely that "the definition of alternatives is the supreme instrument of power."[7]

In a follow-up article to the "Two Faces of Power" Bachrach and Baratz coined the term "non-decision making" to refer to the effort to control the "definition of alternatives," that is, to prevent certain matters from ever becoming an object of political decision making. As Lukes notes, they defined a "non-decision" as "a decision that results in suppression or thwarting of a latent or manifest challenge to the values or the interests of the decision-maker."[8] As Lukes also notes, pluralist critics were quick to pounce on the ambiguity of this definition, claiming that if the challenge was "latent," that is, "hidden," "concealed," or a mere "potential," then there was no way to actually identify it, and thus no way empirically to demonstrate the existence of a "non-decision." In this case, they argued, the so-called "non-decision" would be impossible to distinguish from a "non-event" from which no inferences about the exercise of power could validly be drawn. Faced with this objection, Bachrach and Baratz conceded that:

> If there is no conflict . . . the presumption must be that there is consensus on the prevailing allocation of values, in which case nondecision-making is impossible . . . [I]n the absence of conflict . . . there is no way accurately to judge whether the thrust of a decision really is to thwart or prevent serious consideration of a demand for change that is potentially threatening to the decision-maker. [If] there appears to be universal acquiescence in the status quo [it is not possible] to determine empirically whether the consensus is genuine or instead has been enforced through nondecision-making.[9]

It is important to understand just how enormous this concession to the pluralists really was. It involves the claim that there is no way to demonstrate that power is exercised over people unless (a) they are expressing grievances and (b) decisions are made that prevent those grievances from becoming live political issues. But isn't the condition of an oppressive society precisely one in which individuals fear the consequences of airing their grievances and thus often refrain from doing so? As Lukes argues, "to assume that the absence of grievance equals genuine consensus is simply to rule out the possibility of false or manipulated consensus by definitional fiat."[10] In other words, where people fail to air grievances because they are afraid of doing so, do we really want to say that there is no way to determine that power is being exercised over them? But this is, in fact, exactly what Bachrach and Baratz say. In a passage from their book *Power and Poverty* they consider a situation "where B, confronted by A who has greater power resources, decides not to make a demand upon A for fear that the latter will invoke sanctions against him," and they "concede the point," made by their pluralist critics, that "B's non-action, based upon his anticipation of A's reaction, is a 'non-event', which is, by nature, impossible of verification."[11] Notice that this situation is essentially identical—at least according to Lindblom—to the relationship between big business and elected politicians in which the politicians refrain from making demands on business that they fear might result in business decisions that might harm the economy on which their electoral success depends. Whereas Lindblom identifies this relationship of dependence of elected officials on big business as the "fundamental mechanism by which a great deal of business control [i.e., power] . . . comes to be exercised over government,"[12] Bachrach and Baratz's methodological concession to the pluralists prevents them even from identifying this relationship as a power relationship.

This brings us to the "three-dimensional" view of power, which Lukes claims as his own. Remember that each view is a different interpretation and application of the same general, "negative" concept of power: A exercises power over B by affecting B in a manner contrary to B's interests. The one-dimensional pluralist view translates "contrary to B's interests" as contrary to the preferences that B expresses on a given issue. The two-dimensional view of Bachrach and Baratz translates "contrary to B's interests" to include preventing B's grievances from becoming political issues. In contrast, Lukes's three-dimensional view translates "contrary to B's interests" as contrary to the *real interests* of B, even if B "may not express or even be conscious of [his] interests."[13] On this view of power, in other words, it is possible to speak of the exercise of power even if no overt conflict exists between those who exercise power and those over whom it is exercised, even if those over whom it is exercised currently express no grievances or complaints about the arrangement. Indeed, Lukes suggests that the absence of such complaints *may* be a sign of what he calls:

> the most effective and insidious use of power [namely] to prevent such conflict from arising in the first place . . . [I]s it not the supreme and most insidious exercise of power to prevent people . . . from having grievances by shaping their perceptions, cognitions and preferences in such a way that they accept their role in the existing order of things, either because they can see or imagine no alternative to it, or because they see it as natural and unchangeable, or because they value it as divinely ordained and beneficial?[14]

Lukes acknowledges that "where there is no observable conflict between A and B, then we must provide other [indirect] grounds for asserting the relevant counterfactual." By the "relevant counterfactual," Lukes means that, since he defines power as the ability of A to get B to do something that she would otherwise prefer not to do, to demonstrate that A exercises power over B in the absence of observable conflict between them "we must provide other, indirect, grounds for asserting that if A had not acted (or failed to act) in a certain way . . . then B would have thought and acted differently from the way he does actually think and act."[15] In other words, to support the claim that A has acted contrary to the "real interests" (but not the expressed preferences) of B, we have to make the case that those expressed preferences would be different in the absence of A's action; we have to provide evidence that B would want different things if he or she had the option that he currently lacks. Thus, in explaining why he describes his view as a "radical view," Lukes asserts that:

> the radical . . . maintains that men's wants may themselves be a product of a system which works against their interests, and, in such cases, relates the latter [their interests] to what they would want and prefer, were they able to make the choice.[16]

Lukes admits, however, that "sometimes . . . it is extraordinarily difficult to justify the relevant counterfactual,"[17] that is, to make the case that—"were they able to make the choice"—individuals would in fact think and act differently than they currently do. But I think he actually underestimates this difficulty. Although he concludes that,

> in general, evidence can be adduced (though by the nature of the case, such evidence will never be conclusive) which supports the relevant counterfactuals implicit in identifying exercises of power of the three-dimensional type. One can take steps to find out what it is that people would have done otherwise,[18]

it seems to me that his own argument suggests that this is not so in the case of the "supreme and most insidious exercise of power." In this case, you will recall, individuals "accept their role in the existing order of things, either because they can see or imagine no alternative to it, or because they see it as natural and unchangeable." What does it mean to say that, under circumstances where individuals cannot even imagine an alternative to the existing system, they would think and act differently if they were not subject to the power of those who control it? Does it mean anything other than: if they had the choice—which they don't—they would choose an entirely different system? Maybe they would, but how would we know this? Lukes refers obliquely to this problem when he asks, "Can we always assume that the victims of injustice and inequality would, but for the exercise of power, strive for justice and equality?" and "Is not such an assumption a form of ethnocentrism?,"[19] but to my mind never satisfactorily answers this question—a question to which we shall return in the section of this book on "Culture and Identity."

To put the point I am making another way, Lukes's commitment to his concept of power, as A making B do what B would otherwise prefer not to do, presupposes an assumption about the inevitable persistence of individual *autonomy* that he doesn't adequately defend and that appears to be called into question by his own account of the "supreme and most insidious" exercise of power. According to that account, the exercise of that "insidious" power precludes the awareness of alternatives and thus *eliminates* the very individual autonomy that the plausible assertion of the "relevant counterfactual," and thus the demonstration of power in the absence of conflict, requires. But if the only way to determine whether power has been exercised in the absence of conflict is to identify a "counterfactual" that presupposes the persistence of individual autonomy, how can Lukes legitimately describe a situation that eliminates individual autonomy as the result of a "supreme and insidious" exercise of power? To put this the other way around, that description would appear to trade on a concept of power whose existence does *not* depend on the persistence of individual autonomy and thus the possibility of identifying the "relevant counterfactual."

This conflict between what might be called his residual individualism and his more radical sociological awareness surfaces in other ways in Lukes's text. He criticizes Bachrach and Baratz for "adopting too methodologically individualist a view of power," that is, for failing to recognize that:

> the bias of the system can be mobilized, recreated and reinforced in ways that are neither consciously chosen nor the intended result of particular individuals' choices [but rather] most importantly, by the socially structured and culturally patterned behavior of groups, and practices of institutions . . . The power to control the agenda of politics and exclude political issues cannot be adequately analysed unless it is seen as a result of collective forces and social arrangements.[20]

Here Lukes argues that the exercise of power does not always, or even "most importantly," depend on the intentions of individuals but rather on the "collective forces and social arrangements" in which they are enmeshed. But he also argues, toward the end of his book, *against* what he calls "structurally deterministic" theories of power: we can, he claims, only speak of the exercise of power when those who exercise it

> have a certain relative autonomy and could have acted differently. [Thus] within a system characterized by total structural determinism, there would be no place for power . . . To identify a given process as an "exercise of power" rather than as a case of structural determinism is to assume that it is *in the exerciser's . . . power* to act differently.[21]

But this appeal to the capacity for choice on the part of those who exercise power does not sit easily with his already quoted claim that the "bias of the system can be mobilized, recreated and reinforced in ways that are neither consciously chosen nor the intended result of particular individuals' choices," which reads like a claim on behalf of the very "structural determinism" he rejects.

To make the ambiguity in Lukes's position clearer, consider whether or not he would argue that big businessmen exercise power over the lives of the individuals who are dependent on the system of production and distribution that those businessmen (in some sense) control. The decisions made by those businessmen will dramatically affect the health and well-being of the people who work for them as well as the people who consume their products, but these decisions are governed by the requirement of profit maximization rather than any conscious intention to affect the health and well-being of their workers or consumers. The businessmen, we might say, are just trying to stay ahead or at least remain on a par with their competition. Can we really say that they have the power to act differently if the consequence of doing so is that they will go out of business? Is there not an important sense in which their decisions are determined by a structure to which they, too, must submit? If so, and if, according to the individualistic version of Lukes's position, structural determinism precludes the exercise of power, we could not conclude that those businessmen exercise power. But this seems counter-intuitive, since, as Lindblom argues, big businessmen have a "privileged position" within the system as a whole. The other, more structural version of Lukes would have to agree. The problem, then, is that Lukes does not appear to agree with Lukes.

16

THE CONCEPT OF POWER II
Normalization versus Communication

To set the stage for my comparison of the concepts of power in Hannah Arendt and Michel Foucault I begin this chapter with a brief review of the concept of "negative" power I ascribed to all three of the positions I examined in the last chapter. According to that concept, power operates to prevent individuals from doing what they otherwise would prefer to do, which implies, of course, that if individuals *were* able to do what they wanted to do—in Lukes's case to do what they *really* wanted to do—then their action would *not* be an effect of power but would rather be unaffected by it. In other words, the negative concept of power assumes an inverse relationship between the operation of power on the one hand and the existence of individual autonomy on the other: the stronger the hold of power on the individual, the less autonomous she is; the more autonomous the individual, the less does power determine her action. There is, in short, an *outside* of power, and that outside is *freedom*.

Both Hannah Arendt and Michel Foucault contest—although in radically different ways—this negative concept of power and the inverse relationship between power and freedom that it establishes. In *On Violence* Arendt takes pains sharply to distinguish her conception of power from violence in particular and what she calls the "command–obedience" relationship in general. The "command–obedience" relationship is Arendt's formulation of the concept of negative power, which she traces back to Max Weber in the early twentieth century and Voltaire in the eighteenth. For Voltaire, "power consists in making others act as I choose"; for Weber, I exercise power when I "assert my own will against the resistance" of others.[1] The problem with this concept of power, according to Arendt, is that it can make no sense of the claim that a republican form of government rests on the "power of the people," or, more generally, of the fact that "it is the people's support that lends power to the institutions of a country, and this support is but the continuation of the consent that brought the laws into existence to begin with."[2] There are two different claims contained in this last sentence. The first claim is that the power exercised by institutions is loaned to them by the people in the form of their support for those institutions. The second is that this support is the continuation of an original consent or mutual agreement that created those institutions in the first place. Thus power, for Arendt, is ultimately generated through mutual agreement, an agreement reached among a plurality of different individuals.

What then is the connection between the consent or mutual agreement of the people and their power? Arendt's answer is that:

> *Power* corresponds to the human ability not just to act but to act in concert. Power is never the property of an individual; it belongs to a group and remains in existence only so long as the group keeps together. When we say of somebody that he is "in power" we actually refer to his being empowered by a certain number of people to act in their name. The moment the group, from which the power originated to begin with (without a people or group there is no power) disappears, "his power" also vanishes.[3]

So Arendt's answer to the question about the connection between mutual agreement and power is that the agreement among a plurality of individuals makes it possible for them *to act in concert*, to act together; the agreement makes it possible for them to do together what they could never accomplish as isolated individuals, as individuals who (somehow) did not belong to the group. To say this is to say that the agreement that forms the group and lends it power is also the condition of possibility for the power of its individual members: if the power of the group increases, so too, and simultaneously, does the power of the individuals who make up the group. Within the group, in other words, my power can increase without a corresponding decrease, indeed, *along with a corresponding increase*, in your power. Taking strength from the group, each of us is capable of acting in ways we could not act alone; each of us is *empowered* through the mutual agreement that makes our participation in the group possible. Thus for Arendt the relationship between power and individual freedom is mutually constitutive rather than conflictual or zero-sum: whereas, as have seen, the negative concept of power proclaims an inverse relationship between power and freedom—freedom exists to the degree that power does not—in Arendt's "positive" conception power and freedom go hand-in-hand and necessarily reinforce one another.

This Arendtian point can be put in another way, using language that is not hers but is entirely consistent with her meaning. According to Hegel—Marx's great early nineteenth-century theoretical teacher and eventual opponent—the development of the individual depends on the recognition that he receives from others. But that individual must also recognize the individuals from whom he receives recognition as worthy of granting it; nobody can feel affirmed by being recognized by somebody he does not respect. Hegel's point is that all individually self-affirming recognition must be reciprocal or mutual.[4] When mutual recognition breaks down the struggle for individual recognition takes the form—the inevitably unsatisfactory, self-defeating form—of a relationship of domination and subordination or of command–obedience in which neither party to the relationship is truly empowered. Thus when power in the sense of command–obedience, that is, in the sense common to the three views of power examined in the previous chapter, comes into being, power in Arendt's sense *disappears*. The power of mutual recognition gives way to one-sided effort to extort recognition, to *make* others do what we want, the extreme form of which—and thus the antithesis of power—is violence.

To put this yet another way, Arendt's concept of power trades on the ancient and specifically Aristotelian distinction between action and production, between social interaction through which individuals reveal or discover something about themselves to others and activity through which individuals make or fabricate something in order to satisfy a material or physical need.[5] Elsewhere in her writings, and in *The Human Condition* in particular, she argues that the modern condition is one characterized by the subordination of action to production, of politics to economics.[6] From this perspective we can say that the conception of power as command–obedience reflects the modern subordination of action to production: we think of power as one person (or group of persons) *making* another person (or group of persons) do something she would prefer not to do, bending or molding that person into an instrument of our will, because in the modern era the logic of material production—of making something—informs and distorts the social and political relationships in which we are engaged. Thus Arendt's alternative—action-based—conception of power can be understood as a challenge to our modern instrumental culture and to the way identity is formed—or rather *not* formed—within that culture.

Michel Foucault is also preoccupied with the problem of identity formation within modern society, although the way that he poses this problem is very different from Arendt. Like Arendt he explicitly rejects the command–obedience concept of power—or what he elsewhere calls the "repressive hypothesis"[7]—that posits an inverse relationship between power and freedom. But if, like Arendt, Foucault understands that there is no freedom outside power, *unlike* Arendt he claims that there is *no freedom inside power* either. Let me attempt to clarify this claim by summarizing what he has to say about what he calls disciplinary power—or simply "discipline"—in the chapter "The Means of Correct Training" from his justly celebrated book *Discipline and Punish*, first published in French in 1975.

The original French title of *Discipline and Punish* is *Surveiller et Punir*—to "Surveille and Punish." This title reflects his emphasis on surveillance—on what Foucault calls "hierarchical observation"—as one of the principal techniques of disciplinary power. He describes the emergence in the eighteenth century of a variety of institutions—including "working-class housing estates, hospitals, asylums, prisons [and] schools"[8]—that were all designed and constructed to make possible the continual surveillance of the people who inhabited them. An architecture was built, he tells us:

> to permit an internal, articulated and detailed control—to render visible those who are inside it; in more general terms, an architecture that would

operate to transform individuals: to act on those it shelters, to provide a hold on their conduct, to carry the effects of power right to them, to make it possible to know them, to alter them. Stones can make people docile and knowable.[9]

Foucault's juxtaposition of "docile" and "knowable" is not accidental. It reflects his view that the same mechanisms that, in his words, "coerce [individuals] by means of observation" are also the means by which these same individuals become objects of a knowledge—a supposedly scientific knowledge—that justifies and reinforces the very techniques that "maintain the disciplined individual in his subjection . . . by the fact of being constantly seen."[10] Thus hospitals and asylums in which patients are constantly under surveillance become the setting within which there develops the medical and psychological knowledge necessary for the disciplinary control of their patients, and schools in which all the students, ideally, can be disciplined by being seen in a single gaze become, as it were, a laboratory for the development of pedagogical knowledge that feeds back into the disciplinary mechanism. The social sciences in particular are born in disciplinary institutions and then function to reproduce them. Thus Foucault speaks of "power/knowledge complexes" or "regimes of Truth": knowledge is not outside power but rather at its very center. As he puts it in an earlier chapter from *Discipline and Punish*, "power and knowledge directly imply one another; there is no power relation without the correlative constitution of a field of knowledge, nor any knowledge that does not presuppose and constitute at the same time power relations."[11] Less abstractly, and more simply put, the claim to speak the truth about individuals simultaneously secures the "expert" status of those who enunciate that truth and prepares them to exercise control over the individuals for whom they have responsibility.

It is important to understand that, for Foucault, the individual is not only the object but also the subject of disciplinary power. He asserts that "discipline 'makes' individuals; it is the specific technique of a power that regards individuals both as its objects and as instruments of its own exercise."[12] By "instruments of its own exercise" Foucault means that the individuals who become the object of disciplinary control *themselves participate* in the exercise of that control: the individual who is surveilled constantly surveilles himself, the body that is disciplined subjects itself to discipline. As he puts it, disciplinary power "is not exercised simply as an obligation or prohibition on those who 'do not have it'; it invests them, is transmitted by them and through them."[13] In short, it works not only on the body but also *through* the body. Disciplinary power thus runs even deeper than the "radical" power that Lukes describes. Whereas Lukes never doubts that the individual always remains something more than a mere effect of power, Foucault goes so far as to claim that the individual "is . . . a reality fabricated by this specific technology of power that I have called 'discipline'," and that "power produces; it produces reality . . . the individual and the knowledge that may be gained of him belong to that production."[14]

Foucault's discussion of the second principal technique of disciplinary power, "normalizing judgments," serves I think to clarify this seemingly outrageous claim. Perhaps the best way to understand what he means by "normalization" is to contrast the power of the norm with the power of the traditional legal penalty that it at least partly supplants. The criminal law *prohibits*; it tells people that they must not do what they would otherwise wish to do. And as long as they obey that prohibition the criminal law leaves them free to do whatever else they want to do; in repressing or excluding one act as illegal it leaves open an entire range of perfectly legal acts that escape its regulation. The norm, in contrast, does not prohibit but rather *incites*: it tells people that if they want to live up to, or ideally exceed, the norm—if they want to be smarter, healthier, stronger, more efficient, etc.—then they should study more, eat better, exercise more, time-manage better, etc. And, since judgments made in the name of the norm—normalizing judgments—are always comparative—because normalizing judgments are always judgments about the relative performance of individuals in relation to other individuals—one can never be smart, healthy, strong, or efficient *enough*. It is always possible, and always desirable, to achieve a higher SAT score, a higher muscle-to-fat ratio, or higher productivity: a higher score serves as a measure of a success that is never quite achieved; an average score indicates that you are merely mediocre; and a low score is a sure sign of failure. Thus, whereas the power of the traditional legal penalty is limited in the sense that it proscribes one activity but does not require others, the power of the norm is totalizing in the sense that it requires a host of activities that must be constantly monitored and evaluated by the individual who engages in them. Listen to Foucault on normalization:

> It refers individual actions to a whole that is at once a field of comparison, a space of differentiation and the principle of a rule to be followed. It differentiates individuals from one another, in terms of the following overall rule: that the rule be made to function as a minimal threshold, as an average to be respected or as an optimum towards which one must move. It measures in quantitative terms and hierarchizes in terms of values and abilities, the level, the "nature" of individuals. It introduces, through this "value-giving" measure, the constraint of a conformity that must be achieved. Lastly, it traces the limit that will define difference in relation to all other differences, the external frontier of the abnormal. The perpetual penalty that traverses all points and supervises every instant in the disciplinary institutions [schools, prisons, factories, etc.] compares, differentiates, hierarchizes, homogenizes, excludes. In short, it *normalizes*.[15]

There is a great deal going on in this passage, but I have space only to emphasize one Foucauldian point: normalization creates an individual whose sense of self depends on a continual comparison with anonymous others that is based on a measure—a purely quantitative evaluation—of their relative performance. To put it bluntly, modern individuals who are increasingly enmeshed in disciplinary institutions increasingly identify self-realization with *achieving the highest score*. Perhaps Foucault's claim that disciplinary power produces individuals is an exaggeration, but anyone who has felt the pressure to score higher—whether on an academic or a physical examination—will recognize that this claim has a certain ring of truth.

This reference to the examination was not accidental, for the examination is the third and last disciplinary technique or "means of correct training" that Foucault considers. The examination, he tells us, "combines the techniques of an observing hierarchy [hierarchical observation] with those of a normalizing judgment."[16] The examination—be it the doctor's examination of the patient, the teacher's examination of the student, or the employer's examination of the job-seeker—subjects the examined individual to the surveillance of an examiner who evaluates the performance of that individual in relation to the performance of every other individual who is examined by the examiner. Thus the examination is designed to measure just how well the examined have absorbed the Truth that the examiner has proclaimed and thus how disciplined they have become by his "regime of Truth." And their performance on the examination produces information for the examiner that only adds to the already considerable but impersonal or objectified knowledge of them that his regular surveillance of them has produced, which knowledge only furthers his effort to subject them to his power/knowledge. "At the heart of the procedures of discipline," Foucault asserts, "it [the examination] manifests the subjection of those who are perceived as objects and the objectification of those who are subjected."[17]

It is important to emphasize, once again, that the subjected are complicit in their own subjection. Who among us don't *want* to do well on an exam? How many of us have succumbed to the tendency to evaluate ourselves as we have been evaluated by the "normalizing judgments" of the academic institutions in which we have participated? How many of us have resisted the temptation to spit back to a professor the Truth that he has "deposited" in us? I suspect that our answers would reveal the *partial* truth in Foucault's claim that nobody is outside (disciplinary) power. I say "partial" truth because I think Foucault exaggerates. It is one thing to say that nobody is *entirely* outside power (as he understands it)—which I think is true—but it is another thing to say—which is what Foucault says—that everybody is *entirely inside* power. In saying this Foucault is, I think, guilty of what might be called a performative contradiction, a contradiction between the content of what he says and the fact of his saying it. By this I mean the following: if Foucault is correct to argue that all truth claims "presuppose and constitute at the same time power relations," then this would also have to be true of the particular truth-claim that Foucault is making about the "correlative" relationship of knowledge and power. But if this is the case, how can Foucault claim that his truth-claim is any less "disciplinary" than the truth-claims he catalogs and deconstructs? And, if it isn't any less disciplinary in its effects, wouldn't it be dangerous for us to take it seriously? On the other hand, if Foucault's particular truth-claim is worth taking seriously, if it doesn't have disciplinary effects, then he can't be right to insist that all truth-claims have a disciplinary effect. But perhaps this is unfair to Foucault. A Foucauldian might argue that all he is saying is that all truth-claims contribute to the constitution of some kind of, but not necessarily specifically disciplinary, power relation, and that Foucault's truth-claim contributes to the constitution of a different, non-disciplinary power relation. This rejoinder implicitly makes recourse, however, to a concept of an emancipatory power—a power that would liberate rather than discipline—that can nowhere be found in Foucault's writings. But it might be found in the writings of Hannah Arendt.

Part III

CULTURE AND IDENTITY

INTRODUCTION

In the Introduction to Part II I argued that the student of Law and Institutions should take a (conceptual) trip to Markets and Power. Now I want briefly to make the case that she also needs to cross over the (artificial) border from Markets and Power to Culture and Identity. In this Introduction to Part III, I highlight those chapters in Part II that have already adumbrated the need for that border crossing. As we shall see, at least some of the questions raised in those chapters will remain open until Part IV. But my hope is that enough light will be shed on them in Part III to conclude that the student of Law and Institutions and Markets and Power also needs to understand the ways in which our identities—who we are—are governed by the culture(s) we inhabit.

Consider first Steven Lukes's ambivalent approach to the concept of power in chapter 15. We saw that at one point he appeared implicitly to include the very "structural determinism" that he explicitly excluded from his definition of power, when he argued that:

> the bias of the system can be mobilized, recreated and reinforced in ways that are neither consciously chosen nor the intended result of particular choices [but rather] most importantly by the socially structured and culturally patterned behavior of groups, and practices of institutions.

Here a couple of things need to be said. First, what I have called Lukes's debate with himself recalls the issue discussed in the General Introduction as to whether "governance" does or does not require a conscious governor. You will recall that I argued that it does not, that conduct is governed as much by structures as it is by conscious intentions. This argument puts me on the side of the Lukes who included "culturally patterned behavior" within the scope of his concept of power. But Lukes nowhere told us what he means by "culturally patterned." To answer this question, clearly, we need to understand what culture *is*. This question is taken up in the first chapter of Part III.

In the course of his ambiguous treatment of the concept of power Lukes raised another issue that will be taken up in Part III. Recall that he argued, against Bachrach and Baratz, that "to assume that the absence of grievance equals genuine consensus is simply to rule out the possibility of false or manipulated consensus by definitional fiat." Thus he claimed, to the contrary, that "the most insidious exercise of power [is] to prevent people . . . from having grievances by shaping their perceptions, cognitions and preferences" to the point where they cannot even imagine an alternative to the "existing order of things." At the same time, he also insisted that to demonstrate the existence of such power it would be necessary to "justify the relevant counterfactual," which in this case would mean plausibly to make the case that, if given the choice, the (oppressed) people would prefer an "order of things" more just or equal than the existing one. In other words, to make this case it would be appear to be necessary to assume "that the victims of injustice and inequality would, but for the exercise of power, strive for justice and equality," but Lukes himself worried that this assumption may be "a form of ethnocentrism." Thus he introduced an issue that will be addressed in chapter 18, "Beyond Ethnocentrism and Relativism" (but not resolved until Part IV, "Conclusion").[1]

A number of other chapters in Part II underscored the specifically modern presuppositions of markets and power, and thus point us in the direction of chapter 19, on the meaning of modernity. In chapter 9 Karl Polanyi argued that a market economy is a post–nineteenth-century exception to the general rule that "man's economy . . . is submerged in his social relationships." For Polanyi, in short, "economic man" is no older than "modern man." He showed, in effect, and against Adam Smith, that people are rationally self-interested maximizers (of material things) not by nature but rather by culture, and by a specifically modern culture in particular. To understand a market economy, then, we need to understand modernity.

The same is true, of course, of that world-wide march of the market economy that is euphemistically referred to as "globalization." In chapter 14 we saw that some of the radical critics reject globalization in the name of a "resacralized" modernity for which the earth would no longer be mere "resource" and the fastest possible exploitation of that resource would no longer be its overriding end. But it was perhaps premature to speak about a fundamental transformation of modernity in the absence of an account of modernity that is more complete than the highly condensed one that the second half of the last sentence just offered. That account, once again, is the subject of chapter 19.

Hannah Arendt's critique of the "command–obedience" concept of power pointed us in the direction of the same chapter. I suggested in chapter 16 that this concept of power reflects the specifically modern subordination of action to production that Arendt identified and called into question in *The Human Condition*: we are likely to think of power as a way to *make* others do what they would otherwise prefer not to do "because in the modern era the logic of production—of making something—informs and distorts the social and political relationships in which we are engaged." Put otherwise, the "command–obedience" concept of power can be understood as an abstract expression of the (perhaps increasingly) instrumental nature of human relationships in a culture that is committed to control.

The culture of control is the subject of Zygmunt Bauman's account of modernity in chapter 19. Bauman argues that modernity is defined by omnipotent pretensions to defeat death that cannot but result in the defeat of life. Bauman's account of the exclusively mortifying nature of modernity will be contested in that same chapter by Anthony Giddens, who recognizes its darker side but insists that modernity also offers life-affirming possibilities that are unavailable in pre- or non-modern cultures. More specifically, Giddens will argue that the unprecedented existential uncertainties of modernity create as many opportunities for fruitful self-definition as they do incentives for emotional retreat.

The claim that identity is uniquely in question under modernity is pursued anew in chapter 20, "Modernity and Identity," in which Charles Taylor highlights the importance of mutual recognition for the sense of self of both individuals and groups. This emphasis on mutual recognition, we saw in chapter 16, was already implicit in the action-based concept of power of Hannah Arendt. I suggested in that chapter that the relationships of command–obedience that Arendt decried can be understood as symptoms of the breakdown of the relations of reciprocal recognition on which genuine (according to Arendt) power depends. According to the concept of mutual recognition, the development of the individual's sense of self is contingent on the recognition she receives from an other whom she recognizes as worthy of granting it. But we also saw in the same chapter that Michel Foucault appears to call into question the very possibility of mutual recognition insofar as he holds that the formation of the individual subject is necessarily bound up with his subjection. The search for a stable, unambiguous identity is, for Foucault, part of the modern problem rather than the basis for a modern solution.

This implicit debate on individual identity between Arendt and Foucault in chapter 16 anticipates the explicit debate on group identity between Charles Taylor and Joan Scott in chapter 20. Taylor argues that the identity of groups is as dependent on public recognition as the identity of individuals is dependent on the recognition of significant others. Following Foucault, Joan Scott decries what she takes to be the inevitably "normalizing" and exclusionary consequences of a politics based on group recognition, or what is often called "identity politics." And Todd Gitlin worries that identity politics distracts attention and energy from what he considers to be the *real* issue, namely the struggle to redress the gross inequalities in wealth and power that inevitably result, he believes, from the unregulated operations of a capitalist market economy. Gitlin's argument is, in this sense, a modern variation on Marx's theme, examined in chapter 10, of the overriding importance of alienated labor and the struggle to overcome it. Thus the summary of Marx in chapter 10 anticipates Gitlin's critique of identity politics every bit as much as the discussion of Foucault in chapter 16 anticipates Scott's critique of identity politics.

The general debate over identity politics becomes more specific in the last four chapters of Part III, which are devoted, respectively, to gender, racial, ethnic, and religious identity. Central to this debate is the opposition between "essentialism" and "social constructionism." Essentialism, as the name implies, is based on the assumption that there are natural, unchanging, or essential sources of human identity—be they gender, racial, ethnic, or religious—that inevitably find social and political expression. Social constructionism (often in the form of post-modernism), argues that essentialist discourse *creates* the very identities that it claims to discover and that the social and political expression of those identities must be contested by unmasking or "deconstructing" the discursive exercise of power that creates them. I argue throughout the last four chapters of Part III that "essentialism" *under*estimates the importance of discourse even as "social constructionism" *over*estimates its importance, and that the opposition between them can and should be transcended by a synthesis that incorporates their respective merits and leaves their respective limits behind. But this synthesis will not be fleshed out until Part IV in the conclusion to this book.

17

WHAT IS (A) CULTURE?

This part of this book is titled "Culture and Identity." But what "culture" means is anything but clear, and among the anthropologists who study culture there is in fact deep and often intense disagreement as to its meaning. My task in this chapter is to introduce you to two radically different conceptions of culture—one associated with the work of Clifford Geertz, the other with Marvin Harris—that also entail two profoundly different understandings of how to study it, of what, in other words, are the goals and methods of a "science" of culture.

Let me begin with a summary of Geertz's argument about what a culture is and how it should be studied. In his "Thick Description," Geertz announces that:

> The concept of culture I espouse . . . is essentially a semiotic one. Believing, with Max Weber, that man is an animal suspended in webs of significance he himself has spun, I take culture to be those webs, and the analysis of it to be therefore not an experimental science in search of law but an interpretative one in search of meaning. It is explication I am after, construing social expressions on their surface enigmatical.[1]

There is a lot going on in this passage, so let me try to unpack it as slowly and systematically as possible. Semiotics is the study of signs—verbal and nonverbal alike—so to describe a concept of culture as "essentially a semiotic one" is to define it as an "interworked system of construable signs."[2] What then is a sign? A sign is a *meaningful* product, a human act that signifies something, that is significant. Consider first a verbal sign, or a word. It is not the purely physical dimensions of a vocalized word—the way our voice-box vibrates and our lips move in order to make the sound associated with it—that determine the meaning of the word and thus what it really is, but rather the context within which it is uttered. This becomes clear once we recognize that the same word, understood as a purely physical vocalization, can mean very different things—for example "cool" can mean "somewhat cold," "great," or "distant," and "hot" can mean "too warm to touch," "currently in vogue," or "sexy"—depending on the sentence in which it is used and the relationship of that sentence to the others that the speaker employs. On the other hand, the fact that different words in a similar context—say "left-handed" or "southpaw" when an announcer of a baseball game is describing how a pitcher throws—can mean precisely the same thing compels the same conclusion. The point is that to understand a word—to grasp its meaning—we have to understand the context within which the word is being used.

The same is true for non-verbal signs as well. This is the point of the philosopher Gilbert Ryle's analysis of the difference between a "twitch" and a "wink," with which Geertz begins his case on behalf of anthropology as "thick description." Although both a twitch and a wink are produced through precisely the same rapid contraction of the eyelid—the same observable physical action—their meanings—what they really *are*—are obviously profoundly different. And to be able to tell the difference between a twitch and a wink requires an understanding of the setting within which the physical action takes place as well as a knowledge of the "public code in which [contracting your eyelids on purpose] counts as a conspiratorial signal."[3] I will come back to the "public" nature of the code. At this point I want simply to emphasize that, according to Ryle, a description of the act of winking that was restricted to "a rapid contraction of the eyelid" would be a "thin description" because it wouldn't really tell you anything about what was really going on. In contrast, a description of that act that was "thick" enough to clue you in on what was actually happening—for example whether the wink was a genuine "conspiratorial signal," a parody of one, rehearsal for one, etc.—would have to uncover what Geertz calls:

> a stratified hierarchy of meaningful structures in terms of which twitches, winks, fake-winks, parodies, rehearsals of parodies are produced, perceived and interpreted, and without which they would not . . . in fact exist, no matter what anyone did or didn't do with his eyelids.[4]

Making explicit the "stratified hierarchy of meaningful structures" that always implicitly informs the behavior of people is for Geertz the object of ethnography, which he identifies with cultural anthropology. To put this another way, Geertz's claim is that there is *no observation without interpretation*. Because "interpretation . . . goes all the way down to the most immediate observational level,"[5] the study of human culture can never be a study of uninterpreted, brute physical facts. Rather the appropriate subject matter for the student of human culture, to return to the language of the first passage I cited, is the humanly spun "webs of significance" in which humans are inevitably suspended.

As I have already intimated, these webs of significance—and this is Geertz's second principal point—are public: they are not inside the head of or the property of any one individual, but rather are the property of the culture as a whole. Meaning is never intra-subjective but always *inter*-subjective. As Geertz puts it, "culture is public because meaning is. You can't wink without knowing what counts as winking,"[6] and what counts as winking—or any other meaningful action—is determined by the culture within which it takes place. Just as the meaning of a word depends on a semantical code that all fluent speakers of a particular language have absorbed, so too a shared cultural code internalized by the native inhabitants of any given society assigns meaning to any of the non-verbal signs they produce. And, just as a student who is trying to learn a foreign language often mistakes the meaning of one word for another, and often winds up saying something very different from what she intended, so a visitor from another culture who hasn't yet mastered the cultural code of his host country often misunderstands the actions of his hosts in ways that can range from the merely comical to the definitely dangerous.

In many respects the anthropologist who studies an "alien" culture is in exactly that position. She tries to make sense of—to *interpret* the meaning of—behavior so apparently different from the society in which she normally lives that it initially appears ambiguous at best and entirely indecipherable at worst. Because she realizes that meaning is inter-subjective, she understands that she will have to master the cultural code before she can be sure that her interpretation of the meaning of any particular action she observes is correct. But of course that cultural code as a whole is never explicitly articulated, never present all at once for the anthropologist to observe. Normally the only way to gain access to it is through an encounter with the particular acts whose meaning is governed by it. This, then, is the anthropologist's dilemma: you have to understand the whole in order to understand the part, but the only way to understand the whole is to understand the part. At first glance this circle—what philosophers call the hermeneutic circle—looks like a vicious circle, but ideally it becomes instead a fruitful spiral. As Geertz describes it elsewhere in his writings, the anthropologist engages in:

> a continuous dialectical tacking between the most local of local detail and the most global of global structures in such a way as to bring both into view simultaneously . . . Hopping back and forth between the whole conceived through the parts that actualize it and the parts conceived through the whole that motivates them, we seek to turn them, by a sort of intellectual perpetual motion, into explications of one another.[7]

This passage might seem obscure, but if we think of what's involved in interpreting a written text—and Geertz tells us that "doing ethnography is like trying to read . . . a manuscript"[8]—I think it becomes much clearer. Consider what happens when reading a novel, or at least a novel of which we have no previous knowledge. We read the first chapter and attempt to understand it by making an initial guess as to what the novel as a whole is about; this tentative understanding of the whole enables us (if we are lucky) to get a better understanding of the next chapter, whose reading leads to a more informed understanding of the whole purpose of the book, which more informed understanding of the whole improves our understanding of the next part, and so on. We understand the novel when we are able to figure out how all the parts fit together, and we only understand how all the parts fit together because we have grasped the point of the book as a whole. Thus do we "hop back and forth between the whole conceived through the parts which actualize it and the parts conceived through the whole which motivates them" and "turn them . . . into explications of one another."

When the anthropologist's reading of the culture reaches this point he has achieved the goal of providing a "thick description" of that culture. But this does not mean that he has arrived at *the* definitive, final, one-true-account of that culture. It is always possible that deeper, longer immersion in its parts could produce a better understanding of the whole and that better understanding of the whole could improve his account of any particular part. It is in this sense that Geertz concludes that "cultural analysis is intrinsically incomplete."[9] But for Geertz the inherent incompleteness of anthropology does not threaten its status as a science, does not mean that anthropological interpretation is hopelessly subjective. Just as there are better or worse interpretations of a novel, so there are better or worse interpretations of a culture. The better interpretations more convincingly "sort winks from twitches and real winks from mimicked ones" and thus more closely "bring us in touch with the lives of strangers."[10]

It is, finally, this goal that clearly animates Geertz's "semiotic approach to culture." He tells us that:

> we are seeking, in the widened sense of the term in which it encompasses very much more than talk, to converse with [those whom we study], a matter a great more difficult, and not only with strangers, than is commonly recognized [and that] the whole point of a semiotic approach to culture is . . . to aid us in gaining access to the conceptual world in which our subjects live so that we can, in some extended sense, converse with them.[11]

Thus Geertz's conception of the science of culture is ultimately governed by his commitment to communicate with others with whom communication would otherwise be impossible. It follows that someone who did not make that commitment to communication a priority would not share Geertz's semiotic approach to culture.

One prominent example of that someone would definitely be Marvin Harris. In his *Cultural Materialism* he proclaims that "the test of the adequacy of [anthropological] accounts is simply their ability to generate scientifically productive theories about the causes of sociocultural differences and similarities," and he defines scientific theories as those that "restrict fields of inquiry to events, entities, and relationships that are knowable by means of explicit, logico-empirical, inductive–deductive, quantifiable public procedures or 'operations' subject to replication by independent observers."[12] To translate into layperson's terms: Harris is committed to a science of human culture that makes use of the same concepts and methods of those natural sciences that are dedicated to the discovery of universal laws that explain and predict the behavior of the things they study. On this understanding of science, of course, Geertz's interpretative, semiotic approach to culture is anything but scientific.

To say this is not to say that Harris rejects the idea that one of the anthropologist's tasks is to attempt to reproduce explicitly the implicit understandings of the people he studies. To the contrary: describing how his subjects make sense of their world and themselves is an important part of the anthropological calling. But, for Harris, this co-called "emic" approach is only a first step, a preliminary to the more fundamental task of providing what is called an "etic" account that *explains* the self-understanding of that culture, that is, that explains why that self-understanding is both similar to and different from the self-understandings of other cultures. The emic account, in other words, is undertaken not, as it is for Geertz, for the purpose of enhancing the possibility of an "extended conversation" with the members of the culture that is being studied but rather simply to produce "data" or the raw material for a scientific explanation of what they *think* they are doing, an explanation that is necessarily framed in terms of concepts of the observer rather than the observed.

The concepts on which Harris relies—and now we move from his general understanding of a science of culture to his particular, "culturally materialist" version thereof—are designed to enable him, in his words, "to build theories about culture that incorporate lawful regularities occurring in nature."[13] The "lawful regularities occurring in nature" result from the fact that humans, like all "bioforms," must expend energy in order to survive, and that, also like all "bioforms," they must propagate in order to reproduce the species. Among humans the first requirement gives rise to what Harris calls the mode of production, by which he means "the technologies and the practices employed for expanding or limiting subsistence production," and the second requirement engenders what he calls the "mode of reproduction," that is, "the technology and the practices necessary for expanding, limiting, and maintaining population size."[14] His theoretical claim, then, is that the mode of production and the mode of reproduction of a society combine to explain the culture of that society. Otherwise put, for Harris the way in which a society fulfills its physical or material needs—the need to fill its stomachs as well as the need to produce its children—ultimately determines the cultural practices they adopt. Hence Harris's description of this theoretical strategy as "cultural materialism."

Harris's explanation for the "origin of the Sacred Cow"—his effort to explain the taboo on eating beef in Hindu India—is an example of the way this theoretical strategy is employed to account "etically" for a cultural practice that is "emically" understood in a very different way. A practicing Hindu would say that she doesn't eat beef because cows are sacred, and would probably connect their sacred character to *ahimsa,* that is, to the Hindu doctrine of the sacredness of life. But Harris points out that during the Vedic period (2000 BC to 800 BC) "oxen appeared to have been eaten freely," and that "even in late Vedic times, it was still customary to kill a big ox to feed a distinguished guest."[15] But this was no longer the case—an absolute taboo on beef eating emerged—by 300 BC. According to Harris, this taboo was the result of a combination of dramatic demographic and ecological changes that occurred prior to that time. Whereas in 1000 BC the population in the Ganges valley was "scanty and spread out in small villages," by 300 BC that valley was the site of "vast irrigation works, great cities, and a population estimated between 50 and 100 million people."[16] At the roughly the same time India "became subject to increasingly severe droughts and famines, due in part . . . to deforestation and settlement of marginal lands"[17] produced by an increasingly large, urbanized population. Those droughts and famines, of course, affected not only humans but also other animals, and in particular cattle, which, Harris argues, had long been valued for their ability to pull plows and thus for their indispensable contribution to Indian agriculture. Under conditions where cattle remained economically necessary but were becoming increasingly scarce, it was no longer rational to eat cows: the costs now outweighed the benefits. Thus, argues Harris, "an animal whose flesh was previously consumed became too costly to be used as food as a result of fundamental changes in the ecosystem and mode of production." The taboos on slaughtering and eating cows, he continues, "reflect the indispensability of cattle as a source of traction under conditions of high preindustrial population and rainfall agriculture. Hence the cow became holy . . . in order to protect its vital function as mother of the bullock."[18]

I leave it to scholars more knowledgeable than I to determine whether Harris's materialist explanation fits the facts he describes. The only question I would ask is whether that explanation reads into the Hindu Indian society of more than two thousand years ago utilitarian assumptions that may be specific to Harris's own—and our—modern culture. Is it the case that Hindu peasant farmers were essentially "economic men" who were careful to calculate the costs and benefits of eating their cattle, or is it possible that Harris is smuggling into his supposedly naturalistic explanation of the origins of the Sacred Cow culturally and historically specific, "economistic" assumptions that, for example, Karl Polanyi would contest? Is it possible, in other words, that in the guise of incorporating "lawful regularities occurring in nature" Harris is guilty of ethnocentrically projecting the mind of the West into the mind of the Rest? To conclude, I think it is worth contemplating the possibility that Harris's culturally materialism is merely the emics of modernity masquerading as an etic—or scientifically objective—theoretical explanation. In the next chapter I take up this issue of theoretical ethnocentrism in much greater detail.

18

BEYOND ETHNOCENTRISM AND RELATIVISM?

At the end of the last chapter I suggested that there may be something ethnocentric about Marvin Harris's cost–benefit explanation of the origins of cow-love in India, and, more generally, something ethnocentric about any explanation that is based on the assumption that human beings choose to adopt, modify, or reject cultural practices according to whether or the extent to which these practices are consistent with their material needs. This suggestion reflects a salutary awareness on the part of at least some Western social scientists since the 1960s that their theoretical categories—the concepts they employ to account for the behavior of people in other cultures—are not necessarily universal or objective but rather might in fact merely be abstract expressions of the particular values of the specifically Western culture to which the social scientists belong. If this were the case, then their supposedly "scientific" explanations of the behavior of other peoples would have to be judged to be a form of conceptual imperialism, an ethnocentric imposition of the values of the West on (what the West all too frequently describes as) the Rest. To their credit, many social scientists in general and political scientists in particular are alert to this danger, and have forcefully criticized ethnocentric explanations for their failure to recognize just how different different cultures really are.

This recognition, even celebration of cultural difference, however, is all too often accompanied by the claim that any one culture is as good as any other. Thus ethnocentrism gives way to its apparent opposite, cultural relativism. Whereas ethnocentrism uncritically assumes the superiority of our cultural values over the values of another culture, relativism assumes that there simply is no non-ethnocentric way to justify the claim that one set of cultural values is any better, any more defensible, then any other set of cultural values. Relativism thus deprives us of the arguments we need to make moral distinctions between, for example, a pacific culture and a violent culture, or between a culture that respects the bodily integrity of female children, and thus honors the innate potential of women fully to experience sexual pleasure, and a culture that thwarts that potential by mutilating the genitals of its young girls. The claim that this cultural practice, along with many other longstanding, deeply rooted practices of male domination, is a violation of universal human rights is likely to ring hollow in the ears of those for whom ethnocentrism and cultural relativism are the only two alternatives. The concept of universal human rights implies, in other words, that there is a common, indeed universal, core of what it means to be human, and that the rulers of Saudi Arabia, China, Myanmar, Sudan, or Guantanamo should be brought to justice for their assault on that common core. But identifying that common core—defending a concept of human nature in the light of which *any* culture, Western or non-Western, modern or traditional, can legitimately be called into question—is no easy task. I am arguing, in short, that it is both necessary and difficult to go beyond the either/or of ethnocentrism versus relativism.

An important exchange between Peter Winch and I. C. Jarvie illustrates this point. Winch argues that we simply cannot understand a primitive society, and the African Azande in particular, if we uncritically assume the standpoint of the Western scientific conception of reality. In his "Understanding a Primitive Society" Winch notes that:

> the Azande hold beliefs that we cannot possibly share and engage in practices which it is peculiarly difficult for us to comprehend. They believe that certain of their members are witches, exercising a malignant occult influence on the lives of their fellows. They engage in rites to counteract witchcraft; they consult oracles and use magic medicines to protect themselves from harm.[1]

Although E. E. Pritchard denied in his classic study of the Azande that their belief in witchcraft is illogical, and thus denied as well the claim of earlier anthropologists that their intelligence is inferior to the intelligence of modern Western people who—supposedly—reject magical in favor of scientific beliefs, Pritchard nonetheless insists that the scientific beliefs are correct whereas the magical beliefs of the Azande are not: "We can say that the social content of our thought . . . is scientific, is in accord with objective facts, whereas the social content of savage thought . . . is unscientific since it is not in accord with reality".[2]

Winch objects to Pritchard's equation of "scientific" with "in accord with objective reality." He points out that there is no way to gain access to reality independent of the concepts we employ in order to describe and understand it. (This does *not* mean that there is no reality independent of those concepts.) This is what Winch means when he says that:

> reality is not what gives language sense. What is real and what is unreal shows itself *in* the sense that language has . . . both the distinction between the real and the unreal and the concept of agreement with reality themselves belong to our language.[3]

Thus the Western scientific world-view cannot be said to agree with "objective reality" because it is only within the context of that world-view that the notion of "agreement with objective reality" makes any sense. Consequently it is ethnocentric to claim that the Azande or more generally the primitive, animistic world-view does not accord with "objective reality."

Defenders of Western science might concede this point but still argue on pragmatic grounds that Western science is superior to Zande magic: after all, the technologies that flow from Western science enable us far more effectively to exercise control over nature than the magical techniques that the Azande employ. Judged instrumentally, in other words, Western science is obviously superior to Zande witchcraft. But it is just this instrumental judgment that is, according to Winch, an ethnocentric "category mistake." It is a "category mistake" because it reflects the belief that Zande magic is designed to achieve the same end as Western science and technology—mastery over nature—and thus the assumption—the fallacious assumption—that the modern Western conception of nature and our relationship to it is the only possible conception. And, of course, once Zande practices are mistranslated into our instrumental categories those practices can only be described as poorer, less developed versions of the ones we moderns have perfected.

If we want to avoid this kind of conceptual imperialism—evaluating different cultures in the light of a supposedly universal standard that is in fact only *our* modern Western standpoint and inevitably finding those different cultures wanting for their "failure" to measure up to that standard—then we have to be open to the possibility that Zande magic is an expression of a very different understanding of and orientation to the natural world than the modern instrumental understanding. This, indeed, is what Winch suggests when he writes that:

> A man's sense of the importance of something to him shows itself in all sorts of ways: not merely in precautions to safeguard that thing. He may want to come to terms with its importance to him in quite a different way: to contemplate it, to gain some sense of his life in relation to it. He may wish thereby . . . to *free* himself from dependence on it;

and that Zande magical rites "express an attitude toward contingencies . . . which involves recognition that one's life is subject to contingencies, rather than an attempt to control these."[4] In other words, whereas so-called "developed" societies assert their supposed independence from nature in the course of their effort to control it, the Azande in particular, and so-called "primitive" people in general, affirm their dependence on a nature that they recognize is generally beyond their control.

In Winch's brief rejoinder to Jarvie's critique of his essay he accuses Jarvie of making the same "category mistake" as the thinkers Winch criticized in that essay, namely the ethnocentric assumption that, "the only standards available to us against which to compare Zande standards are the standards involved in the practice of *scientific* work."[5] This fallacy is evident, according to Winch, in

Jarvie's insistence that Western scientific rationality is superior to Zande ratio-nality because the former is "an open and critical intellectual system" and the latter a "closed and unrevisable system of beliefs." Thus the Western scientific world-view makes possible, as the Zande world-view does not, a "learning from experience, and especially from mistakes"[6] that is a minimal condition for genu-inely rational action. But Winch argues—to me not entirely persuasively[7]—that Jarvie's emphasis on "mistakes" implies that he thinks that the Azande are try-ing to so *the same thing* as modern Western people, only they do it the same way over and over again, repeating the same mistakes. In other words, according to Winch, Jarvie still assumes that the category of "doing things" or technique is the relevant category by which to make sense of the Azande, and thus fails, like the thinkers Winch criticized in his first essay, to understand that there are different, non-technical ways to relate to the world.

If we fail to recognize this, not only can we not understand primitive societ-ies but we rob ourselves of the opportunity of learning from them:

> What we may learn by studying other cultures are not merely possibilities of different ways of doing things, other techniques. More importantly we may learn different possibilities of making sense of human life, different ideas about the possible importance that the carrying out of certain activi-ties may take on for a man, trying to contemplate the sense of his life as a whole.[8]

Or again:

> the concept of *learning from* which is involved in the study of other cultures is closely linked with the concept of *wisdom*. We are confronted not just with different techniques, but with new possibilities of good and evil, in relation to which men may come to terms with life.[9]

Rather than ethnocentrically assume that so-called primitives are "less devel-oped" and therefore need to learn from us, we should rather assume that in certain respects their understanding of life may actually be more developed than ours, and that we need to learn from *them*. Thus, according to Winch, "seriously to study another way of life is necessarily to seek to extend [i.e., to broaden or enlarge] our own—not simply to bring the other way within the already existing boundaries of our own."[10]

This equation of "serious study" of other ways of life with "extending" our own implies, of course, that there is something narrow, inadequate, or incom-plete about our own way. Winch does not say much about this, except when he criticizes

> the general difficulty [among Western social scientists] of thinking about such matters [as Zande magic] except in terms of "efficiency of produc-

tion"—production that is, for consumption. This . . . is a symptom of what Marx called the "alienation" characteristic of man in industrial society . . . Our blindness to the point of primitive modes of life is a corollary to the pointlessness of much of our own life.[11]

This reference to "the pointlessness of our own life" suggests that Winch has a vision of a society that would have more of a point, that would be less alienated, a vision that implies, in turn, a concept of human nature in the light of which the judgment of pointlessness or alienation is made. But Winch never makes that theory of human nature explicit. He does argue that there are three "limiting notions" or inescapable concepts with which *all* human societies must come to terms: (1) the concept of death, which gives rise to the problem of what it means to live in the face of our mortality, of the fact that we will die; (2) the concept of sex, which engenders (Winch rather quaintly insists) the problem of the heterosexual relationship, the relationship between women and men; and (3) the concept of birth, which presents the problem of inescapable, unchosen ethical obligations to those who have given us life. These three "limiting concepts"—mortality, sexuality, and natality—"will necessarily be an important feature of any human society and . . . conceptions of good and evil in human life will necessarily be connected with such concepts."[12] So Winch gestures in the direction of a universalism that assumes that *all societies face and must attempt to solve the same fundamental problems.* But this gesture is incomplete at best and hollow at worst because he never provides criteria in the light of which it would be possible to determine that some societies solve these universal problems better than others. Thus his argument is vulnerable to the objection that he leaves the door open for the very cultural relativism that he explicitly rejects.

What we need, I think, and what Winch doesn't give us, is a concept of human nature that incorporates the best that both primitive and modern societies have to offer and that leaves the worst of each of them behind, a synthesis or "third way" that—as I already suggested in chapter 14—would be a fuller expression of what it means to be human than either of the polar opposite elements of which it is composed. The virtue of the "primitive" world-view, in my eyes, is that it affirms our dependence on and solidarity with the other beings with whom we share the planet; its vice, on the other hand, is that its insistence on the oneness of the world tends to ignore or at least underestimate the undeniable difference between the human and non-human parts of that world. The modern world-view, in contrast, acknowledges, even celebrates, that difference, but at the cost of denying any kinship between human and non-human nature and transforming the difference between them into a hierarchical opposition: humans are subjects for whom nature is merely an object. In short, modernity transforms difference into domination. Much more on modernity in the next chapter. For now I conclude with the suggestion that what we need is neither pure identity nor pure difference but rather a union of identity and difference, one that would, on the one hand, enable human beings to feel at home in the world but that would, on the other hand, be a properly human place.

19

MODERNITY

The goal of this chapter is to introduce you to, and help you make sense of, two very different contemporary accounts of the distinctively modern culture that we all inhabit. These accounts of modernity are difficult to comprehend not merely or mainly because of the perhaps unfamiliar language they employ, but also, more importantly, because it is always difficult for people who are inside a culture to see it, as it were, from the outside, that is, to understand one's own culture as an anthropologist attempts to understand a more obviously alien culture. Getting sufficient distance from our way of life in order to understand it merely as *one* way of life rather than the way life *is*, in other words, is no easy task, but it is just this task that you are asked to perform when you read and think about Anthony Giddens's and Zygmunt Bauman's interpretations of modernity.

Bauman's account of modernity is far bleaker than Giddens's. For Bauman "modernity is drive to mastery; a mode of being shot through with hope, ambition and confidence—a behavioral–attitudinal complex correlated with [the] subordination and appropriation of nature."[1] This "behavioral–attitudinal" commitment to subdue nature is the outcome of a process that the great early twentieth-century sociologist Max Weber called the "disenchantment of the world."[2] By the "disenchantment of the world" Weber meant the seventeenth- and eighteenth-century Western European overthrow of the teleological conception of nature that prevailed in that part of the world prior to that time (and that is still dominant in non-modernized parts of the world today). The root Greek word of the adjective "teleological" is *telos*, which means end, goal, or purpose. So to speak of a teleological conception of nature is to speak of a nature that is understood to be informed by or tend toward an end or a purpose, an end or purpose in the light of which humans are expected to live their lives. Within the context of a teleological world-view, in other words, people find meaning in their lives in their participation in what they take to be a meaningful world. The "disenchantment of the world" refers to the conceptual (and emotional) process of stripping nature of meaning or purpose and transforming it into a purposeless object that exists for the sake of the human subject, that is raw material for human production, a pure means for uniquely human ends. In short, once nature is deprived of subjectivity the only possible human relationship with it is an objectifying one: under these conditions the effort of humans to achieve meaning in their lives necessarily takes the form of the effort to make nature *useful*, to achieve the maximum possible mastery over nature.

"Mastery over nature," Bauman informs us, "could mean nothing else but emancipation from necessity."[3] By "necessity," Bauman means anything on which human beings are dependent, any natural contingency that resists human control. To say that modernity is dedicated to emancipation from necessity is thus to say that, in Bauman's words, modernity "suffers resistance badly";[4] what remains resistant to human control "scandalizes" the omnipotent pretensions of a modernity that seeks to make the world an entirely predictable place. And the greatest scandal of all is, of course, that most natural and therefore most inevitable of all natural contingencies, namely death. As Bauman puts it:

> Of all adversities of earthy existence, death soon emerged as the most persistent and indifferent to human effort. It was, indeed, the *major* scandal. The hard, irreducible core of human impotence in a world increasingly subject to human will and acumen. The last, yet seemingly irremovable, relic of fate in a world increasingly designed and controlled by reason.[5]

Modernity responds to this scandalous "relic of fate" in two different but related ways. First, it banishes death from public view: the dying are moved from the homes in which they used to die and are sequestered in hospitals where they no longer have to be seen, and the dead are moved from the easily accessible graveyards of central-city churches to the less accessible outskirts of town. Corresponding to this spatial segregation of the dead and dying is a psychological separation that takes the form of the inability of the living to speak with, or even about, the dying: "Death has become unmentionable,"[6] except perhaps euphemistically in such expressions as the "passing" of a relative or the "loss" of a friend.

Second, Bauman argues that this

> conspiracy of silence has been protected by the expedient of the *analytical* deconstruction of mortality . . . From the existential and *unavoidable* predicament of humanity, mortality has been deconstructed into diverse events of private deaths, each with its own *avoidable* cause; death as the fact of *nature* has been deconstructed into a set of outcomes of many and varied, yet unmistakably and invariably *human*, actions.[7]

By this Bauman means that modernity attempts to sidestep death, as it were, by concentrating attention on its individual causes. Although "death is omnipotent and invincible . . . none of the specific cases of death is." All of these individual cases have determinate causes, and therefore they are all, in principle, preventable, all amenable to human control. As Bauman notes:

I can do nothing to defy mortality. But I can do quite a lot to avoid a blood clot or a lung cancer. I can stop eating eggs, refrain from smoking, do physical exercises, keep my weight down . . . And while doing all these right things and forcing myself to abstain from the wrong ones, I have no time left to ruminate over the *ultimate* futility of each thing I am doing,[8]

namely, that I eventually *will* die. Thus does the celebration of the "ever new triumphant battles" [over T.B., heart disease, cancer, etc.] make the "news of the lost war" [against death] inaudible."[9]

The inevitable and ironic consequence of this effort to deflect death by deconstructing it into its humanly avoidable causes is that death weighs far more heavily over life in modernity than it did over life in earlier or different cultures. Whereas in those cultures death was or is something that merely came or comes at the end of life, in modernity, Bauman argues, "it is there from the start, calling for constant surveillance and forbidding even a momentary relaxation of vigil . . . fighting the *causes* of dying turns into the meaning of life."[10] In other words, an ever-increasing amount of individual time, energy, and money is devoted to protecting our *health* against the many and diverse things that threaten it. On the one hand, this modern *health consciousness* defends us against the awareness that, in the end, we must die, and thus from coming to grips with that inescapable fact of life: as Bauman puts it, "the existential worry can now be all but forgotten in the daily bustle about *health*."[11] On the other hand, this effort to deflect death only serves to mortify life, which is lived increasingly "in the shadow of death":

Death is a momentary event, but defence of health and vigilance against its enemies is a lifelong labour. If death comes at the end of life, the defense of health fills the whole of it. The price for exchanging *immortality* for *health* is life lived in the shadow of death; to postpone death, one needs to surrender life to fighting it.[12]

Thus are modern individuals defeated by their very effort to defeat death.

Finally, this morbid war against mortality inevitably culminates, at least according to Bauman, in a never-ending war against those who are (seen as) less modern than the individuals who wage it. Thus he claims that "the price of the specifically modern way of coping with death anxiety—putting mortality in an institutional and mental confinement and keeping it there—is a constant demand for the 'dangerous other' as a carrier of contagious and terminal disease."[13] By this Bauman means that modernity projects its unacknowledged and thus unresolved fear of death onto other, different people, who unwittingly become, as it were, the "degenerate," that is, less than fully human, targets for its mortal rage: "killing of the appointed disease-carriers is a symbolic surrogate of death-killing."[14] Hence his altogether pessimistic but not altogether persuasive conclusion that "all too often . . . the audacious [modern] dream of killing death turns into the practice of killing people" and that "the specifically modern project of deconstructing mortality . . . infuses modern society with its unyielding and probably incorrigible genocidal drive."[15] I say "not altogether persuasive" because we have also, and all too recently, witnessed this "genocidal drive" in societies—Rwanda, for example—that are anything but modern.

Anthony Giddens might respond to this fact by suggesting that Bauman misses the essential meaning of modernity. What is definitive of modernity, according to Giddens in *Modernity and Self-Identity*, is not the fact—which Giddens does recognize as a fact—that modernity seeks to rid the world of contingencies, but rather the fact that in attempting to do so it actually *produces* more contingencies than it eliminates. Although, according to Giddens, "the original progenitors of modern science and philosophy" *were* committed to the goal of "offering a sense of certitude in place of [what they considered to be] the arbitrary character of [premodern] habit and custom,"[16] in fact, argues Giddens, "the anticipation that the social and natural environments would increasingly be subject to rational ordering has not proved to be valid." We moderns live instead in a world in which not only is change "continuous and profound," but "change does not consistently conform either to human expectation or to human control."[17]

According to Giddens, this "runaway" character of the modern world is in important part a result of what he calls the "reflexivity of modernity." By the "reflexivity of modernity" Giddens means "the susceptibility of most aspects of social activity, and material relations with nature, to chronic revision in the light of new information and knowledge. Such information or knowledge is not incidental to modern institutions, but constitutive of them."[18] In other words, scientific knowledge about the operations of modern institutions increasingly shapes the very operations on which it reflects. And, since, as Giddens notes, "science depends, not on the inductive accumulations of proofs, but on the methodological principle of doubt," it follows that any given "revision" of social or institutional activity that is based on scientific reflection on that activity is necessarily open to further revision. In short, "the reflexivity of modernity actually undermines the certainty of knowledge." Thus Giddens concludes with the observation that there is "an integral relation between modernity and radical doubt [that] is not only disturbing to philosophers but is *existentially troubling* for ordinary individuals."[19]

Under these conditions, the forging of a sense of self or individual identity becomes far more problematical than it was or is in more traditional cultures. In those cultures there were or are of course transitions—for example from the stage of childhood to the stage of adolescence to the stage of adulthood to the stage of being an elder—but the expectations associated with each of these stages were more or less fixed from generation to generation. Under the conditions of what Giddens calls "high modernity," in contrast, the meaning and requirements of these transitions and the identities associated with them come up for grabs: "the social conditions of modernity enforce on all of us . . .

a process of 'finding oneself.'"[20] Thus "the question 'How shall I live?' has to be answered in day-to-day decisions about how to behave, what to wear, and what to eat . . . and many other things"[21] that the members of traditional cultures did not have to make. These decisions, moreover, are increasingly influenced by the various systems of expertise that transmit the latest scientific knowledge about these matters to the ordinary individuals who make them. And, since—as we have seen—this knowledge is subject to "chronic revision," so too are the identity-defining decisions that are shaped by them. Thus Giddens argues that "the reflexivity of modernity extends into the core of the self . . . in the context of a post-traditional order, the self becomes a *reflexive project*."[22]

This reflexive process entails both great risks and potentially great rewards. Since, on the one hand, or so Giddens claims, "an indefinite range of potential courses of action . . . is at any given moment open to individuals,"[23] these individuals are constantly faced with the necessity of choosing among alternatives—Giddens calls this "counterfactual thinking"—whose eventual benefits and costs are never entirely clear. Thus identity formation under modernity is *risky* in a way that it never was in pre-modern societies. On the other hand, this very fact means that there are "opportunities . . . for self-expression lacking in many more traditional contexts."[24] Giddens is aware that "some people," faced with the risks and accompanying anxieties inherent in modern identity formation, "take refuge in a sort of resigned numbness."[25] Indeed, elsewhere in his writings he argues that the compulsive character of the over-consumption endemic to modernity is, in effect, a defense against—a way to numb oneself to—the anxiety that painfully accompanies the intrinsically uncertain, unstable process of modern identity formation.[26] But, on the other hand, he also argues that "many are also able more positively to grasp the new opportunities which open up as pre-established modes of behaviour become foreclosed, and to change themselves."[27] They often do so with the aid of therapy or other forms of counseling that enable them to mourn lost identities the better to be able to embrace new ones. Thus Giddens interprets what Philip Rieff called "the triumph of the therapeutic"[28] in largely positive terms: although he does not entirely dismiss the Foucauldian claim that psychotherapy is a modern, secular form of the traditional confessional that subjects the confessor to the priest to whom she confesses,[29] he argues that it is more usefully, and generously, understood as a means by which individuals draw on expertise in order better to cope with, and respond productively to, the anxieties that might otherwise prevent them from being open to, and taking advantage of, new possibilities. Therapy is, in short, an "expression of the [modern] reflexivity of the self."[30]

Bauman might well criticize Giddens for failing to emphasize the sense in which death—or rather the denial of death—hangs heavily over this "reflexive project." That is, he would undoubtedly argue, as we have seen, that the many decisions that modern individuals are daily obliged to make about, for example, what to eat and how or whether to exercise are made in the name of a preoccupation with health that is, according to him, merely a surrogate for a spurious, impossible immortality. Yet Giddens could counter that death is certainly one of the losses that many modern individuals confront either in or out of therapy, and he could point to the growing public discourse about the need for and meaning of a "good death" as evidence for a slowly growing capacity of modern people to confront rather than evade their mortality. Indeed, whereas Bauman argues that modernity only offers "surrogate solutions to the existential predicament that allows no solution,"[31] Giddens specifically argues in the last chapter of *Modernity and Self-Identity* that efforts to confront this as well as other existential questions are absolutely central to what he calls the "life politics" that increasingly shape the modern political landscape.[32] Modernity is mortifying for Bauman but potentially life-affirming for Giddens. Their contestation reminds one of the famous ending of Freud's *Civilization and its Discontents*, where Freud calls on *Eros—the life instincts*—to counter the work of *Thanatos*—the destructive manifestation of the *death instinct*—and concludes that the outcome of this contest is anything but certain.[33]

20

MODERNITY AND IDENTITY

We saw in the last chapter that Anthony Giddens argues that modernity problematizes individual identity by virtue of its inherent tendency to undermine traditional forms of life through which earlier identities were more or less automatically established. Charles Taylor in his *The Politics of Recognition* agrees that the collapse of pre-modern hierarchies and the values associated with them—especially, for Taylor, the value of *honor*—partly explains why the issue of identity becomes so central to modern life. But he adds that its centrality is also the consequence of what he calls "the massive subjective turn of modern culture, a new form of inwardness, in which we come to think of ourselves as beings with inner depths,"[1] a subjective turn that he thinks Rousseau was the first major thinker clearly to articulate. From Rousseau's writings—not so much from the *Social Contract* but rather from his *Discourse on the Origin of Inequality* and his *Emile*—comes the idea—the altogether modern idea—that we have an authentic inner self that is all too often distorted or repressed by the crass competition of a modern, increasingly commercial, society. Thus the very modernity that buries our identity under the weight of what Tocqueville called the "tyranny" of majority opinion incites us to uncover the true self that underlies it.

Taylor also emphasizes what Giddens did not, namely the sense in which individual identity is dialogically rather than monologically established. Even if we think that our identity is entirely inwardly generated, the fact is, according to Taylor, "the crucial feature of human life is its fundamentally *dialogical* character," by which he means that "we define our identity always in dialogue with, sometimes in struggle against, the things our significant others want to see in us."[2] Similarly, he claims that "my own identity crucially depends on my dialogical relations with others."[3] In other words the self, as I argued in the section of chapter 16 devoted to Arendt's concept of power, is formed only through the *recognition* it receives from the other. This has always been the case, but "in the earlier age recognition never arose as a problem [because it] was built into the socially derived identity by virtue of the very fact that it was based on social categories that everyone took for granted."[4] It is, in short, only with the modern destruction of those social categories that recognition is recognized as a problem to be solved or a goal to be achieved. Thus the preoccupation with recognition and the preoccupation with identity are two sides of the same modern coin.

What is true of individual identity is also true, Taylor argues, of the identities of groups: their identity is as dependent on public recognition as individual identity is dependent on the recognition of significant others. And, just as unequal recognition in interpersonal relationships is harmful to the individuals in those relationships, so unequal group recognition is damaging to the members of those groups:

> Equal [public] recognition is not just the appropriate mode for a healthy democratic society. Its refusal can inflict damage on those who are denied it . . . the projection of an inferior or demeaning image on another [group] can actually distort and oppress, to the extent that the image is internalized.[5]

Thus it should come as no surprise that what Taylor calls "the politics of recognition"—the struggle for equal public recognition of group identities—has come to figure prominently in, if not dominate, the contemporary political landscape.

In the remaining parts of his essay Taylor takes up and attempts to answer the question of whether or the extent to which the effort to achieve equal group recognition—what he and other observers call the "politics of difference"—is compatible with the Liberal principle of equal individual rights and obligations (in the eyes of the law), or what he calls the "politics of universal dignity." The politics of universal dignity, as the label implies, is based on the assumption that respect for the inherent dignity of every individual requires that they all share "an identical basket of rights and immunities" and thus on the claim that preferential or discriminatory treatment of particular individuals is a violation of their dignity. But with "the politics of difference," Taylor emphasizes, "what we are asked to recognize is the unique identity of this individual or group, their distinctness from everyone else."[6] From the perspective of the members of groups committed to the politics of difference, as Taylor puts it, "the supposedly neutral set of difference-blind principles of the politics of equal dignity is in fact a reflection of one hegemonic culture,"[7] that is, a reflection of the values of dominant groups masquerading as universally human values and thus functioning to deny recognition to—thus to marginalize—the members of subordinate groups whose values happen to be different. Thus Taylor notes that "the politics of difference often redefines nondiscrimination [from being "blind to the ways in which citizens differ"] as requiring that we make these distinctions the basis of differential treatment."[8] The question, once again, is whether it is possible to reconcile the commitment to treat different groups differently with the politics of universal dignity.

Taylor's answer is a qualified "yes." He takes up this general question in the specific context of the demand of many Quebecois—French Canadians who live in the majority Francophone province of Quebec—for constitutional recognition of Quebec as a "distinct society" and for laws that recognize and defend its distinctness. In fact such laws have existed for some time, and include language laws that prohibit Francophones from sending their children to English-language schools, require businesses with more than fifty employees to be run in French, and prohibit commercial signage in any language other than French.[9] These laws, as Taylor points out, are designed to protect Francophone culture from the threat of assimilation to the dominant, surrounding Anglophone Canadian (and American) culture by ensuring that "future generations continue to identify as French-speakers."[10] From the Francophone perspective, in other words, these laws that prescribe differential treatment of Francophone and Anglophone Quebecois are essential for the survival of French culture, which cultural survival they identify as an unambiguous good that the government should seek to preserve and enhance. But for Anglophones who are committed to the politics of universal dignity or what is sometimes called "procedural liberalism"—the idea that the state must not favor any particular, substantive way of life but must be neutral with respect to them—Quebec language laws that single out Anglophones and Francophones for different treatment and in some cases give preferential treatment to Francophones are a clear violation of the principles of non-discrimination and equal rights for all. Thus the politics of difference—in this case the recognition of (Francophone) cultural difference— and the politics of universal dignity appear to be at odds with one another.

Taylor argues that this need not be the case. He suggests that a modified politics of universal dignity can in fact accommodate the demand for group recognition embodied in the Quebec language laws and, by extension, other laws designed to ensure the cultural survival of other groups. By a modified politics of universal human dignity—a modified Liberalism—he means one that distinguishes "fundamental rights [such as the right to *habeas corpus*, life, liberty, due process, free speech, free practice of religion] from the broad range of immunities and presumptions of uniform treatment that have sprung up in modern cultures of judicial review." When it comes to fundamental rights, Taylor argues, differential treatment in the name of cultural survival is never justified. But in the case of less fundamental rights that fall under the category of "presumptions of uniform treatment," such as the right to use commercial signage in the language of one's choice, it *is* legitimate "to weigh the importance of certain forms of uniform treatment against the importance of cultural survival, and opt sometimes in favor of the latter."[11] Thus Taylor's modified Liberal position is, in effect, an effort to strike a balance between a procedural liberalism or a politics of universal human dignity that ignores demands for group recognition and a politics of difference or what is often called a communitarianism for which the requirements of the group or particular community typically trump the requirement of equal treatment for all, group members and non-members alike.

Of course the strength of Taylor's position depends entirely on the plausibility of distinction he draws between "fundamental rights" and less fundamental "privileges and immunities," a distinction that, he acknowledges, he does not adequately defend in his essay. And this distinction might turn out to be more difficult to defend than Taylor believes. Perhaps the right to use commercial signage in the language of one's choice is not really so fundamental—after all, the sign "Charcuterie Hebraique de Montreal" doesn't stop the throngs of English speakers who regularly patronize Montreal's most popular Jewish deli—but what about the right to send one's children to a school of one's choice? Abridging the right to determine the language in which one's children will be instructed is surely a more serious matter than prescribing the language in which one advertises one's business in a bilingual society. Perhaps the need to ensure a continuing community of French speakers and thus the survival of French culture *should* trump the right of individual Francophones to send their children to English-speaking schools, but that I think would be a more difficult case to make.

At any rate, in this essay, as I have already said, Taylor doesn't attempt to defend that case. Rather his sympathetic treatment of one form of the politics of difference is followed by a critique of another, he thinks more extreme, form of that politics. Here Taylor has in mind not merely the demand that we recognize the right of particular cultures to survive but also the demand that "we *recognize* the equal value of different cultures; that we not only let them survive, but acknowledge their *worth*."[12] This latter demand, according to Taylor, is simply unreasonable, because it asks us to suspend our critical judgment in favor of an *a priori* and therefore arbitrary cultural relativism that is really more condescending than respectful: in uncritically assuming from the start that one culture is as good as any other, it actually fails to engage, and thus to learn from, the culture whose demand for recognition of equal worth it far too easily concedes. Wary of ethnocentrism, Taylor is willing to grant longstanding cultures the presumption that they are worth taking seriously, the presumption that "all human cultures that have animated whole societies over some considerable stretch of time have something to say to all human beings."[13] But granting them this presumption, he insists, is a far cry from deciding that they have equal value, which decision requires a serious and sustained examination of their merits and limits. Thus Taylor concludes that "there must be something midway between the unauthentic and homogenizing demand for recognition of equal worth, on the one hand, and the self-immurement within ethnocentric standards, on the other."[14] We are back, in other words, to the need to go beyond ethnocentrism and relativism.

If Taylor is basically sympathetic to at least the less extreme forms of the politics of difference—or what is more commonly called "identity politics"— both Joan Scott and Todd Gitlin are decidedly less so, although for different reasons. Scott worries principally about what she thinks are the exclusionary implications of the assumption of a politics organized around group identity. In "Multiculturalism and the Politics of Identity" she claims that both sides to the current debate over "multiculturalism" share what she calls a "unified concept of identity."[15] By a "unified conception of identity" she means "an inescapable trait that . . . is inherently a part of one's being" as a member of a particular group or cultural category.[16] "Multiculturalism," she argues, "pluralizes the notion of an American identity by insisting [in academic or educational settings] on attention to African-Americans, Native Americans, and the like" but assumes in the process that there is something like a single, essential, unambiguous African-American, native-American, etc., identity. Thus it mirrors the argument of anti-multiculturalists that the multiculturalist preoccupation with group difference leads to the "unmaking" or unraveling of a unitary *American* identity: the multiculturalist critique of an undifferentiated American identity "leaves in place" the very "unified concept of identity" that it would appear to contest.[17]

The political problem with this concept of identity, according to Scott, is that it is exclusionary. That is most obvious in the case of the hegemonic assertion of a unified American identity to which all sub-cultures are supposed to assimilate on pain of being considered un-American. But it is equally true, argues Scott, of the specification of the supposedly unitary identity of so-called "subalterns," that is, members of subordinate groups that continue to suffer from discrimination, as the privileged experience or position from which to utter the Truth:

> The exclusionary implications . . . are twofold: all those not of the group are denied even intellectual access to it, and those within the group whose experiences or interpretations do not conform to the established terms of identity must either suppress their views or drop out. An appeal to "experience" of this kind forecloses discussion and criticism, and turns politics into a policing operation: the borders of identity are patrolled for signs of non-conformity; the test of membership in a group becomes less one's willingness to endorse certain principles and engage in specific political actions . . . than one's ability to use the prescribed languages that are taken as signs that one is inherently "of" the group. That all of this is not recognized as a highly political process is troubling indeed, especially because it so closely mimics the politics of the powerful, naturalizing and deeming as discernably objective facts the prerequisites for inclusion in any group.[18]

As against this process of "naturalizing" or "essentializing" identity groups, Scott—clearly influenced by Foucault—proposes that these identity groups are produced by the very power relations against which their members seem to struggle. Referring to a New York State report on multicultural education, Scott notes that "the report assumes that people are discriminated against *because* they are already different, when in fact . . . it is the other way around: difference and the salience of group identities are produced by discrimination."[19] In other words, rather than assume that the identity of people as Black, Women, Gay, etc. precedes the discrimination that is visited on them, we should understand that it is precisely the discrimination from which they suffer that gives rise to a sense of having a Black, Feminist, Gay identity in the first place. According to Scott, one of the virtues of this "alternative strategy—to historicize the question of identity—is . . . to call into question the autonomy and stability of any particular identity as it claims to define and interpret a subject's existence."[20] It is, in short, a conceptual strategy designed to combat what she believes, as we have seen, are the inevitably exclusionary effects of the "essentializing" accounts she contests.

However it would also appear to be a conceptual strategy that undermines the possibility of progressive political organization on the basis of group identity. Scott appears to assume that if an identity group is the consequence of the problem of, for example, racism, sexism, or homophobia, then it can't possibly be part of the solution to racism, sexism, or homophobia. Indeed, she calls "for a more complicated strategy than organizing political campaigns around identity groups," which, she concludes, might "in the current context [she is writing in 1995] in this country at least . . . be all to the good."[21]

I have space for only two quick rejoinders to Scott's provocative but I think overstated argument. First, the mere fact that group identities are created in response to a history of discrimination in and of itself says nothing about whether or not those identities and the sensibilities associated with them can serve as reliable sources for effective resistance to the discrimination from which the members of those groups suffer. It all depends, it seems to me, on the precise nature of those identities and sensibilities: if those sensibilities are infused with envy and what Nietzsche called *ressentiment*—if in other words the identity of the subordinate group is defined *against* the identity of the dominant group and thus is merely its mirror image—then political organization on the basis of that identity can come to nothing good. But if the sensibilities of the identity group are generous and loving—if the members of the group have learned over generations that to *be* a member of the group *means* to reject relations of domination and subordination rather than merely to exchange places with the dominant—then I see no reason why organization on the basis of *that* identity should be considered suspect. Second, and relatedly, if the shared identity of the group is an essentially loving, generous one, then I see no reason why we should assume that that identity is necessarily "exclusionary." Why can't a sense of what all group members have in common go hand in hand with respect for the differences that otherwise exist within the group? I will come back to this question again in the context of my specific examinations of racial, gender, national, and religious identity in the next four chapters, as well as in Part IV. The point I am making now is that I do not think it is either logically necessary or politically helpful to react—as Scott reacts—to the undeniable and unfortunate excesses of *some* identity politics by dismissing identity politics in its entirety.

In *The Twilight of Common Dreams* Todd Gitlin also dismisses identity politics, but for different reasons. Whereas, as we have seen, Scott is principally concerned with its *internal* exclusionary effects, Gitlin is troubled by what might be called its *external* exclusionary effects, that is, with the way in which particular "identity obsessions"[22]—the term is his—prevent people with different racial, sexual, ethnic, or religious identities from becoming aware of, and uniting on behalf of, what they have in *common*—namely, according to him, an interest in reducing the escalating economic inequality from which almost all of them suffer. "It is [the] mobilization for equality and against arbitrary power that is the Left's main business," but, he insists, "the mind-set of identity politics . . . aborts the necessary discussion . . . the obsession with difference stands in the way of asking the right questions," that is, questions about how it might be possible to make the economy work more equitably and democratically. The consequence of "affirming the virtues of the margins," he continues, is that "identity politics has left the centers of power uncontested."[23] In short, identity politics deflects political attention away from the reality of *class* rule and thus helps to reproduce it.

I think there is some truth in this critique, but I also think that the implicit assumption that underlies it—namely that economic interests are more important than group identities—is both undefended by Gitlin and difficult to defend. People need bread in order to live, but—as the saying goes—"man does not live by bread alone." The modern translation would be: people need both redistribution *and* recognition. A Left that realized this and organized around it might truly be a force to be reckoned with.[24]

21

GENDER IDENTITY

In the last chapter we became familiar with the general debate over the merits and limits of identity politics, the debate between such scholars as Charles Taylor, who emphasize the importance of politically recognizing and accommodating group identities, and those, such as Joan Scott and Todd Gitlin, who argue that a politics organized around those identities is necessarily either exclusionary or diversionary. In this chapter I examine how this debate plays out in the specific context of the issue of gender identity. As we shall see, Carol Gilligan in her *In a Different Voice* argues that there is a fundamental difference between the way women and men think about moral questions related to an equally fundamental difference in their early experience within the family. Against this claim that women have, in effect, a distinct identity, Nancy Fraser and Linda Nicholson argue in "Social Criticism without Philosophy" that this and other so-called "essentialist" claims are philosophically and political suspect, and that feminist scholars must therefore avoid making them. Finally, Susan Bordo in "Feminism, Postmodernism, and Gender-Scepticism" will take Fraser and Nicholson to task for laying down an "anti-essentialist" law that arbitrarily rules out of court even the possibility that some generalizations about gender might be correct and that thus dogmatically deprives feminist scholars of the intellectual weapons they require.

In her widely read *In a Different Voice* Carol Gilligan argues that her in-depth interviews with both women and men demonstrate that the moral "voice" of women is radically different from the moral "voice" of men. Men, she argues, tend to approach moral issues—such as the issue of whether someone without money should steal a drug that is necessary to save the life of a family member—by assuming an inevitable conflict of interest and relying on abstract, general principles in order to resolve the conflict—in this case, for example, the principle that the right to life is more important than the right to property and that the individual therefore has a right to steal the drug. Women, in contrast, according to Gilligan, typically assume that moral problems arise from the breakdown of relationships—in this case the relationship between the pharmacist and the impoverished individual—and that the solution to the moral problem therefore requires a restoration of that relationship—in this case, perhaps, a conversation between the individual and the pharmacist that might lead to an agreement that the latter willingly give the drug to the former in return for some work that he or she might subsequently do at the pharmacy.

This preoccupation with the restoration of relationships requires that women pay close attention to the concrete needs of particular individuals, the very context from which men abstract in their effort to arrive at the general principles that are supposed to arbitrate what are assumed to be inevitably conflicting claims or rights. Thus Gilligan contrasts what she calls the disproportionately female "ethic of care" (or "morality of responsibility") with a disproportionately male "ethic of rights," and she argues that psychologists from Freud to Lawrence Kohlberg who identify abstract principled moral thinking as the highest level of moral development have illegitimately equated what is in fact a distinctively masculine mode of moral thinking with moral thinking in general, thus transforming—in characteristically patriarchal, male-dominant fashion—a different, equally legitimate mode of moral reasoning into an inferior female version of the male mode.[1]

Gilligan argues that the difference between the male "ethic of rights" and the "female ethic of care" is the inevitable result of "the fact"—and here she quotes Nancy Chodorow, the author of the enormously influential *The Reproduction of Mothering*—"that women, universally, are largely responsible for early child care."[2] Under these conditions the development of the gender identity of girls and boys takes a different path. Girls are initially identified with someone of the same sex—their mother—and thus the development of their gendered sense of self is consistent with, and can be based on, that initial identification or sense of oneness with their mother. They can tell themselves, in effect, I am a female like my mother. This persistent identification with the mother, moreover, is reinforced by the fact that "mothers tend to experience their daughter as more like, and continuous with, themselves"[3] and therefore treat them accordingly. For both reasons girls are likely to experience an intimate relationship with first the mother, and then others in general, as essential for the completion of their sense of self.

It is otherwise for the boy. Like the girl, the boy is initially identified with the mother, on whom he too is entirely dependent in his earliest life. But, unlike the girl, the boy ultimately comes to experience his initial female identification as incompatible with his emerging, bodily based sense of himself as male. Thus he must dis-identify from his mother—must deny his sense of being like her—in order to become a "man." He must tell himself "I am a man *unlike* my mother." This internal pull toward dis-identification, moreover, is likely to be accompanied by an external push from his mother, who experiences him as different from herself and is therefore far more motivated to encourage his separation from her than her daughter's.[4] Thus for both internal and external reasons the boy is likely to define his first intimate relationship—and subsequent intimate relationships as well—as incompatible with his gendered sense of self. As Gilligan summarizes Chodorow's conclusions:

For boys and men, separation and individuation are critically tied to gender identity since separation from the mother is essential for the development of masculinity. For girls and women, issues of femininity or feminine identity do not depend on the achievement of separation from the mother or on the progress of individuation. Since masculinity is defined through separation while femininity is defined through attachment, male gender identity is threatened by intimacy while female gender identity is threatened by separation.[5]

In other words—and this Chodorowian claim has long since become a staple of supposed commonsense thinking about gender—women are more "relational" than men and men are more "oppositional" than women.[6] It is this difference, Gilligan argues, that is reflected in the difference between the moral thinking of women and men: "relational" women are far more likely to problematize the breakdown of relationships than men and thus far more likely to propose moral solutions that are designed to repair broken relationships, whereas "oppositional" men are far more likely to assume an inevitable opposition between competing parties and thus to elaborate abstract, formal rules designed to resolve that opposition. In short, "the morality of rights differs from the morality of responsibility in its emphasis on separation rather than connection."[7]

As I have already suggested, Gilligan's gender generalizations are called into question by Fraser and Nicholson. They claim that "to the extent that [Gilligan] described women's moral development in terms of *a* different voice; to the extent that she did not specify which women, under which historical circumstances have spoken with the voice in question; and to the extent that she grounded her analysis in the explicitly cross-cultural framework of Nancy Chodorow, her model remained 'essentialist.'"[8] By "essentialism," as this last sentence indicates, Fraser and Nicholson mean (in this context) any theoretical approach that is based on the assumption that there is a single, unchanging, a-historical essence to what it means either to be a woman or a man. Thus Gilligan's theory is essentialist because it assumes that there is a unitary female and a unitary male moral voice, and the Chodorowian theory on which Gilligan relies for an explanation of the difference in these two moral voices is essentialist because it assumes that "relationality" is an essential feature of what it means to be a woman and "oppositionality" is an essential feature of what it means to be a man.

According to Fraser and Nicholson these essentialist assumptions are both conceptually and politically problematical. Conceptually problematical:

[F]or a theorist to use such categories to construct a universalistic social theory [i.e., a theory that purports to be true in all places and all times] is to risk projecting the socially dominant conjunctions and dispersions of her own society onto others, thereby distorting important features of both.[9]

Thus they claim that Chodorow's assumption that women are "relational" transforms the specific historical fact that "many women in modern Western societies have been expected to exhibit strong concern with . . . types of interactions associated with intimacy, friendship, and love" into a universal female orientation, an orientation that, they *assume*, simply did not exist prior to the birth of the "notion of private life specific to modern Western societies of the last two centuries." Rather than employ inevitably historical categories that—like Chodorow's—falsely claim universality, social theorists should *historicize* any and all theoretical categories that pretend to universality and undermine their claims to universality in the process: "Social theorists would do better . . . to construct genealogies of [their] *categories* . . . before assuming their universal significance,"[10] that is, they should identify the specific historical conditions that have made it possible to conceptualize a single gender identity (or any other unitary group identity), rather than assume the universal—cross-cultural and trans-historical—"truth" of that category.

According to Fraser and Nicholson, the failure to historicize the category of gender identity also creates political problems:

> While gender identity gives substance to the idea of sisterhood, it does so at the cost of repressing differences among sisters. Although the theory allows for some differences among women of different classes, races, sexual orientations, and ethnic groups, it construes them as subsidiary to more basic similarities. But it is precisely as a consequence of the request to understand such differences as secondary that many women have denied an allegiance to feminism.[11]

Here Fraser and Nicholson allude to the critique of "essentialist" feminism made by women of color, of different cultures, of different sexual orientations, and so forth, namely that they do not find that their own experience is adequately reflected in the general category of "woman" to which that feminism attaches overriding importance. Black women, it is argued, experience a fundamentally different reality from white women; poor women a radically different condition from rich women; third world women a very different set of circumstances from first world women; gay women inhabit a social world that is qualitatively different from straight women; and so on. Thus the general category of "woman" is exclusionary in the sense that it marginalizes the experience of those women whose experience does not fit that general theoretical category. This marginalization obviously makes the feminist movement far less attractive to black women, gay women, poor women, third world women, etc. than it would otherwise be.

The post-modernist theoretical strategy—post-modernist because it is committed to calling into question, rather than *proving* or verifying, universalistic truth-claims—recommended by Fraser and Nicholson is designed to remedy this political problem. It is designed to harmonize with the fact that, given the very different interests of the very different women to which I have just referred, contemporary feminist political practice

> is increasingly a matter of alliances rather than one of unity around a universally shared interest or identity . . . Thus, the underlying premise of this practice is that, while some women share some common interests and face common enemies, such commonalities are by no means universal; rather they are interlaced with differences, even with conflicts. This, then, is a practice made up of a patchwork of overlapping alliances, not one circumscribable by an essential definition.[12]

It follows, according to Fraser and Nicholson, that an anti-essentialist feminist theory that is sensitive to historical and cultural differences among women and refuses to subordinate those differences to the unitary category of "women" is likely to be far more useful for contemporary feminist practice than the essentialist theories that are the object of their critique.

But it seems to me—and to Susan Bordo—that there is something both conceptually and politically dogmatic about that critique. To begin with, although it is certainly true that so-called essentialist gender generalizations *may* turn out to be unfounded, and probably also true that some of them *have* been shown to be incorrect, it is another matter entirely to argue, as Fraser and Nicholson argue, that they are *by definition* theoretically suspect. Whether any given gender generalization is correct or not should be treated as an entirely open *empirical* question, namely a question for which only historical and cross-cultural research can provide the answer. Consider once again Chodorow's theoretical hypothesis that the (purportedly universal) fact that women are more relational than men and men are more oppositional than women is a consequence of the fact that women have always been the primary care givers of both very young girls and very young boys. It is in fact the case, anthropologists tells us, that in all cultures, women—either the biological mother or one or more female mother-substitutes—have been disproportionately responsible for the care of children under the age of three or four,[13] and it *may* in fact also be the case that in all cultures women are more relational (in Chodorow's sense) than men. Once again, only historical and cross-cultural research can determine whether Chodorow's hypothesis is correct or whether Fraser and Nicholson's alternative hypothesis, namely that women's greater relationality holds only under specifically modern Western conditions, is correct. The problem, however, is that Fraser and Nicholson do not treat their alternative as an hypothesis that—like Chodorow's—might turn out either to be right or wrong. Rather they assume its truth—"*surely*," they write, female relationality "presupposes a notion of private life specific to modern Western societies of the last two centuries"[14]—just as they assume the untruth of the Chodorowian hypothesis they (prematurely) reject.

To put this another way, unless we *assume*—in advance of an empirical investigation of the historical and cultural facts—that all universal gender generalizations are incorrect, what grounds are there for insisting that social theorists *should* "construct genealogies" of their theoretical categories rather than test them for their truth by attempting to see whether they fit the cross-cultural and trans-historical facts? Fraser and Nicholson's insistence that the former intellectual strategy is preferable to the latter strikes me—as it does Susan Bordo—as not only intellectually arbitrary but intellectually authoritarian, which is what Bordo argues when she criticizes them for "legislating the appropriate terms of all intellectual efforts . . . determining who is going astray and who is on the right track."[15] Bordo also argues, correctly to my mind, that Fraser and Nicholson's methodology, "which eschews generalizations about gender on *a priori* [that is, prior to empirical investigation] grounds, is in danger of discrediting and disabling certain kinds of feminist cultural critique."[16] She reminds Fraser and Nicholson that, even though some women are obviously more privileged than others, "*all* of us, as women, also occupy subordinate positions, positions in which we feel ignored or denigrated."[17] An extreme but all too frequent example of this denigration is the fact—the cross-culturally universal fact—that women are raped by men and that all women—rich or poor, gay or straight, third world or first world, and so on—are therefore obliged, at least on some level, to contend with that terrifying possibility. Fraser and Nicholson's a priori ban on universal gender generalizations would make it impossible for feminist scholars to explore the causes of this and other forms of physical and emotional abuse endured by the world's women.

Bordo also rejects—again correctly I believe—Fraser and Nicholson's claim that a focus on what all women share necessarily leads to the neglect and the marginalization of the differences among them. She acknowledges that "generalizations about gender can obscure and exclude," but insists, once again, that "such determinations cannot be made by methodological fiat but must be decided from context to context."[18] Thus nothing *in principle* prevents generalizations about what women have in common from also recognizing the differences—racial, class, ethnic, etc.—that divide them. In other words, by privileging difference over commonality Fraser and Nicholson apparently fail to understand that commonality and difference can—and should—go hand in hand. Thus there is no reason why poor, black, third world, gay, etc. women should feel excluded by gender generalizations that emphasize what they have in common as long as those generalizations are accompanied by an awareness of what distinguishes them from one another. Indeed, without a notion of gender commonality—of gender identity—it would be impossible to understand the sense of the word "Sisterhood" in the famously empowering phrase of so-called Second Wave Feminism, "Sisterhood is powerful."

Bordo also points out, finally, that there is something contradictory about the insistence of Fraser and Nicholson, as well as other post-modernist feminists, that universal gender generalizations obscure the reality of class, racial, ethnic, etc. differences. To argue, for example, that women are different by virtue of their race is to make an implicit racial generalization, but, if racial generalizations are permitted, why not gender generalizations? Alternatively, if we accept the argument that gender generalizations are *a priori* intellectually illegitimate, then we would also have to discount the possibility of racial as well as all other identity generalizations. As Bordo argues, Fraser and Nicholson's argument,

> although designed to display the fragmented nature of gender, in fact deconstructs race, class and historical coherencies as well. The inflections that modify experience are endless, and *some* item of difference can always be produced which will shatter any proposed generalizations. If generalization is only permitted in the *absence* of multiple inflections or interpretive possibilities, then cultural generalizations of *any* sort—about race, about class, about historical eras—are ruled out.[19]

Taken to its logical conclusion, then, the anti-essentialist, post-modernist feminism of Fraser and Nicholson asserts the impossibility not only of a feminist social science but of social science in general. But the fact that the target of their anti-essentialism is restricted to gender generalizations—the fact that they problematize only feminist knowledge-claims, and problematize them just at that point in history when feminist gender generalizations such as Gilligan's have succeeded in calling masculine knowledge-claims into question—obliges Bordo to ask the question—the question with which I conclude this chapter— "Could feminist gender-scepticism . . . now be operating in the service of the reproduction of . . . male knowledge/power?"[20]

22

RACIAL IDENTITY

W. E. B. Du Bois's classic study, *The Souls of Black Folks*, was published in 1903 and even today remains one of the most influential, widely read works on race and racism in America. The enduring influence, indeed canonical status, of this text was recently confirmed with the publication in 2003 of a volume called *The Souls of Black Folks: One Hundred Years Later*.[1] Many of the essays in that volume focus on Du Bois's simultaneously celebrated and controversial concept of the so-called "double-consciousness" of the American black or African American. To understand what Du Bois means by "double-consciousness," consider what is undoubtedly one of the most frequently cited passages in all of the American literature on race and race relation:

> It is a peculiar sensation, this double-consciousness, this sense of always looking at one's self through the eyes of others, of measuring one's soul by the tape of a world that looks on with amused contempt and pity. One ever feels his two-ness—an American, a Negro; two souls, two thoughts, two unreconciled strivings; two warring ideals in one dark body, whose dogged strength alone keeps it from being torn asunder.[2]

It is important, first of all, to recognize that the "two-ness" or "double-consciousness" from which Du Bois claims American blacks suffer is not merely the result of "always looking through the eyes of others," because, as we have seen, all individuals—at least according to Hegel and Charles Taylor—establish their identities in relationship to the way in which they are recognized by others and thus inevitably view themselves through the eyes of others. What is distinctive about double-consciousness is that it is established by viewing oneself through the eyes of others who "look on in amused contempt and pity," that is, through the eyes of white Americans for whom individual blacks are merely personifications of their white racist stereotypes. This becomes clear when Du Bois refers to "this American world—a world which yields him no true self-consciousness, but only lets himself see himself through the revelation of the other world." And the "revelation of the other world"—what white Americans see in black Americans—is clouded and distorted by a "veil" that not only prevents blacks from entering that world but also prevents the inhabitants of that world—white Americans—from seeing blacks as they really are. In other words, the veil is a veil of (white) ignorance that precludes the possibility of genuinely reciprocal or mutual recognition between whites and blacks and thus "yields [blacks] no true self-consciousness."[3] Thus Du Bois's concept of "double-consciousness" is designed to explain just how difficult—but also, we shall see, just how necessary—is the formation of a stable, undivided African-American identity.

On the one hand, insofar as blacks internalize white racist stereotypes that reflect what Du Bois calls "the all-pervading desire to inculcate disdain for everything black from Toussaint [the leader of the late–eighteenth-century Haitian slave revolt against the French] to the devil," white hatred of blacks is transformed into a debilitating self-hatred that is the very antithesis of "true self-consciousness": "the facing of so vast a prejudice," Du Bois argues, "could not but bring the inevitable self-questioning, self-disparagement, and lowering of ideals which ever accompany repression and breed in an atmosphere of contempt and hate."[4] On the other hand, all too often, from Du Bois's point of view, the reaction of blacks to this "atmosphere of contempt and hate" is an effort to prove to whites that they really are no different from them, that blacks are "as American" as whites. But this "assimilationist" impulse, however understandable, comes at the price of a denial of valuable cultural difference, the repudiation of the distinctive qualities of American blacks—Du Bois mentions their egalitarian commitments, their musical contributions, their sense of humor, and their spirituality—that have been cultivated under the harsh conditions of slavery and Jim Crow and that are ultimately rooted in mother Africa.[5] And, even if assimilation or the loss of the African half of the self were worth this price—which Du Bois denies—it is a goal that is likely to remain elusive in the face of white racist stereotypes that, like all stereotypes, are notoriously resistant to the intrusion of reality.

This resistance on the part of whites to the assimilationist efforts of blacks, in turn, often gives rise to a repudiation of integration in the name of a cultural nationalism, separatism, or Afro-centrism that valorizes, or even claims superiority for, the very cultural differences that are denigrated in the white racial imaginary. But this privileging of the African half of the black self comes at the cost of the denial or at least the underestimation of the importance of the American half of that self, a failure to appreciate the fact that, as Du Bois points out, "before the Pilgrims landed we were here";[6] in other words, that African Americans really *are* Americans who helped build America and who identify with the best—including the "pure human spirit of the Declaration of Independence"[7]—that America has to offer.

Thus assimilation and cultural nationalism are merely different, polar opposite forms of the "two-ness"—the "two unreconciled strivings"—that plague African Americans. Overcoming two-ness or double-consciousness thus requires a refusal of this fateful either–or—either American *or* African—in favor of an African-American identity that would, as Du Bois puts it, "merge his double self into a better and truer self" and thus fulfill his "longing to attain self-conscious manhood." According to Du Bois:

> In this merging he wishes neither of the older selves to be lost. He would not Africanize America, for America has too much to teach the world and Africa. He would not bleach his Negro soul in a flood of white American-ism, for he knows that Negro blood has a message for the world. He simply wishes to make it possible for a man to be both a Negro and an American, without being cursed and spit upon by his fellows, without having the doors of opportunity closed roughly in his face.[8]

Thus an authentic African-American identity would entail a synthesis—Du Bois too was influenced by Hegel—of the opposing elements of which it is composed. And this synthesis on which the development of an authentic African-American identity depends would also be—as the reference to "Negro blood [that] has a message for the world" implies—a contribution to American society as a whole: the realization of "the ideal of human brotherhood, gained through the unifying ideal of Race." Thus Du Bois looks forward to the day when "on American soil two world-races may give each to each those charac-teristics both so sadly lack."[9]

Notice how the claim that American whites are just as *lacking* as American blacks turns the conceptual and political table on whites who assume that they have everything to teach to, but nothing to learn from, blacks. Du Bois argues, to the contrary, that American whites have much to learn from American blacks:

> We the darker ones come . . . not altogether empty-handed: there are to-day no truer exponents of the pure human spirit of the Declaration of Indepen-dence than the American Negroes; there is no true American music but the wild sweet melodies of the Negro slave; the American fairy tales and folk-lore are Indian and African; and, all in all, we black men seem the sole oasis of simple faith and reverence in a dusty desert of dollars and smart-ness. Will America be poorer if she replace her dyspeptic blundering with light-hearted but determined Negro humility? Or her coarse and cruel wit with loving jovial good humor? Or her vulgar music with the soul of the Sorrow Songs [Negro Spirituals]?[10]

American society, in short, would be a far better society if white Americans were able to grant to black Americans the recognition they are due. Thus Du Bois lifts the veil that prevents white Americans from seeing the "spiritual striv-ings" of black Americans not only in order to liberate blacks but to liberate whites as well. However much the white racist might deny it, the fate of the black race and the fate of the white race are inextricably intertwined.

It is precisely this continuing Du Boisian commitment to the concept of "race" that Anthony Appiah's "The Uncompleted Argument: Du Bois and the

Illusion of Race,"[11] written roughly eighty years after *The Souls of Black Folks*, vigorously contests. Appiah demonstrates that even though Du Bois had doubts as early as 1897—five years before the publication of *Souls*—about the scientific status of the concept of "race," he was never able entirely to free himself from the assumption—for Appiah the fallacious assumption—that racial differences are biologically based. Thus even as Du Bois emphasized the sense in which "Negroes" were a "sociohistorical community"—a group of people united by a common history and culture—he continued to speak in *Souls*, as we have seen, of the message that "Negro *blood* . . . has for the world." As Appiah shows, the idea of "common blood" implies "shared ancestry," which presupposes, in turn, "common features by virtue of a common biology derived from a common descent."[12] But—quite apart from the ambiguity, to which I will return—in the notion of a "common biology," the problem is that this criterion does not in fact correspond to the culturally defined criteria that actually assign people to distinct racial categories. According to those categories, Du Bois was black, but if "common biology" were the criterion for racial assignment then Du Bois, whose mother was African-American and whose father was Dutch, could just as easily have been assigned to the category of what he calls the "Teutonic" race as to the "Negro" race, or perhaps to some "mixed-race" category. That he was nevertheless defined as unambiguously "black" in early twentieth-century America has little if anything to do with biology and everything to do with the so-called "one-drop rule," the arbitrary cultural rule that automatically assigned—and in America generally still (despite the movement to establish an official mixed-race category) defines—someone with *any* African ancestry whatsoever to the category of "black."[13] The effect of this rule is that many people with skin as light and hair as straight as many so-called "whites" will nonetheless be considered "black." This means that so-called "phenotypical" differences—the observable physical differences among different individuals—are not in fact the effective basis for the assignment of those individuals into existing racial categories. The same point is evident when we consider that racial categories often differ dramatically from society to society: under South African Apartheid, for example, people of "mixed" parentage were defined not as "black" but as "colored," which means that people who were physically indistinguishable from light-skinned American "blacks" were assigned to an entirely different racial category from their African-American counterparts. Thus it will not do to argue that "race" is biologically based, if by "biologically based" we mean based on phenotypical differences.

Nor, according to Appiah, are racial categories based on what are called "genotypical" differences, that is, on genetic differences among individuals assigned to different racial categories. He points out that "every reputable biologist will agree that human genetic variability between the populations of Africa or Europe or Asia is not much greater than those within those populations."[14] For example:

the chances of two people who are both Caucasoid [i.e., considered "white"] differing in genetic constitution at one site on a given chromosome are about 14.3 per cent, while, for any two people taken at random from the human population, they are about 14.8 percent.

Thus "the conclusion is obvious: given only a person's race, it is hard to say what his or her biological characteristics will be, except in respect of the 'grosser' features of color, hair and bone,"[15] features that, we have already seen, do not suffice unambiguously to assign people to different races.

Once we realize that "race" is an "illusion"—a cultural construction with no basis in biology—we can complete the argument (remember the title of his essay is "The Uncompleted Argument") that, according to Appiah, Du Bois "never quite managed to complete." That is, we should speak in terms of "civilizations" or "cultures" rather than race:

> The truth is that there are no races: there is nothing in the world that can do all we ask "race" to do for us. The evil that is done is done by the concept and by easy—yet impossible—assumptions as to its applications. What we miss through our obsession with ["race"] is, simply, reality.[16]

The "evil" that is done by the concept of "race" is done through what Appiah calls the "biologizing [of] what *is* culture,"[17] that is, the transformation of what in fact are cultural realities into supposedly natural realities. Cultural realities can be changed whereas natural realities cannot. Thus to equate cultural differences with racial differences is necessarily to suggest that those cultural differences cannot be changed and that it is therefore not even worth trying to change them. Thus does the concept of "race" work to help reproduce the gross cultural inequalities that existed during Du Bois's time and that persist even today. The concept of race, Appiah might say, is inherently racist. It follows that those who are committed to the overcoming of racism should also be committed to the overcoming of racial identity.

This, Eric Lott might say, is easier said than done. He argues in his *Love and Theft*, which is a study of blackface minstrel shows in the first half of the nineteenth century in America, that the immense popularity of this form of entertainment—in which white actors blackened their faces and mimicked the music, jokes, gestures, and speech of blacks—can be understood only if we understand the way in which *white* racial identity was—and still is—defined in ambivalent opposition to the qualities that whites project onto blacks. Whereas most of the earlier studies of blackface condemned it as a demeaning rip-off of black culture by racist whites, Lott argues—as the title of his book implies—that there was both love and theft involved in this form of cultural appropriation. The enormous pleasure that the mainly but not exclusively working-class white audiences experienced as they watched white actors impersonate (what they took to be) the ways of uneducated blacks suggests an intense attraction to those ways that coexisted with the more obviously contemptuous and derisive attitude toward them. Thus Lott claims, perhaps counter-intuitively, that "negrophobia [fear of negroes] and negrophilia [love of negroes] . . . are not at all contradictory."[18]

Negrophobia and negrophilia are "not at all contradictory," according to Lott, because the "store of images and fantasies" contained in the "white Imaginary . . . is virtually constituted by the elements it has attempted to throw off."[19] More specifically, Lott argues that the qualities that whites attribute to blacks—such as prodigious sexuality and aggressive animality—for which blacks are denigrated as less than fully human—are in fact qualities that whites split off from themselves in order to define themselves as more civilized and intelligent than blacks. Thus, by controlling blacks, whites are able indirectly to control the parts of themselves they do not accept. At the same time, however, with blackface whites are temporarily able to recapture the very qualities that they have lost: they are able to experience the intense, transgressive pleasure of vicarious participation in the forbidden ways of the body that their commitment to "whiteness" has prevented them from experiencing directly. But all from a safe and denigrated distance. Thus white attraction to blackface is as much the loving "return of the repressed" as it is the re-enactment of repression.

I close this chapter with a brief reflection on the implications of Lott's insightful analysis for the question of racial identity. We have seen that Appiah argues that racial identity is, in effect, part of the problem of, rather than the solution to, racism: because there is no *real* basis for the category of "race," we should drop this category and speak instead of different "civilizations" or "cultures." But Lott's argument suggests that racial categories serve emotional or psychological functions and that they are not so easily dropped. You can, in other words, talk to people until you are blue in the face about how race and racial identity are "illusions" with no basis in reality but they will continue to believe deeply in these categories as long as they need them to help control parts of themselves that they are unwilling or unable to embrace. This suggests that the overcoming of "race" and "racism" depends on the emotional development of those people who currently believe in race and racism. In the case of racist whites, Lott implies, this would entail the integration of the more physical, embodied dimensions of human existence that they currently split off and project onto blacks. On this account, to conclude, an end to white racism would require that those whites get their emotional act together.

23

NATIONAL IDENTITY

The study of national identity has been dominated of late by the debate between "social constructionist" and "ethnosymbolic" approaches to the study of nations and nationalism. The social constructionist approach emerged in the 1960s and beyond as a reaction against an earlier approach to national identity that is often called "primordialism" or "perennialism." That earlier approach, as its names implied, assumed that the nation was "a given of social existence, a 'primordial' and natural unity of human association outside time."[1] To quote a recent critic, "the primordialist argues that every person carries within him through life 'attachments' derived from place of birth, kinship relationships, religion, language, and social practices that are 'natural' for him,"[2] attachments that are, so to speak, the "organic" basis for the nations that are assumed inevitably to grow out of them. According to the primordialist approach, then, national identity is an essential and therefore inevitable component of what it means to be human.

The social constructionist approach thoroughly repudiates this essentialist assumption: as the name of this approach implies, it argues that the nation and national identity are socially constructed rather than essential or natural political realities. According to Anthony Smith, one of its critics, social constructionism includes the following ideas:

1 "The assumption that nationalism created, and continues to create nations, rather than the opposite."[3] Whereas primordialists assumed that the ideology of nationalism is an expression of pre-existing nations and national identity, social constructionists argue that nations are brought into being by those who are committed to nationalism, that is, to an ideology that assumes

   that the world is divided into nations, each possessing a distinctive character, history and destiny; [that] political power resides solely in the nation, and loyalty to the nation overrides all other obligations; [that] to be "free" human beings must identify with a nation [that has] maximum autonomy; [that] world peace and justice can be built only on a society of autonomous nations.[4]

Unless and until this set of assumptions emerges, spreads, and eventually becomes dominant, nations and national identity simply do not exist. Thus for social constructionists the "nation" is, above all, an *ideological* construction.

2 It is, moreover, a relatively recent construction. For social constructionists such as Benedict Anderson and Ernest Gellner, "nations are recent and novel products of modernity."[5] Almost all nations, they point out, are products of the eighteenth century and later, and presuppose for their existence conditions—such as a capitalist economy, modern time-consciousness, widespread literacy, and formal legal structures—that are specific to the modern era. In other words, we should interpret the term "nation-state" to mean that the (modern) state creates the nation, rather than the nation creates the state.

3 "A view of nations as social constructs and cultural artifacts deliberately engineered by elites."[6] Nationalism is an ideology of modernizing *elites* that serves their modernizing purposes rather than a sentiment that springs up spontaneously among the masses, and so too therefore are the nation and national identity that nationalism engenders.

4 "The idea that nationalists 'invent' and 'imagine' the nation by representing it to the majority through a variety of cultural media and social rituals."[7] The so-called traditions that nations are assumed to re-enact are in fact largely fabricated to serve the instrumental purposes of the modernizing elites; the supposed continuity between the political present and the distant past is invented by elites who often falsify actual history to achieve that end.

Anthony Smith, a proponent of the ethnosymbolist approach, argues that social constructionists (a) dramatically overstate the degree of rupture between the (supposedly) exclusively modern nation and the forms of social life that preceded it, and (b), as a consequence of (a), are unable to explain the intensity of mass support for the nationalist project. As to (a), Smith concedes that most (but not all) nations are modern, post–eighteenth-century realities—prior to that time most people lived within, and were loyal to, small communities, tribal or otherwise, that may or may not have been parts of large empires—but argues that modern nations are almost always based on sentiments and traditions that flourished for hundreds if not thousands of years—what he calls the *longue durée*—in those pre-national communities. This argument turns on the distinction that Smith draws between the ethnic community or what he calls the *ethnie*, on the one hand, and the nation on the other. He defines the *ethnie* as

a named human population with myths of common ancestry, shared historical memories, one or more elements of a shared culture, a link with a homeland, and a measure of solidarity, at least among elites. While *ethnies* share with nations the elements of common name, myths and memory, their center of gravity is different: *ethnies* are defined largely by their ancestry myths and historical memories; nations are defined by the historic territory they occupy and by their mass, public cultures and common laws. A nation must possess a homeland; an *ethnie* need not—hence the phenomenon of diaspora *ethnies*.[8]

This distinction between *ethnie* and nation enables Smith to determine the merits and limits of both the primordialist and social constructionist approaches and thus to forge a kind of synthesis between them. Because ethnic communities are not modern constructions—because they are rooted in historical memory and myths of common ancestry that long antedate the advent of modernity—the primordialists are correct to argue that nations and nationalism presuppose ancient, enduring emotional attachments that are widely shared and seen as entirely "natural." But what the primordialists fail to understand is that the attachments and loyalties that unite members of an *ethnie* are the necessary but *not sufficient* conditions for nations—as the examples of Kurds, Palestinians, and other *ethnies* that lack a defined national territory and associated state demonstrate. *Ethnies* become nations, in other words, only by virtue of successful national projects that create a territorial state with a single economy. This is the relative truth, so to speak, of the social constructionist approach, but that approach errs in its failure to understand that nationalist projects are successful in creating a (stable) nation only if they are able to draw on pre-existing ethnic loyalties that are deeply rooted and enduring rather than the mere invention or fabrication of modernizing elites. To put this another way, as Smith does, neither the primordialists nor the social constructionists understand that "the concept of the nation includes both ethnic and civic elements: shared myths and memories but also common laws, a single economy, a historic territory, and a mass, public culture."[9]

The failure of the social constructionist to recognize the dependence of nations and the nationalist projects that helped to create them on pre-existing, deeply felt, so-called primordial attachments prevents them from understanding why nationalist projects are so successful, why nationalist appeals made by political elites strike such a responsive chord in the underlying population. All the elite efforts to play the nationalist "card," in other words, would come to naught if that game did not resonate profoundly with the needs of the mass of "players" whose support the elites are attempting to mobilize. As Smith argues, "constructing the nation away [which, in effect, is what the social constructionist does] misses the central point about historical nations: their powerfully felt and willed presence, the feeling shared among so many people of belonging to a transgenerational community of history and destiny."[10] Similarly, Smith asks why "should so many people . . . choose to lay down their lives for an elite construct and artifact, even after it has been deconstructed by the postmodernists?," and he argues, correctly to my mind, that constructionists are "unable to grasp . . . the emotional depths of loyalties to historical nations and nationalisms," unable to explain why "human beings [are] prepared to sacrifice their possessions and lives for the 'defense of the motherland' (or fatherland)."[11]

This reference to the language of kinship is worthy of pause. The fact that nations are typically figured in maternal or paternal, that is, in parental, terms, suggests that loyalty to them runs even deeper than Smith is able to fathom. There is, I am suggesting, a connection between the normally taken-for-granted but actually quite peculiar willingness of people to die for their country or nation and the fact that the nation is symbolized as either a mother or a father, in any case as a parent. If we assume—with psychoanalysis—that this linguistic link between nation and parent is a conscious expression of an unconscious experience of the nation as mother or father, then it would follow that the citizen who loves his country and would risk his life to defend it does so unconsciously in order to protect his family, and especially his beloved parents, from harm. From this psychoanalytic perspective the persistence of national identity and loyalty might be considered the persistence of a not-entirely-outgrown need for parental protection. Thus the "pre-existing symbols and cultural ties and sentiments"[12] on which Smith places so much explanatory weight might themselves call for a specifically psycho-dynamic explanation, one however that Smith does not provide.

That psycho-dynamic explanation might have something important to say about a recent debate between Michael Ignatieff and Robert Fine over the possibility of a "benign nationalism." Both Ignatieff and Fine agree that nationalism is often anything but benign—consider all the destruction that has been wrought and all the blood that has been spilled in its name—but Ignatieff is much more optimistic than Fine about the prospects for a so-called civic nationalism that would be free from the more obviously malignant manifestations of nationalism over the past several hundred years. By a "civic nationalism" Ignatieff means a commitment to "a community of equal, rights-bearing citizens, united in patriotic attachments to a shared set of political practices and values."[13] A "patriotic attachment[] to . . . shared . . . practices and values": like nationalists in general, civic nationalists would *love* their country, but, unlike many nationalists, they would love their country only because or insofar as it embodies broadly liberal political principles. Thus the civic nationalist, like all nationalists, claims that a nation is a community of shared *feelings* rather than the culmination of a purely rational social contract, but, unlike the nationalist who is committed to "my country, right or wrong," the civic nationalist seeks to direct and mobilize patriotic feelings exclusively on behalf of political principles that are also rationally defensible. To put this another way, a civic nationalism would detach the ethnosymbolic elements that, Smith argues, have always been one side of national identity from the civic elements that are, according to Smith, its other, equally important side, and would dispense entirely with the former in favor of an exclusive commitment to the latter.

Ignatieff is aware, however, that the distinction between the ethnic and civic dimensions of national identity is a leaky one—he admits that "most 'civic' nationalist societies depend on certain 'ethnic' elements to sustain nationalist commitment; while most 'ethnic' societies ostensibly safeguard a host of 'civic' principles."[14] On the one hand, countries such as Britain that are supposedly "civic" draw important sources of support from what it often assumed to be a unitary "English way of life," and supposedly "ethnic" states such as Croatia do claim to respect constitutional norms and human rights. Since, Ignatieff acknowledges, "most [national] allegiance fuses the two . . . the ideal of differentiating the 'civic' side of nationalism from the 'ethnic' side might seem hopeless." But this would be the case, he goes on to argue, only if "civic nation-states happened to be mono-ethnic or mono-religious in their composition," and "mono-ethnic nation states are now the exception rather than the rule." Under the increasingly common conditions of multicultural nation-states, where "common ethnicity no longer provides the glue which bonds the nation to the state and vice-versa,"[15] it is both possible and necessary to link nationalism exclusively to its civic elements. According to Ignatieff, its "civic elements" include "democracy, accountability, rule of law, procedural fairness [and] opportunity for all." Until "nationalism becomes truly civic" in this sense, "it cannot be benign."[16]

Yet at the same time Ignatieff admits that civic nationalism is itself not necessarily benign. He points out that the history of British, French, and American imperialism reveals that "there is no necessary relation between the 'civic' character of the national identity and peaceful behavior toward foreign nations and neighbours." A messianic drive to export civic values to other parts of the world, we are surely now in a position to understand, can be just as deadly and destructive as the more obviously malignant projects of the ethnic cleansers. Thus Ignatieff acknowledges that " 'civic' . . . doesn't necessarily mean 'benign.'"[17]

But if civic nationalism is not necessarily benign, what then do we make of Ignatieff's claim that unless nationalism becomes truly civic it cannot be benign? What his argument amounts to is the claim that an exclusively civic nationalism is the *necessary but not sufficient* condition for its being benign. In other words, his conclusion is that, whereas all ethnic nationalisms are inherently malignant, only civic nationalism is *potentially* benign. But Ignatieff has nothing to say about what might determine the malignancy or benignity of any given civic nationalism. Thus his argument is vulnerable to the criticism that his ideal of a benign civic nationalism fails to clarify the conditions under which that ideal could actually be realized.

Robert Fine questions whether it *ever* could be realized. He presses some of the very same points that Ignatieff, in effect, makes against his own case on behalf of civic nationalism, including the leaky or muddy distinction between ethnic and civic nationalism and the "violence [that] infuses civic nationalism when it becomes a principle of unlimited, self-expanding power."[18] But unlike Ignatieff his conclusion is not a defense of certain—albeit under-specified— kinds of civic nationalism but rather "that nationalism in all its forms is a danger to human rights, and that the right to have rights must be guaranteed by humanity itself."[19] All nationalism is suspect because "it is a dangerous principle to place feeling and enthusiasm rather than reason at the heart of our political commitments."[20] The danger of all nationalism—civic or otherwise—is that "it attracts us through images of home, hearth, warmth and love, but it displaces emotions which belong to our personal lives onto political life, and thereby robs both of their value"[21] Thus Fine argues on behalf of a rationally based "cosmopolitanism" that echoes Montesquieu's famous insistence that:

> If I knew something useful to my homeland and detrimental to Europe and Humankind, I would consider it a crime . . . All *particular* duties cease when they cannot be accomplished without offending *human* duties . . . The duty of a citizen is a crime when it leads one to forget the duty of *man*.[22]

Although Fine is aware that this kind of cosmopolitanism too—like everything—has its dangers, he applauds its "great virtue of making us think about the limits of every form of nationalism."[23] And for Fine those limits, we have seen, have to do with the fact that nationalism privileges feeling over reason and displaces "emotions which belong to our personal lives onto political life." But here it seems to me we have to ask the following questions: Is there ever pure reason that is not grounded in feeling? Can or should political life ever be purged of emotions that are rooted in our most intimate, and perhaps our earliest, personal lives? If the answer to these questions is, as I think it should be, "no"—if political life is inevitably infused with passions or emotions—then the possibility of a healthy political life would depend decisively on the *quality* of those passions or emotions. This insight re-opens the question of whether a benign national identity—a national identity that was not opposed to but consistent with a cosmopolitan identity, a reconciliation of love of country and commitment to humanity—is possible, and suggests that the realization of this possibility requires the emotional development of those who claim that identity. I will return to this link between emotional development and cultural–political development in the last section of this book.

24

RELIGIOUS IDENTITY

The subject of this, the concluding, chapter of this part, is the relationship between modernity and religious identity. For more than a century and a half, the scholarly consensus has been that this relationship is an inverse one: the *more* modern the society, it is argued, the *less* religious it becomes. This, in a nutshell, is the "secularization thesis," the thesis that the social—and perhaps—individual significance of religion declines along with the modernization of society. This thesis has been challenged recently in the light of both the stubborn persistence of religiosity in the United States and the global resurgence of religious fundamentalism, be it Christian, Jewish, or Islamic. Critics of the secularization thesis who have focused on the case of the United States have argued that the fate of religious movements and institutions has less to do with how modern a society is and more to do with how pluralistic it is, that is, on whether or the extent to which the society allows or encourages religious competition: the more individuals are able to choose among a large number of diverse religious organizations, the argument runs, the more likely are they to affiliate with any particular religious organization and to devote their time and energy to it. Thus, according to the proponents of this position, the presence of religious pluralism in the United States and the relative absence of religious pluralism in many Western European societies explain why religiosity has declined dramatically over the last century in Western Europe yet remains so vibrant in the United States. This so-called "market" approach, in turn, has been called into question on a number of theoretical and empirical grounds, in favor of an updated, somewhat modified version of the secularization thesis. But—as we shall see—it is not clear that either the religious "supply-siders" or the new "secularizationists" can explain the late–twentieth-century–early-twenty-first-century rise of religious fundamentalism. Thus the purpose of this chapter is not only to familiarize you with the debate between them but also to underscore the limits of this debate.

The late–twentieth-century proponents of the secularization thesis—the sociologists Peter Berger, Brian Wilson, and David Martin[1]—are all deeply indebted to nineteenth- and early-twentieth-century social theorists, including

Marx, Weber, and Freud. Even as religion flourished at the time of their writing, each of these master thinkers predicted that it would eventually "wither away." Marx claimed, of course, that religion was the "opium of the people," in the twofold sense of dulling their perception of (bourgeois) reality and making that reality somewhat more bearable than it would otherwise be. It is less well known that he also called religion "the soul of soulless conditions,"[2] by which he meant that religious belief and practice express needs for human solidarity that, as we have seen, he believed could not be satisfied in an alienated capitalist society. It followed, for Marx, that the elimination of capitalist alienation and the creation of a dis-alienated socialist society would eliminate the need for religion. Max Weber argued that modernization entails the instrumentally rational "disenchantment of the world," a world in which questions of ultimate meaning or ends are increasingly supplanted by technical questions or questions of means that squeeze out any room for religious reflection.[3] And Freud also argued that religion and science are inversely related, that even as religion satisfies essentially infantile needs for parental, especially paternal, protection the slow but steady maturation of society, facilitated by the diffusion of psychoanalytic awareness, would eventually enable science to supersede religion.[4]

In the cases of both Marx and Freud—less obviously so in the case of Weber—the predictions of the ultimate demise of religion were accompanied by the assurance that this would be a *good thing*. Belief in God, they assumed, merely reflected the immaturity of Man. Religion did not express universal, genuinely human needs but rather the needs of people in a less than fully human, less than fully rational, society. Thus the early secularization thesis was as much a brief *in favor* of secularization as it was a prediction about its inevitable progression. The late–twentieth-century advocates of the secularization thesis, in contrast, did not necessarily share the normative judgments of Marx and Freud, but, as supposedly more detached, "objective" sociologists, simply argued that mid- and late–twentieth-century religious developments amply confirmed their empirical prediction. Thus they pointed to the steady erosion since the 1960s of church attendance in almost all Western European societies, and to studies that showed that belief in God and life after death in those countries declined significantly in the second half of the twentieth century.[5] Whereas, for example, in 1947, a majority or near-majority (49 percent in the case of two countries) of the citizens of nine Western European democracies professed a belief in an afterlife, by 2001 that belief was shared by a majority of citizens in only *one* of those countries.[6] Similarly, by the end of the twentieth century only about 20 percent of the people in those societies declared that religion was "very important" in their lives.[7] These as well as other related data persuaded the great majority of students of religion that secularization was an established fact. And they tended to *explain* this fact along essentially Weberian lines. What was common to the accounts of Berger, Wilson, and Martin was the argument that industrialization brought with it a series of social changes—the fragmentation of the life-world, the decline of community, the rise of bureaucracy, technological consciousness—that together made religion less arresting and less plausible than it has been in pre-modern societies. That is the conclusion of most social scientists, historians, and church leaders in the Western world.[8]

But this conclusion does not seem to fit the American case. The United States is obviously a modern Western society in which industrialization has brought with it all the social changes referred to in the preceding passage, but religion has clearly *not* become "less arresting and less plausible" in that society. A full 94 percent of Americans surveyed in 2001 professed a belief in God, exactly the same percentage as in 1947. In 2001 somewhat *more* Americans—a full 76 percent—believed in an afterlife than fifty years earlier.[9] Similarly, there has been no overall decline in U.S. church attendance during the period of its decline in Western Europe: as Roger Finke shows in his "An Unsecular America," the decrease in the membership of the "mainline" Protestant denominations since the early 1970s has been matched by an increase in the size of conservative and evangelical churches.[10] In fact Finke shows that rates of religious attendance in the United States are actually *higher* now than they were at the beginning of the twentieth century.[11]

There are also important indications of the increasing *political* significance of religious identity in the United States. Whereas prior to the 1970s presidential candidates were often reluctant to discuss their religious beliefs in public, since that time they have been effectively obliged to wear their faith on their sleeve to have any chance of being nominated or elected. Under the administration of George W. Bush, the wall between church and state was arguably penetrated by religious rhetoric and government funding of "faith-based" initiatives. And "in the 2000 US presidential election . . . religion was by far the strongest predictor of who voted for George W. Bush and who voted for Al Gore."[12] All of these facts clearly call the secularization thesis into question.

So too do the data reported by Finke comparing church attendance in urban and rural areas of the United States. According to the logic of the secularization thesis, rates of religious adherence should be higher in rural areas, since presumably those areas have been less affected by industrialization and its attendant changes than urban areas. But Finke shows that "the results are quite the opposite of what it predicts": since 1890 church attendance in rural areas has *never* been higher than in urban areas, and in 1906 and 1926 attendance was actually *lower* in the countryside than in the cities.[13] Similarly, Finke found no support for the secularization thesis when he examined the relationship between rates of attendance and the percentage of the labor force in manufacturing (in both rural and urban areas): contrary to (what he takes to be) the prediction of the secularization thesis, "the adherence rate *increases* in areas where a higher percentage of the labour force is employed in manufacturing."[14]

In this respect as well, America appears to be a striking exception to the rule of secularization in the West.

Finke's explanation for American "exceptionalism" draws on Tocqueville's observation in *Democracy in America* that religion in that country is so strong precisely because it appears to be so weak. By its apparent weakness Tocqueville meant the constitutionally enforced separation between church and state that prevented churches from directly exercising the political power they exercised in his own and other European countries in the middle of the nineteenth century. But this apparent weakness of American religion, Tocqueville argued, was actually the source of its unparalleled strength: since the different denominations were not allied and identified with particular political parties, they did not have to worry about and defend themselves against the "animosity which the latter excite" and could instead devote their energies entirely to what Tocqueville felt was their proper task, namely "direct[ing] the manners of the community."[15] Consequently religion in the United States was far more powerful in "regulating domestic life" than it was in countries, such as France, where its morally regulatory efforts were burdened by politically motivated anti-religious hostility. And, Tocqueville immediately added, "by regulating domestic life, [religion] regulates the State."[16] Thus the prohibition on a direct political role for religion paradoxically results in its enormous and enduring indirect political influence: "Religion in America takes no direct part in the government of society, but it must nevertheless be regarded as the foremost of the political institutions of that country."[17]

Finke agrees with Tocqueville's claim that religion will flourish when it is separate from and unregulated by the state. Under these conditions, he argues, a variety of religious movements and organizations will compete with one another to satisfy (what he assumes are) the enduring religious needs of the people:

> [The] lack of regulation in the USA leads to a proliferation of new sectarian movements each trying to meet the needs of some segment of the population. And although only a handful of the numerous movements ever become sizeable denominations, their presence forces all denominations to compete for adherents. Moreover, the lack of regulations allows sects to serve as a testing ground for religious innovation. Most will fail, but a few succeed.[18]

Thus a "free market" in religious "products" increases the supply of those products and maximizes the satisfaction of religious "consumers," thus ensuring their loyalty and commitment to the particular religious "producer" of their choice.

As I indicated at the outset of this chapter, this market model has been challenged on both empirical and conceptual grounds. To come first to the empirical problems: the purported correlation between religious diversity or pluralism and religious strength does not seem to hold in many parts of the world other than the United States. On the one hand, there are a number of countries that are now quite religiously pluralistic—such as England—where secularization has nevertheless proceeded apace, where church attendance and religious commitment are quite weak, often as weak as or weaker than in countries where there is *more* state control of religion.[19] On the other hand, there are countries characterized by heavy state regulation or even control of religion that are anything *but* secularized, countries in which religion is far more salient to people's lives than in more religiously pluralistic societies—a number of Middle Eastern countries come immediately to mind, but the same is true of a number of countries in Latin America. The proponents of the market model might respond to this problem by limiting their theory to the West, but in so doing they would of course have to explain why their assumption that religious commitment is a rational choice that is conditioned by the supply of religious "products" applies in the West but not elsewhere in the world.

The conceptual critique questions whether religious commitment can be understood as a "rational choice," whether in the West or anywhere else. The economic explanation of religion is effectively identical to Marvin Harris's materialist explanation for Hindu "cow-love" that we examined in chapter 17, and is therefore vulnerable to the same objection that was raised against Harris. Just as I asked whether it makes sense to assume that Hindu peasant farmers were essentially "economic men" who carefully calculated the costs and benefits of eating their cattle, so we can ask whether the decision to join a particular religious organization is akin to the consumer's decision to purchase one material product rather than another. Isn't this a case of utilitarian or economic thinking run amuck among contemporary sociologists of religion? The defender of the religious market model might respond by arguing that his theoretical assumptions merely reflect the ubiquity, even dominance, of economistic thinking among ordinary modern Western people—that Western Man has in fact become economic Man—and that this is why the model can explain religious adherence in the West but not elsewhere. But religious people in the West, like religious people generally, are religious precisely insofar as they insist on the *limits* of reason, so it seems peculiar, perhaps even perverse, to attempt to reduce their religious commitment—their leap of faith—to a rational economic choice.

These and other problems associated with the market model have encouraged scholars who remain committed to the secularization thesis to modify that thesis in order to account for the American exception on which the "free-marketers" have placed so much explanatory weight. Some of the new "secularizationists" have also argued that a satisfactory account of what is, after all, a disproportionately if not exclusively *European* secularism must also explain why most of the rest of the world is anything but secular. Thus Pippa Norris and Ronald Inglehart in their recent *Sacred and Secular: Religion and Politics Worldwide* advance a version of the secularization thesis that attempts to explain both American "exceptionalism" (relative to Europe) and European "exceptionalism" (relative to most of the non-Western world). Their basic assumption is that religiosity is a response to what they call "existential insecurity," by which they mean vulnerability to risks "ranging from environmental degradation to natural and manmade disasters such as floods, earthquakes, tornadoes, and droughts, as well as . . . disease epidemics, violations of human rights, humanitarian crisis, and poverty."[20] They also assume that these sources of "existential insecurity" are far less prevalent in modern industrial and especially "post-industrial" societies than in less modern or so-called "developing" societies in which "humanity remains at the mercy of inscrutable and uncontrollable natural forces."[21] In the absence of the ability to control those forces, people in poor countries rely on religion—they believe in God—to assuage their anxiety or reduce their existential insecurity. When those natural forces come under "human control,"[22] as they do, according to Norris and Inglehart, in modernized societies, people become far more secure and thus no longer look to God to alleviate their insecurity. This explains, according to Norris and Inglehart, why people are far more religious in the developing world than they are in the modern West. And, because the birth rate in poor religious countries (in part for religiously related reasons) is so much higher than in rich secular countries, *"the world as a whole now has more people with traditional religious views than ever before."*[23] Thus do the decrease in *Western* religiosity and the increase in *global* religiosity go hand-in-hand.

It follows from the logic of Norris and Inglehart's explanation that American religious "exceptionalism" must be the result of an "existential insecurity" that is significantly higher in the Unites States than elsewhere in the Western world. This, indeed, is precisely what they argue:

> Relatively high levels of economic insecurity are experienced by many sectors of U.S. society, despite American affluence, due to the cultural emphasis on the values of personal responsibility, individual achievement, and mistrust of big government, limiting the role of public services and the welfare state for basic matters such as healthcare covering the working population. Many American families, even in the professional middle classes, face risks of unemployment, the dangers of sudden ill health without adequate private medical insurance, vulnerability to becoming a victim of crime, and the problems of paying for long-term care of the elderly. Americans face greater anxieties than citizens in other advanced industrial societies [where there is] an expansive array of welfare services, including comprehensive healthcare, social services, and pensions.[24]

It might be added—although Norris and Inglehart do not add—that the influx of immigrants during the last three decades of the twentieth century from non-industrial countries with strong religious traditions also contributed to the continuing vitality of American religion during that period.[25] This argument might be considered a "friendly amendment" to Norris and Inglehart's theory, since that theory would explain the intense religiosity of those migrants as a result of the high levels of "existential insecurity" that they (supposedly) experienced growing up in their poor country of origin.

Whether Norris and Inglehart's theory offers an adequate explanation for American religious exceptionalism is open to question. It ignores, among other things, the fact that the United States was founded by religiously motivated immigrants, and that for several hundred years religious institutions played a singularly important role in helping to "civilize" the ever-expanding American frontier. It also suffers, it seems to me, from a problematical account of (the sources of) "existential insecurity" that compromises its explanation not only of American exceptionalism but of European exceptionalism as well. According to that account, once again, existential insecurity declines with the advent of modernity and the control over nature that it (supposedly) brings in its wake. But if we recall Anthony Giddens's concept of "manufactured uncertainty," discussed in chapter 19, we have good reason to question this claim. Giddens argues that modernity actually produces *more* contingencies than it eliminates, and that there is "an integral relation between modernity and radical doubt [that] is *existentially troubling* for ordinary individuals."[26] If Giddens is correct, then, there is no good reason to believe that people in modern societies are more existentially secure than in traditional societies. Yet most of them are, at least by all the standard measures, far more secular than their traditional counterparts. This suggests—again if Giddens is right—that we would need a different explanation for secularization than the one offered by Norris and Inglehart.

Finally, and relatedly, it seems to me that Norris and Inglehart's materialist theory of religion cannot explain, and is in fact called into question by, the resurgence of specifically fundamentalist religious movements and institutions throughout the early–twenty-first-century world. By "materialist theory" I mean, in this case, a theory that assumes that religious or spiritual needs are merely a substitute or surrogate for physical or material needs, for what Norris and Inglehart call the "basic conditions of survival."[27] At bottom, their assumption is that people are religious only when their material needs go unmet; when those needs are met they no longer need religion. Thus their theory effectively privileges the material over the spiritual. But this privilege of the material over the spiritual is precisely one that the features of modernity that contemporary fundamentalists—be they Christian, Jewish, or Islamic—find so profoundly offensive. Is it possible for a theory that starts from an assumption that fundamentalism rejects to explain the power of a fundamentalism that rejects that assumption?

Of course fundamentalists reject many other features of modernity as well—including the equality of women and the free expression of personal and political beliefs. Those of us who are committed to these features of modernity but share fundamentalism's distaste for its materialism are therefore obliged to think through the possibility of a synthesis—a "third way"—that would incorporate the virtues and leave behind the vices of both the modern and the traditional worlds. I have adumbrated this synthesis at a number of earlier points in this book and will flesh it out in my concluding chapter. Whether this synthesis would be sufficient to defuse the many and all too deadly dangers of a militant fundamentalism is unclear. But what is clear, at least to me, is that it—or something like it—is the only thing that could.

Part IV

CONCLUSION

INTRODUCTION

The first three parts of this book have left us with large and as yet unresolved questions concerning the nature of human beings and their relationships with the other beings with which they share the planet. What does it mean to be a human *subject*, both in relation to other people and in relation to the world to which the human subject belongs? These are the two interrelated questions that I attempt to answer in the concluding part of this book. In this Introduction to Part IV I pave the way for that attempt by reviewing the many ways in which these two questions have forced themselves onto our attention in the course of the previous twenty-four chapters.

Let me begin with the question of the nature of human relationships. In fact competing claims about the nature of these relationships resonate throughout the first three parts of this book. On the one side we have frequently encountered the claim that individual passions are inevitably self-seeking, compelling, or at least inclining people to experience other people as mere means to, or as obstacles that inevitably impede their successful pursuit of, selfish advantage. Hobbes's claim, referenced in chapter 1, that by nature humans seek ever greater power over others was echoed in chapter 2 both by Montesquieu's assumption that "every man invested with power is apt to abuse it" and by Madison's claim that "power is of an encroaching nature." It was, you will recall, Madison's distrust of the passions that led him to argue either (in *Federalist 49*) that those passions should be regulated by a government that is (somehow) committed to reason or (in *Federalist 51*) that conflicting passions should be arranged in such a way that, in effect, they cancel themselves out. This latter argument was renewed in chapter 6, in which, starting from the assumption that the "latent causes of faction are . . . sown in the nature of man," Madison in *Federalist 10* recommends the multiplicity of competing factions in an "extended" republic as the antidote to the formation of an organized and effective majority faction and thus as the only guarantee that the public interest will prevail.

Madison's argument in *Federalist 10* was, in effect, the political analogue of the economic argument of Adam Smith that we encountered in chapter 9. You will remember that Smith argued that the "hidden hand" of the market guaranteed that the general interest would (normally) be the unintended consequence of the universal pursuit of economic self-interest, that is, of individual material gain or profit. We also saw that Smith's argument about the virtues of self-interest became the assumption underlying both the Friedmans' and Hayek's case (in chapters 10 and 11, respectively) against the (supposed) vices of governmental regulation and redistribution.

On the other side, we have seen that the primacy of "possessive individualism"[1] was challenged in many of the same chapters in which it was proposed. In chapters 2 and 4 we encountered Rousseau's claim that a society that is a mere collection of selfish individuals is not really a human society at all. Thus a state that merely regulates or moderates the pursuit of selfish interests cannot be legitimate. In a genuinely good society individuals would be united by a social bond formed by the *common* interest that they share, and "it is uniquely on the basis of this common interest that society ought to be governed." Thus for Rousseau the only legitimate state is one in which individuals transcend self-interest in favor of a commitment to the general interest and thereby function as *citizens* rather than merely private persons. We also saw in chapter 4 that Rousseau's rejection of a state based on self-interest was echoed in Benjamin Barber's disdain for politics as "zoo keeping." Rousseau's commitment to an "elevating" citizenship was renewed in Barber's brief on behalf of a "strong democracy" in which citizens develop their faculties and sensibilities in the course of their common deliberations. And this critique of the politics of self-interest in favor of a "civic republican" celebration of a "thicker," active citizenship was paralleled in chapter 16 in the form of Hannah Arendt's critique of the "command–obedience" concept of power in the name of a power based on a mutual agreement that enables people to act in concert.

Similarly, we have seen that the Smithian assumption that individuals are above all motivated by material gain was challenged in a number of different ways by Polanyi, Marx, and John Rawls. Polanyi argued that material gain was not in fact the principal passion motivating production until the nineteenth century. Prior to that time, "man's economy [was] submerged in his social relationships" and the individual acted "so as to safeguard his social standing, his social claims, his social assets and value[d] material goods only insofar as they serve this end." Thus capitalism ushered in a "great transformation" that substituted the motive of material gain for the more obviously social motives that prevailed in pre-market societies. Marx characterized this transformation as the emergence of a system of wage labor that alienated individuals from their simultaneously creative and social natures, and envisioned yet another "great transformation" through which individuals would come to affirm, rather than deny, their mutual dependence. For Marx, in other words, the individual is a social being whose freedom is a function of the quality of the social relationships in which he is engaged. We have seen, finally, that, although Rawls tried to demonstrate that the "difference principle" (and the justification for redistribution it provides) would be supported by individuals who are "mutually disinterested," he also argued that the difference principle expresses a "conception of reciprocity" and an application of the idea of "fraternity." Thus even as Rawls's concept of justice pays tribute to material self-interest it appeals to motives—more social motives—that transcend it.

There are considerable merits *and* limits to both sides of the debate I have just reviewed. The partisans of "social man" are correct to insist that a society that rewards egotism and competition is an historically and culturally specific exception to a more general rule of societies that privilege dependence on and cooperation with others, and that an awareness of these (more often than not) earlier and more "social" societies compels us to question the complacent equation of what currently exists with what always *must be*. The vision of a future society to which they are either explicitly or implicitly committed, moreover, has much to recommend it. But the partisans of "social" man, in my judgment, simply have no convincing way to explain why the motivations and behavior of actually existing individuals depart so dramatically from that vision. We saw, for example, that Marx's claim that egotistical individuals and competitive social relationships are the product of alienated labor begs the question why human beings who are supposedly social in nature would have ever created a society that so encourages a-social or even anti-social behavior. To answer this question, I suggested at the end of chapter 10, would require that we modify Marx's (as well as other thinkers') insistence on the sunny side of human nature with an appreciation of its darker side as well.

A capitalist society, moreover, is by no means the only society divided by this darker side. As Marx himself emphasized, capitalist societies are only one species of a broader genus of class societies, and competitive relationships based on individual egotism are only one historical form of universal or near-universal relationships of domination and subordination. Most—if not all—of the more "social" societies, in other words, have been societies in which one person or group of persons exercises power *over* others. Even Polanyi's societies based on gift-exchange are no exception to this general rule. The "Big Man" of Polynesian tribal societies, you will recall, became "big" precisely because he was able to give more away to others than anyone else, securing their indebtedness to him in the process. The general point is that—however much we might be attracted by the vision of a society based on mutual empowerment—we are obliged to acknowledge that for most of human history power relationships have been anything but mutual. And we need to understand *why* this is the case if the vision to which we are attracted is to become anything but a vain hope. Dreams of solidarity will never become reality unless we understand why they have been for so long deferred. In short, if we want to grasp the possibilities of liberation we need to plumb the depths of domination.

Here the (supposedly more "realistic") partisans of egoism are of some help. Although the authors we have reviewed characteristically conflate domination with the specifically capitalist (i.e., individualistic) form thereof, at least they look with clear eyes at the persistent tendency of people to exercise power over others. They teach us that any adequate theory of human nature must make room for that tendency, and their dedication to institutions that are designed to contain it reminds us that *any* future society no matter how different from the current one must forever be on guard against it. In the light of history it would be foolish not to be properly skeptical about dreams of a better world. Yet one can be skeptical and hopeful at the same time. But cynicism kills hope, and cynicism (about the possibility of a different world) is exactly what the ostensibly "realistic" partisans of egoism preach. That, moreover, is not their only problem, for even in this world there are elements of compassion and mutual empowerment that their one-sided focus does not allow them to acknowledge. If we want both to look beyond this world and to discern the elements of the new one already present within it, it is to the partisans of "social man" that we must turn.

The foregoing suggests that we need a synthesis that overcomes the opposition between the partisans of social man and the partisans of egoistic man. As I explained in earlier chapters, by a synthesis I mean a theory that incorporates the merits and leaves behind the limits of each of the elements out of which it is developed. We need an account of human nature that does justice to both the brighter and the darker sides of the human condition. For that account I turn in Part IV to the psychoanalytic assumptions of Melanie Klein and her followers.

As we shall see, Klein assumes that by nature all human beings are motivated *both* by loving or compassionate *and* by hostile or envious passions, and that our central emotional challenge is to integrate these conflicting passions in order to sustain realistic and mature relationships with the various important others we encounter. To translate the Kleinian assumption into specifically political terms: the individual whose aggression is tempered by generous, reparative sensibilities is the subject with a well-governed soul, and the subject with a well-governed soul is the person who is willing and able to enter into rewarding relationships of mutual empowerment or reciprocal recognition. The individual with an ill-governed soul, in contrast, is unable to integrate his love and hate and is therefore driven either to demonize or to idealize the others he encounters: suffering the psychology of either the master or the slave, he craves one-sided relationships of recognition in which he either exercises power over others or submits to their exercise of power over him. For Klein, then, the seeds of both the social man and the anti-social man are planted in the soil of the human condition itself.

We shall also see that she helps us understand the conditions that determine which of these seeds will sprout. Whether the child (and then the adult) overcomes or succumbs to the splitting of love and hate depends in important part, she argues, on the type of treatment she receives from the first and most significant other she encounters, namely, for Klein, her mother. But Klein both under-specifies the maternal practices that matter and takes for granted, and therefore fails to consider the consequences of, the fact that the first significant other *is* typically the mother (or female mother-substitute). Thus we will have to look to other thinkers who follow in her footsteps to develop a more complete account of the way in which both the structure and the practices of parenting engender the government of the soul.

This account, when properly modified, will also enable us to resolve some of the unresolved issues from Part III, "Culture and Identity." The opposition between the partisans of a-social man and the partisans of social man in Parts I and II resurfaced in somewhat different guise in Part III. In chapter 20, for example, the question was not whether individual relationships are inevitably self-interested and competitive but rather whether a politics based on *group* identity has necessarily "normalizing" and externally exclusionary consequences. On the one hand, we saw that Charles Taylor argued that group membership is a necessary condition for individual identity and that justice may therefore require public recognition of and support for endangered groups. In effect, Taylor extended the Hegelian model of reciprocal recognition to the relationships among groups, and argued that the state sometimes has an obligation to compensate for the absence of reciprocal group recognition when the survival or even the flourishing of insufficiently recognized groups is at stake. Thus he gave us a (qualified) defense of what has come to be called identity politics.

On the other hand, Joan Scott in that same chapter and then Fraser and Nicholson in the next denounced identity politics and the supposedly "essentialist" claims underlying them as destructive of the integrity of the very individuals on whose behalf these claims are typically made. Scott argued that the multiculturalist critique of an undifferentiated American identity relies on the same "unified concept of identity" that it would appear to contest, proclaiming in the process a norm of authentic (subaltern) group membership that effectively polices "the borders of identity for signs of non-conformity." In response to this danger she asked us to "call into question the autonomy and stability of any particular identity as it claims to define and interpret a subject's existence." This same appeal to individual difference, we saw, was at work in Fraser's and Nicholson's complaint against gender generalizations that (supposedly) deny the variegated reality of the many different individuals who are grouped under the category of "women." And, like Scott, they recommended genealogies of that and other "essentialist" categories that would historicize and destabilize them. Thus, although neither Scott nor Fraser and Nicholson are partisans of a specifically egotistical form of individualism, they are nevertheless committed to the position that theoretical references to a stable "ascriptive" group identity inevitably do violence to the irreducible particularity of the individual subject. It is in this sense, then, that they can be said to defend the individual against the group.

You will perhaps recall that at the end of chapter 20 I argued, against Joan Scott, that there are no good reasons to assume that a politics based on group identity is per se exclusionary or normalizing. Whether struggles for group recognition reproduce the very domination against which they struggle, I suggested, depends decisively on whether the identity claimed by the group is infused with love or poisoned by *ressentiment*. If the identity of the group is a loving or generous one, the commitment to that common identity in no way would negate, but in fact would entail respect for, whatever differences exist among its individual members. Everything depends, in short, on the nature or quality of the identification that binds the members to the group. And, just as Klein will help us understand whether and why the predominant passions of the individual are benign or malign, so the extension of her account to the analysis of groups can go a long way to clarifying the conditions under which the emotions that hold the group together encourage or discourage respectful relations with other groups as well as with its own members.

The same is true of national identity. We saw in chapter 23 that Robert Fine argued, against Michael Ignatieff, that there is no such thing as a benign nationalism. This argument was based on the assumption that nationalism necessarily "place[s] feeling and enthusiasm rather than reason at the heart of our political commitments." You will remember that I called into question the hierarchical opposition that this assumption establishes between reason and passion in favor of the claim that reason is inevitably infused with passion and that the possibility of a healthy politics therefore depends decisively not on the exclusion, but rather on the *quality*, of those passions. Thus I reopened the possibility of a benign nationalism that Ignatieff proposed but Fine foreclosed, and suggested that the realization of promise of a national identity that was consistent with a cosmopolitan identity was contingent on the emotional development of those who claim that identity. At the same time, I also speculated that at least certain forms of national identity might be based on an essentially infantile need for parental protection. The combination of these two points leads us to the conclusion that a benign nationalism would be an emotional identification with a nation that is no longer an omnipotent parental protector, or, to put this another way, is no longer the object of an idealization that is inevitably purchased at the price of the demonization of enemies of its own making. As I have already intimated, a Kleinian analysis of group development will help us identify the conditions under which this dream of a benign form of nationalism might become a reality.

The debate between Du Bois and Appiah that we reviewed in chapter 22 reproduced in certain respects the contest between the partisans and the critics of identity politics to which I have just referred. As we saw, Du Bois affirmed, whereas Appiah attempted to deconstruct, the notion of an authentic African-American racial identity. Whereas for Du Bois that racial identity would be a synthesis of the best that America and Africa have to offer the world, for Appiah the very idea of a racial identity trades on a decidedly problematical concept of "race" that is, for him, part of the problem of racism rather than the basis for its solution. You will recall that I argued that Appiah's deconstruction of the concept of race only postpones the problem of why people continue to cling to (what he takes to be) such a thoroughly discredited concept; the racist white American for whom that concept satisfies deep-seated emotional needs is hardly likely to follow Appiah's advice that the concept be "dropped." Following Eric Lott, I suggested that racist fantasies enable whites to control parts of themselves that they are unwilling or unable to embrace, and that only an emotional development that enabled whites to embrace those rejected parts that are currently split off and projected onto blacks would consign those fantasies to the death they deserve. This was already an implicitly Kleinian treatment of the problem of racial identity, one that points to the more explicit and somewhat more detailed account I offer in Part IV.

Chapter 24 on religious identity, finally, brings us to the second large issue left unresolved in the first three parts of this book: the relationship between human beings and the other beings with which they share the planet. In that chapter (as well as in chapters 14 and 18), you will remember, I speculated about the possibility of an alternative, "resacralized" modernity that would incorporate the virtues and reject the vices of both the actually existing modernity and its fundamentalist antagonist. In a resacralized modernity, I suggested, relationships between humans and (non-human) nature would be as reverential as those that prevail in many traditional societies, even as the relationships among human beings would be as tolerant, equal, and unrestricted as they are (at least in principle) in most modern societies. The commitment to overcome the domination of "man" over man, in other words, should be complemented by a commitment to overcome the domination of man over nature. This commitment points to the need for an account of the domination of nature that can clarify the conditions under which that domination could be overcome. We shall see in Part IV that an extension of a Kleinian theory of human nature to the relationship between human beings and nature can help satisfy the need for that account.

25

THE SUBJECT

I argued in the introduction to this section that we need a theory of human nature that explains the persistence of human domination even as it clarifies the possibilities for human liberation. What is required, in other words, is an account of what it means to be a human subject that rejects both the unwarranted cynicism of the proponents of a-social man and the ungrounded utopianism of the partisans of social man in favor of a synthesis that satisfies both the social and the a-social sides of the human condition. I also claimed that this simultaneously realistic and optimistic synthesis can be derived from the psychoanalytic assumptions of Melanie Klein. It is now time to make good on this claim.

Freud had located the Oedipal triangle as the crucible in which the self is shaped: the child—or at least the male child, who serves as the model child in what was later challenged as Freud's "phallocentric" account—loves the mother, whom he wants to monopolize, hates the father for enforcing the prohibition on incest, and eventually resolves this Oedipal conflict by internalizing the paternal prohibition in the form of a harsh "superego." Thus for Freud it is the father who represents civilization against the erotic impulses of the child—what he called the "reality principle" against the "pleasure principle"—and it is on the identification with the father that the reproduction of civilization depends.

For Klein, in contrast, it is the *mother* who enforces both the pleasure principle *and* the reality principle. Even a mother who is deeply dedicated to satisfying the imperious oral and other needs of her infant necessarily frustrates those needs as well. Thus—long before the father typically enters the scene— it is the mother who becomes the target of both the infant's love and its rage (Klein assumes that maternal gratification and frustration only reinforce innate libidinal and aggressive impulses, or what the later Freud called the life and death drives, but most contemporary analysts influenced by Klein have jettisoned this assumption). But in its earliest months the infant is unaware that the source of its dramatically different sensations of pleasure and pain is one and the same person. Lacking what cognitive developmental psychologists call "object permanence," the infant, Klein inferred from her pioneering analysis of young children, imagines both a "good breast" and a "bad breast" as separate sources of the antithetical experiences of blissful maternal presence and terrifying maternal absence. She also argues that the infant reacts to its otherwise self-destructive rage by projecting it onto the "bad breast," against whose imagined aggression the infant protects itself with further imaginary attacks. Thus Klein calls this initial infantile emotional position the "paranoid-schizoid" position: schizoid because the infant's experience of reality is radically split between an all-good and an all-bad "object," paranoid because its rage against the latter is felt as coming from the outside rather than from within the infant itself.

When the infant acquires object permanence (Klein locates this as early as the third month of life but we now know that it typically doesn't emerge until the last third or even quarter of the first year[1]), it enters into what she calls the "depressive position," the successful negotiation of which becomes for Klein and those who follow her the chief task on which the emotional development of the child depends. Klein argues that the realization that the mother of gratifica-tion and the mother of frustration—the target of both its worshipful love and its murderous rage—are in fact the same person engenders the terrifying anxiety of having destroyed (in fantasy, but at this point the child makes no distinction between fantasy and reality) the very mother to whom it is so ardently attached and on whom all its feelings of goodness and security depend. This profound "depressive" anxiety, in turn, is normally associated with an equally pronounced sense of guilt. Depressive guilt, according to Klein, entails genuine concern or "pity" for the mother and "remorse" for having harmed her.[2] Thus "depressive" anxiety and guilt will typically induce the child to attempt (first in fantasy and then in reality) to repair the damage to the mother, whose positive responses to these reparative efforts will serve to reassure the child that the mother has, after all, survived his aggression, thus inaugurating a benign cycle of love given in return for love. If all goes well, then, depressive anxiety and guilt are self-limiting, and culminate in the child's recognition that the mother—as well as the self, which Klein assumes is the product of "introjections" of aspects of the mother—is neither all-good nor all-bad and therefore worthy of care.

Thus the Kleinian message is that the child inevitably hurts the one he loves, and that the prospects for a relationship with the mother that is free from debilitating anxiety or guilt will depend on the development of his capacity to repair the damage he has done. Reparative capacities are, in short, the key to the child's rewarding relationship with (first) the mother and (then) the others with whom he will interact. More specifically, the child in whom these reparative capacities are well developed will become the adult who is prepared emotion-ally to endure, even embrace, the ambivalence that lies at the heart of all human relationships and to recognize others (and the self) for the inevitable amalgam of positive and negative qualities they possess. Thus the relationships of mutual empowerment or reciprocal recognition to which the partisans of social man are committed depend decisively on the development of the reparative capaci-ties of first the child and then the adult.

But these reparative capacities, Klein argues, are countered by defensive mechanisms that threaten to destroy them: the child may be tempted to defend against depressive anxiety and guilt in ways that suppress her reparative inclinations and thus permanently postpone the task of integrating her love and hate. Chief among these defenses are "idealization" on the one hand and what Klein calls "manic denial" on the other. Idealization wards off depressive anxiety and guilt through the fantasy of a mother who is too perfect ever to be the object of rage; typically the rage is "split off" and directed against the self and/or others. In this way the child is also able to evade the deeply difficult but necessary task of mourning the loss of the all-good internal mother of the paranoid-schizoid position.

The child who resorts to manic denial—as the name implies—defends against depressive anxiety and guilt by denying any dependence on, or love for, the mother and omnipotently transforming her into an object of contempt and control.[3] Children who succumb to either of these defenses—as well as a number of others—will be plagued as adults by unstable, unrealistic "object relations," alternately idealizing or demonizing the others they encounter and unable to develop or maintain mature relationships with them. More specifically: the child who defends against depressive anxiety and guilt through manic denial typically becomes the "adult" who needs to dominate others, whereas the child who defends against depressive anxiety and guilt through idealization ordinarily becomes the "adult" who needs to be dominated by them. Both lack the well-governed soul of the depressively integrated individual. Their souls are literally split.

Klein argues that most children will eventually negotiate the depressive position more or less successfully, and thus avoid this fate.[4] But she also insists that our hold on the depressive position is vulnerable to the various losses we will inevitably suffer throughout our lives: any significant loss, whether real or intra-psychic, will trigger the paranoid-schizoid tendencies of even the most securely depressively integrated adult and thus confront him with the task of "rebuilding [his] inner world,"[5] that is, of regaining his threatened hold on the depressive position. According to Klein this requires that he mourn his losses rather than defend against them by either idealizing or demonizing what has been lost. Thus the successful negotiation of the depressive position is a difficult and life-long task.

Dorothy Dinnerstein insists that this task is even more difficult than Klein believes. In *The Mermaid and the Minotaur* she argues that (what she somewhat unhappily calls) "mother-dominated child rearing"—the hitherto culturally universal fact that either the mother or a female mother-substitute is disproportionately responsible for the care of very young children—creates a serious *structural* obstacle to the successful negotiation of the depressive position. According to Dinnerstein, the fact that the father (or substitute father) of the mother-raised child is "innocent of the association with the inevitable griefs of infancy," and is therefore available as a "blameless" refuge from the mother, enables both the boy and the girl to "dodge the work of healing the split between good and bad feelings toward the first parent."[6]

The direction of the dodge differs, however, depending on the gender of the child. The boy's depressive anxiety is compounded by his anxiety over the difference between his mother's gender and his own. He not only fears that he has permanently destroyed the mother he so desperately needs but is also unable to acknowledge that he needs her without feeling like a girl. Ordinarily the boy relieves both his depressive and his gender anxiety by "dis-identifying" from his mother and identifying with his father, that is, by simultaneously denying his dependence on her and affirming that he is a "man" like him. This paternal identification prepares the boy for participation in a masculine world within which his still intensely ambivalent feelings toward his mother can be kept safely under control. Thus the emotional stage is set for his treatment of the women who come to represent her as objects from which he will attempt to establish a "principled . . . more or less derogatory distance."[7] Maintaining this distance typically requires the exclusion of women from positions of public power and prestige. Thus do men seek to ensure that they will never again have to encounter the female authority they so painfully experienced as children within the family. Manic denial (of their dependence on women) is, in other words, the path of retreat from the depressive position taken by most mother-raised men.

The mother-raised girl will also find it difficult, if not impossible, to attain this position. *Her* depressive anxiety is exacerbated by problems resulting from the *identity* between her gender and the gender of her mother. Because the girl's early "pre-Oedipal" identification with her mother is experienced as the source of, rather than an obstacle to, her sense of herself as female, that identification (as we saw in chapter 21) will normally be both more intense and more persistent than her brother's. The difficulty for the girl is precisely that—unlike the boy—she cannot rely on any obvious physical difference to help disentangle herself from a relationship with her mother that is even more overwhelming than his. What she *can* and usually does do is to "transfer to the father . . . much of the weight of [her] positive feelings [toward her mother], while leaving the negative ones mainly attached to their original object."[8] By transforming the split between the "good mother" and the "bad mother" into the split between the "bad mother" and the "good father," the girl "gains a less equivocal focus for her feelings of pure love, and feels freer to experience her grievances against her mother without fear of being cut off altogether from . . . a magic, animally loved, parental being." But the price she eventually pays for falling in love with her father is a "worshipful, dependent stance toward men" to whom she will sacrifice her agency in order to repudiate her mother's.[9] Thus are women psychologically prepared to submit to the very men who are emotionally committed to their domination.

It follows from Dinnerstein's diagnosis of the "traditional symbiotic emotional equilibrium"[10] between women and men that co-parenting is the only possible treatment for this problem. When men come to participate with women as equal partners in the process of gratifying and frustrating the vital needs of their infants and young children, fathers will join mothers as the object of both their love and their hate. With mothers no longer the exclusive target of infantile rage, women would "stop serving as scapegoats . . . for human resentment of the human condition."[11] With fathers no longer available as an "apparently blameless category of person" to whom children can turn to evade their intense ambivalence, "split off feelings of love and anger . . . would have to be integrated within each individual person."[12] Thus co-parenting would open the door to Klein's "depressive position" and enable "our infantilism [to] be more easily outgrown."[13] Having truly grown up, men would no longer need to dominate women and women would no longer need to be dominated by men.

We have seen that the Kleinian message is (a) that relationships of reciprocal recognition or mutual empowerment depend on the development of the reparative inclinations and capacities of the participants in those relationships and (b) that demonizing and idealizing defenses suppress those reparative inclinations and capacities and thus emotionally prepare people for relationships of domination and subordination. What Dinnerstein adds to Klein is the understanding, first, that men are disproportionately vulnerable to demonizing defenses and women are disproportionately vulnerable to idealizing defenses, and, second, that the development of the reparative inclinations and capacities that enable people to defeat these gender-related defenses depends decisively on a fundamental change in the structure of child rearing that Klein takes for granted (and that has prevailed in every known culture up to this point in time). Dinnerstein acknowledges, however, that even with this transformation to co-parenting "it is possible . . . that we will prove unable to marshal the strength for [depressive] integration."[14] Thus she understands co-parenting as a necessary but not necessarily sufficient condition for the successful negotiation of the depressive position. Indeed, I will argue that unless the transformation in the *structure* of parenting she envisions is accompanied by what Donald Winnicott calls "good-enough" child-rearing *practices*, we should *not* expect that transformation to have the effect for which she hopes.

Klein herself did not entirely ignore, but tended rather to underestimate, the role of child-rearing practices in either hindering or facilitating the development of the child's reparative tendencies and thus the depressive integration that both depends on and results from them.[15] Although she insists that "a good relation to its mother and to the external world helps the baby to overcome its early paranoid anxieties" and thus successfully to work through the depressive position,[16] she is noticeably vague about the precise meaning of a "good relation" to the mother. Here Winnicott is of considerable help. He argues that "good-enough" mothering—which includes "holding" the child in order to facilitate the formation of a coherent, basic sense of self, "mirroring" the child's autonomous efforts in order to foster an initially grandiose sense of agency, and "optimally frustrating" the child in order eventually to reduce that sense of agency to more realistic dimensions—is a prerequisite for the child's ability to integrate his or her love and hate for the mother. Let me consider each of these dimensions of (what Winnicott assumes is an exclusively) maternal care in the order in which I have introduced them.

1: Holding

Winnicott employs this term "to denote not only the actual physical holding of the infant, but also the total environmental provision" during the period when the infant "has not separated out a self from the maternal care on which there exists absolute dependence in a psychological sense."[17] At this, the earliest stage of post-natal life, the infant is entirely dependent on the mother to protect it from unpredictable "impingements" from the world that would disrupt its "continuity of being" and thus preclude the formation of a stable sense of self: "the holding environment . . . has as its main function the reduction to a minimum of impingements to which the infant must react with resultant annihilation of personal being."[18] In other words, a mother who responds lovingly, predictably, and quickly to, and even anticipates, the needs of her infant encourages the experience of a safe world in which it has a secure place. In contrast, the improperly "held" infant who has not been protected from disturbing environmental "impingements" will suffer a debilitating anxiety that prevents it from trusting either the world or the self. In Kleinian terms, an infant who has been properly held will be able to form an internal representation of a "good mother" (and thus eventually of a "good self") that will eventually motivate the child to make reparations to her for the harm he will inevitably do to her, whereas the improperly held infant who lacks the internal representation of a good mother will become a child (and later an "adult") who lacks both the inclination and the capacity to make reparations. This is the sense in which successful negotiation of the depressive position depends decisively on the quality of maternal—but we should say parental—holding.

2: Mirroring

The same is true of what Winnicott calls "mirroring." The child's confidence in his creative capacities—his sense of himself as an *agent* able to affect the world—will flourish, Winnicott argues, only if his mother reflects back to him (with a smile or the glint of her eyes) her pride in his early efforts to explore that world. Thus the "creative capacity" of children whose efforts are not mirrored or recognized by their mothers—children with a "long experience of not getting back what they are giving"—will eventually "atrophy."[19] More specifically: if their efforts are met by a mother who is emotionally absent they will associate self-assertion with maternal withdrawal and the anxiety it produces, and will substitute a compliant for a creative relationship to reality, experiencing the "world and its details . . . as something to be fitted in with or demanding adaptation."[20] Now, a compliant child who lacks confidence in his ability to affect the world is scarcely in a position to expect that his efforts to repair the damage he has done to his mother will be effective. Thus even if he felt "pity" and "remorse" for his mother it would be unlikely that he would be motivated to make reparations to her. And even if he were, an emotionally absent mother who is unable to mirror her child is not likely to match the child's reparative efforts with lovingly reassuring efforts of her own.

We have seen that Klein's message is that relationships of reciprocal recognition or mutual empowerment depend on the successful negotiation of the depressive position, and that the successful negotiation of the depressive position depends on the strength of the reparative inclinations and capacities of the child. Winnicott adds that the strength of reparative tendencies depends, in turn, in important part on proper mirroring by the mother. Thus the capacity of adults to participate in rewarding relationships with others depends on the quality of the recognition they received as children from their mothers.

3: Optimal Frustration

Even the most supportive mother will—indeed should—frustrate the demands of her child and will therefore become the object of his rage. The way in which she responds to her child's rage, in turn, will affect the intensity of his depressive anxiety and guilt. A mother who calmly withstands her child's rage is far more likely to foster an internal representation of a caring mother who has survived his destructiveness than a mother who either retaliates or falls to pieces in the face of that rage. Thus through "optimal frustration" the child learns to distinguish between the mother whom he has destroyed in his fantasies and the real mother who has survived his aggressive assaults, which helps him learn that the damage he has done is not irreparable and therefore contributes to his confidence in capacity to repair that damage. But a child of a mother who responds in either an overly repressive or an overly indulgent manner to his anger is never in a position to learn this lesson. In the first case her efforts to suppress her child's rage will teach him that it is unacceptable to express it and thus discourage him from "owning" it, short-circuiting from the very outset the task of integrating it with his love. In the second case the mother's capitulation teaches the child that he has, in effect, destroyed her, which is likely both to intensify his already considerable anxiety and guilt and to increase the difficulty of distinguishing between the real and fantasized mother.

Optimal frustration, then, teaches the child the distinction between fantasy and reality and thus prepares her to cope with the inevitable resistance of the world to her wishes. In Winnicott's words, "destructiveness, plus the object's survival of the destruction, places the object outside the area of objects set up by the subject's projective mental mechanisms . . . outside the area of the subject's omnipotent control."[21] This lesson in transforming omnipotent fantasies into a creative relationship with reality is not available to either the overly repressed or the overly indulged child. The former learns to suppress her wishes and the latter never learns to adjust them to the requirements of reality; the first learns a lesson in impotence and the second in omnipotence. Neither will become an adult with a really potent, that is, simultaneously realistic and creative, relationship with world.

This world includes, of course, the world of other people. To participate with them in relationships of reciprocal recognition the subject must be prepared confidently to express his wishes *and* to acknowledge the legitimacy of the wishes of a really separate other, to treat the other as "an entity in its own right [and] not as a projective entity."[22] But the overly repressed individual is likely to project hostility (from his mother) onto the others he fearfully and defensively encounters, and the overly indulged individual will ordinarily expect others to (like his mother) surrender to his wishes and will reject them when they (since in reality they *are* separate) do not. Thus does the "sub-optimal" frustration of the child contribute to the distorted "object relations" of the "adult" who is unprepared for relationships of mutual empowerment or reciprocal recognition.

4: Desirable Discipline

To Winnicott's catalogue of "good-enough" parenting practices I add my own entry: desirable discipline. It should go without saying that even the parent who "lays down the law" in an optimal way should expect that the child will at least occasionally violate that "law." Disobedience is a challenge with which every parent will have to deal, and the way that he copes with that challenge will significantly affect the chances that his child will achieve depressive integration. It is by now commonplace, perhaps even clichéd, to insist that when a child misbehaves the parent's remonstrative reaction should be directed exclusively to his action and not to his being: what the child has *done* is bad but *he* is not. Underlying this by-now standard advice is an important psychological truth, namely that condemning the child's being evokes *shame* whereas condemning the child's act evokes *guilt*. There is no constructive way that the child can respond to shame; the child who is shamed will either internalize the judgment that he is "bad" or react defensively against it. But guilt is something that can motivate the child, where possible, to make reparations for the damage that his deed has done. Punishments that are tailored to the harmful actions of the child, in other words, are far more likely to encourage his reparative inclinations and capacities than wholesale criticisms of his person.

Perhaps it is not going too far to say that the primary purpose of punishment should be precisely to encourage the reparative tendencies of the child. Parents implicitly recognize this when they insist on an apology from their children and forgive them when that (hopefully genuine) apology arrives. Punishment that encourages an apology that culminates in forgiveness teaches children that harm cannot be condoned but that harm can be repaired. It is a lesson that prepares them for the many reparations that responsible adults will have to make for the damage they cannot but do. "Love means never having to say you're sorry," on the other hand, is perhaps the worst, and certainly the least Kleinian, lesson that it is possible to learn.

At the beginning of this chapter I argued that we need an account of the human subject that synthesizes the competing claims of the partisans of social man and the partisans of a-social man, one that does justice both to the desire of the subject to exercise power over others (or to submit to that exercise) and to the commitment of the subject to participate with others in mutually empowering relationships of reciprocal recognition. It is time briefly to review the distance we have traveled in the direction of that synthesis. I have argued that (a) children who defend against depressive anxiety and guilt through manic denial and idealization will be psychologically predisposed as adults to participate in relationships of domination and subjection; (b) children who have been raised more or less exclusively by their mothers in their earliest years are vulnerable to manically denying and idealizing defenses that prepare them emotionally for "adult" relationships of domination and subordination; and (c) children (whether mainly mother-raised or not) who have not been optimally held, mirrored, frustrated, and disciplined are likewise liable to defend destructively against depressive anxiety and guilt and subsequently to succumb to relationships of domination and subordination.

Conversely, children (a) whose reparative inclinations and capacities are stronger than their defensive tendencies and are thus able to achieve depressive integration will be psychologically prepared as adults for relationships of reciprocal recognition; (b) who have been co-parented are (everything else being equal) likely to have stronger reparative tendencies and are thus more likely to achieve depressive integration and the adult relationships of mutual recognition for which that integration is a prerequisite; and (c) who have been properly held, mirrored, frustrated, and disciplined are likewise likely to manifest the reparative sensibilities necessary for depressive integration and thus for adult relationships of reciprocal recognition or mutual empowerment. So we can sum up our Klein–Dinnerstein–Winnicott synthesis with the conclusion that "good-enough co-parenting" is the child-care condition most conducive to the development of a subject with the psychological strength to enjoy genuinely rewarding relationships with others—most likely, in short, to produce a person with a well-governed soul.

Thus a commitment to the transformation of the prevailing mode of child care in favor of "good-enough-co-parenting" is the political culmination of my theoretical synthesis. I have argued elsewhere that this political commitment would also have to include a reform of the many—economic, institutional, and cultural—conditions that currently stand in the way of the realization of this child-care ideal. A movement to transform the prevailing structure and practices *inside* the family can only be as successful as movement to transform the structures and practices *outside* the family that support those inside it.[23] But even as these extra-familial factors influence the intra-familial factors, so too do the latter influence the former. Indeed psychoanalysis teaches us that individuals relive their earliest interactions with their parents inside the family in the course of their subsequent relationships with others outside it, that is, that their supposedly adult relationships are at least in part *transferential*. In *An Autobiographical Study* Freud defines transference as the individual *"re-experiencing emotional relations which had their origin in his earliest object-attachments during the repressed period of his childhood,"* and he warns that although the analyst relies on the patient's transference it would be a mistake to assume that transference is confined to the analytic setting. Rather, Freud argues, transference "is a universal phenomenon of the human mind . . . and in fact dominates the whole of each person's relations to his human environment."[24] This argument authorizes the application of psychoanalytic concepts to the dynamics of groups or collectivities. But it is not on Freud's concepts, but rather on Klein's, that I will mainly rely for this application.

26

THE SUBJECT IN THE GROUP

In the more than four decades since Klein's death Kleinians have applied her account of the dynamics of individual development to the dynamics of groups, or even entire societies. Freud and Freudians assume that groups are bound by attachments to leaders that are rooted in feelings for the father.[1] Kleinian social theorists, in contrast, have explored the way in which the relationship between the individual and the group reproduces the relationship between the child and its mother.[2] They have argued that individuals unconsciously experience groups as simultaneously gratifying and frustrating mothers that inevitably evoke their gratitude and their rage. Thus the group that is loved is also necessarily the group that is hated. The development of the group demands that its members learn to respond reparatively to the anxiety and guilt aroused by this ambivalence, that is, that they come to understand that their group is neither all-good nor all-bad but nonetheless worthy of care. But this happy outcome is always threatened by the temptation of individual members to defend against the group equivalent of depressive anxiety and guilt, either by denying one's dependence on the group (the group analogue of manic denial) or by denying one's rage against it (the group analogue of idealization). Manic denial leads to dropping out of the group but often entails an obsessive preoccupation with, and denigration of, the very group from which one has dropped out. (Think of the former Leftist and now militantly right-wing David Horowitz!) Idealization creates a demonized out-group that unwittingly becomes a target for all the rage that cannot be expressed within the in-group. Thus the Kleinian message is at once hopeful and ominous. It reassures us that harmonious relations among groups *are* possible if group members cultivate their capacity to acknowledge and work through, rather than defend against, the ambivalence and guilt that inevitably accompany membership in their group. But is also warns us that the failure to cultivate this capacity can culminate in exploitative, even murderous relations between groups. Group development, in short, is possible but precarious.

Dinnerstein's feminist modification of Klein's account of individual development has implications for a Kleinian account of group development as well.

Dinnerstein reminds us that it is the mother and not the father—a woman and not a man—who is normally our first representative of political authority, the "first, overwhelming adversary"[3] of our will that we encounter. Thus she assumes that our feelings about authority relationships will always reflect our feelings—our intensely conflicted feelings—about our mothers. And the fact that the father (or father-figure) is typically uninvolved in early child-care, and is therefore available as a "blameless," idealized refuge from maternal power, makes it possible (she argues) for both mother-raised boys and mother-raised girls to evade the deeply difficult task of integrating these intensely conflicted feelings about the first authority they encounter.

The idealization of the father within the family, in turn, psychologically prepares men and women to idealize (mainly) male political leaders outside the family. Freud had argued that "the great majority of people have a strong need for authority which they can admire, to which they can submit, and which dominates or even ill-treats them," and identified this need as a "longing for the father that lives in each of us from his childhood days."[4] Dinnerstein's point, however, is that this "longing for the father" is not an original longing but rather a longing for a less boundless, less overwhelming, less frightening form of authority than the one first exercised by our mothers, a search for a "reasonable refuge from female authority."[5] For Dinnerstein, in other words, the willingness of "adults" to embrace authoritarian politics is an expression of a continuing dependence on the mother that the turn to, and idealization of, the father has displaced, permitted us to deny, and prevented us from outgrowing. Thus are mother-raised men and women emotionally primed to idealize the (mostly male) leaders of the groups to which they belong. (These idealized leaders, moreover, will typically encourage their followers to idealize the groups they lead rather than encourage them to own and work through their inevitably conflicted feelings about the group.) Under conditions of mother-monopolized child rearing, then, we should not expect that the group analogue of depressive integration will be easy to achieve. Rather we should expect that love for the in-group will all too often be purchased at the price of hate for an out-group.[6]

We should also expect that individuals who *can* tolerate or even embrace emotional ambivalence—individuals who have successfully negotiated the depressive position—are unlikely to idealize an in-group and demonize an out-group. By now we should not be surprised to learn that Dinnerstein expects that co-parented children will be far less likely to idealize the groups to which they belong, and thus far more likely to achieve the group equivalent of depressive integration, than conventionally raised children.[7] Nor should we be surprised that a follower of Winnicott would add that—even under co-parenting—this adult achievement presupposes a childhood encounter with "good-enough" holding, mirroring, frustration, and discipline. Combining Dinnerstein and Winnicott, we can say that the development of healthy groups is as dependent on "good-enough" forms of co-parenting as is the development of healthy individuals.

But if healthy individuals are necessary, they are not sufficient, for healthy groups. Depressively integrated individuals will be reluctant to devote their emotional energies to groups if the groups themselves are not structured in ways that facilitate "owning" and working through the intense ambivalence that inevitably accompanies life in groups. On the assumption that the group is unconsciously experienced as a mother, it should be possible to identify group practices that facilitate the depressive integration of groups that parallel the maternal practices that (I argued in the previous chapter) facilitate the depressive integration of individuals. What follows, then, is an account of what I take to be the group analogues of maternal holding, mirroring, optimal frustration, and desirable discipline.

1: Group Holding: Community

Just as the protection of the "good-enough mother" is the ultimate source of her infant's trust in a safe world within which it can find a secure and stable place, so the support of what we might call the "good-enough group" makes it possible for its members to feel that they are part of something larger than themselves that lends meaning to their individual lives. This concept of "group holding," it might be said, is merely a restatement of the "communitarian" claim that individuals are, after all, social beings, the quality of whose individuality depends in important part on the quality of the communities in which they participate. But what the concept of group holding adds to this by now commonplace observation is, first of all, the understanding that the ties that bind individuals to their communities are, in Freud's words, "the work of Eros . . . these collections of men are to be libidinally bound to one another. Necessity alone, the advantages of work in common, will not hold them together."[8] Solidarity, in short, has a sensual source. The individual literally loves the group that holds her.

The love of the individual for his group, second, is the necessary condition for her reparative response to the damage (fantasized or real) that she will inevitably do to his group. This aggression, I have already suggested, follows from the frustration that even the most gratifying group imposes on its members. More on the source of this frustration shortly. For now the point is that, in the absence of loving feelings for the group on the part of those whom the group has aggrieved, we should not expect the aggrieved to feel sorrow or pity for the group that has aggrieved them. In Kleinian terms: an internal representation of a "good group" is a prerequisite for the flowering of reparative feelings for the group and thus for the group analogue of depressive integration.

2: Group Mirroring: Democracy

Democratically organized groups are, I argue, more likely to encourage depressive group integration than undemocratically organized groups. We have seen that proper maternal mirroring engenders the child's sense of himself as an agent, and that this sense of individual agency is the source of the child's confidence in his capacity to repair the harm he inevitably does to his mother. The group analogue of the child's sense of agency, I would suggest, is the member's confidence that he *matters* to the group and thus that he can help determine its direction. His confidence that he can affect the group, in turn, will depend on whether the group is designed to encourage and enable him to do so. Thus democratically organized groups that recognize or "mirror" the wishes of their members are far more likely than hierarchically organized groups to foster the political agency or efficacy of their members. And the group member who lacks this sense of political efficacy will likewise lack the confidence that his reparative responses to any (real or fantasized) damage he does to the group will in fact be able to repair that damage. He will therefore be far more tempted to defend against the group equivalent of depressive anxiety and guilt through idealization and demonization than his more reparatively inclined democratic counterpart.

The same reasoning that leads us to expect that democratic groups are less likely to be plagued by (in-group) idealization and (out-group) demonization than undemocratic groups leads to the expectation that "thicker" or more directly democratic groups are less vulnerable to this danger of group splitting than "thinner" or less directly democratic groups. Whatever makes democratic citizens feel that their voice and vote matter will increase their sense of political agency and thus their confidence in their reparative capacities. And, I would suggest, democratic citizens are far more likely to feel that their voice and vote matter if they have regular opportunities to participate in decisions that significantly affect their lives. But in a "thin" democracy in which, to return to the words of Benjamin Barber, "politics . . . become[s] what politicians do; what citizens do (when they do anything) is vote for the politicians,"[9] the feelings of political efficacy on which reparative confidence is based are hardly likely to flourish. "Thin" democracies, in other words, encourage the perception of powerlessness, and the perception of powerlessness is a recipe for resentment rather than reparations.

At the same time it is true that, as I pointed out in chapter 5, even the thickest, most participatory democracies are obliged to reply on representation. Hannah Pitkin argued in that chapter, you will remember, that the representative should represent both the wishes and the welfare (as perceived by the representative) of her constituents, but was unable to make good on her claim that those wishes and welfare will normally coincide. Our neo-Kleinian interpretation of groups sheds light on this particular problem. Consistent with Pitkin, it insists that proper representation requires an appreciation of the distinction between the wishes and the welfare of the represented. But it draws this distinction in a different and more specific way than Pitkin. From a Kleinian point of view, the welfare of the represented is depressive integration and the reparative tendencies that both encourage and result from it. Thus the representative who is committed to the welfare of her constituents will always act in ways that encourage their reparative sensibilities and discourage their tendencies to split, that is, to idealize the group to which they belong and demonize the groups to which they do not.[10]

This suggests that Pitkin overestimates the ability of the representative regularly to harmonize her commitment to both the welfare and the wishes of the represented. Since idealizing and demonizing tendencies are, to one degree or another, always present within the represented, the reparative representative's commitment to their welfare may, to the same variable degree, conflict with what her constituents may wish. If their wishes are, in Kleinian terms, paranoid-schizoid, we should expect that the representative's commitment to their (reparatively defined) welfare will in fact *preclude* a commitment to their wishes. To put this the other way around: the reparative representative's commitment to the wishes of her constituents presupposes that these wishes are themselves reparative rather than idealizing or demonizing.

3: Optimal Group Frustration: Good-Enough Norms

No group can exist without norms that distinguish between acceptable and unacceptable behavior and that encourage the former and discourage the latter. Any group must protect itself and its (norm-abiding) members from other members who would violate those norms. Yet these necessary norms are necessarily a source of frustration to some of the very members who are protected by them. This is obviously true in the case of norms that are undemocratically imposed on those who are obliged to adhere to them. But it is also true in the case of democratically organized groups whose members have, at least in principle, freely chosen the norms by which they are governed. The republican principle that "obedience to the law one has prescribed for oneself is liberty"[11] will not prevent some group members from experiencing constraint if they are obliged to follow norms or (in the case of the state-group) obey laws that are, in practice, made by a majority of members with whom they happen to disagree. Majority rule is, in short, a recipe for minority frustration. Although it is true that this frustration may be tempered by the prospect of eventually becoming part of a new majority, that prospect is unlikely entirely to dissipate the dissatisfaction: the *possibility* of a future victory is generally insufficient to salve the wounds of the *actuality* of an ongoing defeat.

The participatory democratic response to this problem is to privilege the democratic process over the outcome and thus to argue that members who reap the rewards of active participation in the process are less likely to be frustrated by an outcome of that process with which they happen to disagree. Agreed. But even the most satisfying process is itself likely to be a source of considerable frustration: the patience of even the most dedicated deliberative democrat will be worn thin by endless meetings, and even the most committed partisan of public discourse does, after all, have a private life. Thus a deliberatively democratic group is no exception to the general rule that the group that gratifies its members cannot but frustrate them as well.

Finally, the fact that any large group—no matter how devoted to participation or deliberation—is obliged to rely on representatives is also a potential source of frustration to its many members. On the one hand, as I suggested above, the task of the reparative representative is precisely to frustrate the paranoid-schizoid wishes of her constituents in the name of their real, that is, reparative interests. On the other hand, even the most reparatively oriented constituents will be frustrated if their representatives pursue interests of their own that conflict with the interests of their constituents. Thus even the group member who consistently finds himself in the majority will be frustrated if his representative ignores or effectively subverts the norms or laws that issue from that majority. The frustration of the represented with their representatives is thus a permanent possibility in a representative democracy.

For all these reasons, then, even the most democratically organized group will necessarily frustrate the very members for whom its "holding" supplies solidarity and its "mirroring" encourages agency. On the assumption that frustration breeds aggression, it follows that even the most democratically organized group will become a target of the aggression of its members. And, just as the good-enough mother optimally frustrates the aggression of her child, so too the good-enough group optimally frustrates the aggression of its members. Recall that the good-enough mother sets limits on her child's aggression that help transform his grandiose fantasies into realistic agency: she steers a course between overly repressive responses to her child's rage that would squelch his agency and overly indulgent capitulations to it that would discourage its socially appropriate assertion. Similarly, we can say that the norms of the good-enough group limit the aggression of its members by encouraging its peaceful, but discouraging its violent, expression. Otherwise put, these norms will uphold the right to *dissent* but deny the (omnipotent) drive to *dominate*.

Just as the mother who calmly withstands her child's rage promotes his awareness that his rage has not in fact destroyed her, thus mitigating both his depressive anxiety and guilt and the temptation destructively to defend against it, so the group whose norms legitimate dissent promotes the perception that the group is strong enough to tolerate, even welcome, his (peacefully expressed) aggression, thus diminishing his fear of the group-destructive consequences of his rage as well as the probability of his defending against it. And norms that validate his dissent also give him more reason to love the very group against which his anger is directed. For both reasons, good-enough norms encourage reparative sensibilities and discourage the tendency either to idealize or to demonize the group: they both express and encourage the awareness that the group is neither all-good nor all-bad and therefore worthy of care.

Not-good-enough norms, in contrast, encourage either the idealization or demonization of the group. It goes without saying that norms that validate the violent expression of dissent threaten the stability or even the survival of the group. It is perhaps less obvious to add that violence directed against the group is likely to intensify the group-depressive anxiety and guilt of the perpetrators of that violence, encouraging them to defend against that anxiety and guilt by manically denying their dependence on and love for the group (which denial, in turn, is likely to intensify the violence they direct against the group). Overly repressive norms that invalidate or demonize dissent, on the other hand, are likely to foster an idealization of the group that is purchased at the emotional price of the demonization of an out-group. Anticipating Klein, Freud argued that "it is always possible to bind together a considerable number of people in love, so long as there are other people left over to receive the manifestation of their aggressiveness."[12] What must be added is that this projection of the "aggressiveness" of group members onto an out-group is far more likely to happen if the in-group is not prepared "to receive [its] manifestations." If it *is* prepared—if its norms welcome forcefully expressed dissent—then we should expect, against Freud, that the group might well "bind a considerable number of people in [mature, non-idealizing] love" *without* having to find an out-group as a target for its hate.

It follows—everything else being equal—that societies in which the rule of law prevails are more likely to be depressively integrated than societies in which it is absent. We saw in chapter 1 that Joseph Raz argued that laws that are prospective, open, clear, general, and relatively stable serve to limit the arbitrary exercise of governmental power and thus provide a "secure framework for one's life and actions" that is lacking whenever citizens are not in a position unambiguously to determine whether their contemplated actions are legal or not. In short, when the rule of law is absent there are reality-based reasons for *fear* that can only reinforce the fearful fantasies that already belong to the paranoid-schizoid position. And fear, Klein has helped us understand, is always a trigger for mechanisms of defense—whether idealizing or demonizing—that suppress the reparative sensibilities on which depressive group integration depends.

If this is so, it follows that the rule of law as Raz understands it is a necessary but insufficient condition for the group integration that depends on it. According to his understanding, you will remember, the rule of law is perfectly consistent with the presence of societal norms that demonize dissent. Only if the rule of law is more expansively defined to include the right of the people to make and change the prospective, clear, open, etc. laws by which they are governed can we say that the rule of law legitimates dissent. This right is enshrined, for example, in the First Amendment to the Constitution of the United States of America, which prohibits laws that "abridg[e] the freedom of speech, or of the press, or the right of the people peaceably to assemble, and to petition the Government for a redress of grievances."

These specifically democratic rights, we might say, institutionalize the principle of hope and thus help to defeat the debilitating, self-defeating fear that things will never change. And the triumph of hope over fear is, as we have seen, the victory of the group-depressive position over the poisonous paranoid-schizoid tendencies that defend against it.

4: Desirable Discipline: Restorative Justice

Just as the parent who sets limits on her child's behavior must discipline him when he oversteps those limits, so the group whose norms regulate the behavior of its members is obliged to discipline its members for transgressing those norms. And, just as good-enough individual discipline encourages the reparative sensibilities of the child by demanding apologies for the damage he has done and extending forgiveness to him when those (hopefully heartfelt) apologies are made, so too, I would argue, good-enough group discipline should be designed to develop the capacity of its norm-violating members to make reparations for the harm they have caused. This, in fact, is precisely the project of the recent and increasingly influential movement for *restorative justice*. Restorative justice starts from the assumption that "crime" is not merely or even mainly an offense against society for which the offender must pay a debt to the state which acts on society's behalf, but rather in the first and perhaps most important instance a concrete harm done to a particular individual (or set of individuals) to whom the offender is obliged to make reparations. The advocates of restorative justice argue that a (professionally mediated) face-to-face encounter between the offender and the person(s) he has harmed, in which the former is personally informed by the latter of the nature and extent of that harm, is far more likely to encourage the reparative sensibilities (and actions) of the offender than more conventional, impersonal forms of punishment that preclude that kind of confrontation and thus make it easier for the offender to defend against whatever guilt he might otherwise feel for his harmful deed.[13] Thus they agree with Nietzsche's claim that it is

> a blunder [to] view . . . punishment as the true instrument of "remorse" . . . True remorse is rarest among criminals and convicts: prisons and penitentiaries are not the breeding place of this gnawer . . . By and large, punishment hardens and freezes; it concentrates; it sharpens the sense of alienation; it strengthens resistance . . . it is precisely punishment that has most effectively retarded the development of guilt feeling . . . in the hearts of the victims of punitive authority.[14]

Translated into Kleinian language, Nietzsche's claim is that (traditional) punishment magnifies rather than mitigates the paranoid-schizoid tendencies to which the offender has (arguably) already succumbed in the course of his offense. Restorative justice, in contrast, is supposed to stimulate both the offender's depressive anxiety and guilt and her reparative responses to it, thus helping the offender to transcend the splitting of the paranoid-schizoid position in favor of the integration of the (successfully negotiated) depressive position.

Thus it purports to contribute to the emotional development of the offender even as it satisfies the need of the victim for reparations, whether material or emotional. This is, to this point, a largely untested claim, although there is a small but growing literature that purports to evaluate it.[15]

There is also a somewhat larger body of literature that considers whether there is or is not an irreconcilable tension between the rule of law and restorative justice.[16] Sentencing under restorative justice is based on the premise that the (restorative) penalty imposed should be geared to the particular situation of the offender as well as the specific harm he has caused; on this premise, different individuals convicted of the "same" (legally defined) crime might well receive radically different sentences. Yet the rule of law is often assumed (rightly or wrongly) to require justice to be "blind" to the very differences on which restorative justice focuses and therefore to treat different individuals who have committed the same (legally defined) crime in the same way. What is at stake, in short, is the question of what "equal justice under the law" means, or should mean. But that is a question for another book.

27

IDENTITY POLITICS REVISITED

In the Introduction to Part IV, I claimed that a Kleinian analysis can clarify the conditions under which a politics based on group identity would be consistent with respect for individual differences among the members to whom that identity is assigned, and would therefore be innocent of the charge of "normalization" and "exclusionism" that the critics of "essentialism" have lodged against it. I am now in a position to make good on this claim. My argument is that the same structures and practices that determine whether a group is depressively integrated will determine whether the identity claimed for that group normalizes or excludes its (potential) members. If the identification that binds the members to the group is an idealizing identification, that is, if love of the in-group is predicated on hate for an out-group, then there is good reason to expect that differences among the members of the in-group will be deemed dangerous and that (as Joan Scott worried) the "borders of identity [will be] patrolled for signs of non-conformity." When the group-self is purchased at the price of a demonized group-other, in other words, expressions of dissent or difference within the former will be experienced as offering aid and comfort to the latter: the need to find traitors within the group goes hand-in-hand with the need to find enemies outside it. Thus all the rage that is projected onto an external target cannot but return to the (unintegrated) group in the form of "witch hunts" that are ostensibly designed to protect it (but that inevitably work to destroy it). And under these conditions the pressure to prove one's loyalty to the group will easily override whatever other identities are important to its individual members.

We should expect a different story, however, if the identification that binds together the members of a group is decidedly reparative. Under these conditions, as we have seen, there is no need to project anger onto a demonized out-group because expressions of anger are tolerated, even welcomed, *within* the group, and if there is no need for an external enemy there will be no need for an internal enemy either. Moreover, if there is no need for an internal enemy there will be no pressure to deny or denigrate the differences among the members of the group that coincide with their commonalities. To put this another way: depressively integrated members of a depressively integrated group will experience one another as real persons rather than as projections of their paranoid-schizoid (group) fantasies and will therefore be mature enough to recognize, even celebrate, the fact that their different identities cannot simply be collapsed into the identity of the group.

Thus whether Fraser and Nicholson were correct to argue, for example, that "gender identity gives substance to the idea of sisterhood . . . at the cost of repressing differences among sisters" depends entirely on whether (female) gender identity is reparatively created and reinforced or not. If the identification of individual women with their "sisters" is established through the demonization of those whom they would deny to be their "brothers"—if their gender identification is idealizing rather than reparative—then we should assume that they will be attracted to feminist groups whose structures and practices reinforce that idealized identification "at the cost of repressing [the] differences" among them. Those feminist groups characterized by not-good-enough holding (community), mirroring (democracy), frustration (norms), and discipline will, for all the reasons I have earlier advanced, discourage depressive integration and encourage (pre-existing) tendencies to split reality into idealized friends and demonized enemies (including the enemy within). But if the feminist group creates a supportive community, encourages the democratic agency of its members, frustrates them optimally, and disciplines them restoratively, then we should not expect that it will succumb to idealizing and demonizing tendencies and to the "repression" of individual differences among them that necessarily accompanies those tendencies. Under these conditions there is no reason to believe that a feminist identity would normally be anything other than benign.

The same can be said, it seems to me, for national identity. My argument is that an identification with a nation whose state properly held, mirrored, frustrated, and disciplined its citizens would not normally depend on the demonization of an other-nation and thus would be generally consistent with (what Robert Fine calls) a cosmopolitan identity. The depressively integrated citizens of that nation-state will be grateful for its gifts even as they acknowledge its imperfections, and rather than deny those deficits they will seek to repair them. When their country does wrong—when it acts unjustly—both their love of justice *and* their love of their country will move them to try to right that wrong. Thus an identification with the nation is perfectly consistent with a cosmopolitan identification as long as that first identification is rooted in reparative rather than idealizing emotions. And national identification will be reparative whenever the structure and practices of the nation-state encourage the depressive integration of its citizens.

To this point my argument might read as support for the case that Michael Ignatieff made in chapter 23 on behalf of "civic nationalism": after all, the political forms that, according to Ignatieff, properly claim the allegiance of the civic nationalist—"democracy, accountability, rule of law [and] procedural fairness"—are among the very political forms that, according to my argument, encourage the depressive integration that is an emotional–political precondition for a "benign" nationalism. But those political forms, I want to argue, are a necessary but *not always sufficient* condition for depressive integration.

Let me explain. Earlier we saw that Klein argues that significant (real or intra-psychic) losses can trigger demonizing and idealizing tendencies in even the most securely depressively integrated individuals and that those individuals are thereby obliged to renegotiate the depressive position to avoid succumbing to those paranoid-schizoid tendencies. The same can be said for normally depressively integrated nation-states: major threats to the integrity of a nation whose democratic, liberal, etc. political forms generally encourage reparative sensibilities can trigger sensibilities that are anything but reparative and thus threaten its hold on the political depressive position. Whether that hold can be preserved—whether nationalism remains benign or becomes malignant—will depend in important part on whether the leaders of the nation reinforce the normally reparative sensibilities of its citizens or fan their newly emergent paranoid-schizoid flames. You will remember that Ignatieff agreed with Fine that "there is no necessary relation between the 'civic' character of the national identity and peaceful behavior toward foreign nations and neighbors" and that, consequently, "civic doesn't necessarily mean 'benign,'" but that he failed to explain what determines whether any given civic nationalism turns out to be malignant or benign. The role of that particular political practice that is leadership is surely one of the determinants that Ignatieff missed.

As a case in point consider the response of President Bush and others in his administration to the terrible national loss of September 11, 2001. A reparative response to the attacks of 9/11 would have encouraged a period of national mourning followed by careful collective and individual deliberation about the best way to bring to justice the individuals (and their supporters) who were responsible for those attacks. In fact a window briefly opened for that kind of response immediately following the attacks when the country came together in grief that was shared by hundreds of millions around the world who declared that they, too, were Americans. (Nous sommes tous des Americains!) But shortly thereafter that window was slammed shut when, on September 21, President Bush declared a "War on Terror" and then warned on November 6 that all those nations that did not join Americans in that war would henceforth be considered as evil as the enemies who attacked American: "you're either with us or against us in the fight against terror." No rhetoric could have been better designed to strengthen the paranoid-schizoid and weaken the reparative sensibilities of the citizens to whom it was addressed. And the rest, as they say, was history, and a most unfortunate history at that. The Unites States endured eight years during which an obsessive search for external enemies made far more of them than were ever brought to justice and predictably resulted in the search for an enemy within, that is, in the demonization of dissent by one of the most lawless administrations in the history of the American Republic. At one point following the invasion of Iraq, the Australian journalist John Pilger (quoting from Arthur Miller's explanation for writing *The Crucible*) quipped that the

American "state has lost its mind."[1] He was exactly right: America had lost its collective hold on reality—its hold on the depressive political position—and embraced the dangerous delusions of the paranoid-schizoid position. Thus did "civic nationalism" become anything but "benign."

The election in 2008 of Barack Obama suggests that the United States may have finally come to its senses. Surely the hallmark of a campaign that officially started almost two years before the election but arguably began with his electrifying keynote address to the Democratic National Convention in 2004 was Obama's consistently Lincolnesque appeal to the "better angels of our [political] nature" and thus his repudiation of the Republican Party's strategy of demonizing America's adversaries along with those Americans who would dissent from that strategy. The fact that this message of hope resonated so strongly with a majority of Americans (hopefully) signaled that they too had had "enough" of the Rovian "politics of division" and were eager for the "politics of addition" that Obama had preached. Thus as I write these words (only months after the election) there is reason to believe that the American nation-state will begin to repair the damage it had done to the political principles and practices that both embody and encourage the reparative sensibilities of its citizens.

The fact that a majority of Americans were willing to support the reparative campaign of an *African American* suggests, moreover, that Obama was the beneficiary of *racially* reparative sensibilities. By racially reparative sensibilities I mean desires on the part of "white" Americans who have either directly or indirectly benefited from the institutions of slavery, Jim Crow, and de facto segregation to repair the awful damage that these peculiar institutions have done to their "black" American counterparts. Thanks to Klein we are now in a position to interpret the demonizing and idealizing white racial fantasies described by Eric Lott as mutually reinforcing defenses against the anxiety and guilt that would otherwise accompany the awareness of this continuing history of harm, that is, as defenses against the successful negotiation of the racially depressive position. Elsewhere I have identified four pairs of demonizing and idealizing white racial fantasies: (1) blacks as "lazy and shiftless" versus blacks as "laid back and cool"; (2) blacks as "dirty and smelly" versus "blacks are beautiful"; (3) blacks as "sexual monsters" versus blacks as "sexual marvels"; and (4) blacks as "animals" versus blacks as "athletes."[2] These are, I argue, the central fantasies that form (what Du Bois called) the "veil" that occludes the vision of racist white Americans and prevents them from experiencing backs as real people whose suffering is worthy of concern. Thus do the demonizing and idealizing stereotypes of the white racial imaginary deaden the reparative sensibilities of those who succumb to them.

On the assumption that whites who voted for Obama are (relatively) free from those stereotypes, there is reason to hope, then, that his victory signals a resurgence of reparative feelings—a collective emotional step forward—that might well weaken the hold of racism on the American imaginary. Indeed, a majority of Americans seem to agree: a *USA Today*/Gallup poll taken the day after the election revealed that two-thirds of Americans predicted that race relations "will eventually be worked out" in the United States, by far the highest number since Gallup first asked the question in 1963, and the same number described themselves as feeling "proud" about Obama's victory.[3]

At the same time, there are reasons to be cautious about this new "wave of optimism about the future of [American] race relations."[4] To begin with, although Obama won slightly more than 52 percent of the popular vote, only 43 percent of white Americans voted for Obama. It is true that this was actually 2 percent more than voted for John Kerry in 2004, but it is reasonable to speculate that a white Democrat running in 2008 and benefiting, like Obama, from a major financial and economic crisis and the lowest approval rating of a sitting president in American history would have done substantially better. This speculation is supported by the fact that, in the Deep South and the Appalachian region, fewer than a third of whites voted for Obama, and that he "won in only 44 counties in the Appalachian belt, a stretch of 410 counties that runs from New York to Mississippi." Indeed, in large swaths of this region McCain actually did *better* among whites than George Bush did in 2004, and in Alabama "the 18 per cent share of whites that voted for . . . John Kerry in 2004 was almost cut in half for Mr. Obama."[5] In short, the election results suggest that traditional white racism is alive and well among many Americans, disproportionately but not exclusively concentrated in the South.

Finally, and perhaps most importantly, it is possible that Obama was not even perceived as "black" by many of the white Americans who voted for him. Certainly his campaign emphasized his biracial status in an obvious effort to assuage racial fears, highlighting his roots in the (Kansas) "heartland" and frequently picturing him with his white mother and the white maternal grandparents who helped raise him. Apparently one way that union organizers for Obama attempted to counter white racist resistance to his candidacy in Ohio and western Pennsylvania was to point out repeatedly that Obama was "as white as he was black." And if their challenge to the "one-drop" rule that defines someone as "black" if *any* of his ancestors were black was often unsuccessful, there is reason to believe that this rule is no longer followed by many of the under-thirty voters who supported Obama by a margin of more than two to one.[6] A generation far more familiar than their elders with inter-racial dating and marriages, as well as the children who result from those marriages, is arguably more likely to think of someone of with a complexion like Obama's as "mixed" rather than "black."[7]

The question, then, is this: if Obama's skin had been considerably darker than it is—if he had been more obviously "black"—would he have been elected, or even nominated in the first place? Given the ample evidence of continuing color prejudice in this country—and even in the "black" community itself[8]—it would be far too optimistic to answer "yes." If in fact it would be more realistic to answer "no"—if it is reasonable to assume that an imaginary, ebony-skinned Obama could not have become President—then it would be worse than premature to conclude that the victory of the real, coffee-colored Obama means an end to racism. Racism based on the one-drop rule may (outside Appalachia and the Deep South) be dying, but a different kind of racism based on a new rule appears to be alive and well. The new rule makes room—as it does in other countries—for more than two races but still assigns less value to those with the darkest skin. And, if dark skin is still denigrated, we are still a long way from Appiah's ideal of the end of racial identity, and, on his assumption, the end of racism as well. This suggests that there is still more racially reparative work to be done in the United States of America.[9]

28

THE SUBJECT IN NATURE

In chapter 19 we saw that modernity encourages "opportunities . . . for self-expression lacking in more traditional contexts"[1] even as it *dis*courages opportunities for the more meaningful relationship with (non-human) nature that normally prevails in those more traditional contexts. In a number of other chapters, you will recall, I envisioned a synthesis of the modern and the traditional world-views that would incorporate the best of each and leave the worst behind: this synthesis would preserve the self-expression of modernity while rejecting its "drive to mastery" over nature and would reject the traditionalist suppression of self-expression while preserving its more reverential relationship to nature. In this chapter I extend my Kleinian account of the human subject to its relationship with nature in order to supply the psychological support for this synthesis.

This account of the subject in nature starts from the assumption that nature is always a source of both gratification and frustration and that "she" is therefore always unconsciously experienced as both a good and a bad mother.[2] On the one hand, nature is loved for the goodness she grants. Just as the infant's life depends entirely on the mother who feeds it, so too nature is the ultimate ground of all the nourishment we need. Just as the mother is a predictably comfortable presence with whom the infant can merge, so too nature is the source of our sense that we are part of something larger and more stable than ourselves. And nature not only "holds" us but "mirrors" us as well: by watching the way it reacts to the way in which we work it, we gain a sense of our competence that parallels the emerging agency of the child whose autonomous efforts are recognized by his mother.[3] In all these ways—and more—nature nurtures us and is therefore loved by us.

But nature is also hated for harming us. Often it is a dreaded threat to the very human survival of which it is the source. Just as the child disdains his discovery that his mother has a separate, independent existence, so we decry the seemingly willful unpredictability of nature—its storms, its floods, its droughts—as an unpalatable indifference to, or even assault upon, our welfare. And, even if we are lucky enough to evade these attacks, we cannot avoid the fact that the very nature that secures our existence also appears to begrudge it. If it is true that nature is the ultimate source of our survival, it is also true that nature is never so bountiful as to prevent us from having to *work* in order to survive. Labor, Hegel tells us, "is desire restrained and checked, evanescence delayed and postponed."[4] Because nature makes us work, it obliges us to postpone gratification. Thus even the most giving nature is a source of frustration and of the aggression to which frustration inevitably gives rise. Like the paranoid-schizoid child, moreover, we tend to project that aggression onto nature, which then becomes an even more monstrous mother than it would otherwise be. Thus the nature we love is also the nature we hate.

Cultural development, I suggest, depends every bit as much on the integration of our love and hate for nature as individual development depends on the integration of love and hate for the mother. Just as the child who successfully negotiates the depressive position painfully comes to the conclusion that his mother is neither all-good nor all-bad, but rather "good-enough" and therefore worthy of care, so culturally depressive integration would entail the symbolization of a nature that is "good-enough" to merit our ministrations. Moreover, just as the depressively integrated child is able to relate to the (m)other not as a "projective entity" but rather as an "entity in [her] own right" with whom it is possible to establish a non-narcissistic object relation, so a depressively integrated culture would be able to achieve a "state of being in relation to [non-human nature] as something outside and separate."[5] This experience of the non-human world as something separate with which we are nevertheless connected, in turn, is as essential for healthy cultural development as the child's non-narcissistic relationship to the mother is necessary for his individual development. As David Abram has written, "we are human only in contact, and conviviality, with what is not human."[6]

But this experience of conviviality does not come easily. In fact it presupposes a work of cultural mourning that parallels the mourning of the child who is *en route* to depressive integration. Just as that child must grieve the loss of the all-good fantasy mother for whom she pines as well as surrender to her sorrow for having harmed (whom she now recognizes as) the real mother, so the culture must relinquish its fantasy of a perfectly nurturing nature as well as confront its sadness and guilt for having harmed the real, imperfect one. When we work, nature winces. This suffering would be a source of considerable anxiety and guilt even if human work were not infused with the aggression that inevitably issues from the frustration that it imposes. But, because work *is* infused with aggression, our anxiety and guilt are compounded by the unconscious fact that the harm we do is harm we *wish* to do.

Precisely because this anxiety and guilt is so stressful, the temptation to evade it is so strong. The difficult work of cultural mourning is threatened by mechanisms of defense that parallel those of the child whose depressive anxiety and guilt is simply too great to grieve. For reasons to which I refer in my *Marxism and Domination*, in pre-modern, "primitive" societies *idealization* is the predominant cultural defense against "natural" depressive anxiety and guilt: nature is typically symbolized as a perfectly benevolent mother on whom one remains forever dependent while nature-hatred is split off and returns in the form of a self-abnegating obligation to give gifts or make sacrifices to her.[7] This intimate identification with an all-good mother-nature excludes any sense of separation from her and thus arguably rules out the development of an authentically autonomous self.[8] Thus what Giddens calls the absence of "opportunities for self-expression" in pre-modern societies is the other side of a coin whose face side is the idealization of nature.

In modernity, in contrast, self-expression flourishes in the flawed form of what Bauman calls the "drive to mastery." In other (Kleinian) words, *manic denial* is the defensive path typically taken in modern societies: modernity defends us against "natural" anxiety and guilt that would otherwise accompany the awareness that we hate the (mother) nature that we love by manically denying our need for nature and transforming it into the denigrated object of our omnipotent control. Having projected its own aggression into (what becomes) an all-bad nature, modernity aggressively defends against this (its own) aggression by treating nature as an enemy that must be conquered, even destroyed. Thus, from a Kleinian point of view, the labor that is celebrated by Marx and other Modernists for its "civilizing" reduction of nature to a pure "object for humankind . . . to subjugate . . . under [its] needs"[9] is anything but a labor of love. That labor is, instead, a demonizing defense against the difficulties of the depressive position and, like any psychological defense, it has a necessarily compulsive character. Could production be anything other than compulsive if, as Marx argues, every production that satisfies existing needs *necessarily* engenders new ones?[10]

We saw in chapter 10 that, for Marx, the ideal culmination of this productive process is that "nature appears as [Man's] work [and] he contemplates himself in a world that he has created."[11] But if we only find ourselves when we look at nature, then it becomes impossible to "imagine that we are part of something larger than ourselves . . . We have deprived nature of its independence, and that is fatal to its meaning. Nature's independence *is* its meaning; without it there is nothing but us."[12] And if, to repeat Abram's claim, "we are human only in contact and conviviality with what is *not* human," then "when there is nothing but us" it is difficult indeed to feel fully human. If, in other words, the meaning of human life can be established only in relation to the meaning of nature, then when we deprive nature of meaning we deprive our lives of meaning as well. Thus the price of modernity's manic defense against "natural" depressive anxiety and guilt is the chronic feelings of meaninglessness that prevail in its midst. As the psychoanalyst Otto Kernberg argues, "in narcissistic personalities, where the normal relations between an integrated self and integrated internal objects are replaced by a pathological grandiose self and a deterioration of internal objects, the experience of emptiness is most intense and almost constant."[13] What goes for a narcissistic personality goes for a narcissistic culture as well: the failure to introject a "good-enough" world precludes the formation of a good-enough self. Hence the modern "epoch of nihilism" of which Nietzsche despaired but to which his celebration of the "will to power" arguably contributed.[14]

But nihilism does not negate, but rather only intensifies, the need for the good mother in the form of an intense "hunger for objects," that according to Melanie Klein is "so characteristic of mania."[15] The message of consumerism, as John Carroll has argued, is "if you feel bad, eat!"—but what the consumer wants, above all, "is to be eaten up, absorbed by a larger universe than that of her lonely self."[16] In Kleinian terms: unable to introject a "good-enough world," the empty self defends itself against depletion through an omnipotent merger with objects that represent the "good mother" murdered by manic denial. Thus the split between the good and bad (mother) nature is transformed into the split between all-bad nature and all-good objects. The desperate drive for (re)union with the perfect mother explains why people will "shop 'til they drop" and accounts as well for the elation—the "commodity euphoria"[17]—they experience when that union is consummated. If compulsive consumers were to speak to their products, here is what they would say: "you are perfect, but I am part of you."[18]

But of course this perfection is not meant to last. Like a lover who disdainfully drops his over-idealized partner as soon as he discovers her inevitable imperfections, as soon as one product goes "out of style" it is quickly rejected and replaced by another. Thus the temporary elation at refinding the perfect mother inevitably gives way to the depletion resulting from losing her over and over again. Compulsive consumption, in other words, is a recipe for perpetual *dis*satisfaction, and it therefore functions to reproduce the very emotional emptiness against which it is supposed to defend. Yet the compulsive consumer knows no other way to fill himself up. If and when he gets sick of this self-defeating cycle, he will omnipotently declare his independence from the very objects he continues to crave. But this impossible struggle to "defeat" the object serves only to defeat the self: his repeated failures to give up the food, clothes, cars, etc. on which he over-depends eventually make him face the humiliating fact that the (apparent) power of the object is far greater than his own. Thus does the guilt that results from damage done to nature culminate in shame that does damage to the self.

To sum up: my argument to this point has been that modernity defends against "natural" depressive anxiety and guilt through a cycle of compulsive production and compulsive consumption that does violence to the world as well as the self. This self- and world-defeating cycle blocks the (ascending) path to a reparative response to that anxiety and guilt, and thus to a more reverential relationship between self and world. In the long term, that reparative cultural development would benefit from those changes in the structure and practices of child rearing I have already identified as conducive to depressive integration. But there are also hopeful *contemporary* signs of a culturally reparative response to natural depressive anxiety and guilt. I would like to close this book by briefly summarizing two such responses that I have described elsewhere at greater length.[19]

A: Deep Ecology

The term "deep ecology" was coined in 1973 by the Norwegian philosopher Arne Naess in order to distinguish forms of environmentalism that were "shallow" in their failure to challenge anthropocentrism from the radical critique of anthropocentrism that he endorsed.[20] Over the course of the last three decades deep ecology has moved "from a proposal in a philosophical journal . . . to a position that is now a bench mark in defining varieties of environmental philosophies."[21] It is an environmental philosophy, moreover, that can justly claim widespread political influence: "It has provided inspiration for resistance against nuclear weapons, nuclear power, military bases, new dams, and logging operations, and is closely related to activist groups such as Greenpeace, Earth First, Friends of the Earth, and Green political parties."[22]

All deep ecologists insist that the modern assumption that nature is a mere means for exclusively human ends, and thus that nature properly becomes the object of the human effort to master it, is a recipe for both natural and human disaster. The particular virtue of Arne Naess, in my judgment, is that he manages to contest modernity's (manic) denial of dependence on and pretension to (omnipotent) control over nature without indulging in its idealization. "The process of identification," he tells us in *Ecology, Community, and Lifestyle*:

> leads us to see much cruelty in nature . . . Nature is not brutal, but from a human point of view, we do see brutality—as we see yellow in the sun; as we see these fantastically blue mountains outside this window.

As an example of such "cruelty" or "brutality" he offers the example of a "desperately hungry wolf attacking an elk, wounding it mortally but . . . incapable of killing it," and tells us that it is "impossible not to identify with and somehow feel the pains of both" the elk that dies "after protracted, severe pains" and the wolf who "dies slowly of hunger." This sorrow, in turn, inevitably triggers the

> search for means to interfere with natural processes on behalf of any being in a state of panic and desperation, protracted pain, severe suppression or abject slavery. But this attitude implies that we deplore much that actually goes on in nature [and] that seems essential to life on Earth.

Thus he concludes that the natural "process of identification" between humans and the other suffering beings on whom they depend precludes "any unconditional *Verherrlichung* [glorification] of life, and therefore of nature in general."[23]

Far from replacing the demonization with the idealization of nature, then, Naess insists that nature is neither all-good nor all-bad: it is, in that sense, "beyond good and evil." As such, nature is the inevitable source of *both* our joy and our sorrow. Or at least it is for people strong enough to feel both of these emotions: "With maturity, human beings will experience joy when other life forms experience joy and sorrow when other life forms experience sorrow."[24] Thus for Naess mourning is as central as celebration to a mature relationship with nature. To both mourn and celebrate with nature, moreover, is to *accept* it as a site of both great pleasure and great pain: "There is a kind of deep yes to nature which is central to my philosophy . . . there is a deep unconditionality, but at the same time a kind of regret, sorrow or displeasure."[25] Without doing any violence to Naess's position we can translate it into the following specifically Kleinian terms: nature is neither all-good nor all-bad and therefore eminently worthy of care. The ecological analogue of depressive integration is the uncon-ditional "yes" to which Naess yields.

It is precisely this simultaneously emotional and cognitive position, I would suggest, that supports the first and most controversial "plank" in the "platform" of deep ecology proposed by Naess and his colleague George Sessions in 1984: "The well-being and flourishing of human and nonhuman Life on Earth have value in themselves (synonyms: intrinsic value, inherent value). These values are independent of the usefulness of the nonhuman world for human pur-poses."[26] Against the claim of some of their critics that treating nature as an end in itself would prevent people from making use of it in order to satisfy their legitimate needs, Naess and Sessions emphasize that "the slogan of 'noninterfer-ence' does not imply that humans should not modify some ecosystems as do other species. Humans have modified the earth and will probably continue to do so. At issue is the nature and extent of such interference."[27] And in Naess's 1973 article inaugurating deep ecology he made it clear that "modifying" nature necessarily includes "some killing, exploitation, and suppression" of the non-human beings who inhabit it.[28] The inevitability of harm to non-human beings is in fact *already* implicit in the third "plank" of the deep ecological platform: "Humans have no right to reduce [the] richness and diversity of [non-human life forms] except to satisfy *vital* needs."[29] It follows from this principle that deep ecology *does* allow for the destructive interference with non-human life when that interference really *is* essential to the satisfaction of those needs.

Of course it follows from Naess's principle of "identification" that even the necessary harm that humans impose on non-human nature would be a source of great regret.[30] If mature human beings suffer from the suffering of the beings with whom they identify, then any harm done to those beings in the course of the satisfaction of vital human needs will inevitably be a source of human (as well as non-human) pain. Thus mature human beings will be motivated either to find alternative, non-destructive ways to satisfy their vital needs or to re-evaluate those needs if in fact benign ways of satisfying them cannot be found. To put this another way: deep ecology is dedicated to dialogue in which individuals attempt to reconcile their needs with what they take to be the needs of nature. It encourages not "irresponsible passivity" but rather an active search

for technologies that, in Naess's words, "satisfy maximally both the requirements of reduced interference with nature and satisfaction of human vital
needs." Naess is aware that "conflicts" between these two goals are inevitable
and that the best we can hope for is a kind of "equilibrium" between them.[31] But
he also insists that the onus is on us to justify any "disequilibrium" that favors
our needs over the needs of nature.[32]

Naess understands that a qualitatively different relationship with nature
implies a qualitatively different relationship with our products. He gestures
in the direction of a critique of consumerism in his *Ecology, Community, and
Lifestyle* when he emphasizes that:

> the [deep ecology] movement encourages the reduction of individual total
> consumption, and will through information, increased awareness, and
> mutual influence attempt to free the individual from the consumer pres-
> sures which make it very difficult for politicians to support better policies
> and a healthier society.[33]

But "information, increased awareness and mutual influence" are no match for
the contemporary *compulsion* to consume. Neither Naess nor (to my knowledge) any other deep ecologist "gets" that over-consumption is a psychological
and not just ideological problem, and that the only way to stop "repeating"
this problem is to "work it through." Working it through is precisely what happens—or is supposed to happen—in twelve-step recovery programs.

B: Recovery

The extraordinary proliferation of self-help or mutual aid groups during the last
quarter of the twentieth century is surely one of the most significant psycho-
social developments of our time. According to the most comprehensive study
of support groups in America, by 1994 "between 8 and 10 million people" or
at least 5 percent of the adult population participated in at least 500,000 self-
help groups in which they "share[d] their problems" and "receive[d] emotional
support." In 1994 almost one-third of the members of these self-help groups,
or between two-and-a-half and three million people, belonged to twelve-step
recovery programs,[34] or as many people as were then receiving help from professional psychotherapists.[35] Since then twelve-step membership has increased
exponentially: a November 2003 report claims that "an estimated 15 million [!]
Americans are currently involved in some form of recovery, making 12-step-
pers more numerous than Episcopalians, Jews, and Muslims combined."[36]

Although the first and largest twelve-step program is, of course Alcoholic
Anonymous, A.A. is only the prototype for (what were estimated in the early
1990s to be) between 120 and 260 different national recovery programs deal-
ing with every conceivable form of addiction.[37] Thus it is no exaggeration to
claim that the original twelve-step philosophy of A.A. has expanded into a

"generalized twelve-step consciousness" that is shared by millions of Americans who "think of themselves as members of a . . . recovery movement."[38] For many of the members of this movement, compulsive consumption—of alcohol, drugs, food, clothes, or whatever—is the problem for which they seek a solution.

When they do so, the first thing they will learn is that "the attainment of humility is the foundation principle of each of [the recovery program's] twelve steps."[39] The first of the twelve steps affirms both the "addict's" dependence on the "drug" he had earlier denied and his consequent lack of control over his life: "We admitted we were powerless over [drug of choice]—that our lives had become unmanageable." With this admission the addict begins to renounce the grandiosity that all twelve-step programs locate at the heart of his addiction. He admits, in effect, that he is not God. But this admission—humbling as it may be—that his own power cannot defeat his addiction is but a prelude to his affirmation in steps two and three that faith in, and reliance on, "a Power greater than ourselves" is the only route to his sobriety.[40] Steps two and three are an even greater insult to the omnipotence of the addict than step one: it is one thing to for him to acknowledge that he lacks the power to conquer his problem, but quite another to admit that something or someone else has the power he lacks.

Yet this admission, according to twelve-step thinking, is essential to her recovery. Without the first step the addict would still be "in denial" of her despair. But without steps two and three there would be no available exit from it: having reluctantly come to the conclusion that she really is powerless over her addiction, the only way in which she can "keep hope alive" is to come to accept that some other power will help her overcome it. Given the twelve-step diagnosis of the problem, moreover, it makes sense to describe this "other" power as a "Power greater than ourselves," a "higher power," or "God as we under[stand] him."[41] If, as A.A. claims, addiction is a self-destructive symptom of a "soul-sickness"[42]—of "personal enslavement to the false ideals of a materialistic society"[43]—then only some sort of spirituality can save the addict's soul from that sickness.

This spirituality is defined as expansively as possible: the appeal to God "as we understand him" in the third step is intended to make room for people who are not religious in any traditional sense of that word. Because virtually any-thing—including the recovery group itself—can serve as the addict's "higher power"—agnostics and even atheists can "work" the steps that are supposed to lead to their sobriety. Non-believers in the ordinary sense of that term can complete steps two and three by coming to the conviction that the power of the group, which after all typically includes many members with many years of sobriety, can help "restore them to sanity" if only they ask for its help and follow its (or their sponsor's) advice. Whether or not the member explicitly affirms the group as the higher power to which he must "surrender," twelve-step programs understand that the support given to him by the group is indispensable to his recovery. In the group he learns—for the first time—that he does not need to hide (which is what the addict always does) but can reveal himself in all his weakness and still be accepted—indeed applauded—by the other, equally vulnerable members of the group. Thus the twelve-step group becomes, in effect, what Winnicott calls a "holding environment" within which a (new) sense of self can be nourished, a "good-enough" mother, as it were, that unconditionally supports the addict's eventual individuation.[44]

Steps four through nine make this crystal-clear. The fourth step asks the addict to undertake "a searching and fearless moral inventory"[45] of himself, a painfully honest appraisal of both his defects and his assets. Here he is challenged to break the cycle of "grandiosity . . . and abjection"[46]—and thus his tendency alternately to demonize others and to demonize himself—from which he suffers in order to see himself and others as he and they really are, that is, as neither all-good nor all-bad and therefore worthy of concern. Psychoanalytically speaking, this step signals the beginning of the end of

> the splitting of the good and bad self and object representation[s]. As the previously split "good" and "bad" self and object representations begin to merge . . . recovering substance abusers become more tolerant of their own shortcomings and that [sic] of others.[47]

In working step four, then, the recovering addict moves from shame to guilt, from the fantasy that she is bad (as well as the fantasies that defend against this feeling) to the reality that some of her actions have been bad, and thus from a position that precludes taking responsibility for those actions to one that encourages it. Thus we can say that step four is a step in the direction of a reparative response to what Klein calls the depressive position, and that the group whose support makes this step possible is like the good-enough mother whose ministrations make it possible for the child to begin to negotiate it.

Steps five through eight move her further down the road toward the righting of the wrongs identified in her moral inventory. Step five asks her to admit these wrongs to both another human being and to her higher power, and is thus at once an additional lesson in humility, the beginning of more honest relationships with others, and public protection against any "denial" of the defects that keeping them private might otherwise promote.[48] Steps six and seven reproduce, in effect, the logic of steps two and three: just as two and three assert that faith in, and reliance on, a higher power is required for her recovery, so six and seven proclaim that she needs help from her higher power in order to begin the difficult reparative work on which that recovery depends.

That reparations are in fact essential to recovery is spelled out in steps eight and nine, which ask members first to make "a list of all persons we have harmed, and become willing to make amends to them all" and then to make "direct amends to such people wherever possible, except where to do so would injure others."[49] Since, according to *Twelve Steps and Twelve Traditions*, "defective relations with other human beings have nearly always been the immediate cause of our [addiction],"[50] the effort to repair those relations is essential to the process of recovering from it. Since the active addict "is like a tornado roaring his way through the lives of others"[51] there is a great deal of damage he has done and many wrongs he will therefore have to try to right. He is, in short, faced with a formidable task indeed. But the recovering addict is assured that the difficulty of the task is more than matched by the rewards for undertaking it. "In nine cases out of ten" he will find that his former lovers, friends, or associates are moved to forgive him by the sincerity of his remorse over, and his willingness (where possible) to make restitution for, the harm he has caused them.[52] With forgiveness comes enormous relief. And even when forgiveness is not forthcoming, the recovering addict at least gains satisfaction from knowing that he has done what he can to "clean house" and "put [his] life in order."[53] Moreover, even when restitution to the other is impossible, in the course of reflecting on the damage he has done to the other he will often become more aware of the damage he has done to himself.[54] Thus steps eight and nine offer recovering addicts the opportunity to make reparations not only to others but also to themselves.

If we assume, with Freud, that "ostensibly normal people do not behave very differently from neurotics,"[55] then we recognize that the difference between the "neurotic" addiction to, and "normal" over-consumption of, a wide range of "stuff" is merely a matter of degree. This recognition authorizes Ernest Kurtz's claim that modernity is "inherently addictive: the striving always harder for the ever more that satisfies ever less."[56] If modernity is, in that sense, "inherently addictive," then we can also say, with Kurtz, that the twelve-step critique of addiction is a "counter-Enlightenment phenomenon antithetical to the central assumptions of . . . modernity."[57] Thus twelve-step recovery programs recommend themselves as programs for what might be called the recovery from modernity.

By now the depth-psychological connection between recovery and deep ecology should be clear: both contest modern omnipotence and are committed to repair the damage that it does. But there is also an organic (or mutually causal) connection between them. If compulsive consumption defends us from the loss of meaning mandated by the denial of our dependence on nature, then the recovery from compulsive consumption ultimately requires the deep ecological effort to reconnect with a world that would no longer be an object of compulsive production. If the insatiable search for "stuff" is an unconscious prop (as well as conscious justification) for compulsive production, the deep ecological challenge to compulsive production must eventually embrace the struggle to recover from the addiction to "stuff." Thus the fate of deep ecology and the fate of twelve-step recovery are, in fact, inextricably intertwined.

I suspect, however, that many of the supporters of both movements might currently contest this fact. On the one hand, to many of the anti-anthropocentric members of the deep ecology movement, the exclusive preoccupation of the partisans of recovery with the repair of the self may look like the same self-centered indulgence that has long plagued the planet. Thus the twelve-step movement is not likely to appeal to deep ecologists until its commitment to repair the self includes a commitment to repair the world on which the self depends. On the other hand, twelve-steppers who suffer through the emotional causes and consequences of their own personal omnipotence are unlikely to embrace a deep ecological movement that has yet to acknowledge that an omnipotent relationship with nature has a psychological source. Unless deep ecology becomes more psychologically sensitive it is unlikely to attract people for whom the struggle to recover their emotional equilibrium is of paramount importance. In short, there are pitfalls on the path to an integration of, or even an alliance between, the deep ecological and twelve-step movements. But a constructive relationship between them is as promising as it is problematical.[58] Together they point to the possibility of a well-governed subject-in-nature.

GLOSSARY OF NAMES

Benedict Anderson (1936–)
Professor Emeritus of International Studies, Government and Asian Studies at Cornell University. He is best known for his book *Imagined Communities*, which established his reputation as one of the leading social constructionist students of nationalism.

Kwame Anthony Appiah (1954–)
Professor of Philosophy at Princeton University. Appiah is a Ghanaian philosopher, cultural theorist, and novelist who is perhaps best known for his critique of Afro-centrism in his widely acclaimed book, *In My Father's House.*

Hannah Arendt (1906–1975)
A German-Jewish refugee from Nazi persecution, she arrived in the United States in 1941 and subsequently taught political theory at the New School for Social Research, Princeton, and the University of Chicago, among other schools. She is probably best known to the public for coining the phrase the "the banality of evil" to describe Adolph Eichman in her *Eichman in Jerusalem*. But it was her *The Origins of Totalitarianism* and *The Human Condition* that established her status as the only woman whose works are typically included in the canon of modern (post–sixteenth-century) political theory.

John Austin (1790–1859)
Considered by many to be the founder of modern jurisprudence, Austin served as Professor of Jurisprudence at the University of London (now University College London) from 1826 to 1832. His command theory of law is elaborated in his *The Province of Jurisprudence Determined*, which greatly influenced the subsequent development of what came to be called "legal positivism."

Peter Bachrach (1918–2008)
One of the leading academic advocates of democratic participation in the 1960s and 1970s, Bachrach taught democratic theory for many years at Bryn Mawr

College and Temple University. His article with Morton Baratz, "The Two Faces of Power," remains the most widely cited article in the discipline of political science.

Morton S. Baratz (1923–1998)
Colleague of and co-author with Peter Bachrach, for many years he was Chair of the Economics Department at Bryn Mawr College until he joined the faculty of Boston University and subsequently served as Vice-Chancellor of the University of Maryland, Baltimore County.

Benjamin Barber (1939–)
Professor of Civil Society and Distinguished University Professor at the University of Maryland, College Park, President and Director of the NGO CivWorld, and Senior Fellow at Demos. His positions at CivWorld and Demos reflect his longstanding commitment to translate democratic theory into democratic practice.

Zygmunt Bauman (1925–)
Bauman lost his Chair in Sociology at the University of Warsaw during the anti-Semitic purge of 1968 and has lived in England since 1971. Now Professor Emeritus at the University of Leeds, where he taught for many years, Bauman is the author of fifty-seven books (!), most of them devoted to the critical analysis of modernity. He is perhaps best known for his *Modernity and the Holocaust*, which argues that the Holocaust was not a regression from but rather the culmination of modern rationalism.

Peter Berger (1929–)
University Professor of Sociology and Theology at Boston University. His *The Desecularization of the World* (1999) calls into question the secularization thesis that he promoted two decades earlier. He is well known for co-authoring (with Thomas Luckmann) *The Social Construction of Reality*, which argues that individuals shape the very social structures by which they are shaped.

Susan Bordo (1947–)
Currently the holder of the Otis A. Singletary Chair in Humanities at the University of Kentucky, Bordo has explored the culturally constructed identification of women with the body and thus the connection between the denigration of the body in Western philosophy and the denigration of women. In her *Unbearable Weight: Feminism, Western Culture and the Body* (1993) she argues that disproportionately female bodily disorders such as anorexia and bulimia are both forms of resistance to, and the debilitating effects of, the cultural construction of the female body.

Robert Bork (1927–)

A conservative legal scholar and advocate of "originalism" who served as Solicitor General and (briefly) as Acting Attorney General under President Nixon and later as Judge for the United States Court of Appeals for the District of Columbia Circuit. In 1987 he was nominated to the Supreme Court by President Reagan but the Senate did not confirm his nomination.

Walter Dean Burnham (1930–)

Professor Emeritus of Political Science at The University of Texas at Austin, he taught for many years at Washington University in St. Louis before coming to the University of Texas in 1988. He is well known for the theory of "critical elections," elections that not only transfer power from one party to another but also inaugurate a profound and lasting change in the ideologies and policies that prevail in the political system.

Nancy Chodorow (1944–)

Feminist sociologist and psychoanalyst who taught for many years at The University of California at Berkeley, from which she retired in 2005. She is best known for her extraordinarily influential *The Reproduction of Mothering: Psychoanalysis and the Sociology of Gender*, which, along with Dorothy Dinnerstein's *The Mermaid and The Minotaur*, is one of the founding texts of "feminist mothering theory."

Robert A. Dahl (1915–)

Professor Emeritus at Yale University, where he taught for over fifty years, Dahl is considered by many to be the "Dean" of American political scientists, both because of his many important book-length contributions to democratic theory and for the large number of prominent political scientist who were his students. In the 1960s his *Who Governs?*, published in 1961, was at the center of the debate among political scientists over the nature of power in America.

Alexis de Tocqueville (1805–1859)

Tocqueville's master work, *Democracy in America*, was published in 1835 following his visit to and travels in the United States. After the fall of the monarchy of Louis-Philippe during the 1848 Revolution, Tocqueville was elected to the Constituent Assembly of 1848 and helped to draft the constitution of the Second Republic (1848–1851). He supported the suppression of the June insurrection of Parisian workers as well as laws passed immediately following the failed insurrection to restrict freedom of assembly and the press.

Dorothy Dinnerstein (1923–1992)

Dinnerstein taught psychology at Rutgers University from 1959 to her death from an automobile accident in 1992. Her major work, *The Mermaid and the*

Minotaur, draws on and modifies the psychoanalytic assumptions of Melanie Klein in order to give a psycho-dynamic account not only of male domination but of political domination and the domination of nature as well. Along the way, a number of important social theorists, including Freud, Marx, Norman O. Brown, and Herbert Marcuse are subjected to incisive yet constructive criticism.

Lisa Disch (1961–)
Feminist political theorist who taught at the University of Minnesota before coming to the University of Michigan, where she specializes in contemporary continental political thought.

W. E. B. Du Bois (1868–1963)
The first African American to earn a Ph.D. from Harvard University, Du Bois went on to become the most prominent "black" intellectual and political activist of the first half of the twentieth century. In 1909 he helped to found the NAACP, for which he worked as editor-in-chief of its publication, *The Crisis*, for twenty-five years. A militant critic of the racial separatism of Marcus Garvey, he was sympathetic to both socialism and Pan-Africanism, and became a citizen of Ghana in 1963, where he died in August of that year at the age of 95.

Ronald Dworkin (1931–)
Currently Professor of Law and Philosophy at New York University, Dworkin previously held Chairs at Oxford University and University College London. In *Law's Empire*, among other works, Dworkin argues that there is an historically evolving relationship between law and morality, and thus contests the sharp separation that positivists such as H. L. A. Hart make between the two. He is a frequent contributor to contemporary debates concerning the relationship between national security and individual rights, particularly in *The New York Review of Books*.

John Ehrenberg (1944–)
Chair of the Political Science Department of the Brooklyn Campus of Long Island University, Ehrenberg's most recent book, *Servants of Wealth*, describes the recent neoconservative effort to use the state to serve dominant economic interests.

John Hart Ely (1938–2003)
Ely taught at Yale Law School and Harvard Law School before serving as Dean of Stanford Law School from 1982 to 1987, where he continued to teach until 1996, when he moved to the University of Miami School of Law. He is one of the most widely cited recent or contemporary legal scholars in the United States, ranking just after Richard Posner and Ronald Dworkin.

Heinz Eulau (1915–2004)

Eulau joined the Department of Political Science at Stanford in 1958 and taught there until his retirement in 1986. He is considered one of the founders of the behavioral movement in American political science.

Robert Fine (1945–)

Fine teaches social and political thought in the Sociology Department of the University of Warwick (UK). He is the author of *Political Investigations: Hegel, Marx, Arendt* and the co-editor of *Social Theory After the Holocaust* and *People, Nation and State*.

Roger Finke (1954–)

Professor of Sociology and Religion at Penn State University, he is best known for his award-winning book, co-authored with Rodney Stark, *The Churching of America, 1776–1990*.

Michel Foucault (1926–1984)

Perhaps the most influential French intellectual of the last half of the twentieth century, Foucault held a chair at the College de France from 1970 to his death in 1984 from Aids-related complications. His "genealogies" of modern medicine, penology, and psychology disclosed the operation of power in and through the very knowledge that is conventionally opposed to it, and led Foucault to insist that the individual "subject" is merely an effect of power/knowledge. At the same time, however, he argued that power necessarily engenders resistance, resistance in which he himself was engaged for some years as a founder and member of the Prison Information Group, which was designed to help prisoners publicize the conditions of French prisons and to support their struggles to improve those conditions.

Nancy Fraser (1947–)

Critical theorist who taught in the Philosophy Department at Northwestern University for several years before becoming the Henry A. and Louise Loeb Professor of Political and Social Science at the New School University. Fraser is best known for her insistence on the centrality of both the redistribution of resources and the recognition of different groups to the struggle for a more just society.

Milton Friedman (1912–2006)

Friedman taught economics for thirty years at the University of Chicago, and was considered the leader of the Chicago School of Economics, which trumpeted the virtues of a "free market" more or less unregulated by the state. He is particularly well known among economists for his monetarism, which argues that the supply of money is more important than investment and government spending in determining the level of production and consumption. His book, co-authored with his wife Rose Friedman, *Free to Choose*, was the best selling non-fiction book of 1980 and has been translated into fourteen different foreign languages. This work as well his *Capitalism and Freedom* provided an intellectual foundation for the efforts, beginning in the 1980s, of Ronald Reagan, Margaret Thatcher, and subsequent "conservative" political leaders to deregulate the economy.

Rose Friedman (1911?-)

Co-author with her husband of *Free to Choose* and *Tyranny of the Status Quo*, she served on the staff of the Federal Deposit Insurance Corporation and the National Bureau of Economic Research after doing graduate work in economics at the University of Chicago.

Clifford Geertz (1926–2006)

Geertz taught anthropology at the University of Chicago for ten years before serving as a professor of social science at the Institute for Advanced Study in Princeton between 1970 and 2000. His "thick descriptions" of a wide variety of cultural practices were based on extensive field work in Southeast Asia and North Africa.

Ernest Gellner (1925–1995)

Born in Paris of Czech-Jewish parents and raised in Prague, he immigrated to England in 1939 and joined the Sociology Department of the London School of Economics in 1949, becoming Professor of Philosophy, Logic and Scientific Method in 1962. In 1984 he became head of the Department of Anthropology at Cambridge, where he remained until 1993, when he returned to Prague as head of the Center for the Study of Nationalism. He first gained academic recognition for his *Words and Things*, a fierce critique of ordinary language analysis, and later was perhaps best known for his *Nations and Nationalism*, an important contribution to the social constructionist approach to nationalism.

Anthony Giddens (1938-)

Giddens taught sociological theory at Cambridge for many years before serving as Director of the London School of Economics from 1997 to 2003. His many works on modernity emphasize the reciprocal relationship between structure and agency and between "macro" processes such as globalization and "micro" processes such as the democratization of intimate relationships. For more than a decade he has explored the possibility of a "third way" between capitalism and socialism, and for some years he served as an adviser to the British Prime Minister Tony Blair. In 2004 he was given a life peerage and now sits in the House of Lords for the Labour Party.

Todd Gitlin (1943–)

A 1960s activist who served as President of Students for a Democratic Society from 1963–1964, Gitlin went on to teach sociology and communications at Berkeley and New York University before becoming Chair of the Ph.D. program in Communications at Columbia University. He is well known for his critical reflections on the New Left and the mass media, as well as the "identity politics" to which (he believes) they both made a contribution.

Alexander Hamilton (1755–1804)

Hamilton was the first Secretary of the Treasury of the United States and the author of fifty-one of the eighty-five essays in the *Federalist Papers*. A consistent supporter of a strong central government, he argued successfully for the creation of a national bank, the assumption by the federal government of state debts incurred during the Revolutionary War, and the founding of the United States Mint, all of which laid the financial foundations of the new Republic. His disagreements with James Madison over (among other things) the role of the central government eventually led to the split between the Hamiltonian Federalist Party and the Democratic-Republican Party of Madison and Thomas Jefferson. In 1804 he was killed in a duel with Aaron Burr, who had served as Vice-President during Jefferson's first term.

Marvin Harris (1927–2001)

Harris taught anthropology for many years at Columbia University before joining the Anthropology Department of the University of Florida, from which he retired in 2000. He is well known for his critical examination of several hundred years of social thought in *The Rise of Anthropological Theory*, and for his controversial account of Aztec cannibalism as a result of a protein deficiency in the Aztec diet in his *Cannibals and Kings*. That account is another (in addition to his explanation of Indian "sacred cows") application of Harris's cultural materialism, which attempts to combine Marx's theory of the determining role of the mode of production with Thomas Malthus's emphasis on the determining role of demography.

H. L. A. Hart (1907–1992)

Hart taught philosophy and jurisprudence for many years at Oxford University. One of the most influential English-speaking legal philosophers of the twentieth century, in his celebrated *The Concept of Law* he united analytic philosophy and jurisprudence to produce a version of legal positivism that subsequently became the object of the criticism of his successor at Oxford, Ronald Dworkin. Dworkin, Joseph Raz, and many other major contemporary legal and political philosophers were among his students.

Friedrich Hayek (1899–1992)
One of the most influential members of the Austrian School of economics, Hayek taught for twenty years at the London School of Economics before teaching at the University of Chicago until he moved to the University of Freiburg, where he taught until his retirement in 1968. He is famous for his critique of centrally planned economies and his defense of classical liberalism and free-market capitalism in his *The Road to Serfdom*, which reached a large popular audience when an abridged version was published in 1945 by *The Reader's Digest*. In 1974 he shared the Nobel Prize for Economics with Gunnar Myrdal, and in 1991 he received the Presidential Medal of Freedom from George Herbert Walker Bush. The Friedmans' *Free to Choose* was heavily influenced by Hayek's account of the price system as a system for transmitting and coordinating knowledge.

Doug Henwood (1952–)
An American journalist whose most recent book is *After the New Economy*, Henwood publishes the newsletter *Left Business Observer* and hosts *Behind the News*, a weekly radio program on New York City's listener-sponsored station WBAI. He is also a contributing editor at *The Nation* magazine.

Michael Ignatieff (1947–)
Ignatieff held a senior research fellowship at Cambridge from 1978 to 1984, when he began his career as a writer and journalist. His documentary series *Blood and Belonging: Journeys into the New Nationalism* (based on his book by the same name) aired on the BBC in 1993. He served as director of the Carr Center for Human Rights at Harvard from 2000 to 2005, when he became the Chancellor Jackman Visiting Professor of Human Rights Policy at the University of Toronto. Elected to the Canadian Parliament as a Liberal Party representative in 2006, Ignatieff became Interim Leader of the Liberal Party in 2008. Initially a supporter of the 2003 American invasion of Iraq, in 2007 recanted his support for that war.

Ronald Inglehart (1934–)
Inglehart is a political scientist at the University of Michigan and director of the World Values Survey, a global network of social scientists who have carried out surveys in more than sixty different societies. The author of *The Silent Revolution*, *Culture Shift*, and *Modernization and Postmodernization*, among others, Inglehart is well known for his theory of "postmaterialism," which argues, based in part on the assumptions of the humanistic psychologist Abraham Maslow, that individuals whose early socialization takes place under conditions of relative affluence are likely to privilege creative and expressive ("post-materialist") concerns over ("materialist") concerns about physical and economic security.

I. C. Jarvie (1937–)
Jarvie is Distinguished Research Professor at York University, Toronto, where he teaches philosophy of science and the sociology of the mass media. In 1959–1960 he was an assistant to the philosopher of science Karl Popper, whose influence is visible in Jarvie's critique of Peter Winch. He is Managing Editor of the journal *Philosophy of the Social Sciences*.

V. O. Key (1908–1963)
Well known for his work on elections and voting behavior, Key taught political science at UCLA, Johns Hopkins, and Yale before moving to Harvard in 1951, where he taught until his death in 1963. His textbook, *Politics, Parties, and Pressure Groups*, which went through five editions between 1942 and 1964, was one of the most widely read works on American politics during that period. His *Southern Politics in State and Nation* is considered a classic by American political scientists who focus on that region.

Melanie Klein (1882–1960)
The most influential twentieth-century psychoanalyst after Freud. Kleinian psychoanalysts are prominent in Britain and much of Latin America, and are influential in continental Europe as well. Born in Vienna of Jewish parents, Klein was the first psychoanalyst to work with very young children. Impressed by her work with those children, in 1926 Freud's colleague Ernest Jones invited her to come to England, where she became a leading member of the British Psycho-Analytical Society until her death in 1960. Considered one of the founders of what came to be called "object relations theory," Klein's theoretical disagreements with Freud's daughter, Anna Freud, led to a split in the training division of the British Psycho-Analytical Society that still exists. In 1988 Klein was the subject of a British play by Nicholas Wright, entitled *Mrs. Klein*, which revolved around the intense and unfortunate conflict between Klein and her daughter Melitta Schmideberg, herself a psychoanalyst. The play was revived in New York in 1995 and broadcast on the BBC in 2008.

Charles Lindblom (1917–)
Lindblom is a Sterling Professor of Political Science and Economics at Yale University, where he taught for many years along with his friend, colleague, and co-author Robert Dahl. Known for his insistence on the artificiality of the disciplinary distinction between political science and economics, Lindblom first championed incrementalism, or what he called the "science of muddling through," but became increasingly aware of the limits of that process over the last three decades of his career.

Eric Lott (1959–)
Professor of English at the University of Virginia since 1990, Lott's *Love and Theft* has garnered a number of prestigious prizes, including the 1994 Avery

236

O. Craven Award from the Organization of American Historians, the Modern Language Association's "Best First Book" prize of 1994, and the 1994 Outstanding Book on the Subject of Human Rights by the Gustavus Myers Center for the Study of Human Rights. Bob Dylan was reported to have taken the title of his album of the same name from Lott's book.

Steven Lukes (1941–)

Currently a professor of politics and sociology at New York University, Lukes previously taught at the University of Siena and the London School of Economics. A social theorist with wide-ranging interests, Lukes has explored the concept of power, the meaning of rationality, and the issue of moral relativism.

James Madison (1751–1836)

Before he became the fourth President of the United States, Madison wrote some of the most influential essays of the *Federalist Papers* and was the principal author of the Constitution of 1789. In 1791 he and Jefferson organized the Democratic-Republican party in opposition to the policies of Federalists such as Alexander Hamilton, who favored a national bank among other centralized governmental institutions. During his second term of office he reversed his earlier stance against the power of the federal government, supporting the creation of a second National Bank, a strong military, and a high tariff to protect new factories opened during the War of 1812.

Charles-Louis de Secondat, Baron de Montesquieu (1689–1755)

The most frequently quoted authority on government and politics in colonial America. Montesquieu's argument in favor of a separation of powers called into question the structure of the French monarchy of his time and exercised an enormous influence over the American founding fathers, and James Madison in particular. His claim that different forms of government embody different principles—monarchies the principle of honor, republics the principle of virtue, and despotisms the principle of fear—anticipates Hegel's concept of the state as "objective mind" as well as the concept of "political culture" within contemporary political science.

Arne Naess (1912–2009)

Generally recognized as the philosophical founder of deep ecology, Naess taught philosophy for three decades at the University of Oslo until 1970, when he left the university to publicize his ecological ideals and participate in political action that was informed by them. In 2005 he was knighted by King Harald of Norway.

Linda Nicholson (1947–)

Nicholson taught feminist theory and history for twenty-five years at the SUNY-Albany before becoming Director of the program in Women and Gender Studies and Stiritz Distinguished Professor in Women and Gender Studies and History at Washington University, St. Louis, in 2000.

Pippa Norris (1953–)

The McGuire Lecturer in Comparative Politics at Harvard University, Norris is the author, co-author, or editor of more than three dozen books, many of which deal with the role of political communication and public opinion in democratic societies. She has also served as Director of the Democratic Governance Group of the United Nations Development Program.

Thomas Patterson (1942–)

The Bradlee Professor of Government and the Press at the Kennedy School of Government at Harvard University, Patterson's *Out of Order* received the 2002 Graber Award of the American Political Science Association as the best book of the previous decade on political communication. An earlier book, *The Unseeing Eye*, was named by the American Association for Public Opinion Research as one of the fifty most influential books on public opinion in the past half-century.

Hannah Pitkin (1931–)

Pitkin is Professor Emerita of Political Science at the University of California, Berkeley, where she has taught political theory for more than three decades. She brings both psychoanalysis and ordinary language analysis to bear on the texts she considers. In addition to *The Concept of Representation* she has written books on Wittgenstein and Hannah Arendt. In 2003 she was awarded the John Skytte Prize in Political Science for her theoretical contributions to the problem of representation.

Karl Polanyi (1886–1964)

Born in Hungary and a supporter of the Social Democratic regime of Mihály Károlyi that was overthrown by the Communist Béla Kun in 1919, Polanyi was forced to flee to Vienna, where he lived and worked as a journalist and tutor until 1933, when he emigrated to England in response to growing fascist influence in Austria. In 1940 he moved to the United States and taught at Bennington College in Vermont while he wrote his master work, *The Great Transformation*. He taught at Columbia University from 1947 to 1953, commuting to New York from Canada because his wife's background as a former communist prevented him from gaining an entrance visa in the United States.

Kenneth Prewitt (1936–)

Prewitt teaches demography and public policy as the Carnegie Professor of Public Affairs at the School of International and Public Affairs at Columbia University. He has also taught at Stanford University, and served for one year as Dean of the Graduate Faculty at the New School University. His distinguished professional career outside the classroom includes positions as Director of the

United States Census Bureau, Director of the National Opinion Research Center, and President of the Social Science Research Council.

Robert Putnam (1941-)

Currently the Malkin Professor of Public Policy at the John F. Kennedy School of Government at Harvard University, Putnam taught at the University of Michigan until moving to Harvard in 1979. Following the publication of his extraordinarily influential book, *Bowling Alone*, Putnam organized a series of meetings among academics, civil society leaders, commentators, and politicians that were designed to help revive (supposedly) declining social capital in America. His most recent work focuses on the relationship between trust within communities and the ethnic diversity of those communities.

John Rawls (1921–2002)

Rawls taught moral and political philosophy at Harvard University for almost forty years, having earlier taught at Princeton and Cornell. His *A Theory of Justice* is widely credited with spurring the revival of the academic study of political philosophy in America during the 1970s and since. His second major work, *Political Liberalism*, works out a political conception of justice that is independent of the arguably "comprehensive" conception of justice of his earlier book, and his last work, *The Law of Peoples*, outlines his vision of a "decent" international political order. Many of the leading contemporary moral and political philosophers studied with Rawls at Harvard.

Joseph Raz (1939-)

Professor of Law at Columbia Law School and Research Professor at Oxford University, where he was Professor of the Philosophy of Law for many years prior to his retirement. His *The Morality of Freedom* won the W. J. M. Mackenzie Book Prize of the Political Studies Association of the United Kingdom and the Elaine and David Spitz Book Prize of the Conference for the Study of Political Thought, New York. Raz was a doctoral student at Oxford under H. L. A. Hart, whose legal positivism he went on to modify with his insistence in *The Authority of Law* on the minimal moral content of the rule of law.

Jean-Jacques Rousseau (1712–1778)

Perhaps the most original and influential thinker of the eighteenth century. Rousseau's *Discourse on the Origins of Inequality* continues to inform contemporary critiques of modernity; his *On the Social Contract* was deployed during the French Revolution to justify Jacobin policies and even today remains a seminal contribution to the Civic Republican tradition; his novel *Emile: or On Education* arguably inaugurated the Progressive movement in education; and his *Confessions* initiated the modern autobiography. A native of Geneva, he lived most of his adult life in France; following the publication of *Emile* his books were banned in both his native city and his adopted country. Forced into exile in England, he returned to Paris in 1770 on the condition that he not publish. In 1794, sixteen years after his death, his remains were moved to the Pantheon in Paris.

E. E. Schattschneider (1892–1971)

Schattschneider taught political science at Wesleyan University from 1930 to 1960. In 1956–1957 he was President of the American Political Science Association, which annually gives an award in his name for the best dissertation in American politics. His book *The Semisovereign People*, published in 1960, exerted an important influence on Walter Dean Burnham, Peter Bachrach, and Morton Baratz, as well as other critics of the Pluralist approach to power who published later in that decade.

Joseph Schumpeter (1883–1950)

Born in Triesch, Moravia, Schumpeter taught economics and government at the University of Czernowitz and the University of Graz before moving to the University of Bonn, where he held a chair from 1925 to 1932. He left Bonn for Harvard in 1932, where he taught until his death in 1950. Although best known among political scientists for his "realist" theory of democracy, among economists (and political leaders influenced by them) he is famous for his concept of "creative destruction," the process, endemic to capitalism, through which new, more innovative enterprises destroy old ones.

Joan W. Scott (1941–)

The Harold F. Linder Professor at the School of Social Science at the Institute for Advanced Study in Princeton, New Jersey, Scott previously taught intellectual history at the University of Illinois at Chicago, Northwestern University, and Brown University, among other schools. She is perhaps best known for her influential article "Gender: A Useful Category of Historical Analysis," published in 1986 in the *American Historical Review*. She is currently exploring the relationship between secularism and gender equality.

Adam Smith (1723–1790)

One of the central figures in the Scottish Enlightenment, Smith held the Chair of Moral Philosophy at Glasgow University from 1752 to 1765. Widely cited as the father of modern economics, Smith famously argued in *An Inquiry into the Nature and Causes of the Wealth of Nations* that the "invisible hand of the market" generally ensured that the public interest would be the unintended consequence of the pursuit of individual self-interest. The metaphor of the "invisible hand" was also employed in his first book, *The Theory of Moral Sentiments*, which was published seventeen years earlier than *The Wealth of Nations* and which proposes a psychology in which individuals find it in their self-interest to develop sympathy for others. Scholars have long debated whether this emphasis on sympathy for others in earlier work is consistent with the emphasis on economic self-interest in the later one.

Anthony D. Smith (1933–)

Currently Professor Emeritus of Nationalism and Ethnicity at the London School of Economics. Smith is a former student of Ernest Gellner, whose conceptualization of nationalism as a specifically modern phenomenon he came to reject in favor of the synthesis of modernism and primordialism that he has propounded for more than twenty years, beginning with his *The Ethnic Origins of Nations*, published in 1987.

Charles Taylor (1931–)

Currently Board of Trustees Professor of Law and Philosophy at Northwestern University, Taylor previously taught at McGill University and Oxford University. One of the most celebrated political theorists of our time, over the past four decades Taylor has produced an influential critique of behavioralism in political science, a lucid interpretation of Hegel, a forceful "communitarian" critique of Liberalism, and a major treatise on the making of the modern self. In all these works he builds bridges between the continental and analytic philosophical traditions, with which he is equally at home. In 2000 he was made a Grand Officer of the National Order of Quebec, and in 2008 he was awarded the Kyoto Prize in the category of Arts and Philosophy, which is sometimes referred to as the Japanese Nobel.

Peter Winch (1926–1997)

Winch taught philosophy at King's College London before moving to the United States in 1984 to become Professor of Philosophy at the University of Illinois at Urbana-Champaign. He is best known for his *The Idea of a Social Science and its Relation to Philosophy*, in which he draws on Wittgenstein's later philosophy, and the concept of language as a "form of life" in particular, in order to develop a forceful if controversial critique of positivism in the social sciences. His argument that the goal of the social sciences is fundamentally different from the goal of the natural sciences not only provoked fierce rejoinders from positivists who identified the two, but also encouraged efforts on the part of other more sympathetic social scientists, including Anthony Giddens and Jurgen Habermas, to develop a philosophy of the social sciences that emphasized both their differences from and their similarities with the natural sciences.

Donald Winnicott (1896–1971)

A pediatrician and psychoanalyst who practiced for forty years at Paddington Green Children's Hospital in London, Winnicott was one of the "middle groupers" in the British Psycho-Analytical Society who took no sides in the intellectual (and personal) conflict between Melanie Klein and her followers, on the one hand, and Anna Freud and her followers, on the other. Although he shared Klein's insistence on the importance of the "depressive position"—which he renamed the "capacity for concern"—he also believed that Klein dramatically underestimated the role that actual maternal practices play in determining whether it is successfully negotiated. He is perhaps best known for his concept of transitional experience, a space (often facilitated by a "transitional object") between infant and mother and between fantasy and reality that he believed was the source of all human creativity.

Robert Yates (1738–1801)

The author of *Letters of Brutus,* which argued against the ratification of the American constitution, Yates attended the Constitutional Convention in Philadelphia but left the convention early and did not sign the constitution. He ran twice for Governor of New York in 1789 and 1795 but lost both elections.

ENDNOTES

PREFACE

1 "A Strategic Plan for the Department of Political Science," May 1995.

GENERAL INTRODUCTION

1 Actually Foucault refers to "government" rather than "governance," and insists that "this word must be allowed the very broad meaning that it had in the 16th century" ("The Subject and Power," Afterword to Hubert L. Dreyfus and Paul Rabinow, *Michel Foucault: Beyond Structuralism and Hermeneutics* (Chicago: The University of Chicago Press, 1983), p. 221). But that meaning, in my judgment, has been irretrievably lost, so automatically do we now associate "government" with the "state." The term "governance," however, has no such statist implication, which is why I prefer it to "government."

2 The "conduct of conduct" has become the standard translation of Foucault's "conduire des conduites," which appears in his *Dits et Ecrits IV* (Paris: Gallimard, 1994), p. 237. The English translation of the essay in which that phrase appears can be found in Dreyfus and Rabinow, *Michel Foucault*, p. 221. In that translation "conduire des conduites" is rendered as "guiding the possibility of conduct" (p. 221).

3 See for example Ira Katznelson and Helen V. Miller, eds., *Political Science: The State of the Discipline* (New York: W.W. Norton & Co., 2002).

4 Foucault, "The Subject and Power," p. 221, emphasis added.

5 Ibid.

6 The caveat that a structure must have been a human creation to count as a governing structure is intended to exclude purely natural structures that constrain human conduct. Thus climate, geography, and genetics, for example, might be considered "governing structures" only to the extent that they have been shaped by human beings.

7 Michel Foucault, *Power/Knowledge: Selected Interviews and Other Writings, 1972-1977* (New York: Pantheon, 1980), p. 97, and Michel Foucault, *Discipline and Punish: The Birth of the Prison* (New York: Pantheon, 1977), pp. 27–28, 192–94. I take up and call into question Foucault's claim in chapter 16 of this book.

8 Strictly speaking, the post-modernist could argue that the most developed or best culture would be one in which there were no culturally shared notion of what it means to lead a good human life, but then we would have to ask whether such a notion is not constitutive of what we mean by culture in the first place.

1 LAW AND THE RULE OF LAW

1 Strictly speaking Hobbes does not claim that *all* human beings are by nature aggressive. What he argues is that all individuals are sufficiently rational to recognize that their security is threatened by those individuals who *are* inherently aggressive and that to eliminate that threat they must act preemptively against them. But whether the motivation for the aggression is innate or "defensive" the result is the same: universal aggression. Thomas Hobbes, *Leviathan* (New York: Penguin Books, 1968), chapter 13, pp. 184–85.

2 Austin's position as stated by H. L. A. Hart, *The Concept of Law*, as cited in Conrad Johnson, ed., *Philosophy of Law* (New York: Macmillan Publishing Company, 1993), p. 88.

3 John Austin, *The Province of Jurisprudence Determined*, as cited in Johnson, ed., *Philosophy of Law*, p. 33.

4 Hart, *The Concept of Law*, as cited in Johnson, *Philosophy of Law*, p. 78, and David Ingram, *Law: Key Concepts in Philosophy* (London: Continuum International Publishing Group, 2006), p. 30.

5 Tom R. Tyler, *Why People Obey the Law* (New Haven: Yale University Press, 1990).

6 Joseph Raz, *The Authority of Law: Essays on Law and Morality*, as cited in Johnson, ed., *Philosophy of Law*, p. 128.

7 Hart, *The Concept of Law*, in Johnson, ed., *Philosophy of Law*, p. 85.

8 Ingram, *Law*, pp. 20–22.

9 Ibid., p. 33.

10 Raz, *The Authority of Law*, pp. 128–30.

11 Ibid., p. 132.

12 Ibid., pp. 126–27.

13 This summary of Dworkin's position is taken from Ingram, *Law*, p. 37.

14 Ibid., p. 43.

15 Robert C. Tucker, *The Marx–Engels Reader* (New York: W. W. Norton & Co., 1978), p. 172 (emphasis in the original).

2 THE SEPARATION OF POWERS

1 Terence Ball, ed., *The Federalist with Letters of "Brutus,"* (Cambridge: Cambridge University Press, 2003), p. 235.

2 Charles de Secondat Montesquieu, ed. David W. Carrithers, *The Spirit of the Laws* (Berkeley: University of California Press, 1977) p. 200.

3 Ibid.

4 Ibid.

5 Ibid.

6 Franz Neumann, editor's introduction to Baron de Montesquieu, *The Spirit of the Laws* (New York: Hafner Publishing Company, 1949), p. lii.

7 Montesquieu, ed. David W. Carrithers, *The Spirit of the Laws*, p. 202.

8 Ibid.

9 Ibid.

10 Ibid., p. 207.

11 Ibid., pp. 210, 209.

12 Neumann, editor's introduction, p. lviii.

13 Ibid.

14 Montesquieu, ed. Carrithers, *The Spirit of the Laws*, p. 211.

15 *The Federalist*, pp. 241–42.

16 Ibid., pp. 242–43.

17 Ibid., p. 242.

18 Ibid., p. 245. Emphasis in the original.
19 Ibid., p 246.
20 Ibid., p. 248.
21 Ibid., pp. 252–53.
22 Ibid., p. 252.
23 Ibid., p. 253.
24 Ibid.
25 Ibid., p. 252.
26 Ibid., p. 254.
27 Beginning with Charles Beard, *An Economic Interpretation of the Constitution of the United States* (New York: Free Press, 1965; first published in 1913). Madison provides ample evidence for this interpretation in *Federalist 10* when he recommends a large republic as protection against dangers that include "a rage for paper money, for an abolition of debts, for an equal division of property, or for any other improper or wicked project" (*The Federalist*, p. 46).
28 *The Federalist*, p. 254.
29 Ibid., p. 255.
30 Jean-Jacques Rousseau, *On the Social Contract* (New York: St. Martin's Press, 1978), p. 59.
31 Ibid., pp. 60, 59.

3 JUDICIAL REVIEW

1   *The Federalist*, p. 377.
2   Ibid., p. 527.
3   Ibid., p. 504.
4   Ibid., p. 525.
5   Ibid., pp. 524, 527.
6   Ibid., p. 529.
7   Ibid. Emphasis in the original.
8   Ibid., p. 378.
9   Ibid., pp. 380–81.
10 Ibid., p. 380.
11 Robert Bork, cited in Ingram, *Law*, p. 67.
12 Robert Bork, cited in Johnson, *Philosophy of Law*, p. 420.
13 Here I follow Ingram, *Law*, pp. 67–69.
14 Bork, cited in Johnson, *Philosophy of Law*, p. 412.
15 This formulation of Ely's argument is from Ingram, *Law*, p. 59.
16 John Hart Ely, *Democracy and Distrust: A Theory of Judicial Review* (Cambridge, MA: Harvard University Press, 1980).
17 Ingram, *Law*, p. 73.
18 Ibid.

4 CONCEPTIONS OF DEMOCRACY

1   Robert A. Dahl, *Polyarchy: Participation and Opposition* (New Haven: Yale University Press, 1971), p. 2.
2   Ibid.
3   Ibid., p. 8.
4   Ibid., p. 4.
5   Benjamin Barber, *Strong Democracy: Participatory Politics for a New Age* (Berkeley: University of California Press, 1984).

6 John Rawls, *A Theory of Justice* (Cambridge, MA: Harvard University Press, 1971), p. 13.

7 Barber, *Strong Democracy*, p. 20.

8 Ibid., pp. 147–48.

9 Joseph Alois Schumpeter, *Capitalism, Socialism, and Democracy* (New York: Harper & Brothers, 1947), pp. 269–70.

10 Ibid., p. 269.

11 Ibid., p. 271.

12 Ibid., pp. 263–64.

13 Ibid., p. 264.

14 Rousseau, *On the Social Contract*, p. 56.

15 Ibid., p. 59.

16 Ibid.

17 Ibid., p. 56.

18 Ibid., p. 102.

19 Rousseau insists that "when an adequately informed people deliberates, the citizens [should] have no communication among themselves" because he fears that that communication would lead to the formation of factions or "partial societies" that would preclude the formation of an authentically *general* will (*On the Social Contract*, p. 61). Because his concept of "deliberation" is in this sense monological rather than dialogical he cannot be considered as an unambiguous predecessor of Barber and later advocates of "deliberative democracy." See note 23, below.

20 Massimo Teodori, ed., *The New Left: A Documentary History* (New York: The Bobbs-Merril Company, 1969), p. 167.

21 Barber, *Strong Democracy*, p. xiv.

22 Ibid., p. 173.

23 Ibid., p. 193. Because Barber emphasizes the centrality of public deliberation to democracy, in one sense his book anticipates the theoretical turn to "deliberative democracy" during the two decades following its publication. But, in contrast to Barber, many of the contemporary representatives of the deliberative turn have de-emphasized the importance of direct citizen participation and have made their peace with a mainly representative system. Thus Amy Gutmann and Dennis Thompson note that "most deliberative democrats . . . do not insist that ordinary citizens regularly take part in public deliberations, and most favor some form of representative democracy" (Princeton, N.J.: Princeton University Pres, 2004), p. 30. They favor, in other words, a modified form of the "thin" democracy that is the object of Barber's critique, which is why I have not given them separate treatment in the body of this chapter. For a "thicker" version of deliberative democracy that is more consistent with Barber's participatory version thereof, see John S. Dryzek, *Deliberative Democracy and Beyond: Liberals, Critics, Contestations* (Oxford: Oxford University Press, 2000).

24 Rousseau, *On the Social Contract*, pp. 101–102.

25 Ibid., p. 102.

26 Ibid., p. 102, 103–104.

27 Robert Paul Wolff was the first to point to this possibility in his *In Defense of Anarchism* (New York: Harper & Row, 1970). For a recent and much more technologically sophisticated version of his proposal for "instant direct democracy," see Majid Behrouzi, *Democracy as the Political Empowerment of the Citizen: Direct-Deliberative e-Democracy* (New York: Lexington Books, 2005).

28 Kirkpatrick Sale, *Human Scale* (New York: Coward, McCann & Geoghegan, 1980).

29 Rousseau, *On The Social Contract*, p. 103.

30 Ibid., pp. 49–50.

5 THE CONCEPT (AND REALITY?) OF REPRESENTATION

1 Hanna Fenichel Pitkin, *The Concept of Representation* (Berkeley: University of California Press, 1967), p. 147.
2 Ibid., p. 147.
3 Ibid., p. 151.
4 Ibid., p. 153.
5 Ibid., p. 154.
6 Ibid., p. 155. Emphases in the original.
7 See my "The Concept of Interest in Marxian and Pluralist Analysis," *Politics & Society* 1:2 (February 1971), 151–77.
8 Ibid., pp. 162–63.
9 Ibid., p. 162.
10 Ibid., p. 165. Emphasis added.
11 Anthony Downs, *An Economic Theory of Democracy* (New York: Harper & Row, 1957); Lisa Jane Disch, *The Tyranny of the Two-Party System* (New York: Columbia University Press, 2002).
12 Pitkin, *The Concept of Representation*, p. 164.
13 Anthony King, "Running Scared," *Atlantic Monthly* 279 (January), 41–61; James A. Stimson, Michael B. MacKuen, and Robert S. Erikson, "Dynamic Representation," *American Political Science Review* 89 (September 1995), 543–65.
14 Susan Herbst, *Numbered Voices* (Chicago: University of Chicago Press, 1993); Lawrence R. Jacobs and Robert Y. Shapiro, *Politicians Don't Pander: Political Manipulation and the Loss of Democratic Responsiveness* (Chicago: University of Chicago Press, 2000); David W. Moore *The Opinion Makers: An Insider Exposes the Truth Behind the Polls* (Boston: Beacon Press, 2008).
15 Kenneth Prewitt and Heinz Eulau, "Political Matrix and Political Representation: Prolegomenon to a New Departure from an Old Problem," in Heinz Eulau and John C. Wahlke, *The Politics of Representation* (Beverly Hills, CA: Sage Publications, 1978), p. 132.
16 Ibid., p. 131.
17 Ibid., p. 137.
18 Ibid., p. 131. Emphasis in the original.
19 Pitkin, *The Concept of Representation*, pp. 148–49.
20 Prewitt and Eulau, "Political Matrix and Political Representation," p. 130.
21 Brian Seitz, *The Trace of Representation* (Albany: State University of New York Press, 1995).

6 POLITICAL PARTIES

1 E. E. Schattschneider, *Party Government* (New York: Holt, Rinehart and Winston, 1942), p. 35.
2 *The Federalist,* p. 41.
3 Ibid.
4 Ibid., p. 42.
5 Ibid., p. 43.
6 Ibid.
7 Ibid., pp. 44–45.
8 Ibid., p. 45.
9 Ibid., p. 46.
10 Schattschneider, *Party Government*, p. 1.
11 Ibid., p. 8.
12 Ibid., pp. 48–49.

13 Ibid., p. 50.
14 Ibid., p. 68.
15 Ibid., p. 69.
16 Ibid., p. 70.
17 Ibid., p. 84. Emphasis in the original.
18 Ibid., p. 85.
19 Disch, *The Tyranny of the Two-Party System*, pp. 127, 7.
20 Ibid., p. 139.
21 Ibid., p. 129.
22 Ibid., p. 14.

7 ELECTIONS

1 V. O. Key, Jr., *The Responsible Electorate* (Cambridge, MA: Harvard University Press, 1966), pp. 7–8.
2 Arthur Maass, "Foreword" to Key, *The Responsible Electorate*, p. xii.
3 Key, *The Responsible Electorate*, p. 91.
4 Arthur Maass, "Foreword" to Key, *The Responsible Electorate*, p. xiii.
5 Key, *The Responsible Electorate*, p. 2.
6 *American Political Science Review* 59:1 (March 1965), 7–28.
7 E. E. Schattschneider, *The Semisovereign People* (New York: Holt, Rinehart and Winston, 1960), p. 68.
8 Ibid., p. 85.
9 Burnham, "The Changing Shape of the American Political Universe," pp. 10–11.
10 Ibid., p. 12. The 2008 presidential election, arguably the most important and exciting in many years, was no exception to this generalization. The turnout rate was (depending on how the number eligible voters is determined) only between 61 and 63 percent, somewhat higher than in previous recent presidential elections but lower than the turnout of 65 percent in 1960, which was the highest turnout since the nineteenth century.
11 Ibid., p. 17.
12 Ibid., p. 9.
13 Ibid., p. 13.
14 Ibid., p. 23.
15 Ibid., p. 22.
16 Ibid., p. 27.
17 Ibid., p. 23.
18 Ibid., p. 27.
19 *Out of Order* (New York: Vintage Books, 1994).
20 Ibid., p. 34.
21 Ibid., pp. 36-7.
22 Ibid., p. 42. At first glance the successful candidacy of Barack Obama in the Democratic Primary contest of 2007–2008 appears to call this pessimistic conclusion into question. An unusually decentralized campaign organization that relied on the financial contributions of millions of people as well as the participation of thousands of volunteers was apparently less dependent on the mainstream media than Patterson's account suggests. But we should not forget that Obama's campaign barely survived the obsessive preoccupation of those media with his arguably irrelevant connections to the Reverend Jeremiah Wright and the former Weather Underground member Bill Ayers.

8 CIVIL SOCIETY

1 Alexis de Tocqueville, *Democracy in America: Volume I* (New York: Schocken Books, 1961), p. lxviii.
2 Ibid., p. lxxi.
3 Ibid., p. lxxvii.
4 *Democracy in America: Volume II*, p. 307.
5 Ibid., p. 25.
6 Ibid., p. 120.
7 Ibid., p. 128.
8 *Democracy in America: Volume I*, p. 314.
9 *Democracy in America: Volume II*, p. 131.
10 Ibid., p. 128.
11 Ibid., p. 143.
12 Ibid., p. 131.
13 *Democracy in America: Volume I*, p. 287.
14 Ibid., pp. 220–21.
15 *Democracy in America: Volume II*, p. 132.
16 *Boy Scouts of America et al.* v. *Dale* (99–699) 530 U.S. 640 (2000). However, in this case, which involved an openly gay Boy Scout troop leader who had been forced to resign and who sued on the basis of New Jersey's laws prohibiting discrimination in "public accommodations," the five–four majority Supreme Court opinion argued that admitting an avowedly homosexual Scoutmaster *would* significantly impede the ability of the organization to carry out its purposes, which include instilling the value of being "morally straight."
17 John Ehrenberg, *Civil Society: The Critical History of an Idea* (New York: New York University Press, 1999), pp. 236, 241.
18 Ibid., p. 233; Grant McConnell, *Private Power and American Democracy* (New York: Knopf, 1966).
19 But see his "That Aristocracy May be Engendered by Manufactures," *Democracy in America: Volume II*, pp. 190–94, and below, Introduction to Part II.
20 Ehrenberg, *Civil Society*, p. 245; Sidney Verba, Kay Lehman Schlozman, and Henry E. Brady, *Voice and Equality: Civic Voluntarism in American Politics* (Cambridge, MA: Harvard University Press, 1995).
21 Schattschneider, *Semisovereign People*, p. 35.
22 *Journal of Democracy* 6:1 (1995), 65–78.
23 Ibid., p. 67.
24 Ibid., p. 77.
25 Ibid., p. 73.
26 See for example Russell Dalton, *The Good Citizen: How a Younger Generation is Reshaping American Politics* (Washington, DC: CQ Press, 2007), chapter 4.
27 Putnam, "Bowling Alone," pp. 74–75.
28 Ehrenberg, *Civil Society*, pp. 247, 248, 249.

INTRODUCTION TO PART II

1 Except that Lindblom at one point appears to hold out the possibility of a "genuine democracy [that] would not be dependent on the market." *Politics and Markets*, p. 169.
2 Tocqueville, *Democracy in America: Volume II*, pp. 191–92.
3 Ibid., p. 194.

9 HUMAN NATURE AND THE MARKET

1 Karl Polanyi, *The Great Transformation: The Political and Economic Origins of Our Time* (Boston: Beacon Press, 1944), pp. 68–69.
2 Ibid., p. 43.
3 Adam Smith, *An Inquiry Into the Nature and Causes of the Wealth of Nations* (Oxford: Oxford University Press, 1976), p. 25.
4 Ibid., p. 26.
5 Ibid., pp. 26–27.
6 Ibid., p. 27.
7 Ibid., p. 28.
8 Polanyi, *The Great Transformation*, p. 43.
9 Ibid., p. 56.
10 Ibid., p. 68.
11 Ibid., p. 53.
12 Ibid., p. 49.
13 Ibid.
14 Ibid., pp. 48–49.
15 Ibid., p. 51.
16 Ibid., p. 46.
17 Ibid.
18 Ibid., p. 57.
19 Ibid., p. 41.
20 Tucker, *The Marx–Engels Reader*, p. 475.
21 Polanyi, *The Great Transformation*, p. 41.
22 Ibid., p. 63.
23 Ibid., p. 73.

10 FREEDOM AND THE MARKET

1 Milton and Rose Friedman, *Free to Choose: A Personal Statement* (New York: Harcourt Brace Jovanovich, 1980), p. 27.
2 Ibid., pp. 28–29.
3 Ibid., p. 12.
4 Ibid., p. 23.
5 Ibid., p. 20.
6 Tucker, *The Marx–Engels Reader*, pp. 71, 72.
7 Ibid., p. 76.
8 Ibid., p. 72. Emphases in the original.
9 Ibid., p. 87. Emphases in the original.
10 Ibid., p. 74. Emphases in the original.
11 Ibid.
12 Ibid., p. 76.
13 Ibid., p. 344.
14 Ibid., pp. 76–77.
15 Ibid., p. 77. Emphases in the original.
16 Compare, for example, his optimistic expectation in his *Critique of the Gotha Program* that, in a genuinely communist society, labor will become "not only a means of life but life's prime want" (Tucker, *The Marx–Engels Reader*, p. 531) with his far more pessimistic insistence in Volume Three of *Capital* that labor will always remain a "realm of necessity" and that the "true realm of freedom" only begins "beyond it" (Tucker, *The Marx–Engels Reader*, p. 441).

11 JUSTICE AND THE MARKET

1 Friedrich A. Hayek, "Equality, Value, and Merit," in Michael Sandel, ed., *Liberalism and its Critics* (New York: New York University Press, 1984), p. 94. Emphasis added.
2 Ibid., p. 90.
3 Ibid., p. 82.
4 Ibid., p. 86.
5 Ibid., p. 87.
6 Ibid., p. 83.
7 Rawls, *A Theory of Justice*, p. 60.
8 Ibid.
9 Ibid., p. 12.
10 Ibid., p. 62.
11 Beginning with the essays in Norman Daniels, ed., *Reading Rawls: Critical Studies in Rawls' "A Theory of Justice"* (New York: Basic Books, 1974). See also Robert Paul Wolff, *Understanding Rawls: A Critique and Reconstruction of a Theory of Justice* (Princeton, NJ: Princeton University Press, 1977).
12 Rawls, *A Theory of Justice*, p. 100.
13 Ibid., pp. 100–101.
14 Ibid., p. 101.
15 Ibid., p. 102.
16 Ibid., p. 103.
17 Ibid., p. 105.
18 Hayek, "Equality, Value, and Merit," pp. 87–88.
19 See Robert Nozick, *Anarchy, State, and Utopia* (New York: Basic Books, 1974), for a "libertarian" critique of Rawls that is influenced by Hayek, and G. A. Cohen, *If You're an Egalitarian, How Come You're So Rich?* (Cambridge, MA: Harvard University Press, 2000), for a socialist critique that is influenced by Marx.

12 DEMOCRACY AND THE MARKET I

1 Charles E. Lindblom, *Politics and Markets: The World's Political Economic Systems* (New York: Basic Books, 1977), pp. 162–66.
2 Ibid., p. 161.
3 Ibid., p. 162.
4 Ibid., p. 165.
5 Ibid., p. 162.
6 Isaiah Berlin, "Two Concepts of Liberty," in *Four Essays on Liberty* (London: Oxford University Press, 1969).
7 Rousseau, as we have seen, is an obvious exception to Lindblom's generalization. But Lindblom argues away this exception with his claim that Rousseau was not a democrat (p. 163).
8 Lindblom, *Politics and Markets*, p. 163.
9 Ibid., p. 164.
10 Ibid., p. 165.
11 Ibid., p. 166.
12 Ibid., p. 168.
13 Ibid., p. 172.
14 Ibid., p. 171.
15 Ibid., p. 172.
16 Ibid., p. 173.
17 Ibid., p. 172.
18 Ibid., p. 187.

19 Ibid., p. 169.
20 Ibid., p. 193.
21 Ibid., p. 175.
22 Ibid., p. 180.
23 Ibid., p. 179.
24 Ibid., p. 180.
25 The major economic crisis that began in 2008 and Obama's presidency will likely combine to produce yet another reversal, this time in the direction that Lindblom predicted.
26 Lindblom, *Politics and Markets*, p. 180.
27 The "blackmail" explanation neglects what is, in my judgment, the relatively independent role of "free market" ideology. Politicians who subscribe to this ideology have another reason, in addition to the fear that business might harm the economy, for giving business what it wants. On the rise of market fundamentalism, see Thomas Frank, *One Market Under God* (New York: Doubleday, 2000).

13 DEMOCRACY AND THE MARKET II

1 Edward N. Wolff, "Recent Trends in Household Wealth in the United States: Rising Debt and the Middle-Class Squeeze," Working Paper No. 502, The Levy Economics Institute of Bard College, pp. 40, 38.
2 Doug Henwood, *Wall Street: How it Works and for Whom* (London: Verso, 1977), p. 257. The quotes within the quote are from Herbert Spencer, "Joint Stock Companies", in J. D. Y. Peel, ed., *Herbert Spencer on Social Evolution* (Chicago: University of Chicago Press, 1972), p. 230.
3 Ibid., p. 289.
4 Ibid., p. 248.
5 Ibid. Of course the financial crisis of 2008 has revealed, all too starkly, that what may appear to creditors to be low-risk strategies may actually turn out to be enormously high-risk strategies.
6 Adolph A. Berle and Gardiner C. Means, *The Modern Corporation and Private Property* (New York: Macmillan, 1933).
7 Henwood, *Wall Street*, pp. 252–53.
8 John Kenneth Galbraith, *The New Industrial State* (Boston: Houghton Mifflin, 1967).
9 Henwood, *Wall Street*, pp. 263–64. The dominant (and baleful) influence of the "financial sphere" was of course all too apparent in the economic crisis of 2008, when a collapse of the credit markets precipitated the worst economic downturn since the Great Depression.
10 Henwood, *Wall Street*, p. 293.
11 Ibid., p. 292.
12 Ibid., pp. 293–94.
13 Robert A. Dahl, *After the Revolution? Authority in a Good Society* (New Haven: Yale University Press, 1970), p. 49.
14 Ibid., p. 102.
15 Ibid., p. 104.
16 Ibid., p. 107.
17 Ibid.
18 Ibid., pp. 114–15.
19 Ibid., p. 110.
20 Ibid., pp. 112–13.
21 Dahl addresses some of these questions in his *A Preface to Economic Democracy*

(Berkeley: University of California Press, 1985). For a more recent defense of market socialism, see David Schweickart, *After Capitalism* (Lanham, MD: Rowman & Littlefield, 2002). For a critique of market socialism from the standpoint of participatory democratic economics, see Michael Albert, *Parecon: Life after Capitalism* (London: Verso, 2003).

14 DEMOCRACY AND THE MARKET III

1 David Held and Anthony McGrew, *Globalization/Anti-Globalization* (Oxford: Polity Press, 2002), p. 55.
2 Ibid., p. 56.
3 Ibid.
4 Joseph Stiglitz, *Globalization and its Discontents* (New York: W. W. Norton, 2002), p. 5.
5 Polanyi, *The Great Transformation*, p. 76.
6 Held and McGrew, *Globalization/Anti-Globalization*, pp. 67–69; Jackie Smith and Hank Johnston, *Globalization and Resistance: Transnational Dimensions of Social Movements* (Lanham, MD: Rowman & Littlefield, 2002).
7 Benjamin R. Barber, *Jihad vs. McWorld: How Globalism and Tribalism are Reshaping the World* (New York: Ballantine Books, 1995), p. 289.
8 Paul Virilio, *Speed and Politics: An Essay on Dromology* (New York: Columbia University Press, 1986), p. 55.

15 THE CONCEPT OF POWER I

1 Steven Lukes, *Power: A Radical View* (London: Macmillan, 1974), p. 27.
2 Ibid., p. 15.
3 Cited ibid., p. 12.
4 Cited ibid., p. 13.
5 Peter Bachrach and Morton S. Baratz, "Two Faces of Power," *American Political Science Review* 56 (1962), 947–52.
6 Cited in Lukes, *Power*, p. 16.
7 See chapter 7, note 7, above.
8 Cited in Lukes, *Power*, p. 18.
9 Peter Bachrach and Morton S. Baratz, Power *and Poverty: Theory and Practice* (New York: Oxford University Press, 1970), pp. 49–50.
10 Lukes, *Power*, p. 24.
11 Bachrach and Baratz, *Power and Poverty*, p. 46.
12 See chapter 12, note 18, above.
13 Lukes, *Power*, p. 25. Emphasis in the original.
14 Ibid., pp. 23–24.
15 Ibid., p. 41.
16 Ibid., p. 34.
17 Ibid., p. 46.
18 Ibid., p. 50.
19 Ibid., pp. 46–47.
20 Ibid., pp. 21–22.
21 Ibid., pp. 54–55. Emphasis in the original.

16 THE CONCEPT OF POWER II

1 Hannah Arendt, *On Violence* (New York: Harcourt, Brace & World, 1969), p. 36.

2 Ibid., p. 41.
3 Ibid., p. 44.
4 G. W. F. Hegel, trans. J. B. Baillie, *The Phenomenology of Mind* (New York: Harper & Row, 1967), pp. 229–40.
5 Aristotle, *Nicomachean Ethics* (Indianapolis: Bobbs-Merril, 1962), pp. 151–52.
6 Hannah Arendt, *The Human Condition* (Chicago: University of Chicago Press, 1958).
7 Michel Foucault, *The History of Sexuality: Volume I* (New York: Pantheon Books, 1978), pp. 17–49.
8 Michel Foucault, *Discipline and Punish: The Birth of the Prison* (New York: Pantheon Books, 1977), p. 171.
9 Ibid., p. 172.
10 Ibid., pp. 170, 187.
11 Ibid., p. 27.
12 Ibid., p. 170.
13 Ibid., p. 27.
14 Ibid., p. 194.
15 Ibid., pp. 182–83.
16 Ibid., p. 184.
17 Ibid., pp. 184–85.

INTRODUCTION TO PART III

1 The attentive reader will remember that this issue was also raised in chapter 1 in the course of a discussion of whether the values embodied in the rule of law are universal or not.

17 WHAT IS (A) CULTURE?

1 Clifford Geertz, *The Interpretation of Cultures: Selected Essays* (New York: Basic Books, 1973), p. 5.
2 Ibid., p. 14.
3 Ibid., p. 6.
4 Ibid., p. 7.
5 Ibid., p. 28.
6 Ibid., p. 12.
7 Cited in Richard J. Bernstein, *Beyond Objectivism and Relativism: Science, Hermeneutics, and Praxis* (Philadelphia: University of Pennsylvania Press, 1983), p. 95.
8 Geertz, *The Interpretation of Cultures*, p. 10.
9 Ibid., p. 29.
10 Ibid., p. 16.
11 Ibid., pp. 13, 24.
12 Marvin Harris, *Cultural Materialism: The Struggle for a Science of Culture* (New York: Random House, 1979), pp. 32, 27.
13 Ibid., p. 56.
14 Ibid., p. 52.
15 Ibid., p. 249.
16 Ibid., p. 251.
17 Ibid., p. 252.
18 Ibid., pp. 252–53.

18 BEYOND ETHNOCENTRISM AND RELATIVISM?

1 Peter Winch, "Understanding a Primitive Society," in Fred R. Dallmayr and Thomas A. McCarthy, eds., *Understanding and Social Inquiry* (Notre Dame, IN: University of Notre Dame Press, 1977), p. 159.

2 Cited in Winch, "Understanding a Primitive Society," p. 161.

3 Winch, "Understanding a Primitive Society," p. 162. Emphasis in the original.

4 Ibid., pp. 180–81. Emphasis in the original.

5 Peter Winch, "Comment", in Dallmayr and McCarthy, *Understanding and Social Inquiry*, p. 208. Emphasis in the original.

6 I. C. Jarvie, "Understanding and Explanation in Sociology and Social Anthropology," in Dallmayr and McCarthy, *Understanding and Social Inquiry*, p. 195.

7 A "mistake," it seems to me, does not necessarily imply that the action to which it refers is an exclusively instrumental one. Mistakes can be made, and learning from those mistakes may be necessary, with respect to non-instrumental, communicative relationships as well.

8 Winch, "Understanding a Primitive Society," p. 182.

9 Ibid., p. 183. Emphases in the original.

10 Ibid., p. 176.

11 Ibid., pp. 182–83.

12 Ibid., p. 186.

19 MODERNITY

1 Zygmunt Bauman, *Mortality, Immortality and Other Life Strategies* (Oxford: Polity Press, 1992), p. 132.

2 Max Weber, "Science as a Vocation," in H. H. Gerth and C. Wright Mills, eds., *From Max Weber: Essays in Sociology* (New York: Oxford University Press, 1958), p. 155.

3 Bauman, *Mortality, Immortality and Other Life Strategies*, p. 133.

4 Ibid.

5 Ibid., p. 134. Emphasis in the original.

6 Ibid.

7 Ibid., p. 137. Emphases in the original.

8 Ibid., p. 138. Emphasis in the original.

9 Ibid.

10 Ibid., p. 140. Emphasis in the original.

11 Ibid., p. 141. Emphasis in the original.

12 Ibid., p. 142. Emphases in the original.

13 Ibid., p. 154.

14 Ibid., p. 156.

15 Ibid., p. 160.

16 Anthony Giddens, *Modernity and Self-Identity: Self and Society in the Late Modern Age* (Cambridge: Polity Press, 1991), p. 21.

17 Ibid., p. 28.

18 Ibid., p. 20.

19 Ibid., p. 21. Emphasis in the original.

20 Ibid., p. 12.

21 Ibid., p. 14.

22 Ibid., p. 32. Emphasis in the original.

23 Ibid., pp. 28–29.

24 Ibid., p. 12.

25 Ibid., p. 13.

26 See, for example, *The Transformation of Intimacy: Sexuality, Love and Eroticism in Modern Societies* (Cambridge: Polity Press, 1992), pp. 70–76, as well as "Living in a Post-Traditional Society," in Ulrich Beck, Anthony Giddens, and Scott Lash, *Reflexive Modernization: Politics, Tradition and Aesthetics in the Modern Social Order* (Cambridge: Polity Press, 1994), pp. 66–74.

27 Giddens, *Modernity and Self-Identity*, p. 13.

28 Philip Rieff, *The Triumph of the Therapeutic* (New York: Harper & Row, 1966).

29 Michel Foucault, ed. Colin Gordon, *Power/Knowledge: Selected Interviews and Other Writings, 1972–1977* (New York: Pantheon Books, 1980), pp. 191, 211.

30 Giddens, *Modernity and Self-Identity*, p. 34.

31 Bauman, *Mortality, Immortality and Other Life Strategies*, p. 159.

32 Giddens, *Modernity and Self-Identity*, pp. 208–31.

33 Sigmund Freud, Civilization *and its Discontents* (New York: W. W. Norton & Company, 1989), p. 112.

20 MODERNITY AND IDENTITY

1 Charles Taylor, *Multiculturalism and the Politics of Recognition* (Princeton, NJ: Princeton University Press, 1992), p. 77.

2 Ibid., p. 79. Emphasis in the original.

3 Ibid., p. 80.

4 Ibid.

5 Ibid., p. 81.

6 Ibid., p. 82.

7 Ibid., p. 85.

8 Ibid., p. 83.

9 Ibid., p. 91.

10 Ibid., p. 93.

11 Ibid., p. 94.

12 Ibid., p. 96. Emphases in the original.

13 Ibid., p. 98.

14 Ibid., p. 101.

15 Joan W. Scott, *Multiculturalism and the Politics of Identity* (New York: Routledge, 1995), p. 5.

16 Ibid., p. 6.

17 Ibid., p. 5.

18 Ibid., p. 10.

19 Ibid., p. 6. Emphasis in the original.

20 Ibid., p. 8.

21 Ibid., p. 11.

22 Todd Gitlin, *The Twilight of Common Dreams* (New York: Metropolitan Books, 1995), p. 227.

23 Ibid., p. 236.

24 See for example Nancy Fraser, "From Redistribution to Recognition? Dilemmas of Justice in a 'Postsocialist' Age," in Nancy Fraser, *Justice Interruptus: Critical Reflections on the "Postsocialist" Condition* (New York: Routledge, 1997), pp. 11–39.

21 GENDER IDENTITY

1 Carol Gilligan, *In a Different Voice: Psychological Theory and Women's Development* (Cambridge, MA: Harvard University Press, 1982), pp. 6–7; 18–21.

2 Cited ibid., p. 7. See also Nancy Chodorow, *The Reproduction of Mothering* (Berkeley: University of California Press, 1978).
3 Chodorow, *The Reproduction of Mothering*, p. 166.
4 Ibid., pp. 104–107.
5 Gilligan, *In a Different Voice*, p. 8.
6 For a modification of this claim, see Isaac D. Balbus, "Masculinity and the (M)other: Toward a Synthesis of Feminist Mothering Theory and Psychoanalytic Theories of Narcissism", in Judith Kegan Gardiner, *Masculinity Studies & Feminist Theory* (New York: Columbia University Press, 2002), pp. 210–34.
7 Gilligan, *In a Different Voice*, p. 19.
8 Nancy Fraser and Linda J. Nicholson, "Social Criticism without Philosophy: An Encounter Between Feminism and Postmodernism," in Linda J. Nicholson, ed., *Feminism/Postmodernism* (New York: Routledge, 1990), pp. 32–33.
9 Ibid., p. 31.
10 Ibid. Emphasis in the original.
11 Ibid.
12 Ibid., p. 35.
13 Michelle Z. Rosaldo and Louise Lamphere, eds., *Women, Culture and Society* (Stanford, CA: Stanford University Press, 1974).
14 Fraser and Nicholson, "Social Criticism without Philosophy," p. 31. Emphasis in the original.
15 Susan Bordo, "Feminism, Postmodernism, and Gender-Scepticism," in Nicholson, ed., *Feminism/Postmodernism*, p. 139.
16 Ibid., p. 135.
17 Ibid., p. 141. Emphasis in the original.
18 Ibid., p. 149.
19 Ibid., p. 150. Emphases in the original.
20 Ibid., p. 151.

22 RACIAL IDENTITY

1 Dolan Hubbard, ed., *The Souls of Black Folk: One Hundred Years Later* (Columbia: University of Missouri Press, 2003).
2 W. E. B. Du Bois, *The Souls of Black Folk* (Chicago: A. C. McClurg, 1903), p. 38.
3 Ibid.
4 Ibid., p. 42.
5 Ibid., p. 43.
6 Ibid., p. 193.
7 Ibid., p. 43.
8 Ibid., p. 39.
9 Ibid., p. 43.
10 Ibid.
11 Anthony Appiah, "The Uncompleted Argument: Du Bois and the Illusion of Race," in Henry Louis Gates, Jr., ed., *"Race," Writing, and Difference* (Chicago: University of Chicago Press, 1986), pp. 21–36.
12 Ibid., p. 26.
13 But see chapter 27, below, for a qualification of this claim.
14 Appiah, "The Uncompleted Argument," p. 21.
15 Ibid., p. 31.
16 Ibid., pp. 35–36.
17 Ibid., p. 36.

18 Eric Lott, *Love and Theft: Blackface Minstrelsy and the American Working Class* (Oxford: Oxford University Press, 1993), p. 103.
19 Ibid., p. 150. See also Isaac D. Balbus, "The Psychodynamics of Racial Reparations," *Psychoanalysis, Culture & Society*, 9 (2004), 159–85.

23 NATIONAL IDENTITY

1 Anthony D. Smith, *Ethnic Origins of Nations* (Oxford: Blackwell, 1986), p. 3.
2 Paul R. Brass, *Ethnicity and Nationalism: Theory and Comparison* (New Delhi: Sage Publications, 1991), p. 69.
3 Anthony D. Smith, *The Nation in History: Historiographical Debates about Ethnicity and Nationalism* (Hanover, NH: University Press of New England, 2000), p. 52.
4 Ibid., pp. 72–73.
5 Ibid., p. 52.
6 Ibid.
7 Ibid. Benedict Anderson in *Imagined Communities: Reflections on the Origins and Spread of Nationalism* (London: Verso, 1991) and Eric Hobsbawm, editor (along with Terence Ranger) of *The Invention of Tradition* (Cambridge: Cambridge University Press, 1983), are two prominent exponents of this idea.
8 Smith, *The Nation in History*, p. 65.
9 Ibid.
10 Ibid., p. 57.
11 Ibid., pp. 61–62.
12 Ibid., p. 75.
13 Michael Ignatieff, *Blood and Belonging: Journeys into the New Nationalism* (New York: Farrar, Straus and Giroux, 1994), p. 6.
14 Michael Ignatieff, "Benign Nationalism? The Possibilities of the Civic Ideal," in Edward Mortimer, ed., *People, Nation and State* (London: I. B. Tauris, 1999), p. 145.
15 Ibid., pp. 145–46.
16 Ibid., p. 147.
17 Ibid., p. 144.
18 Robert Fine, "Benign Nationalism? The Limits of the Civic Ideal," in Mortimer, ed., *People, Nation and State*, p. 152.
19 Ibid., p. 153.
20 Ibid., p. 158.
21 Ibid., p. 154.
22 Cited ibid., p. 156. Emphases in the original.
23 Fine, "Benign Nationalism? The Limits of the Civic Ideal", p. 160.

24 RELIGIOUS IDENTITY

1 Peter Berger, *The Sacred Canopy: Elements of a Sociological Theory of Religion* (Garden City, NY: Doubleday, 1967); David Martin, *A General Theory of Secularization* (Oxford: Blackwell, 1978); Bryan Wilson, *Religion in Sociological Perspective* (Oxford: Oxford University Press, 1982).
2 Robert C. Tucker, ed., *The Marx–Engels Reader*, 2nd edn., p. 54.
3 Weber, "Science as a Vocation," p. 155.
4 Sigmund Freud, ed. James Strachey, *The Future of an Illusion* (Garden City, NY: Anchor Books, 1961).
5 Pippa Norris and Ronald Inglehart, *Sacred and Secular: Religion and Politics Worldwide* (Cambridge: Cambridge University Press, 2004), pp. 86–91.
6 Ibid., p. 91.

7 Ibid., p. 58.
8 Steve Bruce, *God is Dead: Secularization in the West* (Oxford: Blackwell, 2002), p. 36.
9 Norris and Inglehart, *Sacred and Secular*, pp. 90–91.
10 Roger Finke, "An Unsecular America," in Steve Bruce, ed., *Religion and Modernization: Sociologists and Historians Debate the Secularization Thesis* (Oxford: Clarendon, 1992), pp. 148–54.
11 Ibid., p. 149.
12 Norris and Inglehart, *Sacred and Secular*, p. 94.
13 Finke, "An Unsecular America," p. 155.
14 Ibid., p. 156. Emphasis added.
15 Tocqueville, *Democracy in America: Volume I*, pp. 368, 360.
16 Ibid., p. 360.
17 Ibid., p. 362.
18 Finke, "An Unsecular America," p. 162.
19 Bruce, *God is Dead*, pp. 60–74.
20 Norris and Inglehart, *Sacred and Secular*, p. 14.
21 Ibid., p. 19.
22 Ibid., p. 20.
23 Ibid., p. 25. Emphasis in the original.
24 Ibid., p. 108.
25 Bruce, *God is Dead*, p. 219.
26 Giddens, *Modernity and Self-Identity*, p. 21. Emphasis in the original.
27 Norris and Inglehart, *Sacred and Secular*, p. 14.

INTRODUCTION TO PART FOUR

1 C. B. Macpherson, *The Political Theory of Possessive Individualism: Hobbes to Locke* (Oxford: Oxford University Press, 1964).

25 THE SUBJECT

1 Daniel Stern, *The First Relationship: Mother and Infant* (Cambridge, MA: Harvard University Press, 1977).
2 Melanie Klein, *Love, Guilt and Reparation and Other Works, 1921–1945* (New York: Dell, 1975), p. 227.
3 Hanna Segal, *Melanie Klein* (New York: Viking, 1980), pp. 79–80.
4 Melanie Klein, *Envy and Gratitude* (New York: Basic Books, 1957), pp. 89–90.
5 Melanie Klein, "Mourning and its Relation to Manic-Depressive States," in *Love, Guilt and Reparation and Other Works*, p. 363.
6 Dorothy Dinnerstein, *The Mermaid and the Minotaur: Sexual Arrangements and Human Malaise* (New York: Harper & Row, 1976), pp. 52–53, 69.
7 Ibid., p. 53.
8 Ibid., pp. 51–52.
9 Ibid., pp. 52–53. According to Dinnerstein, the idealization of the father is the typical, but not the only, solution available to the girl. Over-idealizing the mother or projecting bad feelings onto the father are other possibilities, but these options run counter to the "traditional emotional equilibrium that is thought of as 'heterosexual adjustment'" (p. 52).
10 Ibid., p. 52.
11 Ibid., p. 234.
12 Ibid., pp. 189, 134.

13 Ibid., p. 191.

14 Ibid., p. 152, n. 22.

15 C. Fred Alford, *Melanie Klein and Critical Social Theory* (New Haven: Yale University Press, 1989), pp. 31–50; Phyllis Grosskurth, *Melanie Klein: Her World and Her Work* (Cambridge, MA: Harvard University Press, 1987), p. 450.

16 Melanie Klein, *Contributions to Psycho-Analysis, 1921–1945* (London: Hogarth Press, 1965), p. 306. See also p. 313, where she argues that "the visible mother . . . provides continual proofs of what the 'internal mother' is like, whether she is loving or angry, helpful or revengeful."

17 D. W. Winnicott, *The Maturational Processes and the Facilitating Environment* (New York: International Universities Press, 1965), pp. 43, 48.

18 Ibid., pp. 46, 47.

19 D. W. Winnicott, *Playing and Reality* (New York: Basic Books, 1971), p. 112.

20 Ibid., p. 65.

21 Ibid., p. 94.

22 Ibid., p. 89.

23 Isaac D. Balbus, *Marxism and Domination: A Neo-Hegelian, Feminist Psychoanalytic Theory of Sexual, Political and Technological Liberation* (Princeton, NJ: Princeton University Press, 1982), pp. 382–84.

24 Sigmund Freud, *An Autobiographical Study*, in Peter Gay, ed., *The Freud Reader* (New York: W. W. Norton & Company, 1989), p. 26. Emphasis in the original.

26 THE SUBJECT IN THE GROUP

1 Sigmund Freud, *Group Psychology and the Analysis of the Ego* (New York: Bantam Books, 1965).

2 For an introduction to Kleinian group theory, see Alford, *Melanie Klein and Critical Social Theory*, pp. 57–103.

3 Dinnerstein, *The Mermaid and the Minotaur*, p. 166.

4 Sigmund Freud, *Moses and Monotheism* (New York: Alfred A. Knopf, 1939), p. 172.

5 Dinnerstein, *The Mermaid and the Minotaur*, p. 175.

6 Freud, anticipating Klein, argued in *Civilization and its Discontents* that "it is always possible to bind together a considerable number of people in love, so long as there are other people left over to receive the manifestation of their aggressiveness" (p. 72). Dinnerstein would amend this argument by adding "always possible *under conditions of mother-dominated child care.*"

7 Thus I disagree with the argument, advanced by Vamik Volkan in *The Need to Have Enemies and Allies* (Northvale, NJ: Jason Aaronson, 1994), pp. 30–33, and apparently shared by Alford in *Melanie Klein and Critical Social Theory*, pp. 68 and 75–76, that group splitting is consistent with, and even facilitates, individual integration. This argument, it seems to me, renders demonizing and idealizing group fantasies immune to individual emotional growth and the conditions that might facilitate it, and thus effectively essentializes group domination and subordination.

8 Freud, *Civilization and its Discontents*, p. 82.

9 Barber, *Strong Democracy*, pp. 147–48.

10 Alford, *Melanie Klein and Critical Social Theory*, pp. 90–91.

11 Rousseau, *On the Social Contract*, p. 27.

12 Freud, *Civilization and its Discontents*, p. 72.

13 For an introduction to restorative justice, see John Braithwaite, *Restorative Justice and Responsible Regulation* (Oxford: Oxford University Press, 2002).

14 Friedrich Nietzsche, *The Genealogy of Morals* (Garden City, NY: Doubleday & Company, 1956), p. 214.

15 Braithwaite, *Restorative Justice and Responsible Regulation.*
16 See, among others, John Braithwaite and Philip Pettit, *Not Just Deserts: A Republican Theory of Criminal Justice* (New York: Oxford University Press, 1990); Heather Strang and John Braithwaite, *Restorative Justice and Civil Society* (Cambridge: Cambridge University Press, 2001); and Andrew von Hirsch, Julian V. Roberts, Anthony Bottoms, eds., *Restorative Justice and Criminal Justice: Competing or Reconcilable Paradigms?* (Portland, OR: Hart, 2003).

27 IDENTITY POLITICS REVISITED

1 John Pilger, "The State Has Lost Its Mind," *New Statesman*, May 12, 2005.
2 Balbus, "The Psychodynamics of Racial Reparations," pp. 167–77.
3 *USA Today*, November 7, 2008.
4 Ibid.
5 Adam Nossiter, "For South, A Waning Hold on National Politics, *New York Times*, November 11, 2008.
6 "Young Voters Lifted Obama to Victory," *Arizona Republic*, February 5, 2009.
7 "Behind the Scenes: Is Barak Obama Black or Biracial?" CNNPolitics.com, June 9, 2008. The site notes that "the 2000 U.S. Census was the first time Americans were allowed to identify themselves as 'multiracial,' and more than six million people checked more than one box in the race and ethnicity category."
8 Kathy Russell, Midge Wilson, Ronald Hall, *The Color Complex: The Politics of Skin Color among African Americans* (New York: Harcourt Brace Jovanovich, 1992).
9 See Balbus, *The Psychodynamics of Racial Reparations*, for an elaboration of this suggestion.

28 THE SUBJECT IN NATURE

1 Giddens, *Modernity and Self-Identity*, p. 12.
2 My assumption is that there is not merely an analogical but also a transferential relationship between the infant's relationship to its mother and the adult's relationship to nature. I assume, in other words, that nature inevitably inherits the explosive mixture of the infant's feelings for the mother, who is normally its first representative of the world. Here I follow Dinnerstein, *The Mermaid and the Minotaur*, pp. 91–114, whose account I extend and modify in my *Marxism and Domination*, pp. 339–44.
3 Richard Louv, *Last Child in the Woods: Saving Our Children from Nature-Deficit Disorder* (Chapel Hill, NC: Algonquin Books, 2006), pp. 92–95.
4 Hegel, *The Phenomenology of Mind*, p. 238.
5 Winnicott, *Playing and Reality*, p. 89.
6 David Abram, *The Spell of the Sensuous* (New York: Pantheon Books, 1996), p. 22.
7 *Marxism and Domination*, pp. 340–41.
8 Norman O. Brown, *Life against Death* (New York: Vintage Books, 1959), pp. 278–85.
9 Karl Marx, trans. Martin Nicolaus, *Grundrisse: Foundations of the Critique of Political Economy* (Middlesex, England: Penguin Books, 1973), pp. 409–10.
10 Tucker, ed., *The Marx–Engels Reader*, p. 156; Brown, *Life against Death*, p. 18.
11 Tucker, ed., *The Marx–Engels Reader*, p. 76.
12 Bill McKibben, *The End of Nature* (New York: Random House, 1989), p. 83, 59.
13 Otto F. Kernberg, *Borderline Conditions and Pathological Narcissism* (New York: Jason Aronson, 1975), p. 220.
14 David Michael Levin, "Psychopathology in the Epoch of Nihilism," in David

Michael Levin, ed., *Pathologies of the Modern Self* (New York: New York University Press, 1987), pp. 21–83.

15 Melanie Klein, "A Contribution to the Psychogenesis of Manic-Depressive States," in Klein, *Contributions to Psychoanalysis*, p. 299.

16 John Carroll, *Ego and Soul* (Sydney: HarperCollins, 1998), pp. 119, 127.

17 The term is from Michael Schneider, *Neurosis and Civilization* (New York: Seabury, 1975).

18 Heinz Kohut, *The Analysis of the Self* (New York: International Universities Press, 1971), p. 27. Thus the commodified images that advertising invents only give voice to, and work on, the preexisting fantasies of perfection that proliferate in modernity.

19 Isaac D. Balbus, *Mourning and Modernity* (New York: Other Press, 2005), pp. 135–48.

20 Arne Naess, "The Shallow and the Deep, Long-Range Ecology Movement: A Summary," *Inquiry* 16:1 (Spring 1973), 95–100.

21 Andrew McLaughlin, *Regarding Nature* (New York: State University of New York Press, 1993), p. 172.

22 Raymond Murphy, *Rationality and Nature* (Boulder, CO: Westview Press, 1994), p. 91.

23 Arne Naess, *Ecology, Community, and Lifestyle* (Cambridge: Cambridge University Press, 1989), pp. 181, 15, 198–99.

24 Stephan Bodian, "Simple in Mean, Rich in Ends: A Conversation with Arne Naess," *The Ten Directions* (Los Angeles Institute for Transcultural Studies, Zen Center of Los Angeles, Summer/Fall 1982).

25 Naess, *Ecology, Community, and Lifestyle*, p. 15.

26 Cited in Bill Devall and George Sessions, *Deep Ecology* (Salt Lake City, UT: Gibbs M. Smith, 1985), p. 70.

27 Arne Naess and George Sessions, "Comments on the Basic Principles," in Devall and Sessions, *Deep Ecology*, p. 72.

28 Naess, "The Shallow and the Deep," p. 95.

29 Devall and Sessions, *Deep Ecology*, p. 70.

30 Naess, *Ecology, Community, and Lifestyle*, p. 168.

31 Ibid., p. 98.

32 Ibid., p. 30.

33 Ibid., p. 91. See also pp. 24–26.

34 Robert Wuthnow, *Sharing the Journey: Support Groups and America's New Quest for Community* (New York: Free Press, 1994), pp. 70–71

35 Robin Room, " 'Healing Ourselves and Our Planet': The Emergence of a Generalized Twelve-Step Consciousness," *Contemporary Drug Problems* 19 (Winter 1992), 737.

36 Heidi Schlumpf, "Recovering Grace," *U.S. Catholic* 68:11 (November 2003), 12. See also Craig Reinarman, "The Twelve Step Movement and Advanced Capitalist Culture: The Politics of Self-Control in Postmodernity," in Marcy Darnovsky, Barbara Epstein, and Richard Flacks, eds., *Cultural Politics and Social Movements* (Philadelphia: Temple University Press, 1995), p. 97, which also cites the 15 million figure.

37 The lower estimate comes from Alfred A. Katz, *Self-Help in America: A Social Movement Perspective* (New York: Twayne Publishers, 1993), p. 11; the higher is cited in Room, " 'Healing Ourselves and Our Planet,' " p. 727.

38 Room, " 'Healing Ourselves and Our Planet,' " pp. 717–22.

39 Bill W., *Twelve Steps and Twelve Traditions* (New York: Alcoholics Anonymous World Services, Inc., 1953), p. 70.

40 Ibid., p. 5.

41 Ibid.
42 Ibid., p. 49.
43 Bill W., *Alcoholics Anonymous Comes of Age* (New York: Harper, 1957), p. 279.
44 See chapter 25 above.
45 *Twelve Steps and Twelve Traditions*, p. 6.
46 Liz Turnbull, "Narcissism and the Potential for Self-Transformation in the Twelve Steps," *Health* 1:2 (1997), 152.
47 Shulamith Lala Ashenberg Straussner and Betsy Robin Spiegel, "An Analysis of 12-Step Programs for Substance Abusers from a Developmental Perspective," *Clinical Social Work Journal* 24:3 (Fall 1996), 307.
48 *Twelve Steps and Twelve Traditions*, pp. 55–62.
49 Ibid., pp. 7–8.
50 Ibid., p. 80.
51 *Alcoholics Anonymous*, 3rd edn. (New York City: Alcoholics Anonymous World Services, Inc., 1976), p. 82.
52 Ibid., p. 78.
53 Ibid., pp. 83, 77.
54 *Twelve Steps and Twelve Traditions*, pp. 79–80.
55 Sigmund Freud, "The Question of Lay Analysis," in David Strachey, ed., *The Standard Edition of the Complete Psychological Worlds of Sigmund Freud* vol. 20, p. 207. See also "Introductory Lectures on Psycho-Analysis," in Strachey, ed., *Standard Edition* vol. 16, p. 457, and *Civilization and its Discontents*, p. 98.
56 Ernest Kurtz, *Not-God: A History of Alcoholics Anonymous* (Center City, MN: Hazelden Educational Services, 1979), p. 171.
57 Ernest Kurtz, "Why A.A. Works: The Intellectual Significance of Alcoholics Anonymous," *Journal of Studies on Alcohol* 43:1 (1982), 39.
58 For a somewhat more developed account of both the promise and the problems, see my *Mourning and Modernity*, pp. 146–48.

BIBLIOGRAPHY

Abram, David. *The Spell of the Sensuous*. New York: Pantheon Books, 1996.

Albert, Michael. *Parecon: Life After Capitalism*. London: Verso, 2003.

Alford, C. Fred. *Melanie Klein and Critical Social Theory*. New Haven: Yale University Press, 1989.

Anderson, Benedict. *Imagined Communities: Reflections on the Origins and Spread of Nationalism*. London: Verso, 1991.

Appiah, Anthony. "The Uncompleted Argument: DuBois and the Illusion of Race." In *"Race," Writing and Difference*, edited by Henry Louis Gates, Jr. Chicago: The University of Chicago Press, 1986.

Arendt, Hannah. *On Violence*. New York: Harcourt, Brace & World, 1969.

Arendt, Hannah. *The Human Condition*. Chicago: The University of Chicago Press, 1958.

Aristotle. *Nicomachean Ethics*. Translated by Martin Ostwald. Indianapolis: Bobbs-Merrill, 1962.

Bachrach, Peter, and Morton S. Baratz. "Two Faces of Power." *American Political Science Review* 56, no. 4 (1962): 947–952.

Bachrach, Peter, and Morton S. Baratz. *Power and Poverty: Theory and Practice*. New York: Oxford University Press, 1970.

Balbus, Isaac D. *Marxism and Domination: A Neo-Hegelian, Feminist Psychoanalytic Theory of Sexual, Political and Technological Liberation*. Princeton, NJ: Princeton University Press, 1982.

Balbus, Isaac D. "Masculinity and the (M)other: Toward a Synthesis of Feminist Mothering Theory and Psychoanalytic Theories of Narcissism." In *Masculinity Studies and Feminist Theory*, edited by Judith Kegan Gardiner. New York: Columbia University Press, 2002.

Balbus, Isaac D. *Mourning and Modernity*. New York: Other Press, 2005.

Balbus, Isaac D. "The Concept of Interest in Marxian and Pluralist Analysis." *Politics & Society* 1, no. 2 (1971): 151–177.

Balbus, Isaac D. "The Psychodynamics of Racial Reparations." *Psychoanalysis, Culture & Society* 9, no. 2 (2004): 159–185.

Barber, Benjamin R. *Jihad vs. McWorld: How Globalism and Tribalism are Reshaping the World*. New York: Ballantine Books, 1995.

Barber, Benjamin. *Strong Democracy: Participatory Politics for a New Age*. Berkeley: University of California Press, 1984.

Bauman, Zygmunt. *Mortality, Immortality and Other Life Strategies*. Oxford: Polity Press, 1992.

Beard, Charles. *An Economic Interpretation of the Constitution of the United States.* New York: Free Press, 1965.

Behrouzi, Majid. *Democracy as the Political Empowerment of the Citizen: Direct-Deliberative e-Democracy.* New York: Lexington Books, 2005.

Berger, Peter. *The Sacred Canopy: Elements of Sociological Theory of Religion.* Garden City, NY: Doubleday, 1967.

Berle, Adolph A., and Gardiner C. Means. *The Modern Corporation and Private Property.* New York: Macmillan, 1933.

Berlin, Isaiah. "Two Concepts of Liberty." In *Four Essays on Liberty,* Isaiah Berlin. London: Oxford University Press, 1969.

Bernstein, Richard J. *Beyond Objectivism and Relativism: Science, Hermeneutics, and Praxis.* Philadelphia: University of Pennsylvania Press, 1983.

Bill, W. *Alcoholics Anonymous Comes of Age.* New York: Harper, 1957.

Bodian, Stephan. "Simple in Mean, Rich in Ends: A Conversation with Arne Naess." In *The Ten Directions,* Los Angeles Institute for Transcultural Studies, Zen Center of Los Angeles. Summer/Fall 1982.

Bordo, Susan. "Feminism, Postmodernism, and Gender-Skepticism." In *Feminism/Postmodernism,* edited by Linda J. Nicholson. New York: Routledge, 1990.

Braithwaite, John. *Restorative Justice and Responsible Regulation.* Oxford: Oxford University Press, 2002.

Braithwaite, John, and Philip Pettit. *Not Just Deserts: A Republic Theory of Criminal Justice.* New York: Oxford University Press, 1990.

Brass, Paul R. *Ethnicity and Nationalism: Theory and Comparison.* Newbury Park, CA: Sage Publications, 1991.

Brown, Norman O. *Life against Death.* New York: Vintage Books, 1959.

Bruce, Steven. *God is Dead: Secularization in the West.* Oxford: Blackwell, 2002.

Burnham, Walter Dean. "The Changing Shape of the American Political Universe." *American Political Science Review* 59, no. 1 (1965): 7–28.

Carroll, John. *Ego and Soul.* Sydney: HarperCollins, 1998.

Chodorow, Nancy. *The Reproduction of Mothering.* Berkeley: University of California Press, 1978.

Cohen, G. A. *If You're an Egalitarian, How Come You're So Rich?* Cambridge, MA: Harvard University Press, 2000.

Dahl, Robert A. *A Preface to Economic Democracy.* Berkeley: University of California Press, 1985.

Dahl, Robert A. *After the Revolution? Authority in a Good Society.* New Haven: Yale University Press, 1970.

Dahl, Robert A. *Polyarchy: Participation and Opposition.* New Haven: Yale University Press, 1971.

Dalton, Russell. *The Good Citizen: How a Younger Generation is Reshaping American Politics.* Washington, DC: CQ Press, 2007.

Daniels, Norman, ed. *Reading Rawls: Critical Studies in Rawls' "A Theory of Justice."* New York: Basic Books, 1974.

Darnovsky, Marcy, Barbara Epstein, and Richard Flacks, eds. *Culture Politics and Social Movements.* Philadelphia: Temple University Press, 1995.

Devall, Bill, and George Sessions. *Deep Ecology.* Salt Lake City, UT: Gibbs M. Smith, 1985.

Dinnerstein, Dorothy. *The Mermaid and the Minotaur: Sexual Arrangements and Human Malaise*. New York: Harper & Row, 1976.

Disch, Lisa Jane. *The Tyranny of the Two-Party System*. New York: Columbia University Press, 2002.

Downs, Anthony. *An Economic Theory of Democracy*. New York: Harper & Row, 1957.

Dreyfus, Hubert L., and Paul Rabinow. *Michel Foucault: Beyond Structuralism and Hermeneutics*. Chicago: The University of Chicago Press, 1983.

Dryzek, John S. *Deliberative Democracy and Beyond: Liberals, Critics, Contestations*. Oxford: Oxford University Press, 2000.

Du Bois, W. E. B. *The Souls of Black Folk*. Chicago: A. C. McClurg, 1903.

Ehrenberg, John. *Civil Society: The Critical History of an Idea*. New York: New York University Press, 1999.

Ely, John Hart. *Democracy and Distrust: A Theory of Judicial Review*. Cambridge, MA: Harvard University Press, 1980.

Fine, Robert. "Benign Nationalism? The Limits of the Civic Ideal." In *People, Nation and State*, edited by Edward Mortimer. London: I. B. Tauris, 1999.

Finke, Roger. "An Unsecular America." In *Religion and Modernization: Sociologists and Historians Debate the Secularization Thesis*, edited by Steven Bruce. Oxford: Clarendon Press, 1992.

Foucault, Michel. *Discipline and Punish: The Birth of the Prison*. New York: Pantheon, 1977.

Foucault, Michel. *Dits et Ecrits IV*. Paris: Gallimard, 1994.

Foucault, Michel. *Power/Knowledge: Selected Interviews and Other Writings, 1972–1977*. Edited by Colin Gordon. New York: Pantheon Books, 1980.

Foucault, Michel. *The History of Sexuality: Volume I*. New York: Pantheon Books, 1978.

Frank, Thomas. *One Market under God*. New York: Doubleday, 2000.

Fraser, Nancy, and Linda J. Nicholson. "Social Criticism without Philosophy: An Encounter between Feminism and Postmodernism." In *Feminism/Postmodernism*, edited by Linda J. Nicholson. New York: Routledge, 1990.

Fraser, Nancy. *Justice Interruptus: Critical Reflections on the "Postsocialist" Condition*. New York: Routledge, 1997.

Freud, Sigmund. "An Autobiographical Study." In *The Freud Reader*, edited by Peter Gay. New York: W. W. Norton & Company, 1989.

Freud, Sigmund. *Civilization and its Discontents*. New York: W. W. Norton & Company, 1989.

Freud, Sigmund. *Group Psychology and the Analysis of the Ego*. New York: Bantam Books, 1965.

Freud, Sigmund. *Moses and Monotheism*. New York: Alfred A. Knopf, 1939.

Freud, Sigmund. *The Future of an Illusion*. Edited by James Strachey. Garden City, NY: Anchor Books, 1961.

Freud, Sigmund. *The Standard Edition of the Complete Psychological Worlds of Sigmund Freud, Volume 16*. Edited by James Strachey. London: Hogarth, 1971.

Freud, Sigmund. *The Standard Edition of the Complete Psychological Worlds of Sigmund Freud, Volume 20*. Edited by James Strachey. London: Hogarth, 1973.

Friedman, Milton, and Rose Friedman. *Free to Choose: A Personal Statement*. New York: Harcourt Brace Jovanovich, 1980.

Galbraith, John Kenneth. *The New Industrial State*. Boston: Houghton Mifflin, 1967.

Geertz, Clifford. *The Interpretation of Culture: Selected Essays*. New York: Basic Books, 1973.

Giddens, Anthony. "Living in a Post-Traditional Society." In *Reflexive Modernization: Politics, Tradition and Aesthetics in the Modern Social Order*, by Ulrich Beck, Anthony Giddens, and Scott Lash. Cambridge: Polity Press, 1994.

Giddens, Anthony. *Modernity and Self-Identity: Self and Society in the Late Modern Age*. Cambridge: Polity Press, 1991.

Giddens, Anthony. *The Transformation of Intimacy: Sexuality, Love and Eroticism in Modern Societies*. Cambridge: Polity Press, 1992.

Gilligan, Carol. *In a Different Voice: Psychological Theory and Women's Development*. Cambridge, MA: Harvard University Press, 1982.

Gitlin, Todd. *The Twilight of Common Dreams*. New York: Metropolitan Books, 1995.

Grosskurth, Phyllis. *Melanie Klein: Her World and Her Work*. Cambridge, MA: Harvard University Press, 1987.

Harris, Marvin. *Cultural Materialism: The Struggle for a Science of Culture*. New York: Random House, 1979.

Hayek, Friedrich A. "Equality, Value, and Merit." In Liberalism and its Critics, edited by Michael Sandel. New York: New York University Press, 1984.

Hegel, G. W. F. *The Phenomenology of Mind*. Translated by J. B. Baillie. New York: Harper & Row, 1967.

Held, David, and Anthony McGrew. *Globalization/Anti-Globalization: Beyond the Great Divide*. Oxford: Polity Press, 2002.

Henwood, Doug. *Wall Street: How it Works and for Whom*. London: Verso, 1977.

Hobbes, Thomas. *Leviathan*. New York: Penguin Books, 1968.

Hobsbawm, Eric, ed. *The Invention of Tradition*. Cambridge: Cambridge University Press, 1983.

Hubbard, Dolan, ed. *The Souls of Black Folk: One Hundred Years Later*. Columbia, MO: University of Missouri Press, 2003.

Ignatieff, Michael. "Benign Nationalism? The Possibilities of the Civic Ideal." In *People, Nation and State*, edited by Edward Mortimer. London: I. B. Tauris, 1999.

Ignatieff, Michael. *Blood and Belonging: Journeys into the New Nationalism*. New York: Farar, Straus and Giroux, 1994.

Ingram, David. *Law: Key Concepts in Philosophy*. London: Continuum International Publishing Group, 2006.

Jarvie, I. C. "Understanding and Explanation in Sociology and Social Anthropology." In Understanding and Social Inquiry, edited by Fred R. Dallmayr and Thomas A. McCarthy. Notre Dame, IN: University of Notre Dame Press, 1977.

Johnson, Conrad, ed. *Philosophy of Law*. New York: Macmillan Publishing Company, 1993.

Katz, Alfred A. *Self-Help in America: A Social Movement Perspective*. New York: Twayne Publishers, 1993.

Katznelson, Ira, and Helen V. Miller, eds. *Political Science: The State of the Discipline*. New York: W. W. Norton & Co., 2002.

Kernberg, Otto F. *Borderline Conditions and Pathological Narcissism*. New York: Jason Aronson, 1975.

Key Jr., V. O. *The Responsible Electorate*. Cambridge, MA: Harvard University Press, 1966.

Klein, Melanie. *Contributions to Psycho-Analysis, 1921–1945.* London: Hogarth Press, 1965.

Klein, Melanie. *Envy and Gratitude.* New York: Basic Books, 1957.

Klein, Melanie. *Love, Guilt and Reparation and Other Works, 1921–1945.* New York: Dell, 1975.

Kohut, Heinz. *The Analysis of the Self.* New York: International University Press, 1971.

Kurtz, Ernest. *Not-God: A History of Alcoholics Anonymous.* Center City, MN: Hazelden Educational Services, 1991.

Kurtz, Ernest. "Why A.A. Works: The Intellectual Significance of Alcoholics Anonymous." *Journal of Studies on Alcohol* 43, no. 1 (1982): 39.

Levin, David Michael. "Psychopathology in the Epoch of Nihilism." In *Pathologies of the Modern Self,* edited by David Michael Levin. New York: New York University Press, 1987.

Lindblom, Charles E. *Politics and Markets: The World's Political Economic Systems.* New York: Basic Books, 1977.

Lott, Eric. *Love and Theft: Blackface Minstrelsy and the American Working Class.* Oxford: Oxford University Press, 1993.

Louv, Richard. *Last Child in the Woods: Saving Our Children from Nature-Deficit Disorder.* Chapel Hill, NC: Algonquin Books, 2006.

Lukes, Steven. *Power: A Radical View.* London: Macmillan, 1974.

Maass, Arthur. Foreword to *The Responsible Electorate,* by V. O. Key, Jr. Cambridge, MA: Harvard University Press, 1966.

Macpherson, C. B. *The Political Theory of Possessive Individualism: Hobbes and Locke.* Oxford: Oxford University Press, 1964.

Martin, David. *A General Theory of Secularization.* Oxford: Blackwell, 1978.

Marx, Karl. *Grundrisse: Foundations of the Critique of Political Economy.* Translated by Martin Nicolaus. Middlesex, UK: Penguin Books, 1973.

McConnell, Grant. *Private Power and American Democracy.* New York: Knopf, 1966.

McKibben, Bill. *The End of Nature.* New York: Random House, 1989.

McLaughlin, Andrew. *Regarding Nature.* New York: State University of New York Press, 1993.

Montesquieu, Charles de Secondat. *The Spirit of the Laws.* New York: Hafner Publishing Co., 1948.

Murphy, Raymond. *Rationality and Nature.* Boulder, CO: Westview Press, 1994.

Naess, Arne. "The Shallow and the Deep, Long-Range Ecology Movement: A Summary." *Inquiry* 16, no. 1 (1973): 95–100.

Naess, Arne. *Ecology, Community, and Lifestyle.* Cambridge: Cambridge University Press, 1989.

Nietzsche, Friedrich. *The Genealogy of Morals.* Garden City, NY: Doubleday & Company, 1956.

Norris, Pippa, and Ronald Ingelhart. *Sacred and Secular: Religion and Politics Worldwide.* Cambridge: Cambridge University Press, 2004.

Nozick, Robert. *Anarchy, State, and Utopia.* New York: Basic Books, 1974.

Patterson, Thomas. *Out of Order.* New York: Vintage Books, 1994.

Pitkin, Hanna Fenichel. *The Concept of Representation.* Berkeley: University of California Press, 1967.

Polanyi, Karl. *The Great Transformation: The Political Economic Origins of Our Time.* Boston: Beacon Press, 1944.

Prewitt, Kenneth, and Heinz Eulau. "Political Matrix and Political Representation: Prolegomenon to a New Departure from an Old Problem." In *The Politics of Representation: Continuities in Theory and Research*, edited by Heinz Eulau and John C. Wahlke. Beverly Hills: Sage Publications, 1978.

Putnam, Robert. "Bowling Alone: America's Declining Social Capital." *Journal of Democracy* 6, no. 1 (1995): 65–78.

Rawls, John. *A Theory of Justice*. Cambridge, MA: Belknap Press of Harvard University Press, 1971.

Rieff, Philip. *The Triumph of the Therapeutic*. New York: Harper & Row, 1966.

Room, Robin. "'Healing Ourselves and Our Planet': The Emergence of a Generalized Twelve-Step Consciousness." *Contemporary Drug Problems* 19, no. 4 (1994): 717–740.

Rosaldo, Michelle Z., and Louise Lamphere, eds. *Women, Culture and Society*. Stanford: Stanford University Press, 1974.

Rousseau, Jean-Jacques. *On the Social Contract*. New York: St. Martin's Press, 1978.

Russell, Kathy, Midge Wilson and Ronald Hall, eds. *The Color Complex: The Politics of Skin Color Among African Americans*. New York: Harcourt Brace Jovanovich, 1992.

Sale, Kirkpatrick. *Human Scale*. New York: Coward, McCann & Geoghegan, 1980.

Schattschneider, E. E. *Party Government*. New York: Holt, Rinehart and Winston, 1942.

Schattschneider, E. E. *The Semisovereign People*. New York: Holt, Rinehart and Winston, 1960.

Schlumpf, Heidi. "Recovering Grace." *U.S. Catholic* 68, no. 11 (2003): 12–18.

Schneider, Michael. *Neurosis and Civilization*. New York: Seabury, 1975.

Schumpeter, Joseph Alois. *Capitalism, Socialism and Democracy*. New York: Harper & Brothers, 1947.

Schweickart, David. *After Capitalism*. Lanham, MD: Rowman & Littlefield, 2002.

Scott, Joan W. *Multiculturalism and the Politics of Identity*. New York: Routledge, 1995.

Segal, Hanna. *Melanie Klein*. New York: Viking, 1980.

Seitz, Brian. *The Trace of Representation*. Albany: State University of New York Press, 1995.

Smith, Adam. *An Inquiry into the Nature and Causes of the Wealth of Nations*. Oxford: Oxford University Press, 1976.

Smith, Anthony D. *Ethnic Origins of Nations*. Oxford: Blackwell, 1986.

Smith, Anthony D. *The Nation in History: Historiographical Debates about Ethnicity and Nationalism*. Hanover, NH: University Press of New England, 2000.

Smith, Jackie, and Hank Johnston. *Globalization and Resistance: Transnational Dimensions of Social Movements*. Lanham, MD: Rowman & Littlefield, 2002.

Stern, Daniel. *The First Relationship: Mother and Infant*. Cambridge, MA: Harvard University Press, 1977.

Stiglitz, Joseph. *Globalization and its Discontents*. New York: W. W. Norton, 2002.

Strang, Heather, and John Braithwaite. *Restorative Justice and Civil Society*. Cambridge: Cambridge University Press, 2001.

Straussner, Shulamith, Lala Ashenberg, and Betsy Robin Spiegel. "An Analysis of 12-Step Programs for Substance Abusers from a Developmental Perspective." *Clinical Social Work Journal* 24, no. 3 (1996): 307.

Taylor, Charles. *Multiculturalism and the Politics of Recognition*. Princeton, NJ: Princeton University Press, 1992.

Teodori, Massimo, ed. *The New Left: A Documentary History*. New York: Bobbs-Merril, 1969.

Tocqueville, Alexis de. *Democracy in America: Volume I.* New York: Schocken Books, 1961.

Tocqueville, Alexis de. *Democracy in America: Volume II.* New York: Schocken Books, 1961.

Tucker, Robert C. *The Marx–Engels Reader.* New York: W. W. Norton & Co., 1978.

Turnbull, Liz. "Narcissism and the Potential for Self-Transformation in the Twelve Steps." *Health* 1, no. 2 (1997): 152.

Tyler, Tom R. *Why People Obey the Law.* New Haven: Yale University Press, 1990.

Verba, Sydney, Kay Lehman Schlozman, and Henry E. Brady. *Voice and Equality: Civic Voluntarism in American Politics.* Cambridge, MA: Harvard University Press, 1995.

Virilio, Paul. *Speed and Politics: An Essay on Dromology.* New York: Columbia University Press, 1986.

Volkan, Vamik. *The Need to Have Enemies and Allies: From Clinical Practice to International Relations.* Northvale, NJ: Jason Aronson, 1994.

Von Hirsch, Andrew, Julian Roberts, Anthony E. Bottoms, Kent Roach, and Mara Schiff, eds. *Restorative Justice and Criminal Justice: Competing or Reconcilable Paradigms?* Portland, OR: Hart, 2003.

Weber, Max. "Science as a Vocation." In *From Max Weber: Essays in Sociology,* edited and translated by H. H. Gerth and C. Wright Mills. New York: Oxford University Press, 1958.

Wilson, Bryan. *Religion in Sociological Perspective.* Oxford: Oxford University Press, 1982.

Winch, Peter. "Understanding a Primitive Society." In *Understanding and Social Inquiry,* edited by Fred R. Dallmayr and Thomas A. McCarthy. Notre Dame, IN: University of Notre Dame Press, 1977.

Winch, Peter. "Comment." In *Understanding and Social Inquiry,* edited by Fred R. Dallmayr and Thomas A. McCarthy. Notre Dame, IN: University of Notre Dame Press, 1977.

Winnicott, D. W. *Playing and Reality.* New York: Basic Books, 1971.

Winnicott, D. W. *The Maturational Process and the Facilitating Environment.* New York: International University Press, 1965.

Wolff, Edward N. "Recent Trends in Household Wealth in the United States: Rising Debt and the Middle-Class Squeeze." Working Paper no. 502, The Levy Economics Institute of Bard College.

Wolff, Robert Paul. *In Defense of Anarchism.* New York: Harper & Row, 1970.

Wolff, Robert Paul. *Understanding Rawls: A Critique and Reconstruction of a Theory of Justice.* Princeton, NJ: Princeton University Press, 1977.

Wuthnow, Robert. *Sharing the Journey: Support Groups and America's New Quest for Community.* New York: Free Press, 1994.

INDEX

Abram, David 218, 219
absoluteness, assumption of 14–15
abuses of power, prevention of: judicial review and 20–21; separation of powers and 11
accountability in judicial review 20–21
affected interests, principle of 101, 102, 103, 108
African-Americans: "double-consciousness" of racial identity 162–3, 164; identity of, synthesis and 164; *see also* racial identity
Afro-centrism 163
After the Revolution? (Dahl, Robert A.) 65–6, 101–4
agency: childhood and emergence of 217; democratic agency 212; motherhood and 196–7; political agency 205; realism in 207; sacrifice of 195
aggression, frustration and 207, 208
Alcoholics Anonymous (AA) 223–4
alienation: freedom and 78, 79; of labor 79, 80, 81–2, 82–3, 85–6; Marx's perspective in 78, 79, 80, 81–2, 82–3, 141, 175
ambition 15–16
Anderson, Benedict 169, 228, 258n7
anthropocentrism 221
anti-essentialist, post-modern feminism 155, 159, 161
anti-globalization movement 108
anti-majoritarianism 17
anti-materialism 109
Apartheid in South Africa 165
Appiah, Kwame Anthony 164–5, 166, 167, 190–91, 216, 228, 257n11
Arendt, Hannah 118–20, 124, 128–9, 148–9, 186, 228
Aristotle 120
assimilation and racial identity 163–4
Athenian democracy 32
attitude surveys 48
Austin, John 4, 228

authoritarian systems, polyarchies and 91–2, 93
An Autobiographical Study (Freud, S.) 201
autocracy and democracy, distinction between 30
autonomy: power and 116, 118; of voluntary organizations 58
Azande in Africa 138–41

Bachrach, Peter 112–14, 116, 127–8, 228–9
Baratz, Morton S. 112–14, 116, 127–8, 229
Barber, Benjamin 33, 65, 92, 107, 108, 109, 186, 205, 229; democracy, conceptions of 27–8, 31
bargaining, human disposition to 70–71
Bauman, Zygmunt 129, 219, 229; modernity, account of 142–5, 146–7
benign nationalism: identity politics and 212–13; national identity and 171–3
Berger, Peter 174, 175–6, 229
Berle, Adolphe 99–100
Berlin, Isaiah 92
Big Man empowerment 73–4, 187
bioforms 135
biology, racial assignment on basis of 165
biracialism 215
birth, concept of 141
boards of directors, role of 98, 99
Bordo, Susan 155, 159, 160–61, 229
Bork, Judge Robert 22–3, 24, 230
British electoral system 44, 45
Bryan, William Jennings 50
Buchanan, Pat 107–8
Burnham, Walter Dean 49, 50–52, 230
Bush, George W. 46, 96, 176, 213
business: confidence of, importance to government of 94–6; groups in, market economies and 93–5; privilege of, development and (part) reversal of democracy 95–6

271

looking' democratic legitimation 25;
fundamentalism, clash with modernity
109–10; global civil society, rise of
107; Global South, representation
for 107; globalization, privilege and
multi-national corporations 96–7,
105; globalization and governance
105–10; industrial democracy 102–4;
interest-group management 103;
international confederation 108;
laissez-faire, internationalization of
105–6; management and shareholders,
conflict of interest between 99–101;
managerialism 99–101; market
economies, control of 93–4; market-
oriented societies, polyarchies and 91–3;
market socialism 102–4; modernity
109–10; multilateral institutions of
global governance 105–6, 107, 108;
negative freedom 92; ownership
from control, separation of 100–101;
paleocons 107–8; people's capitalism,
rhetoric of 98–9; polyarchies 91–3;
positive freedom 92; poverty, escalation
of 106; private-enterprise market
economy, internationalization of 106–7;
property ownership, market economies
and 93–4; public decision-making,
polyarchal control and 94, 98; reformers
of economic globalization 107, 108–9;
representative democracy, individual
liberty and 92; revolutionary movements
92; self-managed enterprises 101, 103;
self-regulating market system, perils of
106–7; shareholder government 100–
101; shareholder's democracy, obstacles
to 99; short-term profit growth,
obsession with 100, 103; state power,
global capital and 105; stockholding
98–9, 100–101; time-anxiety 108–9;
worker-controlled enterprises 101, 102,
103
Democracy in America (Tocqueville, A.de)
54–8, 68, 177
Democratic National Convention 214
Democratic Party 46, 50, 52
demonization (out group): group dynamics
205, 206, 207–8; identity politics 211,
213, 214; nature, human beings and 225
demos (people) 26
dependence, denial of 224
depressive anxiety: consumerism as defense
against 219–20; group equivalent in
group dynamics 202; guilt and 193–4,
194–5, 202
depressive integration: identity politics and
211; of individuals, facilitation of 204–10
difference: commonality and difference

in gender identity 160–61; cultural
difference, celebration of 137–8;
difference principle of justice 87, 88–90,
186–7; genotypal differences 165–6;
politics of 149–50, 151
In a Different Voice (Gilligan, C.) 155–7
Dinnerstein, Dorothy 200, 203, 230–31;
promotion of co-parenting 194–6
direct democracy 31, 32
Disch, Lisa 45–6, 67, 231
disciplinary power 120–21; control,
individual participation in 121;
normalization and 122–4
Discipline and Punish (Foucault, M.) 120–24
Discourse on the Origin of Inequality
(Rousseau, J.-J.) 148
discrimination: gender discrimination 58;
homosexuality, legal discrimination
against 249n16; identity groups and
152–3
disobedience 199
dissent, legitimation of 207
distributive justice 84–6
diversity and strength, correlation between
177–8
division of labor 68, 73, 83; human nature
and the market 69–71; redistribution
and 72
Du Bois, W.E.B. 162–5, 190, 214, 231
Dworkin, Ronald 8, 9, 63, 231

earth as resource 109
Earth First 221
eco-friendly technologies 110
Ecology, Community, and Lifestyle (Naess,
A.) 221–3
economics: American Republic, social
and economic diversity of 43; capitalist
market economy and civil society
60; centrally planned economies,
polyarchies and 91–2; economic
globalization, rejection of 107, 109;
inequality, political parties 41; inequality
and privilege in civil society 59; laissez-
faire market economies, dangers of 75;
liberalization, consequences of 106;
market economies, control of 93–4;
maximum gain, human behavior in
anticipation of 69, 71; private-enterprise
market economy, internationalization
of 106–7; property ownership, market
economies and 93–4; reformers of
economic globalization 107, 108–9;
socio-economic equality, and Hayek's
argument against political promotion of
86–7; state and, regulatory relationship
between 74–5
education: early education, enforcement of